PALGRAVE STUDIES IN THEATRE AND PERFORMANCE HISTORY is a series devoted to the best of theatre/performance scholarship currently available, accessible, and free of jargon. It strives to include a wide range of topics, from the more traditional to those performance forms that in recent years have helped broaden the understanding of what theatre as a category might include (from forms as diverse as the circus and burlesque to street buskers, stage magic, and musical theatre, among many others). Although historical, critical, or analytical studies are of special interest, more theoretical projects, if not the dominant thrust of a study, but utilized as important underpinning or as a historiographical or analytical method of exploration, are also of interest. Textual studies of drama or other types of less traditional performance texts are also germane to the series if placed in their cultural, historical, social, or political and economic context. There is no geographical focus for this series, and works of excellence of a diverse and international nature, including comparative studies, are sought.

The editor of the series is Don B. Wilmeth (Emeritus, Brown University), PhD, University of Illinois, who brings to the series over a dozen years as editor of a book series on American theatre and drama, in addition to his own extensive experience as an editor of books and journals. He is the author of several award-winning books and has received numerous career achievement awards, including one for sustained excellence in editing from the Association for Theatre in Higher Education.

Also in the series:

Undressed for Success by Brenda Foley
Theatre, Performance, and the Historical Avant-garde by Günter Berghaus
Theatre, Politics, and Markets in Fin-de-Siècle Paris by Sally Charnow
Ghosts of Theatre and Cinema in the Brain by Mark Pizzato
Moscow Theatres for Young People by Manon van de Water
Absence and Memory in Colonial American Theatre by Odai Johnson
Vaudeville Wars: How the Keith-Albee and Orpheum Circuits Controlled the Big-Time and Its Performers by Arthur Frank Wertheim
Performance and Femininity in Eighteenth-Century German Women's Writing by Wendy Arons
Operatic China: Staging Chinese Identity across the Pacific by Daphne P. Lei
Transatlantic Stage Stars in Vaudeville and Variety: Celebrity Turns by Leigh Woods
Interrogating America through Theatre and Performance edited by William W. Demastes and Iris Smith Fischer
Plays in American Periodicals, 1890–1918 by Susan Harris Smith
Representation and Identity from Versailles to the Present: The Performing Subject by Alan Sikes
Directors and the New Musical Drama: British and American Musical Theatre in the 1980s and 90s by Miranda Lundskaer-Nielsen
Beyond the Golden Door: Jewish-American Drama and Jewish-American Experience by Julius Novick

American Puppet Modernism: Essays on the Material World in Performance by John Bell
On the Uses of the Fantastic in Modern Theatre: Cocteau, Oedipus, and the Monster by Irene Eynat-Confino
Staging Stigma: A Critical Examination of the American Freak Show by Michael M. Chemers, foreword by Jim Ferris
Performing Magic on the Western Stage: From the Eighteenth-Century to the Present edited by Francesca Coppa, Larry Hass, and James Peck, foreword by Eugene Burger
Memory in Play: From Aeschylus to Sam Shepard by Attilio Favorini
Danjūrō's Girls: Women on the Kabuki Stage by Loren Edelson
Mendel's Theatre: Heredity, Eugenics, and Early Twentieth-Century American Drama by Tamsen Wolff
Theatre and Religion on Krishna's Stage: Performing in Vrindavan by David V. Mason
Rogue Performances: Staging the Underclasses in Early American Theatre Culture by Peter P. Reed
Broadway and Corporate Capitalism: The Rise of the Professional-Managerial Class, 1900–1920 by Michael Schwartz
Lady Macbeth in America: From the Stage to the White House by Gay Smith
Performing Bodies in Pain: Medieval and Post-Modern Martyrs, Mystics, and Artists by Marla Carlson
Early-Twentieth-Century Frontier Dramas on Broadway: Situating the Western Experience in Performing Arts by Richard Wattenberg

Early-Twentieth-Century Frontier Dramas on Broadway

Situating the Western Experience in Performing Arts

Richard Wattenberg

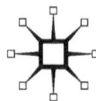

EARLY-TWENTIETH-CENTURY FRONTIER DRAMAS ON BROADWAY
Copyright © Richard Wattenberg, 2011.

All rights reserved.

First published in 2011 by
PALGRAVE MACMILLAN®
in the United States—a division of St. Martin's Press LLC,
175 Fifth Avenue, New York, NY 10010.

Where this book is distributed in the UK, Europe and the rest of the world, this is by Palgrave Macmillan, a division of Macmillan Publishers Limited, registered in England, company number 785998, of Houndmills, Basingstoke, Hampshire RG21 6XS.

Palgrave Macmillan is the global academic imprint of the above companies and has companies and representatives throughout the world.

Palgrave® and Macmillan® are registered trademarks in the United States, the United Kingdom, Europe and other countries.

ISBN: 978–0–230–11144–8

Library of Congress Cataloging-in-Publication Data

Wattenberg, Richard, 1949–
   Early-twentieth-century frontier dramas on Broadway : situating the western experience in performing arts / Richard Wattenberg.
      p. cm.—(Palgrave studies in theater and performance history)
   ISBN 978–0–230–11144–8 (alk. paper)
   1. Theater—New York (State)—New York—History. 2. American drama—20th century—History and criticism. 3. Broadway (New York, N.Y.)—History. 4. Frontier and pioneer life in literature. 5. West (U.S.)—In literature. 6. Myth in literature. I. Title.

PN2277.N5W38 2011
792'.097471—dc22   2010040327

A catalogue record of the book is available from the British Library.

Design by Newgen Imaging Systems (P) Ltd., Chennai, India.

First edition: May 2011

Dedicated to the memory of
My inspiring mentor, Esther Merle Jackson, who showed me that the American theater was my theater, and that the American faith in human possibility was my faith
&
My good-hearted friend, John Steven Paul, whose devotion to the theater as an instrument of enlightenment and hope never flagged

Contents

List of Images	ix
Acknowledgments	xi
Introduction	1

Part I The Axes of Analysis: Frontier Western Discourse and Theater Practice

1	Frontier Western Discourse at the Turn of the Nineteenth to the Twentieth Century	21
2	The Turn-of-the-Century American Theater Context	53

Part II The Plays

3	Discipline and Spontaneity: Clyde Fitch's *The Cowboy and the Lady* and Augustus Thomas's *Arizona*	83
4	Drama from Novels: *John Ermine of the Yellowstone* and *The Virginian*	109
5	Variations on the Frontier Myth: Edwin Milton Royle's *The Squaw Man* and David Belasco's *The Girl of the Golden West*	141
6	From Melodrama to Realism: William Vaughn Moody's *The Great Divide* and Rachel Crothers's *The Three of Us*	169
	Conclusion	201
	Notes	209
	Index	259

Images

Plate 1	A 1900 poster for Augustus Thomas's *Arizona* representing the Act IV court-martial scene. Note the fortresslike gates enclosing Henry Canby's ranch house, stables, and courtyard. (Library of Congress Prints and Photographs Division, Washington, D.C. 20540)	105
Plate 2	Dustin Farnum as the Virginian in the play of that name by Owen Wister and Kirke La Shelle (1904). (The Billy Rose Theatre Division, the New York Public Library for the Performing Arts)	130
Plate 3	Act IV of David Belasco's *The Girl of the Golden West* with Blanche Bates as Minnie, the Girl, and Robert Hilliard as Dick Johnson (aka Ramerrez). (The Billy Rose Theatre Division, the New York Public Library for the Performing Arts)	165
Plate 4	Act I of William Vaughn Moody's *The Great Divide* with Henry Miller as Stephen Ghent and Margaret Anglin as Ruth Jordan. (The Billy Rose Theatre Division, the New York Public Library for the Performing Arts)	175
Plate 5	Act II of William Vaughn Moody's *The Great Divide* with Henry Miller as Stephen Ghent and Margaret Anglin as Ruth Jordan. (The Billy Rose Theatre Division, the New York Public Library for the Performing Arts)	176

Acknowledgments

As is usual in a project of this sort, I owe a great debt of gratitude to many colleagues and friends who shared ideas and offered thoughtful insights as I developed this study. I especially appreciate my colleague William Tate for reading the introduction and offering valuable feedback.

I would also like to thank the Portland State University Interlibrary Loan office for the assistance provided in gathering important research materials. I am equally indebted to Karen Nickeson, acting curator of the Billy Rose Theatre Division of the New York Public Library for the Performing Arts, in Lincoln Center, and all of the various librarians with whom I worked in the Billy Rose Theatre Division for generously assisting. I am also grateful for the thoughtful and patient assistance provided by Stephan Saks and others in the Photo Services Department of the New York Public Library for making it possible for me to study unpublished materials while living three thousand miles from New York and for facilitating the process of gathering supporting photographic images.

Finally, I offer many thanks to all those at Palgrave for their support, and especially to Don Wilmeth, editor of Palgrave Studies in Theatre and Performance History, for his encouragement and Samantha Hasey, Kristy Lilas, and Rohini Krishnan for making the production process run so smoothly.

The material on Clyde Fitch's *The Cowboy and the Lady* in Chapter 3 appeared in an earlier form in the article "Taming the Frontier Myth: Clyde Fitch's *The Cowboy and the Lady*," for *The Journal of American Culture* (16.2 [1993], 77–84), and the discussion of David Belasco's *The Girl of the Golden West* in Chapter 5 appeared in an earlier form in the article "'Local Colour' Plus 'Frontier Myth': The Belasco Formula in *The Girl of the Golden West*," in *Essays in Theatre/Etudes Theatrales* (11.1 [1992], 85–97). I am grateful to both journals for permission to reuse this material.

Plate 1 is reproduced from the Library of Congress Prints and Photographs Online Catalog. Plates 2–5 are reproduced by permission of the Billy Rose Theatre Division of the New York Public Library for the Performing Arts.

Introduction

Since colonial times, the American frontier has provided New World artists and literati—especially those in what has become the United States—with a rich source of narrative material. Frontier themes and motifs have been a primary focus especially for Euro-American artists and writers in search of a distinctly American experience. Even as events associated with the settlement of the western frontier have slipped further and further into the past, the impact of western frontier imagery on how Americans define themselves has remained. There are numerous instances of the lingering power of the frontier mystique. One might note the periodic resurgence of Western movies exemplified in the early 1990s by such popular and well-received films as *Dances with Wolves* (1990) and *The Unforgiven* (1992), as well as the two versions of the Wyatt Earp story, *Tombstone* (1993) and *Wyatt Earp* (1994), and in the new century by such highly praised movies as *Open Range* (2003), *3:10 to Yuma* (2007), *Appaloosa* (2008), and *True Grit* (2010). One might also consider the successful HBO television series *Deadwood*, launched in 2004.

Outside the entertainment industry, frontier imagery has continued to resonate. For example, one might reference the late-twentieth-century debates about the rhetorical power of the Marlboro Man with respect to the marketing of cigarettes. Not only did this western cowboy image help to market filtered cigarettes to males,[1] but a similar figure could also be used to disabuse smokers, as a California antismoking billboard campaign of the late 1990s exemplified.[2] Perhaps more significant here are the rugged western cowboy personas developed by U.S. presidents like Ronald Reagan in the 1980s and George W. Bush in the 2000s. In the case of the latter, frontier mythology was used both as a means of asserting policy (Bush's pledges to take Osama bin Laden "dead or alive" may come to mind) as well as parodying it in political cartoons.

Frontier western imagery and themes have remained a continuous presence in American culture, but what most distinguishes the manner in which this fascination has been manifested in American culture over the past fifty years is the degree to which it has become a self-conscious preoccupation. In fact, over the past half century, the burgeoning American Studies field has provided the impetus for a plethora of studies examining how the western frontier experience was and is represented in American culture. Henry Nash Smith, Leslie Fiedler, Richard Slotkin, Annette Kolodny, John Cawelti, and Jane Tompkins are just a few of the many historians and cultural critics who have contributed to this area of study.[3]

Interestingly, mainstream theater and drama have only a marginal place in such studies. Scholars with an American Studies perspective generally focus on either the more "serious," canonized literary or artistic products,[4] on the one hand, or popular art forms such as dime novels and pulp fiction, Wild West shows, and the Western movie genre,[5] on the other. The so-called legitimate theater often seems to fall outside these two groupings, neither elevated enough to figure as "highbrow" art nor accessible enough to be treated as popular culture.

Although American Studies scholars often ignore the theater, the stage has been the site of vivid frontier representations, and, over the past half century, several theater scholars have offered broad-based studies examining how theater practitioners have come to grips with the frontier experience. In his unpublished 1954 dissertation, "The Representation of the West in American Drama from 1849 to 1917,"[6] Stuart Wallace Hyde considers several hundred plays divided among five subject categories: the Indian barrier and the settlement of the Great Plains, the Mormon frontier, the mining frontier, the cattlemen's frontier, and miscellaneous types. In her 1972 dissertation, "Rhetorical, Dramatic, Theatrical, and Social Contexts of Selected American Frontier Plays, 1871 to 1906,"[7] Rosemarie K. Bank examines a sample of twelve plays written over thirty-five years. While the scope of her study is narrower than Hyde's, Bank makes the case that frontier drama formed a "coherent tradition consisting of shared structural elements which are designed to achieve specific aesthetic or social ends."[8] More recently, Roger A. Hall's study *Performing the American Frontier: 1870–1906* (2001)[9] represents the first published study focusing primarily on American frontier theater. Hall covers a wide range of plays and shows, culminating in a chapter on plays written from 1899 to 1906. Among these latter plays were a number of the most significant frontier plays ever to appear on the American stage. In fact, during this period, some of the most prestigious Broadway theaters—venues that by the nature of their admission prices were obviously catering to audiences drawn from the more prosperous classes—as well as more popular-priced Eighth Avenue or Bowery theaters,[10] housed extraordinarily successful plays dealing with the frontier. Premiering on

Broadway within a brief seven-year period were such triumphant examples of frontier drama as Augustus Thomas's *Arizona* (1900), Owen Wister and Kirke La Shelle's *The Virginian* (1904), Edwin Milton Royle's *The Squaw Man* (1905), David Belasco's *The Girl of the Golden West* (1905), William Vaughn Moody's *The Great Divide* (1906), and Rachel Crothers's *The Three of Us* (1906). As Hall points out, all of these were highly praised by New York reviewers and were distinguished by long, lucrative Broadway runs.[11] Moreover, all went on to enjoy prosperous tours throughout the country, earning both extraordinary profits and national critical esteem, as well as generally contributing to the kind of cultural environment that made possible the continued success throughout the twentieth century of Wild Western pulp fiction and movies.

Indeed, the six plays listed above were among the most successful Broadway plays of the first years of the twentieth century. Their long New York runs, successful tours, and the fact that their popularity prompted parodies such as *The Squawman's Girl of the Golden West* (1906) and *The Great Decide* (1906), always a sure sign of success, suggest that these plays not only met a particular demand for dramas about the frontier, but also succinctly addressed the attitudes about the Wild West that their audiences brought to the theater in the early twentieth century. Indeed, at that time, when the actual frontier was supposedly disappearing, the mythic frontier became a major national preoccupation. In this regard, the appearance of these plays is coincident with a major shift in how Americans viewed the frontier experience. In the years immediately following Frederick Jackson Turner's presentation of his celebrated paper "The Significance of the Frontier in American History" to the American Historical Association convening at Chicago's Columbian Exposition in 1893, his ideas resonated through intellectual circles and the mass media. Turner's "frontier thesis" became the focus of a new understanding of the impact of the Western experience on American culture. The success of frontier plays like those of Thomas, Wister and La Shelle, Royle, Belasco, Moody, and Crothers resides in the fact that their authors wrestle with and finally help to assimilate this new approach to the Western adventure in theatrically cogent ways.

The intent of this study is to extend previous critical evaluations of these and other similarly significant plays in order to understand more completely how the changing vision of the frontier experience was both integrated into and actually constructed within the American theater of the late nineteenth and early twentieth centuries. In other words, this study examines how these key plays both reflected and shaped new views of that frontier experience. In this regard, the central portion of this inquiry will consist of careful analysis of Clyde Fitch's *The Cowboy and the Lady* (1899) and the 1903 dramatic adaptation of Frederic Remington's novel *John Ermine of the Yellowstone* (1902), as well as the six plays mentioned above. The goal here, however, is not simply the close study of plays, once well received but with little production value anymore. By focusing on how these plays represent the intersection of period ideas about the nature of the frontier process with prevailing dramatic/theatrical practices, I hope to set the frontier perspective offered in these theatrical works within the larger context of late-nineteenth- and early-twentieth-century American culture.

Appearing during the first decade of the twentieth century—a period of social upheaval and cultural transformation—these plays contributed significantly to the development of new attitudes about both the frontier experience and American exceptionalism. The eight frontier dramas that are highlighted in this study were performed before educated, well-to-do audiences in first-class theaters; that is, they were performed before members of the new professional middle class and managerial elite as these groups were asserting cultural hegemony at the start of the twentieth century. Providing entertainment for powerful American politicians and statesmen as well as leading figures in the new mass communication industries, these plays helped to shape and reinforce the patterns of thought that motivated the new ruling elite. In short, while these plays were molded by the social and cultural contexts in which they were created, they, in turn, and perhaps more importantly, helped to condition the American culture of the early twentieth century.

Examining the ways in which the frontier vision is presented in early-twentieth-century frontier plays provides insight into deeply felt American ideals, but one mustn't conclude that these plays offer a unified or monolithic point of view on the frontier process. These frontier representations share certain perspectives about the nation and the world, but these plays are distinguished from each other in that each registers subtle, and not-so-subtle, shifts in the meaning associated with still-contested concepts like "frontier," "civilization," and "savagery." These plays are not identical in vision, but as a group they delineate the parameters of a coalescing frontier discourse that shaped and has continued to shape American rhetoric and ideology.

The views of the frontier experience that were taking shape in these plays are still a very significant part of how Americans see themselves—how they distinguish themselves from the rest of the world. To be sure, the assumptions that underlie these plays continue to inform contemporary attitudes and concerns, despite the deconstructing assaults that have been leveled at them over the past twenty-five years by "New Western Historians" like Patricia Limerick and Richard White.[12] To view the influence of the frontier discourse, one needn't look far. Mind-sets forged out of late-nineteenth- and early-twentieth-century frontier discourse impose themselves on current public debates, such as those revolving around the continuing U.S. involvement in Iraq and Afghanistan, as well as those regarding national health-care reform or energy policy. The thinking of the past is still with us.

* * *

As important as the frontier plays of Fitch, Thomas, Wister and La Shelle, Belasco, Royle, Moody, and Crothers may be with regard to American representations of the Western experience, these were not the first successful American dramatic works dealing with frontier themes to hit the boards of America's legitimate stages. On the contrary, these plays represent the culmination of a long line of American plays representing the frontier western experience. To be sure, the western frontier has provided attractive material for playwrights since early in the development of American drama. In fact, the frontier wilderness was the background of one of the first plays written by a colonial American, Major Robert Rogers's *Ponteach* (1766).

For the most part, Rogers's play seems to be cut from the cloth of conventional heroic tragedy. He offers the native chief, Ponteach, as an honorable, self-sacrificing warrior king who contrasts sharply with the play's English characters, who are, as Ponteach laments, members of "A proud, imperious, churlish, haughty Band/...false, deceitful, knavish, insolent...."[13] Ponteach attempts to free his people from the incursions of the tyrannic British, but his hopes are undermined by the passionate vengeance that his two conflicting sons, Philip and Chekitan, visit on each other. Rogers, who was himself not entirely sympathetic to the Indian's plight,[14] nonetheless seems to suggest in this play that the innocent, natural Indian had been devastatingly victimized by selfish, hypocritical white colonizers. Although this play was not performed during Rogers's lifetime, it can be seen as the prototype for what became in the first half of the next century a very popular American theatrical form, the "Indian play."

Plays such as John Nelson Barker's *The Indian Princess, or La Belle Sauvage* (1808), George Washington Parke Custis's *The Indian Prophecy* (1827), and, perhaps the best known of this genre, the Edwin Forrest vehicle, John Augustus Stone's *Metamora* (1829), offered American audiences heroic "noble savages" in the mold of James Fenimore Cooper's Unkas or

Henry Wadsworth Longfellow's Hiawatha and idealized Indian princesses in the picturesque Pocahontas tradition.[15] The Indian play remained very popular until the 1840s, when the success of parodies of the genre, like John Brougham's *Metamora, or the Last of the Pollywogs* (1847) and *Po-Ca-Hon-Tas, or the Gentle Savage* (1855) indicate that audiences may have finally grown tired of it.[16]

The popularity of the Indian play during the first half of the nineteenth century suggests that American theater practitioners and audiences were hungering for a drama that would express the distinctiveness of the New World experience; nevertheless, these plays were clearly a product of European tradition—embodying the basic principles of the European romantic movement. In keeping with the romantic fascination with the exotic, the popular Indian plays were set in a relatively distant past (for instance, popular stage characters such as Metamora and Pocahontas belonged, like their historical prototypes, to the seventeenth century) and focused on characters who were wondrously novel to the predominantly Euro-American audiences. More important, the central character of these plays, the noble savage, while often speaking a language that was highly conventionalized and overtly rhetorical, was meant to appear as a specimen of virtuous simplicity, as a character very much in harmony with the pure, uncorrupted nature that romantics cherished.[17] Even so, the Indian plays were more preoccupied with idealizing their Indian subjects than with representing European-American frontier experience.[18]

While not as celebrated as Indian plays, frontier plays dealing with the exploits of white pioneers also appeared on the American stage during the first half of the nineteenth century. Indeed, historians of the American drama, and more specifically of the frontier western drama, usually cite James Kirke Paulding's character comedy, *The Lion of the West* (1831), as the first popularly acclaimed play to revolve around a pioneer protagonist.[19] This piece was, however, less an exploration of frontier themes and issues than an attempt to capitalize on the popularity or notoriety of the self-promoting Tennessee congressman Davy Crockett.[20] Also a product of the early nineteenth century was Louisa Medina's 1838 adaptation of Robert Montgomery Bird's novel *Nick of the Woods* (1837). While focusing on the exploits of a white Indian hater, Bird, and Medina after him, offered a contrasting view to the idealized Indian of the James Fenimore Cooper and Indian play tradition.

Despite the existence of early works like these, the American frontier experience did not have a significant impact on American drama until the second half of the nineteenth century. In "The Representation of the West in American Drama from 1849 to 1917," Hyde claims that it wasn't until the discovery of California gold turned the nation's attention westward that the frontier adventures of American—that is, European-American—protagonists began to appear with some regularity on the American stage.[21] Even so, frontier plays of the 1850s and 1860s—plays like Alonzo Delano's rather unpolished *A Live Woman in the Mines* (1857)—were not as a whole popular with either audiences or critics. In fact, Hyde as well as both Rosemarie Bank and Roger Hall suggest that it wasn't until after 1870 that the real development of a drama dealing with the frontier West appears.[22] In his search for frontier plays written during the 1849–1917 period, Hyde gathered 1,200 drama titles. Of these, a disproportionate majority come from the years following 1870. While Hyde's list may not be entirely accurate due to imprecise modes of recording titles in the nineteenth century,[23] it is clear that the West had become a significant source of inspiration for American playwrights during the last decades of the nineteenth century and the first decade of the twentieth century.

The increased interest in Western subject matter in American drama and theater during the last decades of the nineteenth century is understandable given the rapid westward expansion of European Americans in the post–Civil War years. After a devastating war, the nation turned to the task of settling the western frontier, and the West became a focus for the renewed activity and expansion of a reunited nation. The completion of the transcontinental railroad in 1869; the land limitations imposed on Native Americans following the Indian wars, which climaxed between 1870 and 1890; and the development of farming methods that enabled agriculture seemingly to take root in "the Great American Desert" opened large tracts of western land for white settlement.[24] In addition to farming and sometimes preceding it, the development of extraction industries, such as mining and timber, as well as cattle ranching attracted migrants and served to further the economic development of the West. Railroads, seeking to finance construction by selling off their federal land grants and, at the same time, to create a continuously growing demand for travel and shipping, lured easterners westward with glowing advertisements. The new migrants, once settled, demanded more railroads to accommodate their transportation needs—thus railroad building and western migration fed off each other and spurred each other on. As the western population grew, so grew the demand for more goods and services, and consequently more merchants and professional people were drawn westward. In short, during the years between 1870 and 1890, the population west of the Mississippi more than doubled.[25] The spread of settlements across the West was so rapid that by

1890, the Superintendent of the Census announced that there was no longer a clear frontier line separating the territory inhabited by Euro-Americans from wild untamed wilderness.[26]

The enthusiasm with which Americans went about settling the West had a profound impact on cultural production, which in turn further fueled the intensity of settlement. Indeed, information regarding the West, especially events of a more dramatic nature, such as explosive Indian-White conflicts, major gold strikes or the discovery of other precious metals, and the important landmarks in the expansion of the railroad, were communicated throughout the country to a rapidly growing urban population by an equally rapidly growing mass media industry consisting primarily of newspapers and magazines.[27] The expanding impact of Western events on public consciousness is registered in the increased popularity of frontier plays in the 1870s. The success of "border" or frontier dramas like James J. McCloskey's *Across the Continent* (1870), Augustin Daly's *Horizon* (1871), Frank Murdock's *Davy Crockett* (1872), Joaquin Miller's *The Danites in the Sierras* (1877), and Bartley Campbell's *My Partner* (1879) in New York City (the hub of the American theater from the late nineteenth century on) testified to the viability of this genre—a popularity that would continue into the twentieth century.[28]

* * *

The increase in the number of frontier plays produced in the popular price as well as the more elite, first-class New York theaters in the years after 1870 paralleled the enthusiasm with which Euro-Americans expanded into the trans-Mississippi western frontier, and this increase would seem to lend credence to the proposition that the theater reflects happenings in the larger world outside the theater, or that the theater functions, in Hamlet's words, "to hold, as 'twere, the mirror up to nature." To be sure, the frontier experience had a very concrete impact on American social and cultural realities, but the full and complex actuality of that experience was not and could not be captured on the late-nineteenth- and early-twentieth-century stages. Rather than view the "frontier" as it appears in American drama and theater of the period as an unmediated representation of the **real** frontier, one should view it as a construction—a by-product less of occurrences in the West than of a series of cultural assumptions, which spoke to the needs and interests of specific audiences. The dramatic representations of the frontier are, in fact, best comprehended when viewed in the general context of late-nineteenth-century efforts to explain the frontier experience.

In this regard, it is important to consider theatrical representations of the western frontier in terms of how they exemplify and, in turn, shape the concerns and modalities of the American frontier western discourse of the late nineteenth and early twentieth centuries. With this in mind, it is necessary to examine the phrase "frontier western discourse."

Generally speaking, frontier western discourse consists of all that might be said about the frontier West at a particular time and place. When one participates in a particular discourse such as that dealing with the frontier West, one builds on what has already been said by contributors to that discourse while accepting sometimes explicitly, sometimes implicitly, the way of interpreting the world that not only pervades that discourse but also makes it possible. In short, a discourse can be understood in terms of the consistency or regularity of thought that conditions the emergence of objects, types of statements, concepts, and themes that it contains.[29] Nineteenth-century frontier discourse consists of all the statements and representations pertaining to the western "frontier," and these statements and representations, though sometimes contradictory, sometimes inconsistent, are nonetheless marked by a certain coherence or regularity.

There are, then, parameters to a discourse such as that dealing with the frontier West—parameters that affect the kind(s) of object(s) discussed and that limit what can be said at any given time about the object(s) of the discourse. In explaining the relationship between the speaker and the nature, or what Michel Foucault called the "positivity"[30] of a discourse, Foucault writes that "positivities are not so much limitations imposed on the initiative of subjects as the field in which that initiative is articulated..., rules that it puts into operation..., relations that provide it with a support...."[31] In other words, the dynamics driving a particular frontier representation should be understood by reference less to the author's individual intentions than to the discursive field in which the representation belongs. When writers and artists addressed the frontier in the late nineteenth century, they entered what, for all intents and purposes, appears to be a prefabricated world of discourse. While they may have eventually shaped discourse, it is discourse that first shaped them—providing them with the intellectual possibilities and structures that govern their contributions to it.

With regard to the late-nineteenth-century frontier discourse, the very idea of "frontier"—a rather unstable concept in its own right[32]—was circumscribed; that is, certain general cultural assumptions limited what could and would be said about it and the experience of it. One of the most cogent late-nineteenth-century statements on the nature of the frontier was made by Frederick Jackson Turner in his seminal 1893 paper, "The Significance of the Frontier in American History." In offering up his revolutionary thesis, Turner was not actually developing an entirely new way of viewing the frontier. His understanding of the frontier was shaped by the modes of thought at his disposal. He defines the frontier as "the meeting point between savagery and civilization."[33] Significantly, this frontier was less a place than a temporal process in which "civilized" eastern Americans or Europeans interacted with "savage" or primitive western conditions and peoples.[34] As such his understanding of "frontier" was clearly bound up with a number of widely circulating intellectual structures and concepts—among the most significant being "savagery," "civilization," and "progress." These concepts circumscribed what Turner said, but also what was said by others about the frontier in the late nineteenth century; however, not everyone entering this discourse viewed the key terms "savagery," "civilization," and "progress" in the same manner. There is in this respect some slipping and sliding of meaning, and yet one sees when viewing the field of this discourse a tangled web of ideas and theories that share a certain regularity. The very fact that participants in this discourse so frequently used "civilization," "East," "savagery," "West," and "progress" even when their understanding of these terms were often diverse suggests the spatial/temporal continuities or regularities that bound them.

One can see an intriguing analogue to this regularity when noting the various complex connections and interconnections that linked the sundry players on this field of discourse. It is more than coincidental that Turner first offered "The Significance of the Frontier in American History" in 1893 at the Columbian Exposition in Chicago even as Buffalo Bill Cody entertained visitors to the fair, including some who might have heard Turner's speech, with his Wild West Show, which was playing right outside the gates to the fair. Here, academic perspectives on the frontier and popular cultural entertainment based on the frontier appeared to butt against each other.[35] But this is just the beginning of an intricate interweaving of representations and representers that helps to define the late-nineteenth-century frontier discourse. Teddy Roosevelt, who wrote a multivolume history of the West, *The Winning of the West* (1889–1896), shared a cordial correspondence with Turner, who wrote reviews of Roosevelt's history,[36] and when Roosevelt chose to play cowboy on the world scene by leading a volunteer unit composed of western cowboys and eastern swells in the Spanish-American War, this regiment was called the Rough Riders—a name appropriated from an equestrian cavalry act in Buffalo Bill's Wild West Show. Long before the Spanish-American War, when he was still at Harvard, Roosevelt developed a lifelong friendship with another Harvard student, Owen Wister, who later became known for his Western novel *The Virginian* (1902) and the play developed from it. Wister in his turn was a friend and collaborator with the Western illustrator and writer Frederic Remington. Not only did Remington provide illustrations for Wister's writings, including the important essay "The Evolution of the Cow-Puncher" (1895), but he also illustrated some of Roosevelt's Western writings, most specifically his account of his experiences in the Dakotas in the 1880s, *Ranch Life and the Hunting Trail* (1887). It was also Remington who prompted playwright Augustus Thomas to turn west for the subject matter of what became his tremendously successful drama *Arizona* (1900).[37] This play opened with a coproducer credit going to Kirke La Shelle, who later collaborated with Owen Wister on his 1904 theatrical production of *The Virginian*. Owen Wister might have found Hamlin Garland arrogant when the latter sent him a somewhat patronizing congratulatory note for his book of short stories *Red Men and White*,[38] but it was Garland (the author of *Crumbling Idols*, an 1894 treatise calling for artists to shift their focus from Europe and the East Coast to the great Middle West, and later of a number of novels dealing with the far West), who led William Vaughn Moody on a trip west that eventually provided the background necessary for his play *The Great Divide* (1906)—a play that became an important vehicle for the actor Henry Miller, who eventually became close friends with a onetime theater rival who later functioned as one of his pallbearers, native westerner David Belasco,[39] author of the frontier play *The Girl of the Golden West*.

Playwrights, historians, novelists, illustrators, and actors are all entangled here in the web that is the late-nineteenth-century frontier discourse. Ivy Leaguers like Harvard graduates Roosevelt, Wister, and Moody, and Yale man Remington mix with westerners, some of whom like Turner (who taught at Harvard from 1917 to 1924) became associated with the Ivy League, to develop a discourse that pervaded the popular media at the turn of the nineteenth into the twentieth centuries. Furthermore, all of these culture producers received the blessing of the new industrial-managerial elite even as they were products of the late-nineteenth-century focus on professionalism fostered by that new elite. These culture producers shared ideas and understandings because they were all working within the same late-nineteenth-century social-cultural context.

The biographical connections linking these various contributors to the late-nineteenth-century frontier discourse can be seen as a concrete manifestation of the discursive links binding their representations. The interconnectedness of frontier representers and representations in the late nineteenth and early twentieth centuries may, however, lead one to conceive frontier discourse in static terms. This rich array of relations and interrelations, viewed metaphorically as a web, suggests a kind of spatial simultaneity and, consequently, would seemingly undercut efforts to construe the complex interweaving of ideas and cultural producers in temporal terms.[40] But discourse is in the world. As Foucault reminds us, it does not first exist as a "pure, neutral, atemporal, silent form," which is then compromised, modified, or suppressed by interaction with other discourses or with nondiscursive historical realities. On the contrary, these factors function primarily as discourse's "formative elements"[41] and as such are so entangled within discourse that distinguishing nondiscursive from discursive factors becomes highly problematic. In the very process of contemplating nondiscursive historical realities, we turn them into discourse. Past and present actualities cannot exist for us in any other form. This is not to say that "reality" or effects of the world are without actual substance, but just that as soon as we ponder these "realities" or "effects," they exist and can only exist for us as elements of discourse. Thinking, speaking, and knowing about events is inherently a process of mediation. Consciousness of an event is ultimately and irrevocably removed from the event in itself. It is because nondiscursive realities and effects can only be comprehended as discourse that distinguishing a pure discourse from one corrupted by nondiscursive or interdiscursive factors becomes extremely difficult. In other words, the themes and strategies that appear within a particular field of discourse may be the result of the impact of nondiscursive practices or events, and in this sense a discourse may be characterized by distinct themes or strategies vis-à-vis the world, but there is no way to make a clean distinction between discourse and the world outside discourse, and ultimately no way to distinguish between undistorted discourse and distorted discourse or between abstract truth and ideological bias.[42]

Who speaks about what, as well as how, when, and where the speaker speaks are important formative elements of discourse. No matter how much the individual speaker pretends to objectivity, what he or she says is circumscribed by the discourse into which he or she enters, and that discourse is stamped with social assumptions and biases. In short, discourse is deeply impressed with social and cultural relations; it cannot be disentangled from the social or cultural practices that informed its development. On the other hand, we see and "know" the world through discourse. There is no fantastic skyhook that will pull us free of the world of discourse to see the actual world as it actually is in its unmediated reality. What we know always exists as—and is consequently limited by—discourse. Knowledge is circumscribed by discourse, but more important, knowledge is power. Simply—or not so simply—put, the construction of knowledge (the "what" that is said) not only provides the speaker (the "who," defined by the "where," "when," and "why" he or she speaks) with power, but also is, in fact, power itself—the power to present or order the "world" in a certain fashion. The way in which a dominant racial, economic, or gender group constructs knowledge cannot help but impose a particular order of things on other subordinate groups. Such an order of things or construction of the world can be forcefully imposed on others or "sold" to others by more subtle means. In other words, those who may not have much to gain from a particular way of understanding the world may be convinced, co-opted, or indoctrinated into accepting that way of viewing reality. Here we see the significance of Antonio Gramsci's concept of "hegemony." For Marxists like Gramsci, the orthodox notion that all discourse was merely part of a superstructure that was narrowly determined by foundational economic realities gives way to a much more complexly conceived notion of the dialectical relations governing economic base and cultural superstructure. Discourse is not merely determined by social realities, but in effect also defines those realities.[43]

Because discourse is always "positioned" and not "neutral" or "objective," one can speak of its ideological dimension, but as Foucault points out, "ideology" is not to be seen as the opposite or distortion of some knowable true state of affairs. Ideology here is to be seen as the particular way in which a so-called truth is organized. Truth and ideology are not opposites, but as Foucault suggests, conflated categories. In retrospect, we may analyze the structure or parameters of an historical "discourse," which for the purposes of this discussion will be referred to as an "object" discourse, but the trick, however, is that we must not forget that the discourse that frames our discussion—that is, our discourse or the "subject" discourse—must also be understood in terms of its "truth" or ideology. In making "discourse" an object of discourse we inevitably view this "object discourse" from the ideological or "truth" perspective of the "subject discourse" in which we set it. Consequently, we are probably saying more about our own ideological bent, our own truths, than about the "object discourse" we study.

There is, nevertheless, good reason to explore the nature of the "object discourse" even if we "know" it only in terms of the mediating structures of the "subject" or framing discourse. What we learn may be partial or incomplete, but it is a way of assimilating past efforts to understand and shape the world. As nineteenth-century American frontier western discourse enters twenty-first-century discourse, it appears to be constructed around certain regularities that produce a series of linked, if diverse, objects, and recurring and related, if diverse, concepts, as well as recurring and related, if diverse, themes and strategies. These commonalities linking the various manifestations of late-nineteenth/early-twentieth-century frontier western discourse suggest a certain way of understanding and discussing the "frontier." This understanding, this "truth," can also be called "the late-nineteenth/early-twentieth-century frontier western ideology." It is ideological, however, not because it distorts or can be distinguished from some transcendent truth. In keeping with Foucault's conflation of ideology and "truth," the parameters of late-nineteenth/early-twentieth-century frontier discourse are best seen by us where they appear to conflict or contrast with what might be referred to as our early-twentieth-first-century frontier western or Western regional discourse.[44] The distance between the two discourses is significant not only in terms of what it says about us, but also in what it reveals about our past.

Ideology/truth, as it is understood here, is sometimes crystallized into a form that takes on a simple narrative and/or imagistic structure—a form that is most powerful and evident in artistic and certainly theatrical representations where reasoned arguments give way to other modes of communication. In this form, ideology can take the shape of myth—where "myth" is not understood as a universally true action or narrative pattern, but as a synthetic or "constructed" narrative pattern that seems true and significant to those who value it. While myth may thus be viewed as concretized ideology, it is useful to separate more purely "ideological" representations from those that are more purely "mythological"—a distinction that the historian Richard Slotkin succinctly draws. Slotkin writes that "ideological statement as such is discursive and propositional in form, and is based on a deliberate abstraction of ideas from the field of cultural materials. The form of mythological statement is apparently metaphorical, but at the core of the mythic metaphor is a narrative structure."[45] Slotkin goes on to claim that mythical metaphors "are condensed versions of cosmology and/or history."[46] As condensed or crystallized ideology/"truth," myth may appear to capture what might be the essence of a discursive formation. Moreover, in its historical or cosmological dimension, it tends to naturalize or universalize these elements of the discourse. Myth is a shorthand way of expressing complex ideas and feelings, and it additionally tends to create the illusion that those ideas and feelings can be fixed as an ahistorical "always true." It is for this reason that the myth of the frontier West has had such power over American culture—it seems to establish our American identity as an unchanging essence.

* * *

Frontier western discourse with its mythic elements has been very much at home in the theater—actually, the theater is uniquely equipped to deal with both the mythic aspects of discourse and its more usual ideological form. However, the shape and scope of frontier western discourse has been affected by its entrance onto the stage; that is, the frontier discourse as it appears in the theater is profoundly influenced by the nature of theater practices, which in themselves may be understood as derivative of an always-shifting theater discourse. Indeed, the theater is not a transparent medium; it does not offer previously developed representations in a manner untouched and unaffected by the technology of the theater itself. In fact, the frontier represented in the nineteenth-century American theater is neither the mirror image of a preexisting external reality nor the undistorted reflection of a preexisting representation of reality. On the contrary, it is a product of what Stephen Greenblatt, in his discussion of Elizabethan theater, has referred to as "representational exchanges"[47]—that is, the theater imposes itself on the representations it gleans from elsewhere and, in turn, offers theatrical representations that help to mold its audience's receptivity to and manner of molding other representations.[48] The nineteenth-century American theater did not passively mirror the ideas and attitudes about the frontier held by American audiences and represented in other venues and media; on the contrary, theatrical representations of the frontier West were part of the dynamic, ongoing nineteenth-century "multilogue" about the frontier West and its significance for the development of the nation as a whole. Nineteenth-century theatrical representations of the frontier exist in the space where nineteenth-century frontier discourse and nineteenth-century theater/drama conventions (which are the practical manifestations of a theater/drama discourse) overlap; that is, theatrical representations of the frontier are thus the products of an ongoing interaction between the ever-changing frontier discourse and the continuously shifting nature of the theater and theater machine in which these representations appear.

It is most important to bear in mind that the nineteenth-century theater was not a static, monolithic institution. The drama developed for the nineteenth-century stage offered representations that spoke to a range of different groups of theatrical practitioners and their audiences—groups that Bruce McConachie has called "theatrical formations"[49] to signify the coherence resulting from shared social and cultural assumptions and expectations. As McConachie explains, "groups of spectators and theater performers produce each other from the inside out as artists-to-be-experienced and audiences-to-be-entertained in a given historical period."[50] These theatrical formations form the social-cultural matrix within which the representations of the frontier offered in specific dramas must be viewed. Consequently, to understand the nature of the early-twentieth-century theatrical representations of the frontier—the nature of the frontier that is represented in major turn-of-the-century plays like Thomas's *Arizona*, La Shelle and Wister's *The Virginian*, Belasco's *The Girl of the Golden West*, Royle's *The Squaw Man*, Moody's *The Great Divide*, Crothers's *The Three of Us*—it will be necessary to explore the turn-of-the-century frontier discourse and the particular theatrical formation for which these plays were written and produced.

The process by means of which these major frontier dramas merge frontier western discourse, on the one hand, and particular theatrical practices and discourse, on the other hand, is often very complex. Frontier western discourse functions as a context for these plays, but these plays are also a part of this discourse and consequently contribute to it. The same can be said for the connections between these plays and the theater in which they appear. For the purposes of analytical clarity, a line will be drawn in the next two chapters. In the first chapter, the intent will be to establish a sense of the larger frontier western discourse that functioned as context for the major frontier plays that appear in New York at the turn of the nineteenth to the twentieth century. In this chapter references will be made to a number of contributing texts—both nonfictional and fictional. In this discussion, however, no reference will be made to the products of the legitimate theater.

In the second chapter, the focus will be on the theater practices and conventions that function as a context for the plays that not only culminate the theatrical attempts to represent the frontier on the early-twentieth-century American legitimate stage, but also—by virtue of the important critical and audience successes of Thomas's, Wister and La Shelle's, Belasco's, Royle's, Moody's, and Crothers's plays—may be seen as a culmination of late-nineteenth/early-twentieth-century American theater. Having set in place what might be viewed as the two primary axes around which this study revolves—the shifting frontier western discourse of the late nineteenth and the early twentieth centuries, on the one hand, and the theater conventions and practices that concretize theater discourse from the same period, on the other—the study will move to an examination of eight plays significant to the developing frontier western discourse.

This section of the study is divided into four chapters, with each chapter examining a pair of plays that are linked both chronologically and thematically. While the plays in the first pair opened in December 1899 and the fall of 1900, the plays of each of the other three pairs opened in the same theater season. More important than the chronological connection between the plays of each pair is the fact that the discussion of each pair focuses specifically on how these plays negotiate a particular issue pertaining to the frontier western discourse or its theatrical representation. The first of these chapters, chapter 3, will concentrate on how Clyde Fitch's *The Cowboy and the Lady* (1899) and Augustus Thomas's *Arizona* (1900) embody the tension between discipline and spontaneity as these two concepts are played out in the western frontier discourse. Chapter 4 explores the impact of theatrical adaptation on two of the most important early-twentieth-century novels dealing with the western frontier: Owen Wister's *The Virginian* (1902) and Frederic Remington's *John Ermine of the Yellowstone* (1902). This chapter focuses on the play versions of these novels put together by Louis Evan Shipman (*John Ermine of the Yellowstone*) and Wister with Kirke La Shelle (*The Virginian*) for the 1903–1904 season. The next chapter investigates the ways in which two of the 1905–1906 season's most successful dramas, Edwin Milton Royle's *The Squaw Man* and David Belasco's *The Girl of the Golden West*, challenged certain aspects of the new frontier myth even as they affirmed it. Finally, chapter 6 will examine the manner in which the aesthetic shift away from melodrama toward the so-called new realism affected the theatrical representation of the frontier. The focus of this chapter will be William Vaughn Moody's *The Great Divide* and Rachel Crothers's *The Three of Us*—two extraordinarily successful plays from the 1906–1907 season.

It is hoped that the careful analysis of how these plays presented the frontier experience to early-twentieth-century audiences will enable students of American Studies and the theater to understand the significant role the theater has played for citizens of the United States as they have sought to define themselves and their culture.

Part I

The Axes of Analysis: Frontier Western Discourse and Theater Practice

1. Frontier Western Discourse at the Turn of the Nineteenth to the Twentieth Century ⁓

Since the first British colonists in North America began to give expression to their New World experiences, the American discourse on the frontier West has taken numerous shapes. Certainly, variations in the who, what, where, when, and why of the discourse have affected its content; nevertheless, the assorted statements and expressions that comprise frontier western discourse have had a certain coherence. From the early seventeenth century, recurring modes of expression, concepts, and strategies or themes have furnished this discourse with a degree of continuity. Most important, the ongoing effort to give American frontier experience some clear shape has provided a continuous source of unity. The geographic nature of the actual frontier may have varied from eastern forests to midwestern prairies to far western plains, deserts, and mountains, but the underlying view of the western frontier as a liminal zone, a borderland, on the edge of civilization has pervaded European-American efforts to represent frontier existence.

The earliest British colonists were well aware that in traveling across the Atlantic they had abandoned the relatively safe and familiar—if, from the Puritan perspective, ungodly or even oppressive—Old World for the primitive wilderness that was often threatening and definitely unfamiliar. These adventurous emigrants were not, however, without intellectual baggage; they arrived in the New World armed with habits of mind born of the Old World they had supposedly left behind. Secure in their own "civilized" virtues, the colonists confronted an unknown "savage" wilderness, and the tension between mind-set and environment was often profoundly unsettling. Seventeenth-century New Englanders reassured themselves by interpreting this tension as a struggle between the forces of civilized piety and light, on the one hand, and savage sin and darkness, on the other.

Indians attempting to defend themselves against European intrusion were construed not as subjects in their own right, but as heathen devils to be suppressed or as scourges of God punishing Christian settlers who strayed from the straight and narrow path. This transformation of a lived, empirical reality into a metaphysical parable is readily apparent in seventeenth-century "captivity narratives," such as that published by Mary Rowlandson in 1682. Recounting her experience of her abduction by Indians through her eventual release from bondage, Rowlandson offered Puritan contemporaries an allegory in which enlightened godliness withstands the horrors of life among godless infidels. As is the usual pattern, experience, in this case frontier experience, enters the realm of discourse via the mediation of previously established categories of meaning—on this occasion categories drawn from the governing theology.[1]

The seventeenth-century "captivity narrative" represents an early effort by English-speaking settlers to give meaning to frontier hardships. During the following centuries, Americans developed other strategies to encompass the tensions of wilderness life, to assimilate the pioneer experience. Although these strategies have shifted over time, what appears to be relatively consistent until well into the twentieth century is the tendency to view the frontier as a place of conflict between European "civilization" and wilderness "savagery." Even as the western frontier disappeared in the nineteenth century, this conflict continued to frame American writers' and artists' attempts to comprehend the frontier legacy. Indeed, the opposition of "civilization" and "savagery" informs nineteenth-century American frontier representations as diverse as those offered in James Fenimore Cooper's Leatherstocking novels (1823–1841), Francis Parkman's autobiographical classic *The Oregon Trail* (1849), countless popular dime novels (written between 1860 and 1900), Wild West shows like Buffalo Bill Cody's (which played from 1883 until 1913), and Frederick Jackson Turner's historical essay "The Significance of the Frontier in American History" (1893).

Like the earlier Puritan "captivity narratives," nineteenth-century frontier narratives revolve around the interaction of civilization and savagery, but the "civilization" and "savagery" that provide structure for these more recent narratives were no more neutrally conceived than in the earlier Puritan tales. In accordance with what post-structuralist theorists have maintained regarding the binary oppositions that structure "texts" (a term used here to indicate human efforts to set experience into communicable form), the binary opposites, civilization and savagery, are never evenly balanced but always appear as hierarchically related categories.[2] In fact, representing different sides of the same coin, binary opposites are defined in terms of each other, with one side generally functioning as the positive center for a text and the opposite acting as a negative, marginalized "other." Although the sharp distinctions made between binary opposites in a text are never as final or stable as they seem to be after a cursory reading—thus opening the door for post-structuralist deconstructions of the text—the hierarchies that shape a text suggest the "ideological" biases or "truth" assumptions inherent in it. For instance, early-nineteenth-century romantics reacting against what they viewed as an inflexible rationalism that bolstered a repressive social/political status quo could tout "savagery" as an original purity, a positive. In this context, "civilization" is a falling away from or a corruption of the primal pure state, and is, consequently, a negative. On the other hand, ambitious Americans seeking to rationalize their appropriation of pristine wilderness lands "inefficiently" used by Native Americans could reverse the terms, viewing "civilization" as a more rational, effective use of resources—and thus a positive term—and "savagery" as the lack of civilized reason and, consequently, a negative term.

Although both the idealized romantic and the exculpatory "realistic" interpretations of the civilization/savagery opposition manifest themselves in nineteenth-century American texts—sometimes both at different points in the same text—the latter approach seems to have been predominant throughout most of the century. Recalling the Enlightenment trust in reason and progress, and capitalizing, later in the century, on the rapid dissemination of the principles of Darwinian evolution, texts informed by this approach presented the frontier in terms of a complex process tracing the progressive movement from savagery to civilization, from darkness to light—a process that encompassed both the land and its inhabitants.[3] In other words, the frontier was viewed as the site of a conflict in which the forces of enlightened civilization displaced natural savagery, which was sometimes viewed as exotic and even noble, but generally understood as inferior to European civilization. Whether this process was conceived in the theological terms of the Puritan "captivity narratives" or couched in the more romantic terms of Cooper's novels, Indian plays like John Augustus Stone's *Metamora* (1829), or epic poems like Henry Wadsworth Longfellow's *The Song of Hiawatha*, it functioned as the dominant organizing principle for American representations of the frontier. Consequently, even while exhibiting a certain amount of ambivalence about the final results, novels such as Cooper's or plays like *Metamora* generally rationalize Euro-American expansion across the continent—a not entirely surprising position given the Euro-American audiences for which these tales and plays were written.

Throughout the first half of the nineteenth century, when this process of civilizing the frontier appeared in American art and literature, it was generally conceived as a confrontation of white civilization and Indian savagery.[4] Even as the Indian challenge to white settlers diminished in the later years of the nineteenth century, the victory of civilization over savagery continued to underlie the Western travel accounts, railroad advertisements, and dime novels, which brought the frontier experience to eastern audiences, as well as the technical and scientific documents written to foster agricultural expansion in the West.[5] Indeed, during the late nineteenth century the representation of civilization's triumph over savagery assumed a central ideological role for the rising American bourgeoisie—both exemplifying and naturalizing the emerging cultural hegemony established by this class. Late-nineteenth-century manifestations of frontier discourse were not only shaped by a prevailing faith in unrestrained economic growth, but they also reinforced the vision of social, economic, and moral progress that framed thinking about the West and about the nation as a whole.[6]

The notion that frontier process represented a triumph of civilization over savagery was an ideologically appropriate expression of the hopes and aspirations of an emerging American bourgeoisie; however, once this class's hegemony was firmly established at the close of the nineteenth century, an apparent shift in how the frontier was viewed by dominant, "mainstream" culture producers took place. The civilization/savagery opposition remained key to turn-of-the-century frontier representations, but the ways in which "civilization" and "savagery" were construed underwent a certain modulation. This change in attitude, coming just as the American bourgeoisie consolidated its cultural hegemony, can be best understood against the background of a series of large-scale social and cultural transformations.

Some of these changes were more obviously a matter of perception than "reality." Most important to the development of American frontier discourse, in this regard, was the fact that according to the superintendent of the census in 1890, there was for the first time in American history no longer a clear western frontier line.[7] Citizens of the United States could no longer distinguish their nation from European nations by pointing to an unsettled margin of "free land."

Paralleling the perception that the frontier had ceased to exist was a general sense that the nation as a whole was making the transition from a rural, agricultural economy to a primarily urban, industrial-based economy. The balance of rural to urban population was swiftly shifting toward the latter (a change evidenced by the 1920 census, which reported more Americans living in towns or cities of 2,500 people or more than in rural environs[8]). Moreover, the nature of urban populations, especially in the East, was changing with the late-nineteenth-century influx of Eastern and Southern European as well as non-European immigrants. These new arrivals frightened members of the earlier waves of immigration from Northern Europe—immigrants who had established or were struggling to establish themselves among the prosperous classes of the United States. Troubled by increased diversity, as well as rapid industrialization and frequent economic panics (such as those in the early 1870s and early 1890s), which resulted in mass unemployment and harsh competition for the remaining jobs, many comfortably assimilated Northern European Americans pressed for immigration restrictions in the early 1890s.[9] Despite these pressures, the modern heterogeneous city became the focus of American social and cultural life.

Indeed, the new industrial city was the hub of a progressively more complex transportation and communication network. Rapidly growing industrial and commercial centers, cities like New York and Chicago gave shape to the new industrial, urban culture, which began to dominate the nation as a whole. To be sure, there was resistance to the development of a mass-produced, centralized national culture offered by late-nineteenth-century advocates of working-class culture and populism.[10] Even so, as historian Gunther Barth has written, in the late nineteenth century, "railroad lines and telegraph wires served as major arteries for spreading patterns of city life everywhere."[11]

The demographic and social changes that accompanied the rise of the United States as a major industrial power—a transformation that brought the new American entrepreneurial elite to cultural hegemony[12]—paradoxically did not call forth a celebration of urban industrial life. Describing the 1890s as a kind of watershed decade marking the beginning of a significant cultural shift in mainstream American values, the historian John Higham notes a growing uncertainty about the value of industrial progress and "a hunger to break out of the frustrations, the routine, and the sheer dullness of an urban-industrial life."[13] This reaction manifested itself in various ways—most significantly in this context was what Higham refers to as a "revitalized interest in untamed nature."[14] Seemingly resisting the urban-industrial transformation that had both advanced the interests of and been fostered by the American bourgeoisie, American bourgeois culture shifted its focus, embracing what appeared to be a kind of counterculture. Finding solace in the kind of relationship to nature that Emerson, Thoreau, and the Hudson River School of painters had exemplified, turn-of-the-century nature worshippers became disciples of what has been dubbed the "wilderness cult."[15]

This yearning for nature might be understood in terms of Renato Rosaldo's notion of "imperialist nostalgia"[16]: Americans immersed in what was becoming a technologically complex urban culture harkened back to a preindustrial wilderness that, unfortunately, was being destroyed by industrial growth. Ironically, Americans hoping to escape the modern urban world and return—if only briefly—to an unsullied nature depended on the products of industrial growth to make this return possible. It was the ultimate symbol of nineteenth-century industrial expansion, the railroad,[17] that provided eastern city dwellers with the means of visiting the still untamed West.

Tourism into the West existed before the 1890s. It had become a significant factor in western development after the completion of the transcontinental railroad in 1869 made traveling to the West easier and more comfortable than when the Conestoga wagon was the primary mode of transcontinental travel. During the 1870s and 1880s, however, tourists traveling by railroad to the West were from the wealthiest social classes in America. A ticket from the East Coast to the West Coast cost about $300—more than most wage earners could afford, especially given the fact that, as an 1874–1875 survey of wage-earning families in Massachusetts reported, the average family's yearly income was a mere $763.[18] To entice the few who could afford the trip, the railroads provided their exclusive clientele with palatial Pullman car accommodations. Although these tourists looked forward to seeing the West's geological and geographical curiosities, they did not want to sacrifice comfort while journeying to these sites. To guarantee ease of travel and to insulate these wealthy wayfarers from anything that might jeopardize the aura of respectability with which they surrounded themselves, exclusive travel companies such as Raymond and Whitcomb arranged tours for carefully screened groups of quality patrons.[19]

In the 1870s and 1880s, elegant resorts often built by the railroads to attract the elite from the East Coast and Europe sprang up across the West. In the early 1870s, General William J. Palmer, owner of the Denver and Rio Grande Railroad began to tout Colorado Springs as a European-style spa offering a healthy climate to well-to-do patrons. Extremely elegant resort hotels like the Del Monte (built by Charles Crocker and the Southern Pacific Railroad in Monterey, California, and opened in 1880), the Antlers (with Palmer as the primary investor, opened in Colorado Springs in 1883), and the Del Coronado (opened in San Diego in 1888) appeared throughout the West, especially on the California coast, advertised as America's Italy, and in the Colorado Rockies, heralded as America's Swiss Alps.[20] While attracting wealthy visitors to the West, these luxurious establishments were intended to protect their patrons from coarse, wilderness conditions. As Anne Farrar Hyde has written:

> Scenery and climate contributed only part of the attraction for a resort area. American tourists demanded architecture modeled after the most well-known European designs. Their concern about emulating Europe made opulent furnishings, elaborate landscape design, and elegant entertainment a requirement. Such attributes insulated them from the wilderness that still made up a large part of the far western landscape.[21]

These sumptuous hotels built in various European styles were meant to wrap their guests in a cocoon of pseudo-European refinement.[22] "Civilization" was not to be sacrificed to "savagery."

In the 1890s, however, inspired by the new wilderness cult's faith in the regenerative powers of nature, many Americans sought less mediated experiences of the wild. This new emphasis on wilderness virtues manifested itself in a sudden proliferation of associations and clubs that stressed the importance of wilderness experiences: the Appalachian Mountain Club (1876), the Boone and Crockett Club (1888), the Sierra Club (1892), the Mazamas (1892), the Campfire Club (1897), the Tribe of Woodcraft Indians (1902), and the Boy Scouts of America (1910). Moreover, the growing desire to experience untamed nature, as well as the belief that outdoor adventures had a beneficial effect on the health and character of the individual, prompted the federal government to guarantee the continued existence of frontier wilderness in at least a limited way by withdrawing federal lands from the reach of private investors seeking to develop these lands for profit. Most significant here was the rapid increase in the number of national parks. In 1889, Yellowstone (established in 1872) was the sole national park, but between 1890 and 1910, a number of parks were inaugurated, including Yosemite (1890), General Grant (1890, but absorbed into Kings Canyon National Park in 1940), and Sequoia (1890) in California; Mount Rainier (1899) in Washington; Crater Lake (1902) in Oregon; and Glacier (1910) in Montana.

Supporting the national parks movement and hoping to take advantage of it were, of course, the railroad owners. Railroads stood to gain from the increase in patronage resulting from easterners traveling west to enjoy the national parks, and consequently, their owners sought to increase the allure by constructing large hotels near or actually within the national parks. The Northern Pacific Railroad opened Mammoth Hot Springs Hotel (1884) and financed the construction of the Old Faithful Inn (opened in 1904) in Yellowstone; the Santa Fe Railroad, with Fred

Harvey, opened El Tovar Hotel at the Grand Canyon in 1905; and the Great Northern Railroad opened Glacier Park Lodge at Glacier National Park in 1913. What distinguished the Old Faithful Inn, El Tovar, and Glacier Park Lodge from the earlier constructed palatial resorts was that in keeping with the wilderness fascination of the tourists visiting these parks, all three hotels were rustic in appearance—designed and constructed to fit into the natural environment and not impose European architectural styles on it. The internal decor and the external design of each were meant to capture a sense of the hardiness of the local terrain. Describing these "American log palaces," Anne Farrar Hyde writes: "Rather than building structures that insulated people from the strange western environment, the railroads and their architects, inspired by the West's beauties, created buildings that celebrated them."[23] In short, the "West's beauties," its uncontaminated savagery, had become a commodity that railroad owners and their business associates sought to sell.

These attractive, mammoth "log palaces" catered to the well-to-do, but during the last decade of the nineteenth century, diminishing transportation costs made the national parks accessible to tourists of more modest means. Reaching for a mass market in the late 1880s, the transcontinental railroads began to develop improved tourist Pullman cars for those who could not afford the price of the more exclusive, palatial accommodations.[24] Moreover, the expansion of branch lines lowered the cost of side trips from nearby cities to wilderness areas. In the 1870s and the early 1880s, an expedition from San Francisco to Yosemite could be made only by stagecoach at a cost of at least $80; by 1907, there was railroad service to within a short distance of Yosemite Valley.[25] The increase in visitors to the parks clearly demonstrates the impact of accessibility. At Yellowstone, for instance, by the end of the 1880s, the park had 6,000 visitors each summer; by the end of the 1890s, the number had risen to 10,000 each year; and by 1915, 50,000 visitors arrived each summer.[26]

Technological advances in transportation made it possible for growing numbers of tourists to experience the wilderness; however, the appetite for this kind of experience was whetted by other manifestations of the new industrial society. The increasing cultural significance of wilderness and "outdoors" activities was stimulated by late-nineteenth-century developments in mass culture. The broad dissemination of new conceptions of "nature" and "wilderness" was, again, the ironic result of the very industrial and technological "progress" from which escape was sought through the "return to nature." Innovations in communication and transportation made the mass production and national circulation of both literary and pictorial representations of the West possible in ways inconceivable before the late nineteenth century.

Of special significance was the rapid development of publishing industries. The written word, or, more specifically, the printed word, became vastly more accessible to the masses than ever before as a result of various technological advances in production and distribution. Certainly the development of the pulp fiction industry contributed mightily to the diffusion of wilderness imagery and Western fantasies, but the revolution in print media is nowhere more apparent than in the proliferation of newspapers throughout the century. The 1840 federal census recorded 138 daily and 1,141 weekly newspapers across the country; these numbers had risen to 1,731 dailies and 12,721 weeklies in the 1890 census[27]—the same census that led to the historical announcement regarding the closing of the frontier. While the growth of the publishing industry was not limited to the expanding numbers of dailies and weeklies, these kinds of publications contributed significantly to the dissemination of the frontier western discourse. Indeed, period newspapers participated in this discourse not only by reporting events and stories related to the West, but also through the positions espoused on editorial pages.[28]

In transportation and communication sectors, technological developments facilitated the consolidation of what might be understood as dominant American managerial-class culture even as the products of this culture, like those fostering the wilderness cult, seemed to assail the very technology that allowed for their circulation, but equally ironic is the fact that the spokespersons for the late-nineteenth-century cultural shift referred to by Higham—a shift that represented a rejection of what Higham referred to as the "authority of professional elites"—themselves often embodied the "authority of professional elites."[29] The late-nineteenth-century expansion of "professionalism" within the larger culture is not entirely surprising given the growing complexity of modern industrial, urban life. As more people took up residence in large heterogeneous metropolises, new areas of knowledge and new skills were required to manage both public and private lives. Specialization and professionalism—representing a new premium placed on expertise—were by-products of the proliferation of knowledge and skills. Moreover, the growing emphasis on specialization and professionalism engendered the need for methods of verifying the actual presence of specialized knowledge. This in turn implied a need for regulation and standardization within occupations—further propelling the movement toward the greater centralization of resources and control that characterized late-nineteenth-century bourgeois culture.[30]

The organization and formalization of knowledge within carefully delineated specialized disciplines was greatly dependent on nineteenth-century developments in higher education. As Burton Bledstein claimed, the university "emerged as the seminal institution within the culture of professionalism."[31] The late-nineteenth-century American university, in short, became the principal site for the construction of diverse fields of knowledge. The university was thus where cultural workers for the newly dominant bourgeois culture laid down the parameters for what was known. It is not surprising, then, that the dominant late-nineteenth-century frontier western discourse received its clearest statement from a young professor who worked at one of the universities that were to become synonymous with research in the twentieth century, and who was himself engaged in the professionalization of his discipline, namely history. At the center of the late-nineteenth-century western frontier discourse was a University of Wisconsin history professor, Frederick Jackson Turner, who was a product of the recently established doctoral program at Johns Hopkins University.[32]

* * *

While the late-nineteenth- and early-twentieth-century frontier discourse is rather heterogeneous in its scope and concerns, Frederick Jackson Turner's "The Significance of the Frontier in American History" might be seen as its center if only because of the attention it has garnered from scholars, artists, and the general public. Turner published notoriously little during his lifetime, but this key essay, which was first presented as a paper at the American Historical Association conference convened at Chicago's Columbian Exposition in 1893 and published a year later, had a far-ranging impact on historiography and on American culture in general. Certainly, Turner was not the first scholar or popular author to attempt to describe the significance of the frontier for American development,[33] but he was the most successful in capturing the imagination of his contemporaries. He rose very quickly to a place of eminence in his chosen field, and it was soon apparent that anyone dealing with the frontier American experience had to come to terms with his work.

Ostensibly, the inspiration for Turner's essay came from the bulletin of the superintendent of the census for 1890, in which Turner read:

Up to and including 1880 the country had a frontier of settlement, but at present the unsettled area has been so broken into by isolated bodies of settlement that there can hardly be said to be a frontier line. In the discussion of its extent, its westward movement, etc., it can not, therefore, any longer have a place in the census reports.[34]

Turner notes the significance of this announcement, claiming that "this brief official statement marks the closing of a great historic movement"; no longer would the nation's development be characterized by "the existence of an area of free land, its continuous recession, and the advance of American settlement westward."[35] In calling attention to this "closing," Turner was shifting the focus of American history from the Eastern Seaboard to the western "free lands"—a proposition that some of his contemporaries might have found radical.[36]

Indeed, Turner maintained that American democracy's distinctiveness was a by-product of the western frontier experience. On the frontier, which Turner defined as "the outer edge of the wave—the meeting point between savagery and civilization,"[37] the civilized eastern pioneer confronts a western savage wilderness that transforms him[38] into a new American type of democratic individual. Turner claimed that this metamorphosis is initiated when the frontier wilderness forces the pioneer to relinquish his connection to Eastern civilization:

> The frontier is the line of most rapid and effective Americanization. The wilderness masters the colonist. It finds him a European in dress, industries, tools, modes of travel, and thought. It takes him from the railroad car and puts him in the birch canoe. It strips off the garments of civilization and arrays him in the hunting shirt and the moccasin. It puts him in the log cabin of the Cherokee and Iroquois and runs an Indian palisade around him. Before long he has gone to planting Indian corn and plowing with a sharp stick; he shouts the war cry and takes the scalp in orthodox Indian fashion. In short, at the frontier the environment is at first too strong for the man. He must accept the conditions which it furnishes, or perish, and so he fits himself into the Indian clearings and follows the Indian trails.[39]

Thus begins the frontier process, according to Turner, but it does not end with the pioneer simply adapting to wilderness demands. On the contrary, once acclimated to the wilderness, the pioneer, in turn, starts to act on the wilderness with significant results: "Little by little he transforms the wilderness, but the outcome is not the old Europe, not simply the development of Germanic germs…. The fact is, that here is a new product that is American."[40] The interaction of eastern pioneer and western wilderness ultimately produced the distinctly American character, which Turner described in the following terms:

> ...that coarseness and strength combined with acuteness and inquisitiveness; that practical, inventive turn of mind, quick to find expedients; that masterful grasp of material things, lacking in the artistic but powerful to effect great ends; that restless, nervous energy; that dominant individualism, working for good and for evil, and withal that buoyancy and exuberance which comes with freedom.[41]

Even as he announced the end of America's frontier period, Turner offered consolation to nationalistic contemporaries by affirming an American exceptionalism. Moreover, his interpretation was embraced by many American historians and literati who thrived on the nostalgic vision of a golden past or hungered for an assertion of American distinctiveness in the present. Indeed, Turner's frontier thesis was a salve easing the anxiety resulting from the rapid industrialization and urbanization of the late nineteenth century—an anxiety that was especially acute during and after the Panic of 1893. Celebrating American pioneer individualism, Turner's frontier analysis offered grounds on which to confront and even overcome social and cultural crises.

It is certainly possible that the impact of Turner's frontier thesis as it was laid out in "The Significance of the Frontier in American History" can be largely attributed to its timeliness, but the place it attained within the larger frontier western discourse suggests that Turner was not only an able synthesizer of current ideas and perspectives, but also well endowed with rhetorical skills. Turner's rhetorical eloquence manifested itself in the vivid imagery and potent examples that he employed throughout his essays.[42] It was equally if not more apparent in the way he organized his arguments—especially the way he organized his arguments around various antitheses or oppositions, a rhetorical devise that, according to Ronald Carpenter, pervades not only Turner's most famous essay but much of his other writing on the West.[43]

While Turner may have utilized antitheses to clarify his ideas in the hope of making them more persuasive, his use of this device suggests another dimension of his rhetorical method: he used the antithesis as a means of distinguishing different ideas, concepts, or images, but also as a starting point in a dialectical practice that would culminate in a new synthesis. The tendency to structure his argument around polar oppositions, which he then sought to reconcile or bridge, might be the most distinctive aspect of Turner's style. Throughout his major essays, he seems to balance or harmonize a number of sharply defined oppositions such as East/West, Europe/America, egalitarianism/individualism, and heredity/environment. In fact, the discursive power of Turner's thesis may reside in its apparently successful resolution of a number of the polar oppositions around which the turn-of-the-century frontier discourse was structured. Perhaps the most important example of this strategy is offered in Turner's delineation of the frontier as "the meeting point between savagery and civilization"—a definitional phrase that both poses and resolves the opposition of concepts that were most pertinent to nineteenth-century discussion of the frontier.

Underlying and supporting Turner's attempts to bridge these various polar oppositions is a larger bridge between two seemingly separate but significant late-nineteenth-century American modes of discourse—one associated with free-flowing American romantic idealism and one related to the more systematic, scientific ordering of phenomena, manifested in Darwinian evolutionary thought. In this regard, Richard Hofstadter insightfully wrote:

> In Turner's preoccupation with the evolutionary stages by which the frontier of the hunter and trapper were superseded by that of the pioneer settler, and then by the increasingly complex communities of villages and small towns, he was forging a link between the Darwinian mentality of his era and the older mythology of Edenic America—joining hopes and aspirations that were as basic to the American outlook as they were poignantly self-contradictory and self-defeating.[44]

The degree to which Turner successfully aligned these two very different perspectives—that belonging to Darwinian evolutionary science and that of American romanticism—may be the true source of Turner's impact on generations of Americans.

* * *

It was probably through his formal education that Turner was initiated into the Darwinian revolution. As a sixteen-year-old lad from the small town of Portage, Wisconsin, he enrolled at the University of Wisconsin–Madison in September 1878. In Madison, Turner would complete his bachelor's and master's degrees before moving on to Johns Hopkins, where he completed his doctorate in history in 1890. The faculties of both these institutions—the University of Wisconsin, though still very small and certainly without the reputation for research that it would eventually garner, and Johns Hopkins, the center of graduate research in America at the time—were animated by the intellectual currents that pervaded the late-nineteenth-century academy. Especially important in this regard was the rapid dissemination of Darwinian ideas on biological evolution. Fewer than twenty years after its publication, Charles Darwin's *The Origin of Species* (1859) was transforming much of what was studied in American universities.

Not only the natural sciences but also the social sciences and humanities were profoundly affected by Darwin's methodology and conclusions. The application of Darwinian modes of thought to areas other than biology was led by the British philosopher Herbert Spencer, whose work significantly impressed Turner's teachers at the University of Wisconsin and Johns Hopkins, as well as Turner himself.[45] Spencer, an advocate of evolution even before *The Origin of Species* had appeared in print, was intensely committed to the notion that the structure and development of societies could be understood in terms of the structure and development of individual living organisms.[46] A similar preoccupation with organic evolution left its imprint on ethnology, which was to become the field of anthropology. Scholars in that field began to seek the origins of basic elements of "civilization" in primitive "savage" cultures. This broad historical approach to the study of society received its most articulate American expression in Lewis H. Morgan's *Ancient Society* (1877), first published the year before Turner matriculated at the University of Wisconsin. Morgan's notion of evolution and especially his understanding of concepts like "savagery" and "civilization" certainly influenced members of the academy in Turner's day.[47]

Subtitled "Researches in the Lines of Human Progress from Savagery through Barbarism to Civilization," Morgan's *Ancient Society* discusses social evolution in terms of seven successive stages or periods, including three stages of savagery, three of barbarism, and one culminating stage of civilization.[48] Morgan notes that each of the seven stages "has a distinct culture and exhibits a mode of life more or less special and peculiar to itself," but he maintains that breaking down social development into these different phases or periods facilitates the discussion of "a particular society according to its condition of relative advancement."[49] In other words, savagery and barbarism are understood in terms of the extent to which they reflect the movement to civilization—or, conversely, they are defined in terms of the degree to which they lack the accouterments of civilization.

The "upward flow of human progress,"[50] according to Morgan, climaxed when the Aryan and Semitic families attained a civilized level of development. Certainly, the ultimate success Morgan attributed to the Aryan and Semitic families could be interpreted in racial, even racist terms. Although racist analyses were very much a part of late-nineteenth- and early-twentieth-century social Darwinism, Morgan claimed that the Aryan and Semitic families arose from barbarism as a result of "the commingling of diverse stocks, superiority of subsistence or advantage of position, and possibly from all together."[51] In other words, he seems to have placed great weight on the environmental context that allowed for a productive intermixing of diverse stocks as well as more accessible subsistence. While the mechanism for evolutionary progress here may have more in common with a Lamarckian understanding of improvement through use than with Darwin's natural selection, this focus on environment rather than heredity as the primary source of change exemplifies how evolutionary ideas could be adapted to explain social development. Such an adaptation of evolutionary discourse informs Turner's interpretation of the role of the frontier in American development.

In making his case for American exceptionalism, Turner used a similarly environmentalist language to challenge the then prevalent understanding of American history, which was based on the belief that American democracy had its only significant roots in Europe. The major spokesman for the latter approach was Herbert Baxter Adams, the Johns Hopkins history professor with whom Turner studied while working for his doctorate. Adams asserted what has been called the "germ" theory of American development: American institutions were understood as having evolved from the germ of democracy that originated in the ancient German "tun." While following an evolutionary approach, the Adams "germ" school focused on the continuity of this germ's development through time and varying conditions.[52] Turner focused less on this continuity than on the dramatic impact of changed environmental conditions. This is most apparent in the initial phase of the pioneer's interaction with the wilderness, during which, as we have seen, Turner maintained, "the environment is at first too strong for the man. He must accept the conditions which it furnishes, or perish...." Using the scientific language of the day, Turner was more explicit when he claimed in an 1896 essay: "The history of our political institutions, our democracy, is not a history of imitation, of simple borrowing; it is a history of the evolution and adaptation of organs in response to changed environment, a history of the origin of new political species."[53]

While Turner appeared to focus on the environment rather than the pioneer germ as the source of American democracy, he was not totally without certain prejudices regarding the nature of that pioneer. Throughout his life he expressed doubts about whether Americans not descended from North European stock could make the kind of adaptation to the wilderness environment necessary for developing and sustaining American democracy.[54]

Not an advocate for the immigration restrictions that other turn-of-the-century Americans sought,[55] and not a public supporter of principles and practices that would appear overtly racist to twentieth-century eyes, Turner nonetheless consistently represented American pioneers as white males—demonstrating his participation in the racial and gender biases that characterize the turn-of-the-century American cultural scene.

Especially problematic is Turner's treatment of Native Americans. As his critics have maintained and even his supporters admit, Indians are not presented as agents or actors in Turner's story. They are simply part of the environment to which the Anglo-Saxon pioneers must adapt. In describing how pioneers must learn the Indian ways or perish in the wilderness, Turner equates these ways, which, as Wilbur Jacobs points out, are certainly cultural products, with environmental factors.[56] In short, Indians and the artifacts of their culture are lumped together with the wilderness as part of the savage environment to which pioneers must adapt before they can develop a distinctly American form of civilization.[57] For Turner, the sequential triad—savagery, barbarism, and civilization—defined by Morgan is reshaped into a dyad of savagery, defined in terms of wilderness environment including Indians and their culture, and civilization, defined in terms of the white pioneer.

Turner's "frontier thesis" is rooted, then, in Darwinian social evolutionary assumptions, which present the movement from simple primitive savagery to complex civilization as unidirectional; however, in Turner's view of the interaction of savagery and civilization, there is movement in both directions. He presents the meeting of civilization and savagery as a process in which civilization returns to savagery in order to cleanse itself before evolving into a new civilization. Insofar as Turner envisioned a purifying wilderness reasserting its value against the claims of civilization, his frontier thesis—and indeed late-nineteenth-century frontier discourse in general—evidences a connection with the American romantic idealization of nature. While Turner's wilderness savagery may sometimes function as a marginalized, negative "other" to civilization, it functions on other occasions as the very positive center of his discourse.

Even as Turner extols American history as the history of human progress in brief, his sense of the positive nature of wilderness savagery is apparent. In "The Significance of the Frontier in American History," he writes:

> The United States lies like a huge page in the history of society. Line by line as we read this continental page from West to East we find the record of social evolution. It begins with the Indian and the hunter; it goes on to tell of the

disintegration of savagery by the entrance of the trader, the pathfinder of civilization....[58]

His choice of the word "disintegration" here, as well as a few pages later when he describes how "the disintegrating forces of civilization entered the wilderness,"[59] suggests that there was a savage wilderness "integration" that could be and was undermined by spreading civilization. It is contact with this primeval integration that, according to Turner, most significantly influences the American character in a healthy, liberating fashion:

> American social development has been continually beginning over again on the frontier. This perennial rebirth, this fluidity of American life, this expansion westward with its new opportunities, its continuous touch with the simplicity of primitive society, furnish the forces dominating American character.[60]

Although Turner valued wilderness savagery, he did not view nature in the mystical or spiritual manner of some of America's transcendentalists; nevertheless, in his youth he treasured Emerson as a favorite author[61] and throughout his life he cherished periods of peaceful escape in the outdoors. In this regard, Turner admitted: "I sometimes am in doubt about 'civilization'.... Perhaps that is because I like to go trout fishing."[62] Turner's biographer, Ray Billington, suggests that this attraction to the outdoors was no simple idle diversion—that, in fact, "physically, Turner required wilderness life as a tonic to rejuvenate a jaded system worn by the pressures of teaching and writing." Billington further elaborated that "those who knew him best recognized the symptoms—a nervous irritability, a far-away look in his eyes—that meant he *must* find solace in the forest or risk serious disorders."[63] In this deep-seated need for wilderness, Turner manifested his own variation of the "imperialist nostalgia" that infected many other Americans seeking escape from their modern urban world by returning, if only briefly, to untouched nature.

As more and more Americans flocked to national parks and explored the wilderness, Turner's claims on behalf of the frontier took on greater resonance. While turn-of-the-century enthusiasm for the outdoors was not just an American phenomenon, the particular American zeal for the wilderness—a zeal that underwrites late-nineteenth-century American frontier discourse—both benefited from and informed Turner's frontier thesis. Balancing scientific discourse with a stance toward nature that incorporates traditional romantic idealization, Turner reconciled two traditions of American thought in a way that may not have always been intellectually coherent, but was certainly emotionally and psychologically satisfying for his contemporaries—both those drawn to scientific analysis and those drawn to old romantic ideals; both those belonging to the new centralized, urban, managerial elite and those who subscribed to the old decentralized, yeoman farmer tradition. In accomplishing this union, Turner demonstrated how late-nineteenth-century capitalist efficiency could walk hand in hand with a romantic faith in wilderness redemption—how culture and counterculture could become one.

* * *

Turner was not alone in linking Darwinian thought and wilderness worship. Like others, he entered a field of discourse in which "civilization" and "savagery" were key, if unstable, concepts. Turner's understanding of "savagery" and "civilization" as well as the larger parameters of the turn-of-the-century frontier discourse within which these terms functioned becomes clearer when his understanding of the wilderness is compared with that of other spokespersons for the new wilderness cult—spokespersons who also helped to define the late-nineteenth-century frontier discourse that the new mass communication technologies disseminated to the American public.

Among the most significant contributors to the wilderness movement was naturalist John Muir. Like Turner, a Wisconsinite who spent his adolescent years in Portage, not far from Turner's home, Muir enrolled in the University of Wisconsin, but in 1860, eighteen years before Turner. Unlike Turner, however, Muir did not complete his degree. He relinquished his seat at the University of Wisconsin in the early 1860s to take his place in the "University of the Wilderness."[64] By the late 1860s, Muir found himself in Yosemite. In the 1870s, Muir's devotion to this wilderness area prompted him to begin writing and speaking on behalf of Yosemite wilderness preservation. Among his more important efforts was a series of articles for *Century*, one of the nation's premier literary monthlies. Largely due to Muir's activism, Yosemite, already a state park, became a national park in 1890. Two years later, Muir was instrumental in founding the Sierra Club, which had as its primary function the protection of pristine wilderness. In 1894, Muir's first book, *The Mountains of California*, was published, becoming, according to writer Gretel Ehrlich, "an instant classic."[65] Awarded honorary degrees from Harvard in 1896 and from Wisconsin in 1897, Muir established himself in the 1890s as a major voice on Western wilderness affairs.

Muir's paeans to wilderness in his various writings offer sure echoes of transcendentalists like Emerson and Thoreau, even though his natural world was far more wild and sublime than the pastoral New England countryside of his predecessors. Like these earlier lovers of the outdoors, Muir read deep but comforting messages in nature. Of the Sierras he could write that "the darkest scriptures of the mountains are illumined with bright passages of love that never fail to make themselves felt when one is alone."[66] Muir believed that those aspects of nature that first appear "lawless" and "ungovernable," "are at length recognized as the necessary effects of causes which followed each other in harmonious sequence—Nature's poems carved on tables of stone...."[67] Certainly, Muir was familiar with Darwin's theory, but rather than characterize nature in the harsh terms of bloody struggle adopted by many Darwinists—especially social Darwinists—he integrated scientific understanding into a vision of benevolent harmony. For instance, in describing trees withstanding a Sierra storm, he wrote:

> All seemed strong and comfortable, as if really enjoying the storm, while responding to its most enthusiastic greetings. We hear much nowadays concerning the universal struggle for existence, but no struggle in the common meaning of the word was manifest here; no recognition of danger by any tree; no depreciation; but rather an invincible gladness as remote from exultation as from fear.[68]

It was to the virtues of this pure and poetic wilderness world that Muir sought to awaken his contemporaries.

Muir viewed wilderness as the necessary cure for those Americans oppressed by overcivilization. In an 1898 essay, he argued the importance of national parks:

> The tendency nowadays to wander in wildernesses is delightful to see. Thousands of tired, nerve-shaken, over-civilized people are beginning to find out that going to the mountains is going home; that wildness is a necessity; and that mountain parks and reservations are useful not only as fountains of timber and irrigating rivers, but as fountains of life. Awakening from the stupefying effects of the vice of over-industry and the deadly apathy of luxury, they are trying as best they can to mix and enrich their own little ongoings with those of Nature, and to get rid of rust and disease.[69]

Living in harmony with wilderness meant living in harmony with nature's law. For Muir, then, wilderness stripped of its horror and viewed as a balm to the overcivilized was to be understood not as a destructive savagery—something for civilization to conquer—but as a positive source for the overcivilized individual's mental health.

While claiming that wilderness served a necessary function for civilization, Muir, like Turner, adopted an evolutionary stance. To be sure, his sense of progress differed considerably from those who viewed progress in terms of a movement from a savage simplicity to a civilized complexity. Instead, Muir called for a new simplicity. In *The Story of My Boyhood and Youth*, written toward the end of his life, Muir confessed an evolutionary faith:

> Surely a better time must be drawing nigh when godlike human beings will become truly humane, and learn to put their animal fellow mortals in their hearts instead of on their backs or in their dinners. In the mean time we may just as well as not learn to live clean, innocent lives instead of slimy, bloody ones. All hale, red-blooded boys are savage, the best and boldest the savagest, fond of hunting and fishing. But when thoughtless childhood is past, the best rise the highest above all this bloody flesh and sport business, the wild foundational animal dying out day by day, as divine uplifting, transfiguring charity grows in.[70]

Muir looked forward to the time when "the wild foundational animal," the animal still prone to violent savagery, would evolve into a civilized human—a human in tune with nature and purified of bloodlust by virtue of a compassion for his or her fellow creatures. Like Turner, Muir believed that the wilderness environment could be instrumental in the evolution of a new kind of "civilization," but perhaps as a result of the rigorous religious discipline that his father imposed on him as a youth,[71] Muir viewed both the frontier wilderness and its impact on civilization in much more spiritual terms than had Turner.

Turner's feeling for the regenerative power of nature lacked the religious dimension of the visionary Muir, but had perhaps even less in common with that of another lover of the wild, Theodore Roosevelt.[72] Because of his political position and extensive writing on the West (including his multivolume history, *The Winning of the West*, published between 1889 and 1896, and more personal histories like his 1888 *Ranch Life and the Hunting Trail*), Roosevelt probably had more impact on the dominant turn-of-the-century frontier discourse than did John Muir. Given Roosevelt's unquestionable place within the eastern establishment,[73] there is, in fact, a certain irony in his close association with the Wild West. The future president made his first extended trip to the West in 1884, when, after suffering personal tragedy (the deaths of his mother and wife in rapid succession) and political setbacks, he took refuge on his ranch in the Dakota Badlands. Here, Roosevelt was reinvigorated by the challenges of western life. Throwing himself fully into the cowboy's life, Roosevelt represented what Earl Pomeroy has described as a "heartily masculine approach to the West, in contrast to the predominantly feminine approach of the Raymond tourists," but, as Pomeroy continues, "there was an adolescent quality to his maleness, a disposition to take the West not in stride but with a leap and a whoop"—that is, for Roosevelt the West was "a great playground,"[74] not a place to live in, as it was for Turner. Always "Mr. Roosevelt," even to his fellow cowboys, it would seem that Roosevelt was never anything but an easterner on vacation even when most involved in the hardy western outdoors.[75]

In speaking and writing, Roosevelt supported his enthusiasm for the western-style "strenuous life"[76] with the rhetoric of social Darwinism. Like Turner, Roosevelt employed a Darwinist perspective to explain the significance of western wilderness for American development, but the "adolescent quality" of Roosevelt's sense of the frontier translated easily into a much more "blood and thunder" attitude than was ever present in Turner. In addresses such as "Biological Analogies in History" (1910) and "The World Movement" (1910), delivered more than twenty years after he first went west, Roosevelt, like Spencer, noted the parallels between the development of species in the animal kingdom and the development of human societies in the human world,[77] and, like Morgan, he traced the development of human society from savagery to civilization, but, most significantly, in these essays he adopted a Darwinian logic to explain why civilization must never lose the "virile fighting virtues" that sustained barbarian societies.[78] This is not to say that Roosevelt believed modern Americans should transform themselves into savage individualists. On the contrary, in his role as a progressive, he believed that unrestrained individualism could descend into a dangerous savagery if not monitored by the new class of expert managers—hence his trust-busting persona. Still, Roosevelt believed that wilderness savagery had been instrumental in the development of a distinctly American character and that the future American society and, in fact, all Anglo-Saxon civilization, which in his mind represented the culmination of social evolution, would decay if it ever lost touch with its savage roots.[79] Unlike Muir, who looked forward to a time when evolution would carry humans beyond their savage early history, Roosevelt felt that evolution and the future of humankind depended on this savage core. Roosevelt, like Turner, sought a civilization bolstered by savage vitality.

For Roosevelt, then, to sustain the Anglo-Saxon male as the agent of historical progress, it was necessary to fend off civilized softness. In this spirit, he helped to create the Boone and Crockett Club in 1888. The club's goal was to foster big game hunting as "the sport for a vigorous and masterful people."[80] In his devotion to a hardy masculinity, Roosevelt became a poster boy for a new perspective on manhood—one that sought to regenerate the modern male who was deteriorating within a debilitating overly tamed, middle-class, white-collar world.[81] Roosevelt's faith in the vigorous Anglo-Saxon and in the West as a training ground for heroic action manifested itself in his own cowboy adventuring as well as in his approach to the organization of his Spanish-American War volunteer regiment, the Rough Riders. The regiment consisted of twelve troops: one was known mostly for its easterners, but members of the other eleven were drawn from the knockabout Wild West. A combination of refined eastern Ivy League swells and rugged western cowboys,[82] his volunteer corps represented a synthesis of civilization and savagery with emphasis on the latter. Roosevelt was certainly no transcendentalist, but his belief in the regenerative function of frontier wilderness was as deep as either Turner's or Muir's and never abated. During Roosevelt's two terms as president, historian Robert Hine writes that "an unparalleled array of conservation activity took place."[83] Roosevelt created national forests, national monuments, and national parks with abandon.

While Roosevelt shared a love of the wilderness with Muir, he was less willing than Muir to separate "wilderness" from brutal "savagery." Interestingly, Muir actually sought to convert Roosevelt to a more compassionate attitude toward the wilderness. When the two went camping together in the Yosemite region in 1903, Muir tried to convince Roosevelt to give up what Muir viewed as his childish affection for hunting—apparently with little success.[84] It would seem that Muir and Roosevelt represented two extremes, between which Turner conveniently fits. Unlike Muir, Turner seemed to think of wilderness and savagery as interchangeable terms. Unlike Roosevelt, Turner viewed the frontier less as an arena of bloody conflict than as an environment requiring hard work in primitive circumstances. As Richard Slotkin has written, Turner's frontier hero was the "farmer," Roosevelt's was the "hunter."[85] Turner's vision of the wilderness, less devout than Muir's, allowed an important evolutionary role for "savagery," and less sensational—or perhaps more grounded in true western experience—than Roosevelt's, rejected the adventure-story romanticization of "savagery."

In short, Turner, Muir, and Roosevelt all negotiated the tension between industrial civilization and wilderness savagery, as well as that between new evolutionary scientific modes of thought and an older, more traditional romantic sensibility. In their separate ways, all three contributed to the late-nineteenth- and early-twentieth-century frontier discourse. Just as important as the fact that the writing of these commentators was circumscribed by concepts like "civilization" and "savagery" is the fact that they viewed these concepts very differently. The range of their views on "civilization" and "savagery" provides some sense of the heterogeneous nature of the late-nineteenth- and early-twentieth-centuries' frontier discourse.

* * *

Even as writers like Turner, Muir, and Roosevelt explored the space separating western wilderness and/or "savagery," on the one hand, and eastern "civilization," on the other, this space took on a very literal geographic significance within late-nineteenth-century American life—that is, differences between West and East provided a convenient lens for interpreting national political, social, and cultural conflicts. As a new western consciousness, manifested politically with the emergence of the Grange and Populist movements, raised itself against what appeared to be the Eastern Seaboard's oppressive economic dominance, the rhetorics of West versus East, of labor versus capital, and of wilderness savagery versus urban civilization became entangled. Indeed, sectional tensions deepened during the depression of the 1890s and came to a head with the bitterly contested 1896 election in which the Democratic and Populist parties' candidate, "the great commoner," Nebraskan William Jennings Bryan, and the Republican candidate and spokesman for traditional northeastern power brokers, William McKinley, vied for the presidency.

In a sense, Turner again seems to encompass this East/West tension. Geographically speaking, he had always focused primarily on the Midwest, which he referred to as the "Old West." This region was, in fact, a bridge between the East and the late-nineteenth-century, trans-Mississippi frontier West. Given its geographical location as an intermediate zone, it is not surprising that Turner's Old West served him so well as the site where eastern civilization and western savagery met. Turner not only linked East and West, civilization and savagery, in his writings, he also did so in his life. His roots may have been in the rural West, but he was definitely drawn to the urbane East. With a doctorate from Johns Hopkins, Turner was unquestionably associated with the eastern professional elite. His connection to the eastern establishment, if ever in doubt, was clearly strengthened when he moved from the University of Wisconsin to Harvard, where he remained from 1910 to 1924. Moreover, his politics in the 1890s seemed to be more in line with the eastern power elite than with western farmers. Somewhat skeptical of the Populists' monetary policies, Turner supported McKinley in 1896. Despite this association with the eastern power structure, the dissemination of Turner's ideas benefited from western sectional pride even as his writings helped to promote it.[86] His ties to the new West are neatly demonstrated by the fact that Turner offered his 1893 address extolling the West's role in American development at the World's Columbian Exposition in Chicago—the first such exposition not presented on the East Coast and, consequently, symbolic of the economic and cultural arrival of the West.

The way in which western sectional pride both shaped and was shaped by turn-of-the-century frontier discourse is apparent not only in the writings of Turner, but also in the cultural assertions of Hamlin Garland. A spokesman for the small western farmer in his struggle against the large eastern financial establishment, Garland lauded the West as a significant factor in American cultural life. In his short volume of critical essays, *Crumbling Idols* (1894), Garland castigated narrow-minded eastern critics and publishers, who turned to Europe for their artistic models. Conversely, Garland praised a variety of regional writers who expressed western perspectives. Included among these were Bret Harte and Joaquin Miller—both of whose writings chronicled the struggles and joys of Northern California miners and were to exert significant influence on late-nineteenth-century frontier drama. Rather than offering secondhand imitations of past European artists, these authors, according to Garland, offered fresh individualistic expressions of true life; they were of and for the present.

Just as Turner claimed American democracy had its source in the "Old West" wilderness, so Garland maintained that true American culture would arise from the heartland, not the Atlantic coast. He boasted about the growing numbers of cities, writers, and "lovers of light and song" in America's interior, and then anticipating how eastern conservatives might respond to his claims for the West, he wrote:

> "Bigness does not count," the East says in answer to the West. Yes, but it does! The prairies lead to general conceptions. The winds give strength and penetration and alertness. The mighty stretches of woods lead to breadth and generosity of intellectual conception. The West and South are coming to be something more than big, coming to the expression of a new world, coming to take their places in the world of literature, as in the world of action, and no sneer from gloomy prophets of the dying past can check or chill them.[87]

In short, Garland insisted that genuine American literature "must come from the soil and the open air, and be likewise freed from tradition."[88] Underlying this distinction of West and East is the belief that American culture, so long dependent on civilized Europe for its models, must find its roots in the real pulsing life of the West. Like Turner, Garland claims that true American "civilization" could not be separated from western "savagery."

Although Garland championed young western artists against the narrow-minded elitism of old-fashioned eastern critics, it is ironic that the two artists Frederic Remington and Owen Wister, who seemed to contribute most to the turn-of-the-century frontier discourse, were, like Roosevelt, both easterners who discovered and embraced the virile Great Plains cowboy life as adults in the 1880s.[89] Remington and Wister may have challenged the old-fashioned eastern critics who embraced European artistic models, but they did so less to push forward the concerns of the hard-working westerner, which had been Garland's primary concern, than to reinvigorate the eastern artistic establishment to which they both belonged. Remington and Wister—Remington in his paintings, both men in countless articles and stories written for prestigious journals and magazines like *Harper's* and *Century*, and both in successful novels—attempted to do for the eastern arts establishment what Roosevelt had attempted to do for the political elite: revitalize it by treating manly western themes. Wister's work, *The Virginian* (1902), the first major modern Western novel, initiated the vogue for that genre and consequently represented the vanguard of an effort to energize American literary culture that had been dominated by the Victorian domestic novel since the midcentury.[90] Referring to *The Virginian* and the "Westerns" that followed in its wake, Jane Tompkins has written:

> And so, just as the women's novels that captured the literary marketplace at mid-century had privileged the female realm of spiritual power, inward struggle, homosociality, and sacramental household ritual, Westerns, in a reaction that looks very much like literary gender war, privilege the male realm of public power, physical ordeal, homosociality, and the rituals of the duel.[91]

In Wister's *The Virginian* and the novels of prolific successors like Zane Grey and Max Brand (the pen name of writer Frederick Schiller Faust), a romanticized "savagery," often embodied by male protagonists, like the Virginian in Wister's novel or Lassiter in Grey's *Riders of the Purple Sage* (1912), liberates an overly restrained "civilization" embodied by women like Molly Wood in *The Virginian* and Jane Withersteen in *Riders of the Purple Sage*.

Wister's novel began a tradition of modern literary Westerns and, along with the first film Western, *The Great Train Robbery* (1903), was largely responsible for establishing the Western as a significant force in twentieth-century popular art and entertainment. Still, as influential as Wister's literary efforts were in this regard, his work, as well as the frontier dramas of first-class theaters (to be discussed in the following chapters), all owed a tremendous debt to earlier nineteenth-century popular forms of Western entertainment. Dime novels, low-priced melodramas, and Wild West shows—themselves influenced by earlier frontier novels like those written by James Fenimore Cooper—contributed significantly to the frontier discourse within which the successful frontier plays of the early twentieth century developed. From the 1860s on, publishers of dime novels, like Beadle & Adams, offered working-class or youthful—usually male—readers heroic western frontiersmen whose adaptation to life on the frontier enabled them to withstand the challenges it posed. Representing the syntheses of civilization and savagery, these heroes were able to protect civilization and its innocent embodiments—women and children—from the savage outlaws and Indians of the untamed West.[92]

The impact of these heroic protagonists was even greater when they had the authenticity of real life—that is, when dime novel authors conflated fiction with historical truth. While dime novel heroes were generally the products of wish-fulfilling fabrication, pulp writers often sought to give wonderfully woven fantasies more credibility by employing true historical western figures like Wild Bill Hickok or Buffalo Bill as protagonists. In these cases, the line between reality and illusion certainly could be muddied. For instance, Buffalo Bill was an actual frontiersman as a young man,[93] was transformed by E.Z.C. Judson (aka Ned Buntline) into the hero of a popular dime novel, *Buffalo Bill: The King of Border Men* (1869), and then, beginning in 1872 played himself in popular melodramas representing his supposed western adventures. This bizarre sequence culminated when Buffalo Bill temporarily left his theater life behind in June 1876 to go west, where he "avenged" Custer's Little Big Horn defeat by fighting, killing, and scalping the Cheyenne warrior Yellow Hand—a "historical act" that Cody may have staged or at least enhanced for the sake of self-promoting publicity, only then to reenact the event as a "theatrical act" for stage melodramas and for his Wild West Show in later years. Truly, legend and history, discourse and reality become so entangled that distinguishing them from each other becomes impossible.[94]

Buffalo Bill Cody was a clever entrepreneur who knew how to profit from such confusions. Taking advantage of audience susceptibilities, his Wild West Show—advertised as a combination of entertainment and education—ran for thirty years, from 1883 to 1913. Publicity for the show always insisted that Buffalo Bill's "Wild West" was the true West. As Nate Salsbury, vice president and manager of Buffalo Bill's Wild West Show, claimed, Bill's show was "history not vaudeville"; it was "not cheap and ephemeral theatrical mimicry," but "the perpetuation and magnificent material re-introduction of a crowning epoch, of transcendent, electrifying Reality, whose natural stage dwarfs that of Caesar's Coliseum and is illumined by the lamps of heaven."[95]

The history that was presented in Buffalo Bill's Wild West Show was the triumphal myth of western conquest. As theater historian Sarah Blackstone has written, "[T]he show was full-blown propaganda—glorifying the process of the winning of the American West and declaring to the world that America had won a resounding victory in its efforts to subdue the wilderness."[96] This perspective pervaded the rather fragmented series of acts that made up the show. Consisting of an elaborate and formal opening, which climaxed with Buffalo Bill's dramatic entry, followed by a series of different acts that Blackstone categorized under six headings—"races, shooting acts, specialty acts, military exhibitions, riding and horse acts, and dramatic spectacles"[97]—the whole program received coherence through the presence of Buffalo Bill Cody himself. It was in the person of Buffalo Bill that the triumphalist message was most fully crystallized.

The unquestioned star of the show, Buffalo Bill, epitomized all frontier virtues. His heroic nature was put on view in the performance and was in turn substantiated by a lengthy souvenir program that contained excerpts from books and articles, as well as a number of well-known Indian fighters' letters establishing Cody's heroic credentials. An 1895 program describes Cody as "a leader among the manly pioneer barriers between civilization and savagery, risking all that the 'Star of Empire might force its westward way.'"[98] Bridging civilization and savagery, Bill embodied the virtues of both. With "natural ease and courtesy of manner," he exhibited a civilized grace. He was, however, not the overcivilized gentleman whom Roosevelt scorned, but the "natural gentleman" who had all the necessary frontier skills. Buffalo Bill is described in the Wild West Show program as the "exemplar of the strong and unique traits that characterize *a true American frontiersman*"[99] and "a beautiful horseman, an unrivaled shot, and as a scout unequaled."[100] Cody's careful negotiation of civilization and savagery is demonstrated by how he presented himself vis-à-vis Indians. On the one hand, he appeared to the public as a heroic Indian fighter, but, on the other, he displayed a compassionate understanding of Indian concerns. His skilled, very civil treatment of Indians was not only illustrated by the fact that Indians like Sitting Bull were members of the show and accorded appropriate respect, but also that Bill was willing—at least in the Wild West Show program—to balance the presentation of Indians as primitive savages with a defense of Indians who were ill-treated by corrupt whites.[101]

Buffalo Bill epitomized the "meeting point between savagery and civilization," but in his Wild West style, he was a hero in the blood-and-thunder Roosevelt vein. Presented as a conqueror of frontier wilderness, he drew the admiration of all classes. In short, the success of Buffalo Bill and his Wild West Show evidences the power of the late-nineteenth- and early-twentieth-century frontier discourse to construct a "reality" that embodied popular "truths." These truths, embracing civilization and savagery as well as romantic idealism and scientific realism, were produced by historians, naturalists, politicians, literary critics, novelists, and Wild West Show performers, and they made their way into the New York legitimate theater.

* * *

Late-nineteenth- and early-twentieth-century frontier discourse was complex and heterogeneous; nevertheless, it would seem that creators of popular culture (such as the Beadle & Adams, Ned Buntline, and Buffalo Bill Cody), literati and artists (such as Hamlin Garland, Owen Wister, and Frederic Remington), and wilderness enthusiasts (such as John Muir and Theodore Roosevelt) all utilized concepts, strategies, and themes drawn from the same discursive field as that in which Frederick Jackson Turner's essay belongs. This is not to say that Turner's now classic essay, "The Significance of the Frontier in American History," was the foundation on which all the others were built. While Turner's essay does explore the major strands of western frontier discourse developed by the others (not only those mentioned in this chapter, but also other writers, artists, historians, statesmen, etc., who participated in the discourse of the frontier), all of these culture producers, including Turner, interacted in a rather complex manner, feeding into and off each others' works in such a fashion as to establish an intricate web of thoughts and images related to the frontier, a complexly interwoven web that can be understood in its heterogeneousness as the late-nineteenth- and early-twentieth-century frontier western discourse.

Most characteristic of this discourse as it is manifested in the works of the various intellectuals, artists, and entrepreneurs discussed in this chapter is, of course, a sense of the American western frontier as a meeting place of "savagery" and "civilization." During this period, the American West was comprehended primarily in terms of the savagery-civilization dichotomy. While the connotations and even denotations of these terms vary from text to text, "civilization" and "savagery" are bound together as two sides of the same proverbial coin—that is, they are defined in terms of each other.

Whether "civilization" signifies material, cultural, moral, or spiritual progress, refinement, and complexity, "savagery" is consistently the coarse, vigorous, simple, sometimes primitive, sometimes unsullied reverse. In some texts, civilization takes center stage, with savagery assuming a marginal role as that which lacks and awaits the blessings of civilization, but often in the waning years of the nineteenth and the early years of the twentieth centuries, savagery is central, with civilization merely representing the diminution of an original healthy savage vitality.

However "civilization" and "savagery" are defined in late-nineteenth/early-twentieth-century writings dealing with the western experience, the relationship of these concepts to each other is generally set within some temporal scheme. Certainly, "frontier" doesn't necessarily imply temporal sequence. One could, for instance, talk of the "frontier" as the borderline between two settled nation states; nevertheless, "frontier" as it appears in the texts discussed here is viewed as the "space" where savagery and civilization meet, and this "space" is generally comprehended in terms of a process taking place in "time."[102] "Savagery" and "civilization" are set within a temporal frame given by evolutionary modes of thought. The cultural producers reviewed in this chapter understand the relationship of savagery and civilization as a sequence climaxing in a new, more vital form of one or the other—most often civilization. The movement is, nevertheless, generally not a simple movement from savagery to civilization. As Richard Slotkin claims, it usually entails the regeneration of a tired civilization by means of a detour through savagery—often, as he specifically claims, a violent savagery.[103] In short, old-world civilization evolves via wilderness savagery into a new American civilization, which, as Turner suggests, can be viewed as a kind of union of old-world civilization and new-world savagery—a union representing a marriage of science and romance, of Darwinian realism and democratic idealism.

While the various culture producers treated here understood the "western" frontier less as a specific place than as an historical process, they also tended to explicate this historical process by means of a pervasive organicism. In short, the frontier evolutionary scheme is identified as an organic growth process. This identification borrowed from Darwin, who used the image of a tree to explain the course of species evolution,[104] and from Spencer, who attempted to describe the structure and development of society by analogy with the structure and development of a biological organism, as well as from the romantic idealization of nature that fueled the wilderness cult, is not often directly stated; however, Theodore Roosevelt made the analogy explicit in several essays, as mentioned above. This organicist perspective underlies Morgan's presentation of a continuous social evolution, which—progressing through various stages of savagery and barbarism—culminates in civilization. Similarly, this organicist perspective informs Turner's description of the various stages of frontier life and is especially apparent when he writes:

> Stand at Cumberland Gap and watch the procession of civilization, marching single file—the buffalo following the trail to the salt springs, the Indian, the fur-trader and hunter, the cattle-raiser, the pioneer farmer—and the frontier has passed.... Thus civilization in America has followed the *arteries* made by geology, pouring an ever richer tide through them, until at last the slender paths of aboriginal intercourse have been broadened and interwoven into the complex mazes of modern commercial lines; the wilderness has been interpenetrated by lines of civilization growing ever more numerous. It is like the steady growth of *a complex nervous system* for the originally simple inert continent. [Author's emphasis][105]

One can hardly miss the pervasive biological metaphors running through passages like this.

What is most significant about these organic, biological metaphors is that they align frontier discourse with natural science, and in the late nineteenth century not only was knowledge largely shaped along lines that emphasized developmental or evolutionary principles, but also natural science held a position as paradigmatic knowledge. By analogizing the movement toward a higher, more complex civilization with nature, contributors to frontier discourse were working within the intellectual structures of the time, and in doing so, they were ostensibly putting their evolutionary schemas beyond question or challenge. Such schemas would appear to have the inevitability of scientific, biological facts.

This last point is important because the frontier evolutionary process depicted by the culture producers discussed here is generally presented from the single perspective of a narrowly defined agent. Indeed, the agent of progress presented in Turner's work as well as that of most other participants engaged in the turn-of-the-century frontier discourse is the white Northern European, male pioneer. Whether it be Turner's early "Old West" settler, Muir's spiritual naturalist, Roosevelt's plains cowboy, or Buffalo Bill Cody, the subject of this frontier discourse was the white male. As historian Patricia Limerick writes in reference to Turner: "English-speaking white men were the stars of the story; Indians, Hispanics, French Canadians, and Asians were at best supporting actors and at worst invisible. Nearly as invisible were women, of all ethnicities."[106]

The ultimate victory of the white male, who adapts himself to savagery to transform it and himself into a higher form of civilization, comprises a narrative that has been called the "triumphalist story" of the Old West. It is certainly an optimistic account of the nation's past. In this regard, Richard White noted that Old Western historians of the Turner ilk "write comedy, in the sense that they provide a happy resolution."[107] From a contemporary perspective, this comedy appears literally as a "whitewashing" of what could be viewed as a thoughtless conquest of the western wilderness.

In its unambiguous simplicity, the frontier story as it is often presented by late-nineteenth-century commentators takes on a mythic structure. Insofar as Turner and others among the turn-of-the-century contributors to this frontier discourse ordered a complex of historical actions and events into a significant pattern or story, which functioned as a way of explaining Americans to Americans, they in fact constructed what Patricia Limerick has described as a "creation myth."[108] To be sure, Turner's historical interpretation can and perhaps should be viewed as a synthetic, man-made myth, but White's assertion that Turner-like Western history is fundamentally comic takes on added significance if this claim is understood in terms of Northrop Frye's discussion of mythical structure—specifically his discussion of comedic structure, which he refers to as the "mythos of spring." Frye claims that the mythos of spring concludes with the joining or marriage of hero and heroine after they successfully overcome all obstacles to their union. At the end of comedy, Frye writes, "[T]he device in the plot that brings hero and heroine together causes a new society to crystallize around the hero, and the moment when this crystallization occurs is the point of resolution in the action."[109] A very similar pattern underlies Turner's analysis of the frontier process. In viewing American character as a product of the meeting of civilization and savagery, he offered an interpretation of American history that is also structured around a culminating "marriage." Turner describes a process in which his hero, the eastern pioneer, interacts with and becomes bound to the wilderness, which Annette Kolodny points out is often presented as feminine[110]—and may therefore be seen as the "heroine" wooed and won (or perhaps even raped) by the pioneer "hero." For Turner and others, the result of this union is that a new and glorious society crystallizes around the hero.

Although Turner's historical analysis is described here as mythic, this frontier myth is not to be seen as having a universal foundation—an example of some essential "always true" aspect of human experience. It does not exist outside time and history—hence its "constructed" nature. This frequently appearing myth represents a condensation of the complex, heterogeneous frontier discourse that pervaded the first decade of the twentieth century—a condensation that receives its particularly optimistic tone as a response to various social and economic circumstances, which were in turn viewed through the lens of this myth. Indeed, with the 1893 panic past and the United States' domestic front attaining encouraging stability and with the American victory over Spain in 1898—a war that could be and was viewed as a further example of American frontier conquest—American self-confidence was sky-high. For the beneficiaries of these circumstances, especially the new bourgeois managerial elite, the frontier myth seemed real and was a useful way of persuading others who may not have benefited as obviously from events to join ranks in a celebration of the new America.

The optimism of many of the contributors to the turn-of-the-century frontier discourse provides a context within which the frontier experience as it appears in the legitimate drama of the first decade of the twentieth century must be seen. Whether as pure comedy or melodrama (which Frye described as "comedy without humor"[111]), frontier drama generally represents an optimistic vision of the American past, present, and future. To be sure, specific plays are often structured around a mythic sense of the West, but while the outline of a constructed frontier myth described here appears coherent in theory, each frontier play presents a unique variation on this formula. Consequently, the examination of different plays will suggest deviations from this basic outline. Indeed, the examination of the eight plays dealt with in chapters 3 through 6 will reveal the range of questions and doubts that permeate early-twentieth-century frontier discourse and that these plays and this discourse seek to resolve. But before looking at specific plays, it is necessary to examine the theater context in which these plays appeared—that is, it is necessary to explore more closely the theatrical conditions, the prevailing conventions and practices, that impose themselves on and contribute to the development of the turn-of-the-century frontier discourse as it appears in the legitimate theater. Without question, the frontier discourse that was evolving in other cultural venues took on unique shapes and forms when impressed with the stamp of turn-of-the-century theater. The nature of this theatrical stamp will be the subject of the next chapter.

2. The Turn-of-the-Century American Theater Context ❦

Circumscribed as it was by diverse period assumptions and intellectual constructs, late-nineteenth-century frontier discourse was, nevertheless, transformed when it entered the theater. As a mode of representation, or (re)presentation, the theater production process inevitably impresses itself on the material with which it deals. In other words, the theater does not function as a transparent window through which either the actual frontier western experience or the experience as it was constructed through nontheatrical discourse can be viewed in its pure state. When set within a theatrical context, the turn-of-the-century frontier western "discourse" was unavoidably recast to meet the needs of prevailing theatrical practices—that is, in the theater, frontier discourse was shaped to accommodate a "vocabulary" and "syntax" specific to the theater of the period. Insofar as this vocabulary and syntax set the parameters of theater representation, they can be seen as the distinguishing elements of what we might call "theater discourse." Late-nineteenth-century frontier western drama should be understood, then, as the product of what Stephen Greenblatt referred to as a complex cultural "negotiation."[1] Drama representing frontier western experience is the outcome of an intersection of two discursive fields: one defining the limits of what was said about the frontier western experience, and the other defining the limits of what constituted theater or what could be expected of theater representations in the late nineteenth century. To be sure, late-nineteenth- and early-twentieth-century frontier dramas utilized objects (cowboys, miners, saloons, Indians, etc.), concepts (evolution, civilization, savagery, etc.), and themes or strategies (the marriage or union of opposites, regeneration through violence,[2] the assertion of independent individualism, the "exceptional" nature of the United States, etc.) that belong to the frontier western discourse in general, but the vision of the frontier offered by these plays is shaped by the prevalent dramatic conventions and practices of scriptwriting as well as by the accepted theatrical conventions and practices governing production and performance.

The impress of dramatic and theatrical conventions/practices on late-nineteenth-century frontier discourse is most apparent in the way that the key components of the late-nineteenth-century frontier discourse—the Euro-American pioneer individual often conceived as the agent of civilization and the western wilderness often viewed as the realm of savagery—were represented in the theater. Ostensibly, the representation of the interaction of individual and place should translate well to the theater, where individual agents of action are set in space; that is, the western frontier wilderness as a physical location in which and on which pioneers act could be neatly signified by the stage space in which and on which performers or actors act. More specifically, there are parallels in how the late-nineteenth-century scientific discourse revolving around Darwinian evolution affected both frontier discourse and stage discourse or practice. In both cases, the individual was diminished. Just as Turner, for instance, focused on the impact that the western frontier environment had on the pioneer from the East, so too late-nineteenth-century theater practitioners following the tenets of dramatic realism and naturalism viewed the stage setting as an environment within which characters/actors had to "live" and with which they had to negotiate. Indeed, the "scientific" mode of thought that fostered environmental determinism at the expense of the efficacy of free will both shaped Turner's frontier discourse and had a corresponding theatrical dimension as late-nineteenth-century theater practitioners began to view scenery less as a background setting against which theatrical action took place than as a space that enclosed and determined stage action. This shift in theater practice is most apparent in the directorial and design work of Georg II, Duke of Saxe-Meiningen, during the 1870s and 1880s, and his successors throughout Europe and eventually America.[3] Under the guidance of these theater innovators, theater practitioners completed the transition from painted scenery to box sets, from flat, raked stages to sculpted stage floors.

This new approach to scenery gave it a more significant dramatic function, but even though the scenic environment assumed a larger role within the dynamics of nineteenth-century theater, the conflict of characters remained most essential to dramatic action. The tension between character and environment—so primary to late-nineteenth-century frontier discourse—was not as central to the theater. Consequently, the conflict between pioneer and wilderness, individual and environment, was often recast as a conflict between character and character in frontier plays; the conflict between characters subsumed that between character and environment. To be sure, the fact that the conflict between characters remained so primary in the theater of the late nineteenth century suggests the degree to which European and American theatrical representation remains linked to its ancestral Greek roots. European and American dramatic forms continued (and, for the most part, continue) to be structured around the conflict or "agon" of two characters, with the frontier tension between pioneer and wilderness often being displaced onto an allegorical plain in the theater.

The nature of this allegorical approach is best understood within the context of nineteenth-century dramatic forms and character types. In this regard, one can hardly avoid a discussion of melodrama, which is certainly a most insistent aspect of nineteenth-century American theater—at least to early-twenty-first-century eyes. Melodramatic techniques and effects pervaded early-nineteenth-century American theater and continued to be in evidence throughout the second half of the century even as elements of dramatic realism began to make their appearance. Significantly, melodrama left its imprint on late-nineteenth-century dramatic characterization, although what appeared to be more subtle and more lifelike approaches made headway with audiences.

Any discussion of nineteenth-century melodrama must begin with two important considerations. First of all, analyses of "nineteenth-century melodrama" must avoid falling into the trap of conceptualizing the genre as a monolithic and uniform entity. As it developed in nineteenth-century America, melodrama took a variety of different shapes—each an outgrowth of a specific social context; that is, the distinctive forms that melodrama took derived from specific theatrical situations, or what Bruce McConachie has referred to as "theatrical formations."[4] On the other hand, if the term "melodrama" is to have any analytical significance, there must be some common denominator(s) linking these diverse forms. In fact, the kind of drama that has come to be designated as melodrama evolved in the late eighteenth and early nineteenth centuries. While melodrama was an outgrowth of eighteenth-century middle class theatrical forms like the British sentimental drama and the French *drame*, it was also closely associated with romantic tragedy—emerging perhaps as a popularization of that more elitist form. Like romantic tragedy, melodrama seemed to depend on a kind of emotional titillation that would have been unacceptable in the more restrained, French influenced neoclassical theater fare of the eighteenth century. This shift away from neoclassicism affected all aspects of the developing form. Nineteenth-century melodrama's threefold dependence on visual spectacle, musical support, and excessive rhetorical expression was aimed toward the arousal of a heightened emotional state in audiences even as the plays focused on the emotional lives of characters often depicted with a new vividness and specificity.

This emphasis on characters' emotional lives cannot be separated from the evolving discursive preoccupation with individualism that accompanied the growing social power of the new bourgeoisie or middle class in the late eighteenth and early nineteenth centuries. Indeed, the advent of melodrama and romantic tragedy around 1800 parallels the advent of the "third estate" across Europe and America. In delving into specific and concrete emotional realities rather than focusing on general and abstract rational truisms as a means of apprehending human action, melodramatists, like romantic tragedians in the tradition of the early "Storm and Stress" Johann Wolfgang Goethe and Friedrich Schiller and the later French playwright Victor Hugo, seem to align themselves with a more democratic social perspective than that of the aristocratic neoclassical theater. From the perspective of an emerging bourgeoisie—a class that from the early eighteenth century began to comprise larger and larger portions of European theater audiences—the tendency to place value on emotional sensibility and subjective experience, neither of which could be viewed as the exclusive property of an aristocratic class, served to undermine the special claims of inherited title or rank. The bourgeois or middle-class individual, whose social standing supposedly depended on his or her own merit, became the agent and subject of drama. This is not to say that melodrama necessarily conveyed a narrowly liberal or radical political and social agenda. As Bruce McConachie has pointed out, the melodramas of the so-called father of the form, French playwright Guilbert de Pixérécourt, and his early-nineteenth-century American imitators like John Payne were informed by a "patriarchal conservatism."[5] Yet even these plays cannot be divorced from what Robertson Davies has discussed as the nineteenth-century's romantic preoccupation with the individual.[6]

The bourgeois affirmation of romantic individualism, which seems to be at the very core of the melodramatic sensibility, nevertheless implies a democratic faith that goes beyond the assertion of the individual's subjective, emotional reality. Melodrama also went a long way toward democratizing virtue by allowing for the possibility that virtue was not the exclusive possession of a landed inherited elite. On the contrary, virtue might properly belong to those humble, or at least merchant-class citizens who are not prejudiced by the artificial traditions driving the old aristocratic ruling classes. Additionally, the virtuous individual's struggle against and frequent triumph over a willful villain suggests a confidence in the potency of the honorable individual. Consequently, not only does melodrama affirm the individual's inner or subjective experience—even though it is often expressed in what sounds to our ears as a heightened and unnatural rhetoric—but it also often affirms the efficacy of the virtuous individual in the outer or "objective" world.

The moral victory of the upright individual over all obstacles posed by a threatening world, a triumph that is central to the melodramatic vision, elicited a positive response from nineteenth-century European and American audiences—but perhaps this was nowhere as true as in the United States. Whether composed of an urban elite drawn to paternalistic, fairy-tale melodramas in the 1820s, a working class drawn to Bowery melodramas in the 1840s, or an emergent middle class drawn to museum melodramas in the 1850s,[7] American audiences embraced melodrama. Certainly, the democratic fervor exhibited by players and audience members varied with different theater contexts: working-class enthusiasm for Jacksonian egalitarian democracy was different from the kind of democratic faith demonstrated in theaters geared to more middle- or upper-class audiences. Yet melodrama seemed to speak to and for both lower- and upper-class Americans, who as a group seemed to pride themselves on their democratic and republican institutions. Noting this affinity of Americans to melodrama, Daniel Gerould writes: "The United States and melodrama came into existence at almost the same time—the late eighteenth century—and for much the same reason—the democratic revolution in thought and feeling."[8] According to Gerould, melodrama affirmed the naively optimistic assumptions of many of the new nation's citizens; it "nurtures a faith in human equality, the power of innocence, the triumph of justice," and most important, it suggests that "if not *every one* can win, *each* human being has the chance in a society unfettered by Old World hierarchies of class and profession."[9]

Gerould may overstate the link between American democratic fervor and the development of melodrama, but some connection seems logical—especially in the late nineteenth century, when democratic individualism was heralded as the ideological cornerstone of U.S. institutions by the likes of historian Frederick Jackson Turner. Certainly, the claims of individualism inherent in melodrama resonated well in late-nineteenth-century America. Inasmuch as the representation of the virtuous or not so virtuous "robber baron like" individual as a power in and of him- or herself was a significant ingredient in the ideological perspective associated with capitalist bourgeois culture, and inasmuch as that ideological perspective attained hegemony in the mid-to-late-nineteenth-century United States, a clear and significant link between the ideology underlying melodrama and American culture is not surprising.

Stated ideology and actual lived experience, however, do not always mesh.[10] There were limits on freedom within the body politic, and it is similarly true that the freedom of opportunity that nineteenth-century American melodrama championed was more illusion than reality. As Jeffrey Mason has argued, the assertion of individual freedom that Gerould finds in melodrama "is valid only *within* the structure of melodrama, taken from the perspective of the [melodramatic] character herself"[11]—and, consequently, as Mason implies, from that of audience members who embraced the character's perspective. From an outside or early-twenty-first-century perspective, this "freedom" seems to be very rigidly circumscribed. The religious strictures and social assumptions, which appeared as acceptable natural laws to nineteenth-century audiences, now appear as highly arbitrary limits on behavior—limits that draw upon prevailing gender, race, and class biases. As modeled in the theater, human conduct was, in fact, shaped by clearly defined hierarchical assumptions and categories.

The melodramatic character's destiny was not open, but was determined by his or her connection with one or other of the terms in each pair of a series of binary oppositions: virtuous/villainous, male/female, white/non-white, serious/comic, prosperous/impoverished. Most important of these oppositions was the virtuous/villainous or good/evil opposition. While the definitions of melodramatic virtue and villainy may not have been constant throughout the century, they were presented as absolutely defined in each play, and indeed the action of each play revolved around the given or implied understanding of virtue and vice. In short, at the heart of melodrama was this binary opposition (providing the ground of its so-called Manichean spirit[12]); characters were distributed on either side of this divide—there being no middle ground possible. In nineteenth-century theater, what twenty-first-century audiences view as the complexity of human conduct was often reduced to fit simple either/or moral categories: characters are either overly idealized or overly demonized.

Given the centrality of the virtue/villainy opposition to the melodramatic vision, it would be very significant if this opposition were conflated with the civilization/savagery opposition when melodrama took on frontier material. Such a pattern of convergence, where either civilization or savagery were consistently equated with virtue in nineteenth-century melodrama, would indicate a specific interpretation of the frontier experience; however, such consistency is not to be found. To be sure, the lack of congruity between the virtue/villainy and the civilization/savagery oppositions as they appear in nineteenth-century melodramas calls attention to the shifting, ambivalent attitude expressed in nineteenth-century melodramas toward the binary opposition that is at the heart of nineteenth-century frontier discourse. On the one hand, civilization—especially in its Euro-American form—is often viewed as a more elevated, positive expression of human possibility than primitive savagery. On the other hand, the legitimacy of the individual's subjective reality is frequently grounded by associating it with a pure nature, a nature uncorrupted by artificial civilization, or, in other words, a nature that embodies a *good*, healthy connection to primitive savage roots. In short, virtue as it appears in nineteenth-century frontier melodramas is sometimes associated with an idealized untouched nature, which embodies elements of savagery and, at other times, even in the same play, it is linked with the kinds of polish or restraint that signify civilization.

Relevant to the fact that the virtue/villainy and the civilization/ savagery oppositions do not overlap is the fact that neither European-Americans nor Indians are consistently tied to either virtue or vice. Exploring the ambivalent attitude toward nature that informs the early-nineteenth-century Indian play, David Grimsted suggests that Indian savagery is not aligned with either virtue or villainy, but with both.[13] Following the "noble savage"/"vicious Indian" dichotomy that runs through a work like Cooper's *The Last of the Mohicans*, in which, for instance, a good Uncas is contrasted with an evil Magua, Indian plays view savagery as both virtuous and villainous.[14] What might be understood as primitive savagery is divided into a binary opposition in which natural harmony is opposed to passionate dissonance. Referring to the contrast of "nature in its desirable form and nature as the wild antithesis of civilization,"[15] Grimsted argues that the noble savage is viewed as the epitome both of virtue and of pure, uncorrupted nature, while the vicious savage, with a tendency toward excessive cruelty, represents a dangerously disruptive force. Only rarely, as in the case of Metamora in John Augustus Stone's 1829 play of that name, does one character embody both aspects of this opposition.[16]

While late-nineteenth-century frontier melodramas continued to treat savagery ambivalently, it is interesting that the Indian character is less central to these dramas. This might partly be a result of audience fatigue with Indian plays. That the genre had perhaps played itself out is indicated by the tremendous success of John Brougham's midcentury parodies of Metamora- and Pocahontas-like characters.[17] To be sure, the marginalization of the "noble savage" Indian character in late-nineteenth-century frontier melodramas may also be attributed to historical factors, including the animosity felt toward Indians during the highly publicized Indian Wars of the 1870s, the growing virulence of late-nineteenth-century racism, and finally the reality that in the years after 1880 the Indian, increasingly restricted to reservations, played less of a role in the experience of frontier residents.

As Indians disappeared from frontier drama, their role in the savagery-civilization interaction depicted in these plays waned. While primitive Indians were not consistently represented as either negative or positive examples of savagery, European-American white characters were not always viewed as idealized representatives of civilization. As Indians played a less significant role in the dynamics of late-nineteenth-century frontier melodramas, white "savage" frontier types take on more significant roles, and not just as comic heroes such as James Kirke Paulding's "Davy Crockett like" title character in *The Lion of the West*.[18] These new savage-like characters are not always villains, and ironically when they are heroes they are often so because of their unrefined qualities.[19] When white melodramatic heroes like Frank Murdock's Davy Crockett in the 1872 play of that title or Bartley Campbell's rough-hewn California miner, Joe Saunders, in *My Partner* (1879) take on savage or wilderness traits, it is not merely a practical matter of demonstrating how whites can only defeat savagery by learning the savage ways. As in the case of Turner's later essay, savagery in these characters is more than a means to an end, the conquest of the western frontier; it is a positive end in itself—a purity that stands above civilization. When white heroes embody this kind of frontier savagery, we generally see something akin to the noble savage tradition, but the savagery inhabited by these white characters is narrowly circumscribed. Befitting the concerns of Victorian audiences, noble savages, like Murdock's Crockett, Campbell's Joe Saunders, as well as frontier heroes we will see in later chapters, are always characterized with a natural chivalry that distinguishes them from "demon savages," who in keeping with late-nineteenth-century ethnocentric ideas on race are often, but certainly not always, represented by nonwhites. In short, from a twenty-first-century perspective racial binary oppositions may function disturbingly with respect to Indian and Euro-American characters in nineteenth-century frontier melodramas, but neither European/Indian nor white/nonwhite binaries are any more synonymous with the civilization/savagery binary opposition than is the virtue/vice opposition.

Interestingly, it is gender in nineteenth-century melodrama more than virtue or race that seems key to the orchestration of the civilization/savagery opposition in late-nineteenth-century melodramas. To be sure, gender and race were both integral to the late-nineteenth-century understanding of civilization/savagery,[20] but in nineteenth-century melodrama the distinction between civilization and savagery came to be more closely associated with popular notions about gender. As nonwhite characters came to embody, but not exclusively, the most heinous of savages, Euro-Americans can be found in the roles of noble and ignoble savages as well as of noble and ignoble representatives of civilization. Gender, however, functioned consistently as a means of communicating civilization/savagery dynamics and character hierarchy. Accordingly, the interaction of melodramatic heroes and heroines often could and did convey popular assumptions about the savagery/civilization dialectic.

For nineteenth-century theater audiences, the melodramatic heroine exemplified the ideal woman, and in mainstream nineteenth-century culture the idealized woman was closely associated with what were viewed as the virtues of civilization. To a certain extent this connection was a compensation for the fact that nineteenth-century woman was believed to find her proper place within the domestic sphere and not in the exciting, albeit dangerous, public sphere. According to the prevailing middle-class nineteenth-century gender ideology, women were too delicate to bear the hardships and responsibilities of the everyday work world. Focusing on the ways in which woman's limited social role was idealized in mid-nineteenth-century America, historian Barbara Welter describes period gender ideology from the perspective of what she calls "the cult of true womanhood." According to Welter, the nineteenth-century male found his place in the materialistic world outside the home, where he was a busy builder of bridges, railroads, and fortunes. On the other hand, the nineteenth-century woman, who was "the hostage in the home," was assigned the responsibility of maintaining the values that men "held so dear and treated so lightly."[21] More specifically, Welter claimed that "the attributes of True Womanhood...could be divided into four cardinal virtues—piety, purity, submissiveness and domesticity."[22] Without these attributes, a woman was in dire straits, but "with them she was promised happiness and power."[23] While this "cult of true womanhood" offers an idealized woman to counterbalance an overly materialistic male, the result is not a balanced binary opposition. A clear hierarchy is present: the woman remains submissive and subordinate to the male who supports her.[24]

The ideal of true womanhood was certainly challenged as the nineteenth century came to an end. The evolving new industrial culture would have a dramatic impact on gender assumptions. Freeing women from grueling domestic labor, breaking down family units, and offering women new opportunities in a growing consumption-oriented culture, the late nineteenth and early twentieth centuries witnessed the birth of the "new woman."[25] Interestingly, Barbara Welter claims that among the circumstances modifying the ideal of true womanhood was westward migration, which "impelled woman...to play a more creative role in society."[26] Still, even as the "True Woman" became the "New Woman" of the twentieth century, Welter claims that the nineteenth-century stereotypes "persisted, bringing guilt and confusion in the midst of opportunity."[27] Woman's place in society was changing, but the cultural and moral power of domesticity and respectability endured.

Although the ideal of true womanhood was occasionally challenged in the larger culture, it still wielded significant power within late-nineteenth- and early-twentieth-century melodramas. Yet it would be inaccurate to maintain that melodramatic heroines invariably epitomize the ideal of true womanhood in all its refinement. To be sure, some playwrights resisted this stereotype. Female characters, like the earthy Possy in Henry C. DeMille and Charles Barnard's *The Main Line; Or, Rawson's Y* (1886), or the title character in stage adaptations of Bret Harte's story "*M'liss,*" represent heroines of a different kind, but the effectiveness of boyish female characters in plays like these lies in the defiance of the norm. Here, the exception proves the rule; in these plays, audiences enjoyed the exotic nature of characters that represent at least a partial inversion of conventional assumptions about femininity. Ultimately, however, even these characters, as instanced by David Belasco's excellent example of this character type, his "Girl of the Golden West," only appear to challenge the convention. At play's end, the girl takes her place by her man as a traditional wife. Women may have begun to infiltrate the public sphere, but the perception that they were subordinate to and dependent on men remained.

Throughout the nineteenth century, the man's place in the public sphere gave him responsibility for and power over women. He might dirty himself in the struggle to earn a living, and he might depend on the women close to him to smooth his rough edges when he returned to the safety of the domestic sphere, but his role was to protect and maintain the women and children in his charge. His manliness was determined by the degree to which he succeeded in this task. Man, therefore, had an arduous responsibility; he had to enter the competitive economic world and earn a living for his family. A "real" man would succeed in this task, and so the idealized man who filled the role of the melodramatic hero would be able and ready to accept the challenges of the world outside the home. Indeed, it is his success in this arena that earned him the right to the heroine at play's end. Again and again, we see the melodramatic hero winning the pristinely good heroine as a reward for his successfully protecting her interests when they were threatened by dangerous outsiders.

Scholars like E. Anthony Rotundo, Michael Kimmel, John Kasson, and Gail Bederman, who have traced changing attitudes about manhood in America, have noted that throughout the first three quarters of the nineteenth century, it was thought that men succeeded in their breadwinner role by demonstrating self-control and clear-sighted reason. In the late nineteenth century, however, attitudes toward manhood began to shift. Writing about the development of a new "passionate manhood" in the late nineteenth century, Rotundo writes:

> ...there was a growing tendency to look at men as creatures of impulse and passion, even as animals or savages.... When late-century men were not being likened to "primitives," they were urging one another to act like them.... more and more affluent men ranged further and further into forest, jungle, and prairie as hunters in the last decades of the century.[28]

This shift in approach to manhood in the late nineteenth century resulted in a new emphasis on muscular, martial values—a response, perhaps, to the slackening of economic and social opportunities for white males, who felt the pressures of corporate and bureaucratic expansion and growing immigration, as well as the challenge posed by women who were no longer willing to remain segregated within a domestic sphere.[29] It is this late-nineteenth-century preoccupation with the "strenuous life" so often associated with Teddy Roosevelt that we saw in the last chapter as a major propelling force in the transformation of the late-century frontier discourse. This refocusing on the more primitive, indeed savage, aspects of manhood also affected the ways in which late-nineteenth-century melodramatic heroes, who represent exemplar men, were shaped.

While prevailing gender assumptions inevitably mold mainstream culture and especially popular manifestations of it—like melodrama—there is a certain irony in how the idealized characters of frontier melodrama often enact the frontier meeting of civilization and savagery. Shaped by nineteenth-century gender constructions, melodramatic heroes and heroines frequently embody a hierarchical structure that seems to run counter to the widely circulating Darwinian view of progress from savagery to civilization. Here the feminized civilization embodied by the heroine depends on the savage vitality of the dominant frontier melodramatic hero for survival. In plays like Bartley Campbell's popular and critically acclaimed 1879 frontier melodrama, *My Partner*, the heroic rough-hewn frontier miner, Joe, saves the educated, refined English (i.e., civilized) heroine, Mary Brandon, from humiliation and defeat at the hands of a merciless villain. In short, Joe and Mary exemplify "the legitimizing function of gender," which Joan Wallach Scott describes as "the idea that conceptual languages employ differentiation to establish meaning and that sexual difference is a primary way of signifying differentiation."[30] In Campbell's play, the ideal man/ideal woman dichotomy is used to highlight popular assumptions about the distinctions between savagery and civilization and the relative merits of each. Joe and Mary's relationship represents the dependence of civilization on the vitality of western savagery, but the melodrama's happy ending also brings hero and heroine together in a union that foreshadows Turner's optimistic description of the "meeting of civilization and savagery" offered fourteen years after the play was written.[31] Abiding by accepted gender roles, Campbell and other frontier melodrama authors, like Frank Murdock in *Davy Crockett*, could use the forms and conventions of melodrama to trace the relations of civilization and savagery.

* * *

Inasmuch as melodramatic oppositions like virtue/villainy, white/nonwhite, and especially male/female were enlisted in the representation of the frontier interplay of civilization and savagery, melodrama provided the theater with a language through which frontier discourse could be presented on stage. Given that melodrama does not represent a monolithic phenomenon—that particular melodramas bear the impress of the particular theater context, or what Bruce McConachie referred to as "theatrical formations," which gave birth to them—this language allows for the communication of subtly divergent messages. To be sure, different playwrights spoke to different audiences, who might view the basic oppositions underlying melodramas in different lights. For instance, shifting tones and nuances such as those resulting from the fascination with realism—a fascination that affected drama presented to the business and political elite audiences of first-class theaters of New York (quickly becoming the theater capital of the United States) during the years following 1870—are registered in frontier melodramas of the period.

The shift toward realism that appeared in first-class theaters is closely linked to other late-nineteenth-century social and cultural transformations. Indeed, as discussed in the last chapter, the rapid industrialization in the years following the Civil War had a dramatic impact on the nation's culture. This period brought a new class of industrial proprietors and managers to the forefront of the American social and cultural scene. As this new bourgeois elite began to establish its hegemony, its values and ideals began to permeate American culture. Progress, or the progress of this class, was understood in terms of industrial and technological development, which in turn was seen as a by-product of a no-nonsense, realistic approach to life. Efficiency and profits, the products of practical scientific ways of thinking, not metaphysics, were the guardian angels of this new moneyed aristocracy and those who followed its lead. Writing in the 1920s from a perspective that was informed by this scientific frame of mind even as he described its development in the 1870s, Vernon Lewis Parrington claimed in his classic *Main Currents in American Thought* that

> ...with the revolutions in economics and industry, with the rise of an urban society, the mind of America was making ready for the reception of science and the realism that was eventually to spring from science.... In the new interpretation after 1870 the emphasis came to rest on the whole rather than the parts: in sociology, upon the historical growth of human societies; in biology, upon the evolution of the higher from lower forms. The individual, thus conceived of socially and politically, is no longer an isolated, self-determining entity, but a vehicle through which is carried the stream of life, with a past behind and a future before. He is a portion of the total scheme of things, tied by a thousand invisible threads to the encompassing whole. From the parts to the totality, from freedom to determinism—such has been the drift of thought that science has laid upon us and from which there is no easy escape.[32]

From this perspective, "science," Darwinian "evolution of the higher from the lower forms," and artistic "realism" are different facets of the same phenomenon. Admittedly, science and art did not have to be so completely conflated with evolutionary thought, but such was the thinking of many among the new managerial elite at the end of the nineteenth century.[33]

Given the late-nineteenth-century commitment to unsentimental Darwinian evolutionary science, there was progressively less sympathy with the unrestrained romantic, emotional outbursts or the overly idealized vision of life that marked many early-nineteenth-century melodramas. To meet the expectations of middle-class audiences who embraced the perspective of the new managerial elite, theater practitioners began to offer stage pictures, which were at least ostensibly free of the artist's subjective interference—pictures that approached something akin to photographic likenesses of life outside the theater.[34] Realism in its most literal form would require that theater artists assume the stance of neutral, "objective" reporters,[35] but even theater artists who were not entirely committed to this aesthetic found that if they wanted to attract the audiences of first-class theaters, they had to embrace a more "realistic," a more "scientific," approach. In other words, during the last decades of the nineteenth century, frontier melodramas, presented to middle- and upper-class audiences, increasingly took on "the look of truth."

For information on real—or what went for "real"—frontier life, playwrights of the 1870s and 1880s could turn to a growing literature on the

West. Travel accounts, railroad advertisements, dime novels, and Western regional literature all were important in this regard, but, as theater historians like Arthur Hobson Quinn and Richard Moody have suggested, most important for late-nineteenth-century playwrights were the stories of Bret Harte.[36] Harte's depiction of the far western frontier—particularly that of California mining camps—was especially influential in shaping the American consciousness of the West, and his being a native of the West only enhanced his credibility as a truthful observer of western life.

Harte's influence is most apparent in the renunciation of the kind of romanticism that characterizes a frontier play like Frank Murdock's 1872 *Davy Crockett*. While this play differs from other late-nineteenth-century frontier melodramas by being set in a location east of the Mississippi—Crockett's Tennessee—the major distinction between this play and later nineteenth-century frontier melodramas is a difference in tone. This play, described by Arthur Hobson Quinn as an "old-fashioned romance...an idyll,"[37] is a lyrical, melodramatic love story. In fact, while the heroic Crockett offered in this play epitomizes some aspects of a Beadle dime-novel hero, he is also a product of early-nineteenth-century romanticism even to the extent of being compared in the text to the hero of Sir Walter Scott's "Song of Lochinvar."[38] Murdock's Crockett is both folk hero and chivalrous knight. As such he is the source of the play's ebullient mood—a mood that is established by the opening chorus:

> When high o'er the mountains
> Field, valley and crag,
> The sun gilds the fountain
> We watch for the stag—
> Crack! Crack! 'mid the covers
> Our free rifles ring,
> Far flies the wild, wild plover
> The eagle takes the wing.
> A thousand bold echoes
> Roll round at our hand,
> And the startled air owns us
> The Kings of the Land.[39]

In this world, individuals like Crockett are "kings," and nothing is impossible.

This openhearted, gentle romanticism is very different from the mood that dominated the representations of the West that Harte offered during the 1870s. In stories like "The Luck of the Roaring Camp," "The

Outcasts of Poker Flat," and "Tennessee's Partner,"[40] Harte depicted a western frontier that lacked the Arcadian overtones that had been so apparent in *Davy Crockett*. Although Crockett and his friends, the "Kings of the Land," were able to tame the Tennessee wilderness pictured in Murdock's play, Bret Harte's characters are not as fortunate on the far western frontier. Rather than dominating their environment, they struggle to accommodate themselves to it. These characters are overcome by floods and blizzards as well as by occasional violence; they are, in fact, extremely vulnerable to the forces of nature. Harte's characters are not as free of environmental forces as is Murdock's Davy Crockett. These new western characters negotiate with an unpredictable nature that envelops them—they are, in fact, "tied by a thousand invisible threads to the encompassing whole."

While, in this sense, Harte's short stories are more "realistic" than Murdock's *Davy Crockett*, the realistic pictures of frontier western life they offer are, nonetheless, still rather tame—at least to the twenty-first-century eye. Like Murdock's Tennessee forests, Harte's Northern California mining towns have been viewed through a sentimental lens, but the distortion of this lens is less obvious than that of Murdock's. To be sure, many of Harte's characters manifest the same idealized traits that belonged to the characters of plays like *Davy Crockett*. A harsher environment and the superficial coarseness of his characters, who often represent social outcasts like prostitutes, drunkards, vigilantes, or gamblers, nevertheless lend Harte's stories a surface realism, and this realism left its stamp on a number of late-nineteenth-century frontier melodramas catering to the middle and upper classes. Among such successful plays, one would find Augustin Daly's *Horizon* (1871), Bartley Campbell's *My Partner* (1879), and Joaquin Miller's *Forty-Nine* (1881).

These plays set in the picturesque far west were peopled with hard-working common men, whose sometimes questionable habits and ways of speaking epitomized for eastern audiences a sense—drawn from sources like Harte—of the rough-and-tumble life of frontier western communities. While New York reviewers often found the plots of these plays to be conventional, they were sometimes startled by the dialogue's lack of decorum. Reviewing Bret Harte's 1876 endeavor to bring several of his short stories to the stage in *The Two Men of Sandy Bar*, the *New York Times* critic expressed dismay not only at the weakness of the play's plot, but also at what he considered to be the gratuitously contemptible nature of the characters' actions and dialogue. Conflating actor and character, this reviewer wrote: "Mr. Murdoch is very drunk all the time, and very blasphemous, using the name of the Deity in a manner and with a coarseness and frequency that is nothing less than shocking."[41]

If the coarseness of Harte's frontier characters could elicit a negative response, the common—if less profane—nature of Bartley Campbell's Harte-like characters in his successful 1879 frontier drama *My Partner* was one source of that play's success. In this regard, the *New York Times* reviewer wrote: "The leading characters...are men and women of the ordinary world—people who have gone forth to tempt fortune in wild solitudes, since fortune had deserted them elsewhere. It is the contrast between these characters and the scenes in which they appear which gives a certain distinct flower to *My Partner*."[42] Praising Campbell's *My Partner*, the *New York Herald* reviewer similarly wrote that in this play, "there are no revolver discussions and lynchings, no eruption of red shirts and slang phrases, but in their place the honest utterances of men and women who, with one or two exceptions, might have lived and had their being anywhere else than in California."[43] This positive response to the play's depiction of ordinary people suggests how welcome the drift toward realism was.

While melodramatic conventions remained the governing norm, the tone of frontier plays, especially as they appeared in the more prestigious theaters that accommodated the new managerial elite, was changing. Late-nineteenth-century frontier plays produced for middle- and upper-class audiences were beginning to fuse melodramatic conventions born of a romantic idealism with a late-nineteenth-century fascination for realism. Not surprisingly, then, in these plays, as well as in later turn-of-the-century frontier plays, one might see some of the same tensions as can be found in Turner's analysis of the American frontier. In both Turner's essay and the plays of the period, romantic idealism and the new scientific sensibility are precariously balanced—resulting in representations of the frontier that affirm the past as much as they offer positive hope for the future.

* * *

Shifting dramaturgical conventions in the 1870s were part of larger national, cultural, and social transformations that occurred in that period. These changes in dramatic form would have had much less impact than they did—indeed, may not even have occurred—if it were not for major changes that took place with regard to the mode of production and delivery of theater in America. To be sure, the worldview of the new industrial and managerial elite influenced late-nineteenth-century melodramas, but this elite also took over the theaters and theater production process in a more direct way. In short, as the nineteenth century came to a close, the new moneyed aristocracy gained control over the means of disseminating the drama that embodied their vision. This turn of events was just another manifestation of the scientific rationalization and bureaucratic centralization that accompanied the technological and industrial expansion of the late-nineteenth-century United States.[44]

Just as the rapid industrialization that closed the century brought about new heterogeneous cities and more efficient modes of transportation and communication, it also facilitated the formation of large corporate structures to oversee the various components of the burgeoning economy. This kind of centralization and rationalization of all aspects of life extended to culture, including theater production. During the last three decades of the nineteenth century, the American theater witnessed a transformation that Alfred Bernheim referred to as "the industrial revolution" of the American theater[45]—a revolution that significantly altered the form and practice of theater business.

In 1870 the basic unit of the American theater was still the permanent resident repertory or stock company—that is, a company of contracted actors who presented a number of different plays during a theater season. This had been the case since shortly after the revolutionary war, when companies took up permanent residence in New York, Philadelphia, Charleston, and Boston. As the nation expanded westward, other cities welcomed permanent stock companies. As late as 1871–1872, there were fifty of these companies residing in numerous cities stretching from the Atlantic to the Pacific.[46] While the standard fare of each of these companies was supplemented by a growing number of visits from touring stars, each company was an independently managed, autonomous entity.

During the 1870s, however, this kind of company became an endangered species. Vainly struggling against the disarray caused by star performers' all too regular visits, by the development of the combination company—a touring production emanating from New York City—and finally by the economic devastation wrought by the Panic of 1873, many stock companies failed.[47] By 1877–1878, there were only twenty such companies left in the United States, and, by 1880 only seven or eight stock companies survived. Even New York's well-known stock companies, Wallack's, Palmer's, Daly's, and Frohman's, which continued to play into the last years of the nineteenth century, had all gone under by 1903.[48]

The place in the American theater left by the disappearance of the locally based stock company was filled by the "combination company." The origin of the combination company is somewhat hazy. It would seem to have developed as touring stars sought greater control over the product they provided audiences. Rather than rely on the resources of the local stock company in the cities they visited, touring stars began to put together complete productions that they then took on the road.[49] Actor/playwright Dion Boucicault, claiming that he could remember no combination companies in America before 1872, maintained that he developed the idea of the combination company around 1860 and implemented it in England in the early 1860s. Actor Joseph Jefferson told a slightly different story: he recalled no combination company in America before 1868, when he and Charles Wyndham simultaneously developed the first American combination companies.[50]

Who the original innovator was is not important; the combination company seemed to make perfect sense given the conditions affecting American theater production in the post–Civil War period. The combination company's utility became all the more obvious with the demise of the stock company in the years immediately following the Panic of 1873. With fewer and fewer resident stock company to depend on for support, it became necessary for touring stars to travel with their own companies. While stars who had toured in earlier periods may have performed in several different attractions, the tendency now was to tour in one play. Even so, transporting a full production was rather cumbersome, and only became cost-effective in the post–Civil War period as a result of extensive railroad expansion. To be sure, a rapid increase in combination companies followed the great burst of railroad building of the late 1860s and the early 1870s. While there were only a handful of road companies in the early 1870s, Bernheim claims that there were "nearly one hundred" combination companies on the road by the 1876–1877 season.[51] In December 1886, 282 companies were touring[52]; a high-water mark seems to have been reached in December 1904, when 420 companies were on the road.[53]

The development of the combination company in the 1870s meant that the decentralized American theater of independent, local stock companies was giving way to a more centralized theater in which New York City was becoming the hub. During the period 1870–1900, the Union Square area, referred to as the Rialto, became not only New York's first theater center, but also the *nation's* theater center.[54] Here, theater managers from all over the country sought attractions to fill theaters no longer housing stock companies. To facilitate the interaction of individual theater managers and producers of particular theater attractions, booking offices appeared in the Rialto. For a fee, these offices sought to meet the scheduling needs of individual theater managers or managers of circuits of theaters, which had either chosen to unite or had been bound together by ambitious entrepreneurs. The chaotic competition among many individual theaters and circuits seeking to contract attractions from New York was somewhat alleviated by booking offices; however, a more efficient and truly centralized system came into being in 1896 with the organization of the Theatrical Syndicate—an alliance of theater entrepreneurs, including Charles Frohman, Al Hayman, Marc Klaw, Abraham Erlanger, S.F. Nixon, and J.F. Zimmerman. Of the six, only Frohman was a theater producer. Even so, these six businessmen controlled enough theaters in major cities and along significant national circuits that they were able to dictate terms to other New York theater producers who wanted to tour plays. Controlling the booking of these productions into theaters across the country, the Syndicate was likewise able to force non-Syndicate theater owners seeking productions for their otherwise empty theaters to toe the Syndicate line. Although some practitioners and artists, such as David Belasco and Minnie Maddern Fiske, initially resisted the Syndicate monopoly, the only true challenge to the Syndicate came from another group of businessmen, the Shuberts, who, allied with Belasco, Fiske, and other artists, launched a theater war against the Syndicate in 1905. The Shuberts eventually gained the upper hand, but they tended to be as monopolistic and despotic as the Syndicate they replaced.[55]

With the advent of the Theatrical Syndicate and then the Shuberts, the reins of America's first-class legitimate theater were gathered into the hands of a few businessmen. Unfortunately, within this new system, there was very little room for theaters that catered to interests other than those of the business classes. Artistic experimentation and controversial social issues did not make for good business and therefore were rejected by powerful theater entrepreneurs. The result was a theater dominated by the tastes of a single class. In short, the transformation of the American theater from a decentralized theater composed of independent stock companies to a centralized theater dominated by business interests meant that the rising American industrial bourgeoisie attained complete hegemony over activity in American first-class theaters.

The impact of this transformation of the mode of theater production on theater practitioners was significant. Actors could no longer find permanent homes within fixed stock companies, nor could any actor expect to be hired to a general "line of business" in such a company as had been past practice. Instead, an actor would seek employment playing a specific role in a specific production of a specific play. Forced to settle for temporary employment in what they hoped would be a long run of a play in a New York theater or in a combination company tour of a single play, actors became what Bruce McConachie referred to as "job actors."[56]

Playwrights, however, might have looked favorably on the new arrangement since they had access to national audiences in a way that they did not have before 1870. Moreover, the focus of a combination company on a single play put a value on individual plays that had not been the case when actors toured with a limited repertory. In fact, this had been Dion Boucicault's intent when he developed his combination companies in the 1860s, as his focus on the play rather than "star" actors in advertising these companies would indicate.[57] As the combination company mode of production developed, the play—especially new plays—became a more significant ingredient in the theatrical equation. Inasmuch as the profits of the combination or single-play company system depended on the play's long run in New York and its long successful tour of the nation following that, the authors of popular plays were in better bargaining positions than ever before in the United States. In this regard, Jeff Poggi claims the combination company system had much to do with the fact that the payment of royalties to playwrights on a fixed percentage basis became common in the years following 1880.[58] Moreover, writing of the success of playwrights in the years after 1870, Poggi cites as an example Bronson Howard—according to tradition, the first American playwright to be able to live off his earnings as a playwright—and claims that "it was no accident that [Howard] began writing just when the combination system took effect and that the height of his prolific and profitable career coincided with the height of activity of the road companies."[59]

Certainly, the successful playwright had more to gain financially within the combination system than within the stock company mode of production; however, in return for financial success, the playwrights had to accept certain aesthetic limits. Insofar as the new system revolved around extended runs and tours of a single play, there was no room for plays that did not have a large appeal. The combination company system inevitably resulted in the development of standardized, "safe" plays. Playwrights may have been able to increase their earnings under the combination system, but as Poggi writes, they were "forced...to appeal to the 'lowest common denominator' in a large middle-class audience scattered throughout the country."[60]

Given the commercial priorities of the late-nineteenth- and early-twentieth-century mainstream theater, it is not surprising that refined literati who sought poetic or "artistic drama" would be disappointed with Syndicate or Shubert productions,[61] but this does not mean that there was no incentive to produce plays that were viewed as having artistic merit. Seeking to appeal to the "'lowest common denominator' in a large middle-class audience" did not necessarily mean that playwrights and their producers ignored the fashionable elite, who thought of themselves as discriminating theater audience members. On the contrary, the approval of the eastern fashionable elite would go a long way toward providing plays with the kind of prestige necessary to attract large middle-class audiences when the plays went on tour, and this was true of all plays, including frontier melodramas. As in other cultural sectors, appeal to elite audiences would constitute the play as an example of what Lawrence Levine referred to as "highbrow." Such a "highbrow" stamp was a selling point among middle-class audiences inasmuch as participation in "highbrow" cultural events was, as Levine argues, a badge of status for middle-class persons who aspired to join the social elite.[62]

Even before the Syndicate came to dominate the road, frontier plays had been seen as appropriate fare for fashionable and would-be fashionable audiences. In 1876, Harte's *The Two Men of Sandy Bar* was staged at Albert M. Palmer's Union Square Theatre, "the most prestigious theatre on the square,"[63] which was then the theater center of New York. Three years later, the eminent Union Square Theatre was the venue for the successful production of Bartley Campbell's *My Partner*. In describing the September 16, 1879, opening of this play, the *New York Daily Tribune* reviewer mentioned that the play was presented before "a numerous, representative, pleased, and often enthusiastic audience,"[64] but the *New York Herald* reviewer referred more specifically to "a large, fashionable, and critical audience."[65]

In the Syndicate/Shubert era, frontier plays opening at first-class New York theaters were sure to attract fashionable audiences. In responding to the 1903 opening of *John Ermine of the Yellowstone*, the *New York Herald* critic concluded his review with a lengthy list of specific luminaries attending the first night.[66] Reporting on the 1905 Washington, D.C., opening of David Belasco's *The Girl of the Golden West*, the *New York Daily Tribune* correspondent noted that "the national capital is renowned for distinguished first night audiences, but its record was rather surpassed on this occasion, when among the box-holders were all the members of the Cabinet now in town, most of the diplomatic corps and the chief figures in official life."[67] A notice like this certainly says something about the elite nature of the play's audience. Moreover, it would be a good advertisement—attracting less wealthy and eminent members of the middle class who wished to emulate their more celebrated contemporaries. For both well-to-do and middle-class playgoers from the East—especially playgoers with little firsthand knowledge of the West—plays receiving this kind of blessing from the eastern political establishment would probably accrue significant cultural power.

Such frontier dramas could go a long way toward confirming, if not shaping, their audiences' ideas about the western experience.

That some turn-of-the-century frontier plays were aimed at the middle class or even more affluent members of society and not working-class audiences was apparent given the ticket prices of the theaters in which they were performed. In the mid-1890s, vaudeville offered popular fare priced from fifteen to fifty cents,[68] and the spectacle- and action-filled, roughly constructed "ten-twenty-thirty" melodramas, as their nickname suggests, were in the same range. The more refined melodramas by Clyde Fitch, Augustus Thomas, and David Belasco, appearing in the first-class theaters built around the new New York theater center at Longacre Square, renamed Times Square in 1904, cost considerably more to attend. In the 1890s, first-class New York theaters charged two dollars for orchestra seats. In the early part of the next decade this price was lowered at some of the theaters. For instance, Harrison Grey Fiske, owner of the Manhattan Theater, cut the price of an orchestra seat to $1.50 in time for the opening of the highly successful production of Owen Wister and Kirke La Shelle's *The Virginian* in January 1904.[69] This price reduction did not, however, become the norm. In his 1910 *The Exploitation of Pleasure: A Study of Commercial Recreation in New York City*, Michael M. Davis, secretary of the Committee on Recreation and Amusements of the New York Child Welfare Committee, noted that two dollars remained the normal price for orchestra seats in high-priced or standard theaters. While top gallery seats were considerably less expensive at fifty cents apiece, both rates were well above ticket prices in low-priced popular theaters, which still generally charged anywhere from twenty cents to one dollar for an orchestra seat and ten to twenty-five cents for a top gallery seat.[70]

Fiske's $1.50 ticket price for an orchestra seat at the Manhattan Theater production of *The Virginian* may have been more reasonable than the standard two-dollar fee, but it would still be high for a working-class family, which according to a 1901 survey of "city wage- and clerical-worker families of 2 or more persons," could expect an average yearly income of only $651.[71] As Davis pointed out in his 1910 study, the working-class audiences were generally limited to the low-priced theaters, which sometimes put on standard plays at popular prices, but generally staged vaudevilles and burlesques. Speaking of the audience of these latter theaters, Davis writes: "[T]he majority of the audiences are of the working class, a minority of the clerical, and a minute remainder is made up of vagrants and leisure-class persons." On the other hand, Davis claims that at the high-priced or the standard theaters, "the leisure class appears to be in a slight majority over the business or clerical, the working class figuring in at about two per cent."⁷² More specifically, Davis describes the audience at high-priced theaters as being composed of the following types:

> There are the fashionable, the literary, and the professional sets. There is the body of middle-class persons of moderate means, who cannot go frequently to high-priced houses and rarely to the high-priced seats, but who take the theatre frankly and seriously as a means of enjoyment and education for themselves and for their elder children. By contrast follows the "sporty" set, numerically not large, but important to theatre managers because it spends money freely. The theatre provides the sporty man with a place whither to take women, see women, and seek prey; and fills in his life the same part that the dance hall does for his brother without a dress suit. Finally, we may name the "out-of-towners," the host of bourgeois visitors to the metropolis. This class is of particular significance. A family in New York for only a short stay will attend the theatre three or four times as often as will the average resident of the same financial status, during the same period of time.⁷³

Given the class differences cited by Michael Davis in his 1910 study, it would seem to follow that in the 1890s and 1900s, working–class audiences interested in frontier melodramas would experience these in the "ten-twenty-thirty" houses.

This is not to say that there was no crossover between first-class and "ten-twenty-thirty" houses. As Davis suggests, it was always possible for audience members to move from one venue to another, and occasionally plays and playwrights would make the transition. Generally, however, as Theodore Kremer, the author of a number of successful "ten-twenty-thirty" melodramas, confessed, there was a clear difference in style. Subtlety was no virtue among "ten-twenty-thirty" audiences: "[I]t is all right for the Broadway audiences to hear that the two met in a train, but the Eighth Avenue ['ten-twenty-thirty'] audiences have to be shown the train and the meeting."⁷⁴

While managers of the first-class theaters shied away from experimental or poetic dramas, they embraced more subtle melodramas than the rough-and-ready "ten-twenty-thirty" variety. Certainly, these more refined melodramas did not lack the action and effects that excited audiences, but the formula for a nationally successful, first-class theater melodrama included more than action for action's sake. Even so, producers were aware that while the audiences who patronized first-class theaters might desire plays with relatively complex characters who spoke lifelike dialogue, they would not accept any tampering with the basic conventions of melodrama. First-class theater melodramas had to end happily and affirm the kind of moral absolutism that audiences living amid the rapid social transformations of the late nineteenth century found reassuring.

* * *

The "melodramatic" aspects of frontier melodramas suited the taste of audiences and producers of the late nineteenth and early twentieth centuries; however, as "frontier" melodramas, these plays had special attractions other forms of melodrama lacked. To begin with, the "frontier" setting offered an escape from unsettling present conditions. It is not coincidental that the late-nineteenth-century wave of plays dealing with the far western frontier experience appeared as the frontier itself was disappearing. To be sure, the disappearance of the wilderness frontier and the concurrent expansion of industrialized urban centers plagued with new and seemingly complex social problems contributed to the increased interest in frontier plays. By definition, the scene of action of these plays, the western frontier, was preindustrial. While generally not as temporally or spatially distant or as idealized as the subject matter of some romantic dramas, frontier melodrama removed the action to a seemingly simpler time and place—a time and place unaffected by modern industrial anxieties. Indeed, frontier melodrama could fulfill the growing interest in realism while also serving the emotional needs of audience members who willingly gave themselves up to what Renato Rosaldo calls "imperialist nostalgia."[75] In an ironic twist, the turn-of-the-century theater, itself organized along industrial lines, offered dramatic fare that appealed to the escapist desires of its patrons.

Secondly, in the late nineteenth century, the frontier experience could and often was presented as an empowering experience. Here average Euro-Americans seemed to control their destinies, but, even more important, their actions seemed to have true historical significance. In fact, the rapid expansion of European-American settlements across the West—despite obstacles posed by climate, geography, and Native Americans—could be viewed, at least from the European-American perspective, as a real-life melodrama. To be sure, Manifest Destiny had a melodramatic dimension; that is, the taming of the continent against great odds could be rationalized as a victory of virtue over evil. Inherent in this victory, however, was a contradiction: the European-Americans' taming of the Wild West resulted in the very conditions from which frontier melodrama provided escape. The civilizing process taking place in the West led inevitably to an industrialized and urbanized America, and, consequently, to a desire for the freedom of a savage frontier.

While this contradiction is not fully resolved in frontier melodrama, its impact is alleviated by the fact that the conquest of the frontier, represented in its diverse stages in various frontier melodramas, was a distinctly American accomplishment—a uniquely American achievement. For a nation in search of a cultural identity, a rallying point could be found in the Euro-American triumph over the wild frontier. Not only were playwrights, who turned to the western frontier for material, fashioning a drama that had a specifically American appearance, they were also fueling a new patriotic nationalism in which all European-Americans could participate. In other words, frontier melodrama contributed to a sense of national coherence and identity that might offset the isolation that plagued many of the victims of industrialization.

Moreover, giving viewers a sense of being a part of a large fulfilling national movement, frontier drama could serve to co-opt the disenchanted who might otherwise disrupt the social order. Frontier melodrama thus functioned, perhaps without the awareness of its producers, as a tool to build the kind of false consensus that Antonio Gramsci described when analyzing the cultural politics of hegemony. In discussing how theater performance makes use of rhetorical devices that allow for the creation of the semblance of this kind of consensus across classes, Bruce McConachie, elaborating on Kenneth Burke's analysis of rhetorical identification, refers to what he calls the "hegemonic we"—an identification "with the action of a character on the basis of taken-for-granted values."[76] Frontier melodrama offered a story of conquest that all classes could buy into, and consequently took on a social and cultural significance beyond that of amusing large numbers of audience members. In short, frontier melodrama offers a "truth" that takes on ideological value. It becomes both a means by which the successful American industrial bourgeoisie could reassure itself and a net to capture the imagination and allegiance of struggling members of the lower middle and working classes (where they could afford to attend the plays). Based on a vision of a triumphant America, frontier melodrama offered American audience members, regardless of class, the opportunity to identify themselves as a "we" with a national mission worthy of the greatest loyalty.

The ideological power of frontier melodrama was certainly notable given the broad geographical range covered by combination companies, which carried it to first-class theaters throughout the country during the period 1870–1920. Frontier drama at first-class theaters served both to affirm the values of the elite and shape its ideas about the frontier and the nation as a whole. It thus helped to form the thinking of the social elite—reinforcing in its members a sense of the nation that they could then use their cultural leverage to further disseminate. Moreover, insofar as the frontier melodramas of first-class theater not only appealed to but also were accessible to members of the middle and lower classes throughout the country, productions of these plays provided audience members who wanted to associate themselves with the prosperity and values of the elite that opportunity. These plays, consequently, helped to mold a consensus approach to fundamental American concerns.

Ironically, however, it was the possibility of broader-reaching and cheaper modes of mass distribution—a further stage in the technological industrialization of entertainment—that marked the end of the golden age of stage productions of frontier melodramas. The development of film as a mass art, and especially the development of the Western movie, seemed to deprive frontier melodrama—both of the first-class theater and of the "ten-twenty-thirty" variety—of its reason to be. By 1910, Michael M. Davis would write: "Whether judged by the number of places in existence or the number of persons reached, the moving-picture show is by far the dominant type of dramatic representation in New York."[77] Moviemakers freely adapted the melodramatic form as well as particular melodramas from the theater. Given the fact that filmmakers were able to capture the sweep of western scenery and action in a way that theater, even with the most elaborate scenic effects, could not, it is not surprising that moviemakers quickly turned to Western material. When John P. Harris and Harry Davis opened their "nickelodeon," the first successful movie theater, in McKeesport, Pennsylvania, in 1905, their first attraction was *The Great Train Robbery*—a Western.[78]

Interestingly, even as Western movies began to appear on large screens and draw theater audiences as well as new audiences, the live theater version of the frontier melodrama attained a kind of consummation. Five of the most successful frontier plays both in terms of popularity and critical reception appeared on the legitimate stages of New York during the period 1900–1906. Augustus Thomas' *Arizona* opened at the Herald Square Theatre in September 1900. Owen Wister and Kirke La Shelle's dramatization of Wister's very successful novel *The Virginian* opened at the Manhattan Theatre in January 1904. In the fall of the following year, Edwin Milton Royle's *The Squaw Man* opened at Wallack's Theatre and David Belasco's *The Girl of the Golden West* opened at the Belasco Theatre. Then, in October 1906, William Vaughn Moody's *The Great Divide* opened at the Princess Theatre. This play was richly praised by reviewers, such as the critic for the *New York Dramatic Mirror*, who claimed that Moody's drama "set a new standard for the American drama."[79] More recent critics with a certain amount of distance and historical perspective have also spoken highly of Moody's play. Noting the realistic qualities of the play and the psychological depth that William Vaughn Moody introduced to his characterization, Richard Moody called it "the first modern American drama."[80] Even as the movie Westerns were on the verge of eclipsing staged frontier melodrama, William Vaughn Moody seemed to be taking frontier melodrama in a new direction—introducing the United States to the new "modern" theater.

Successful plays like *Arizona, The Virginian, Squaw Man, The Girl of the Golden West*, and *The Great Divide* embodied the social and cultural changes and debates that distinguished the late-nineteenth- and early-twentieth-century American scene. In these plays, however, as in earlier frontier melodramas, the celebration of European-American conquest of the untamed West pervaded the presentation of the frontier. While this triumphant vision provided the rough outline of the turn-of-the-century frontier myth as it was presented in the legitimate theater, these major plays each present a somewhat different perspective on that frontier western myth. To comprehend the theatrical parameters of early-twentieth-century frontier discourse, it will now be useful to examine closely the variations on this triumphal vision registered in particular plays.

Part II
The Plays

3. Discipline and Spontaneity: Clyde Fitch's *The Cowboy and the Lady* and Augustus Thomas's *Arizona*

The opposition of savagery and civilization functioned significantly as a way of distinguishing characters from each other and motivating plot development even in early frontier drama. To be sure, the shape of the action in early-nineteenth-century plays like *Metamora* (1829) and *The Lion of the West* (1830) depended heavily on the civilization-savagery contrast. Later frontier plays, like *My Partner* (1879), had even begun to explore the possibility of bridging this opposition by bringing together in marriage at play's end the characters representing civilization and savagery, East and West, respectively. As the nineteenth century gave way to the twentieth century, however, the possibility of a reconciliation of civilization and savagery crystallized into a major preoccupation both of writers of frontier drama and of other artists and intellectuals who pondered the frontier experience. This turn-of-the-century frontier western discourse to which Turner, Roosevelt, Wister, and Remington were key contributors provides a context within which the frontier visions presented in plays like Clyde Fitch's *The Cowboy and the Lady* (1899), Augustus Thomas's *Arizona* (1900), Frederic Remington and Louis Evan Shipman's *John Ermine of the Yellowstone* (1903), and Owen Wister and Kirke La Shelle's *The Virginian* (1904) can be profitably analyzed.

All four of these plays, originally produced in first-class New York theaters before audiences drawn primarily from among the more prosperous citizens, represent the frontier as a meeting place of civilization and savagery, and all four plays interpret this meeting in terms of comedy—that is, each play suggests that the resolution of the tension between civilization and savagery is not only possible, but also inevitable. In this regard, all four plays exemplify the optimistic mood of the first decade of the twentieth century. After all, affluent Americans seeking diversion in what was becoming the new theater center of New York and of the country in general—Longacre Square, which was renamed Times Square in 1904[1]—had much to celebrate. The panic and depression of the 1890s with their consequent labor disputes seemed to have given way to a vigorous economy in the first years of the twentieth century, and American international prestige had been boosted by a quick victory in the short Spanish-American War of 1898.

Despite the generally optimistic tone of these four frontier plays, there are differences in how they present the evolutionary process associated with the frontier experience; that is, these plays can be distinguished from each other by how each embodies "civilization" and "savagery" and how each represents the confrontation and the resolution of the civilization/savagery opposition. In this regard, the four melodramas can be seen as two pairs of closely related plays: on the one hand, *The Cowboy and the Lady* and *Arizona*, and on the other, *John Ermine of the Yellowstone* and *the Virginian*. The authors of the first two plays, Clyde Fitch and Augustus Thomas, were among the most successful and respected playwrights of the period. The second two plays were drawn from novels written by Frederic Remington and Owen Wister. Neither of these two authors were known as playwrights, but while Remington and Wister were natives of the East, both were much more closely associated with Western subject matter than either Fitch or Thomas. Although all four of the plays represent the western frontier experience according to the conventions of "eastern" theater, the contrast between the first and second pair of plays echoes the distinction between civilization and savagery that is at the heart of all four plays. Epitomizing the eastern theater establishment as Fitch and Thomas do, and the "Wild West" (at least as it was understood and commodified in the East) as Remington and Wister do, these two pairs of authors came at the frontier experience from very different directions.

* * *

Especially noted for his urbane social comedies, Clyde Fitch[2] was born in Elmira, New York, in 1865 and spent most of his formative years in the Northeast, receiving his education at Hartford Public High School and Holderness School in New Hampshire before attending Amherst College. He was an enthusiastic theatergoer and participant in college theater productions while a student at Amherst. After graduating, Fitch eventually found his way to New York City, where he very soon demonstrated his finely tuned skills as a playwright. In fact, he was extraordinarily successful during the years 1890–1910, when he created one hit after another. In 1901, he could boast that four of his plays (*The Climbers, Captain Jinks of the Horse Marines, Lovers' Lane,* and *Barbara Frietchie*) were running in New York simultaneously.[3]

After his death in 1909, however, Fitch's reputation rapidly declined. Perhaps his waning prestige can be explained by his being outshone by successors like Eugene O'Neill. More likely, Clyde Fitch's fall from grace can be attributed to factors inherent in his work. Montrose Moses touches on some of these:

> We could more readily describe Fitch by saying that he was a typical New York dramatist, than a typical American dramatist; for the conventions running through his plays are those of a society which was common to New York City in the eighteen-nineties.[4]

More specifically, Fitch's success depended on his ability to mirror the needs and interests of turn-of-the-century New York high society.[5] His plays spoke primarily to a small elite at a particular time and place in American history. Still, this elite, drawn from the successful business and management classes, had a cultural power disproportionate to its numbers. Indeed, among this elite one would find the entrepreneurs who drove the new publishing and entertainment industries, as well as others with social and political authority.

The stamp of this New York upper class is clearly present in Fitch's frontier western play *The Cowboy and the Lady* (1899). Discussing this play in his unpublished dissertation on Fitch's theater work, Thomas Hellie writes that the playwright was less concerned with western than eastern life and values.[6] To be sure, Fitch—a frequent traveler to Europe, but never to the American West—took advantage of the exotic appeal of the frontier without really knowing the West. His play, however, is more than an exploitation of western scenery and costumes. It represents an eastern response to the western frontier myth. To be sure, Fitch's variation of the frontier myth was especially suited to the needs and interests of an eastern commercial establishment that sought to rationalize its control of American resources. Fitch's *The Cowboy and the Lady* and other of his plays dealing with frontier issues thus become important examples of how a developing fascination with the West could be co-opted or domesticated for the purpose of disseminating what might be called the "eastern frontier myth."

Fitch begins the process of co-optation by apparently adopting the conventions of frontier drama. The connection between *The Cowboy and the*

Lady and earlier frontier melodramas was noted in the headline of the *New York Times* 1899 review. Here, Fitch's play is referred to as a "new mining camp drama."[7] Like mining camp drama, Fitch's play is set in the untamed West; however, Fitch's play, interestingly, is not a mining camp frontier drama at all. Instead, it is set on the cowboy-ranching frontier. The inaccuracy of the *New York Times* review is telling. It suggests the East's cavalier attitude regarding western social and geographical distinctions and, equally important, implies an awareness of the way in which Fitch's play is linked not only to cowboy-ranching plays, but also to all frontier western dramas. The kinship between Fitch's play and western frontier dramas dealing with mining camps is especially obvious when one considers how much the plot structure of Fitch's play's resembles that of what was perhaps the most well known mining camp play at the time, Bartley Campbell's *My Partner* (1879).[8]

The action of *My Partner* revolves around the slowly developing courtship of the hero, Joe Saunders, and the heroine, Mary Brandon. Joe has lived the free, rough life of a miner in California for many years and has fully adapted to the wilderness environment. Consequently, he can be seen as a representative of western coarseness or "savagery." On the other hand, the refined Mary, an English native, exemplifies the culture and concerns of eastern civilization. She has come west with her father, the owner of a relatively prestigious hotel. During the play, the villain, Josiah Scraggs, who perhaps represents the most insidious elements of the eastern commercial establishment, tries to destroy Mary's father both financially and emotionally. To this end, he creates a number of difficulties for the young lovers. Most significantly, he accuses Joe of murdering his own partner, Ned Singleton. Joe goes to trial, but before he can be found guilty, new evidence comes to light that proves his innocence and Scraggs's guilt. In typical melodramatic fashion, virtue prevails over vice, and hero and heroine are happily joined in conjugal bliss.

While the "savage" Joe and the "civilized" Mary seem to be modeled on traditional—if now outdated—gender types,[9] their marriage represented a new acceptance of the westerner in American consciousness. Henry Nash Smith has written about the problematic nature of marriages between frontier westerners and cultivated easterners in nineteenth-century American literature. He describes "how slowly the Western hunter gained sufficient social standing to be allowed to marry the heroine. This fictional emancipation of the Wild Westerner was not clearly worked out before the late 1870s."[10] In *My Partner*, not only is the westerner "emancipated," but, as suggested in chapter 2, the relationship of easterner and westerner parallels the kind of interaction that Turner described when discussing the interaction of eastern pioneer and western environment. During the course of the play, Joe learns to appreciate civilization, which, interestingly, he equates with the arrival of women on the frontier,[11] while Mary comes to understand the tolerance and flexibility that life on the frontier breeds in pioneers. Joe may be a low-class, raw white male pioneer, but as such he has ties with the "noble savage" tradition and, consequently, he can be redeemed; that is, he is not so removed from the sense of civilized virtues that he can't enter into the civilized world. On the other hand, the narrow restraints of Mary's civilized world are loosened after contact with Joe's free, natural spirit. Having been involved in a scandalous premarital relationship with Joe's partner, Ned, Mary—in accordance with Victorian morality—considers herself doomed until she is reassured by Joe that in the frontier West, "where civilization has not built its temples, above the green groves of God—where men live nearer him—wimmen have an equal claim with men to the charity that covers a great mistake."[12] Transforming each other, Joe and Mary have a relationship that represents a true marriage of civilization and savagery—a marriage that in the spirit of Frye's understanding of the mythos of comedy (discussed at the end of chapter 1) signifies the development of a new healthy American society.[13]

While the action of Fitch's play is moved from Campbell's California to Colorado and the present occupation of the play's hero is not miner but cowboy, *The Cowboy and the Lady* adopts a formula similar to that presented in *My Partner*. Indeed, his title suggests a focus on the opposition and relationship of East and West. Not only do the two plays appear to revolve around the romance of a hero who embodies the rough traits of western life and an eastern heroine who embodies civilized refinement, but also the lovers of both plays are confronted with similar obstacles. The heroine of each is, at first, intimately involved with another, if less dependable, lover. For Mary in *My Partner* it is Ned; for Jessica Weston in Fitch's play it is her philandering husband. When, in both cases, this other lover is murdered, the hero is the most obvious suspect, and only after he is found innocent can the hero and heroine be united.

Despite similarities, there is one obvious difference between these two plays. While Fitch's hero, Teddy North, is a ranch owner and the cowboy of the title, he is, in fact, not the westerner that Campbell's Joe is. A New Yorker and a Harvard graduate, he is, on the contrary, closely associated with the East. At least, Teddy appears to be an easterner in the vein of his namesake, Teddy Roosevelt. Like Roosevelt he is a man of physical interests and skills. For instance, he is an able fighter who "put all the amachure sluggers to sleep outside of Boston fur three years."[14] Early in the play, a newly hired cowboy challenges him to a wrestling match. Teddy throws his opponent to the ground after a brief bout, thus demonstrating his athletic superiority to the native cowboys. At the end of Act I, we are again apprised of his physical prowess when we hear how he saves Jessica Weston, who was left desperately clinging to a ledge after her horse stumbled over a cliff.

Fitch's Teddy may have some of the characteristics of the would-be cowboy and soon-to-be-president Teddy Roosevelt, but he also manifests other rough-and-tumble traits that easterners associated with the western frontier. Teddy's strength dwarfs that of the cowboys who work for him, and his language is reputed to be far coarser than theirs. As one of his cowboy friends says, their language is "all Sunday-school books compared with" (14) that of this Harvard graduate. Seemingly uninhibited by polite taste, Teddy is notorious for his cussing and his dirty stories. Finally, if there is any question about Teddy's place among rough-hewn westerners, Fitch binds him to the frontier by virtue of an artificial family association. Teddy legally adopts the frontier girl, Midge, as his sister. In adopting Midge—the "champion woman rifle shooter of Colorado" (10)—Teddy becomes her protector and deepens his claim to being a family member of the western frontier community.

Despite these links to frontier western life, Teddy's eastern background is never far from view. From the very start, he is spoken of as a kind of "dude." Teddy's clothes are a source of humor for those who do not know him well. Even Jessica makes light of what was apparently an incongruous costume. While he may be mocked as one who dresses more appropriately for "lawn tennis or croquette" (27) than for ranch work, Teddy is far from being ashamed of his high, starched white collars. He adopts western wear only as a joke. He arrives at the dance, which is the setting for Act II, in the oversized cowboy togs of his ranch hand, Joe. Significantly, during the course of the act, he removes these clothes on stage to reveal himself in fashionable formal attire. This unveiling has symbolic significance: the true easterner comes out from under the superficiality of so-called western habits. Here lies the major distinction between the image Teddy Roosevelt projected of himself and that of Fitch's Teddy. Roosevelt suggested that the strenuous life of the West stripped the participant of overcivilized constraints, revealing the true rugged individual beneath the civilized facade; Fitch's Teddy strips himself of his cowboy costume, revealing himself as the quintessence of eastern civilized manners, free of cowboy attributes. For many, Teddy Roosevelt represented a new virile manhood; however, Fitch's Teddy only appeared to embody this new masculinity. He is in reality a model of the kind of Victorian restraint that epitomized the understanding of civilization throughout most of the nineteenth century; that is, he embodies the genteel manliness that historian Gail Bederman describes as the male ideal in the years before a new primitive masculinity supplanted it at the end of the nineteenth century.[15]

As the play progresses, Fitch's Teddy assumes more of the polish of the refined eastern-bred hero. This is most evident with regard to his language. In the first act, Teddy is accused of swearing more than anyone else on his ranch. Bearing in mind his own definition of a swear—"Beginning with damn, everything that goes before and after" (14–15)—Teddy swears five time in the first act, but never again in Acts II or III. Moreover, his language loses whatever coarseness it had earlier. The "ain'ts" disappear and the masculine jocularity becomes more tame—especially in Act III, which is set in a courtroom. Here, where Teddy is forced to defend himself against the accusation of murdering Mr. Weston, he assumes a verbal facility that is typical of most articulate urban and urbane late-nineteenth-century melodramatic heroes.

More than clothing or a polished mode of expression finally distinguishes Teddy from native westerners: he holds the kinds of values that in this play define eastern civilization. Most significantly, Teddy defends civilized law and order against the lynch law practiced by his cowboy friends. At the very start of the play, Teddy is apparently opposed to the lynching of Midge's father, which has just occurred offstage. In fact, it was this opposition to lynching that the western Joe claims was "the only real grudge the boys hez ag'in'" (89) him. As Teddy claims, he has "always been on the side of law and order" (90). In his relationship with his ward Midge as well as with the other cowboys, Teddy takes on the role of civilizer. Rather than being one of the "boys," he becomes the monitor of their conduct.

It would seem, then, that despite the suggestiveness of the play's title, Fitch was not interested in presenting a conjunction or marriage of western coarseness and eastern refinement. In this play, when it comes to marriage, regional lines are not crossed; on the contrary, likes do and should attract. The easterner Teddy will mate with the recently widowed Mrs. Weston, but Teddy's adopted sister, Midge, rejects the advances made by Teddy's eastern friend, Bill Ransom, to accept the proposal of the native westerner, Joe. Fitch's eastern prejudices dictate, however, that the westerners Midge and Joe, whose marriage represents the climax of a farcical subplot, should not be taken too seriously. In fact, the westerners are treated with a condescension befitting their lack of civilized refinement.

Eastern society is, nevertheless, not viewed as entirely positive in *The Cowboy and the Lady*. In this play, as in other of his plays, such as *The Moth and the Flame* (1898) and *The Climbers* (1906), Fitch condemned the casualness with which many so-called civilized easterners treated marriage and divorce. In *The Cowboy and the Lady*, Fitch seems to censure Mr. Weston for his willingness to disregard his marriage vows—vows upon which civilized law and order depend. A noted philanderer, Weston not only pursues Molly Larkins, the proprietress of a local dance hall, but also the innocent Midge. Midge responds with a scathing attack on Weston. She claims that "there's never no cowboy—no, nor half-breed—on or near Silverville as hes said to me such things as him, nor done as he tried" (74). In his single-minded pursuit of sensual pleasure, Weston undermines civilized order and lowers himself below the level of the most savage westerner. Although Weston may partially redeem himself in the audience's eyes when he makes a dying plea, heard only by the audience, for Mrs. Weston's forgiveness, it is his pursuit of a "savage" and seemingly lascivious promiscuousness that costs him his life.

While Weston's unrestrained amorousness may represent a breakdown of civilized standards of conduct, Jessica Weston herself demonstrates what might have appeared to turn-of-the-century audiences as an overabundance of spirit. She is described as a noted flirt; however, her flirting with the cowboys in no way suggests a failure to take the institution of marriage seriously. Moreover, her response to Weston's philandering is unequivocal. After hearing about Weston's advances on little Midge, Jessica determines to leave him. Weston warns her: "I'm not sure I can't force you by the law to live with me so long as we remain man and wife" (76). Jessica's response is simple and to the point: "I don't *believe* that *is* the *law*" (76). When Weston threatens to enlist her church on his behalf, Jessica insists on her rights, telling him that he can't prevent her from leaving him. Civilized society depends on law, and it is that law that Jessica expects will protect her from her husband's savage, egoistic behavior.

Together Jessica and Teddy represent civilized law and order standing strong against savagery—whether it be that of the wild western lynch mob or of the urban eastern hedonist. In typical melodramatic fashion, law and order triumph in the final act of *The Cowboy and the Lady*. Not only is the dangerous decadence of the East overcome with Weston's demise, but also, and perhaps more significantly in this context, the savage wildness of the western frontier gives way to civilized respect for law and order. In short, savagery viewed as a childish, self-indulgent individualism yields to the seemingly necessary social discipline, which is the essence of civilization as it unfolds in this play.

The danger of western lawlessness is most clearly embodied not by the humorous cowboys, but by Jim, a "half-breed" with "an Indian cast of features" (5). Madly and jealously in love with Weston's mistress, Molly Larkins, Jim murders Weston at the end of Act II. At this point, Jim supplants Weston as the play's most serious villain. In fact, the problematic nature of Weston's savagery, his selfish inability to live according to social law, is revealed in all its purity in Jim. While Weston's death makes a marriage between Teddy and Jessica possible, Jim's murderous act—less a product of cold-blooded villainy than uncontrolled animal passion—represents a threatening menace to society. Weston's dangerous desires and western lynch-mob brutality are joined in Jim. There is certainly more than an undertone of racism in the fact that this "half-breed"—the play's only nonwhite character—is so closely associated with a violent savagery that should and must be controlled if a predominantly white eastern civilization is to flourish. The victory of this civilization over savagery is assured when Molly Larkins's loyalty to justice and/or race prompts her to inform on Jim, thus exonerating Teddy, who had been charged with Weston's murder.

The victory of civilized law and order over savage violence that this play as a whole represents is exemplified by the progression from the offstage lynching of Midge's father at the start of the play to the courtroom victory of Teddy and Jessica that marks the play's resolution.[16] Moreover, the shift from frontier to courtroom allows for a visual accentuation of this progression. While the play's first two acts are set in scenic environments that obviously capitalize on the exoticism of frontier life (Teddy's ranch and Molly Larkins's dance hall), the last act is set in the Silverville courtroom. Judging from the set descriptions that precede the three acts, Fitch was interested in stage realism. What is most significant in this context is the fact that the court scene, with its heavy dependence on symmetry, provides a visual correlative to the Act III vindication of law and order:

> A pleasant, sunny room with warm brown walls. At C. back is the JUDGE'S desk and seat. On each side of him are two square windows through which the morning sky and some trees are seen. L.C. is the prisoner's seat; at L. are the seats for the Jurors; at R.C. is the place for the witnesses to give their evidence; at R. are rows of benches for the public. At R.B. is the room where the witnesses are. (85)

With the Judge's position providing a center, a balanced stage picture is clearly attained. Associated as a courtroom is with cultural assumptions about justice, and functioning as it does as a place where opposing parties meet in an attempt to peaceably resolve disputes, this setting provides a visual metaphor for the kind of order eastern civilization brings to the frontier West.[17]

The courtroom milieu not only dictates a particular setting, but it also determines the way in which the incidents of Act III are organized. The free flow of the first two acts—exemplified, for instance, by the seemingly irrelevant entrance and exit of the gunman Dick Rod in Act II (62–4)—gives way to a more rigid courtroom structure with its dependence on carefully articulated and generally understood conventions of behavior. Witnesses appear in a preestablished order, and speakers have the floor only when court rules allow. In this regard, the shift from the colorful Act I ranch and Act II dance hall sets to the Act III courtroom becomes emblematic of the larger transition accompanying the settlement of the West—the transition from the wild, open frontier to a well-ordered but closed society.

The last-act courtroom milieu, with its rigid court procedures, emphasizes the victory of civilization over savagery, but, additionally, the court proceedings function as a means of expediting the union of the two equally civilized protagonists, Teddy and Jessica. Jessica first confesses her love for Teddy only under oath. Trying to prove that her testimony in his favor is not biased, Teddy, acting as his own lawyer, asks Jessica if she loves him. Her affirmative admission hurts his case temporarily, but he is overjoyed all the same. At the play's end, after Teddy is found innocent, he challenges Jessica to stand by what she said under oath:

> TEDDY: ... You know what you said under oath you'll have to stick to!
> MRS. WESTON: I'm game!
> TEDDY: Bully! (*Music swells*.)
> QUICK CURTAIN (112)

Their final union is thus closely associated with the legal procedures that epitomize the civilized law and order they both cherish.

Teddy and Jessica are united in a marriage with very different connotations than the climactic marriage of eastern civilization and western savagery in *My Partner*. Fitch's play concludes with a marriage of East and East—representing a "new society" that has overcome dangerous western savagery and that is governed by the principles of civilized law and order. Rather than celebrate a marriage of East and West, Fitch's play celebrates a victory of eastern civilization over western savagery. This victory of civilized order over savage spontaneity is reproduced on a variety of levels—levels pertaining to plot development and organization, character development, and spectacle. In short, in action and production, civilized order is vindicated at the expense of savage freedom.

In fact, *The Cowboy and the Lady* gives dramatic form to a variation of the frontier myth that is similar to the version which cultural historian Richard Slotkin claimed the developing mass media disseminated in the years before 1890. In his analysis of the myth of the frontier as it developed during the period 1800–1890, Slotkin claimed: "At the core of the Myth is the belief that economic, moral, and spiritual progress are achieved by the heroic foray of civilized society into the virgin wilderness, and by the conquest and subjugation of wild nature and savage mankind."[18] Slotkin goes on to write that, "according to this Myth, the meaning and direction of American history...is found in the metaphoric representation of history as an extended Indian war."[19] Writing that this form of the myth was generated during the economic crises of the 1870s,[20] Slotkin argued that the myth of a total war against savagery—Indian or otherwise—provided a rationale for imposing discipline and order on wild Indians or recalcitrant industrial workers. This popular myth, which was promulgated by the dispensers of mass culture from the Northeast, was very useful as a way of deepening the hold of the "managerial ideology" necessary for rapid industrial growth. Not surprisingly, as Slotkin points out, many of the editors and publishers who were so instrumental in molding this popular myth were based in New York, which had become the center of communication for the United States, and were or became members of the elite society of that city.[21] They were thus members of the same elite whom Hamlin Garland attacked and for whom Fitch wrote at the turn of the century.

Ironically, even though Fitch elevated eastern civilization at the expense of western savagery, eastern civilized audiences did not approve of *The Cowboy and the Lady*, which did not do well in New York City, having only a modest run of forty-four performances after opening at the Knickerbocker Theatre on December 25, 1899. Most of the New York City newspaper reviews were negative.[22] For instance, in his December 31, 1899, follow-up review for the *New York Times*, Edward Dithmar was less than enthusiastic; however, he wrote:

> It is a great mistake to suppose that this play is objected to because it is a drama of Western life, because it deals with coarse characters, because it is melodramatic. Its fault is that it lacks any sort of defined character, any vraisemblance that is more than pictorial.[23]

Other than weaknesses in the character development of Teddy and Jessica, Dithmar complains about the "horrible and needless"[24] offstage lynching of Midge's father and the "inherent improbability"[25] of Jessica's courtroom confession of love and Teddy's joyous response to it—two incidents that are extremely significant to the development of Fitch's version of the frontier myth. For Dithmar, it would seem character consistency and proper decorum were more important than the play's underlying ideological structure, and despite his disclaimer his rejection of the offstage lynching may suggest a certain squeamishness.

While *The Cowboy and the Lady* was not very well received in New York City, it had previously had a relatively successful out-of-town tour during the spring of 1899. As James Murray has demonstrated in his dissertation, "The Contribution of Clyde Fitch to American Theater," the play gathered especially positive reviews in eastern cities like Philadelphia, where it had its official opening on March 13, 1899, and Providence, Rhode Island.[26] Not surprisingly, the western critical response was not entirely favorable. Murray quotes the reviewer from the *Chicago Chronicle*, who laments, "[I]t is sad to believe that they accepted it in Philadelphia as a picture of the 'Wild West.'"[27]

Whatever success *The Cowboy and the Lady* had either in or out of New York, the attitude toward the frontier presented in this play is suggested in other Fitch plays that were certainly well received in New York City. For instance, one can find echoes of the view of the frontier presented in *The Cowboy and the Lady*—more significantly, the view Slotkin later described as total war against savagery—in Fitch's non-Western play, *Her Own Way* (1903).[28] In this play, the civilized, refined Georgiana Carley is pursued by two suitors: the westerner Sam Coast and the easterner Richard Coleman. Like Campbell's Joe, Fitch's Sam is a miner, but this time a miner who has made an incredible fortune. He is presented, however, as crude in taste and uncontrollably savage in his desire, wanting to win Georgiana at all costs, even destroying her family if necessary.[29] Georgiana, of course, rejects Coast, who returns to the West for Dick. Dick is an army lieutenant who has fought on behalf of civilization against the savagery represented both by unhappy American workers and foreign natives. Before the play begins, he had been involved in suppressing a streetcar strike in Brooklyn, and he spends most of the play abroad fighting to defeat native resistance to U.S. rule in the Philippines. In carrying the Indian War mentality into labor disputes and across the Pacific, this warrior for civilization exemplifies how the frontier myth presented in *The Cowboy and the Lady* was assimilated into other areas of concern. In concluding *Her Own Way* with the union of Georgiana and Dick, a marriage of East and East, Fitch once again demonstrates the victory of civilized law and order over western savagery.

In *Her Own Way*, Fitch thus reiterates the version of the frontier myth that appears more fully developed in *The Cowboy and the Lady*. While *The Cowboy and the Lady* utilizes a plot pattern similar to *My Partner*, Fitch adapts this plot structure so as to represent the gradual and necessary victory of eastern civilized discipline over western spontaneity—that is, Fitch affirms the "colonizing" ideology of the eastern establishment. At a time when the Turner frontier analysis was beginning to reshape the way Americans viewed their frontier past, Fitch helped to disseminate a narrowly eastern version of the frontier myth. Even though Fitch's hero Teddy seems to mirror Teddy Roosevelt, Fitch's character, unlike Roosevelt, gains very little from his exposure to the primal aspects of the frontier experience. On the contrary, he is an easterner who seeks to completely tame the West. Despite the suggested synthesis of East and West conveyed by the play's title, Fitch's sense of the American frontier experience was not that of Turner, Roosevelt, Remington, Wister, and others contributing to the turn-of-the-century frontier discourse.

* * *

On September 10, 1900, less than nine months after Fitch's *The Cowboy and the Lady* opened in New York, Augustus Thomas's *Arizona* opened at New York City's Herald Square Theatre.[30] Thomas's play was an unquestionable critical success and very profitable for Thomas. While citing the financial success of *Arizona* as an example of the exorbitant sums playwrights could make in the theater in the years after 1870, Jack Poggi claims that Thomas received royalties of $175,000 for *Arizona*. According to Ronald J. Davis, *Arizona* "grossed more than any other play until then produced in America, with royalties amounting to a quarter of a million dollars for the first five years of its performance."[31] Regardless of which of the two income estimates is more accurate, there is little question that Thomas's play was one of the first-class New York theater's biggest hits during the early years of the twentieth century.

As a frontier play, *Arizona* has a very different tone than *The Cowboy and the Lady*. Thomas was not a playwright whose work was geared narrowly toward the genteel New York elite. While Fitch was most successful when examining the manners and social conventions of the well-to-do, Thomas seemed willing to take on more broadly significant controversial issues. A native of St. Louis, Missouri, who served as a page in Washington, D.C., for the Forty-First Congress, studied law, and worked as a journalist for a number of newspapers,[32] Thomas manifested a greater concern with politics and larger social questions than did Fitch. Distinguishing these two playwrights from each other, Montrose Moses suggested that Thomas's plays had more of "the vigor of the masculine," while Fitch's "dealt with the feminine."[33] Whatever one may think of Moses's use of gender distinctions, he does provide a useful commentary. While both Fitch and Thomas were firmly entrenched in the New York theater by 1900, Thomas's more hard-nosed approach to his material clearly contrasted with Fitch's urbanity.

More concretely, the two playwrights were different in their typical choice of settings for plays. *The Cowboy and the Lady* was somewhat of an anomaly for Fitch, who was primarily known for his plays about New York City life. Thomas's early theater successes, on the other hand, were set in regions well beyond the pale of New York. *Alabama* (1891) and *In Mizzoura* (1893) struck critics who had never been to those locales as sharply etched pictures of unfamiliar regions.[34] No doubt, the onetime journalist Thomas brought a reporter's eye to his subject matter. In fact, when it came to writing his play about Arizona, Thomas wrote from experience. Again, unlike Fitch, who never went west, Thomas required an elaborate trip to Arizona before writing.

This trip was to have an important impact on Thomas's playwriting career. For Thomas, as for his very good friend Frederic Remington—as well as for Roosevelt and Wister[35]—the Wild West was to prove to be the source of a personal regeneration. After the less-than-successful runs of two relatively hard-hitting, probing dramas dealing with the American political scene, *New Blood* (1894) and *The Capitol* (1895), Thomas went through a dry period. As he later recalled in his autobiography, *The Print of My Remembrance*, he wondered at the time if he weren't "written out."[36] Prompted by Remington's encouragement and enthusiasm, Thomas in 1897 "resolved again to go for a subject to the plain and primitive things as far as one could find them"[37]—that is, he decided to travel to Arizona in search of new material. The success of *Arizona* is emblematic of the revitalization that Thomas the playwright experienced as a result of this trip west. As he immersed himself in the rough-and-tumble life of the West, he found an antidote to his writing difficulties. Like others embracing the West as a panacea, he found life in this region offered a remedy for the stresses of that in the civilized—perhaps too civilized—East. In short, Thomas's view of the western frontier and its impact on the country as a whole was very different from Fitch's.

Their frontier visions may have been different; however, both Thomas and Fitch depended on melodramatic techniques to sustain audience interest in their plays. Set in the still wild Arizona territory, the plot of *Arizona*, like that of *The Cowboy and the Lady*, revolves around the heroics of a traditional upright hero who sacrifices himself to protect a woman in distress. In this case, the hero, Lieutenant Denton, prevents his frontier post's commanding officer's young wife, Estrella Bonham, from running off with the dishonest cad, Captain Hodgmen. Unfortunately, late at night, right after Denton has caught Hodgman in the Bonham house, forced him to give up Estrella's jewels, which were to have been used to finance the adulterous lovers' escape, and chased him from the Bonham house, and even as Denton is eliciting a promise from Estrella never to see Hodgman again, the very jealous Colonel Bonham unexpectedly returns home having just been recalled from a trip that he was supposed to take to Los Angeles. Finding Denton alone with Estrella, Colonel Bonham suspects the worst. To protect Estrella's reputation, Denton claims that he had come to the Bonham house to steal Estrella's jewels. Out of loyalty to Denton's father, the Colonel's old comrade in arms, Bonham allows Denton to resign his commission and thus escape court-martial. The civilian Denton takes a job as a wrangler at the ranch of Henry Canby, Estrella's father, so he can be close to Estrella's sister, Bonita, who is his true love. After Hodgman tries to sabotage Denton's chances with Bonita by suggesting to Canby that Denton had threatened Estrella's honor, the play quickly moves to its final climax. In the end, of course, Hodgman is foiled, and the good Denton wins Bonita and regains his position in the cavalry.

Providing dimension to this very conventional melodramatic plot was the colorful, turn-of-the-century Arizona frontier setting. Thomas's Arizona frontier is very much a "meeting point between savagery and civilization"— civilization/savagery and East/West oppositions permeate the play. Unlike Campbell and other playwrights of the period, Thomas, however, did not express these oppositions primarily through gender differences. Certainly, the female characters, like Estrella, Bonita, and Lena (the daughter of Colonel Bonham's ever-loyal Sergeant Kellar), are generally more restrained in their behavior than the male characters, but this distinction, though in keeping with period gender constructions, adds little to the East/civilization versus West/savagery contrast as it is developed in this play. For instance, the rough, somewhat slapdash manner of the old rancher Henry Canby is balanced by his wife's attempts to monitor his appearance and her preoccupation with the fine clothes and jewelry that she possesses but never has the opportunity to wear; nevertheless, this contrast reveals much less about the relationship of savagery and civilization than does the distinction drawn between Canby and Colonel Bonham, or more specifically between Canby's cowboys and the Colonel's cavalry.[38]

In *The Print of My Remembrance*, Thomas provides much insight into the connection of the Bonham-cavalry/Canby-cowboys contrast, on the one hand, with that between eastern civilization and western savagery, on the other.[39] What is particularly interesting here is the impact that Thomas's friend and New Rochelle neighbor, Frederic Remington, had on him as he planned for and later assimilated the experience of his trip west. In fact, Thomas brought to his western journey, and subsequently his play, assumptions shaped by Remington's understanding of the frontier.

Ironically, however, Thomas seemed to have misunderstood aspects of Remington's frontier vision. In describing Remington's attitude toward the great influx of immigrants at the close of the nineteenth century, Thomas alluded to Remington's understanding of the military's role in the settling of the West. He wrote that Remington

> ...refused to believe that the overflowing tide of ignorance was destined to inherit the fruits of the earth. He disliked the growing influence of the unassimilated immigrants. He hated the political herding of them. He loathed all politicians because they talked. He loved the soldiers because the military acted promptly and without debate. In his day in the West the local advent of troopers meant sudden and inflexible order. He saw humanity's future safe only under military discipline. We differed, but I liked his mettle and his impatience with conditions.[40]

Certainly, Remington did demonstrate in his life and writings the kind of xenophobia that Thomas ascribed to him, but if Remington did "refuse to believe that the overflowing tide of ignorance was destined to inherit the fruits of the earth," this refusal was more in the order of wishful thinking than certainty—a fact that is especially apparent after the turn of the century, as Remington's novel *John Ermine of the Yellowstone* (1902) indicates. More important in this context, however, is the fact that Thomas seems to have misread Remington's fascination with the military. Thomas seems to have viewed this interest in the military as an unambivalent assertion of eastern civilization over western savagery—while in fact, Remington, like Roosevelt and Wister, appeared to feel a certain attraction to the western savagery, which instilled new vigor into those who immersed themselves in it.[41] Certainly, Remington believed that civilization would eventually overcome savagery, but if it were to be robust, civilization would have to assimilate some of the savage vitality. It was Remington's loss of faith in this possibility that led to a tragic climax in the novel *John Ermine of the Yellowstone*.

Thomas may not have grasped the fundamental ambivalence underlying Remington's frontier vision, but he nevertheless duplicated it in *Arizona*. In this play, Colonel Bonham and the cavalry represent inflexible order and discipline, but like Remington, Thomas apparently believed that the civilized, eastern sense of inflexible order and discipline needed to be balanced by at least some savage-like western freedom and spontaneity. In *Arizona*, Thomas offers Canby and his cowboys as that balance. Describing the living rancher who served as the model for Canby, Thomas wrote:

> Henry C. Hooker was a quiet little man who had been some twenty-five or thirty years in that locality selling beef to "government and Apaches"; at times on the defensive, and at other times on friendly terms with his savage neighbors. He had known the old Apache chief, Cochise, the predecessor of Geronimo, and had a hundred interesting tales of his experiences with Indians, and cowboys, and soldiers.[42]

In a similar vein, Thomas's Canby was a man who fully understood the savage, undisciplined life of the West; he had assimilated what was best in the savage wilderness—the freedom from artificial rules and conventions. Concerned with sharpening the connection between Canby and the muscular side of the frontier West, Thomas transformed the real Hooker, who was "under the average height of the American, was slight and quiet," and was, consequently, inappropriate for the role he wanted him to play in *Arizona*. Thomas confessed he "took the liberty of replacing him in [his] mind with a more robust and typical frontiersman."[43]

The contrast between Colonel Bonham, an embodiment of civilized restraint, and the more freewheeling Henry Canby is apparent from the play's opening dialogue:

> CANBY: [*As* COLONEL *draws last of julep through straw*] Have another?
> COLONEL: No, I think not.
> CANBY: Well, if you only *think* not— [*calls*] Sam—
> ....
> Sam, fix two more of these, and don't put quite so much whiskey in the Colonel's.
> ....
> COLONEL: I really oughtn't to take another *one*, but it's been a year since I had a *smell* of mint.[44]

Canby, age sixty, and Bonham, age fifty-two, are very neatly delineated here. Canby freely indulges his pleasures, whereas Bonham's pleasures are circumscribed by his sense of duty, by what he "ought" to do. The power of the "ought" with regard to alcohol is demonstrated again later in the play. When the Colonel and his troops visit Canby's ranch on their way to the Gulf, where they will apparently embark for Cuba and the Spanish-American War, Canby offers the Colonel and his officers champagne. The Colonel accepts only a bottle of beer and requests coffee for his officers.

The point here is not that Colonel Bonham is a closet teetotaler. He is a man of discipline, and, Thomas suggests, sometimes that discipline is valuable. Denton confesses to Estrella:

> I tried to knock off whiskey once, and it was a deuce of a pull. Used to say to myself, "I'll bet I won't drink this," even while I was pouring it out. Finally got so I'd bet I hadn't drunk it, after I had. Then one day the Colonel slapped me on the back, and told me to pull up. Stumbled occasionally after that, but he put his arm around me, and now I go in for golf—and tea.... Most anybody can pull up if the Colonel's with 'em. (79)

In this regard, Colonel Bonham embodies the restraint necessary to curb dangerous passions and urges. He epitomizes the civilized discipline that Fitch affirmed in *The Cowboy and the Lady*.

For Thomas, however, discipline lacking in tolerance was harmful, and it was that tolerance that could be learned in the West from characters like Canby. Indeed, Canby and his fellow cowboys are not slaves to the rules and conventions that mark eastern civilization. The savage conditions of life in the West demand a much more flexible and practical approach. Canby tells Denton:

> We take a man on here, and ask no questions. We know when he throws his saddle on his horse, whether he understands his business or not. He may be a minister backslidin', or a banker savin' his last lung, or a train-robber on his vacation—we don't care. A good many of our most useful men have made their mistakes. All we care about now is, will they stand the gaff? Will they set sixty hours in the saddle, holdin' a herd that's tryin' to stampede all the time? (124)

Moreover, this tolerance is not limited to hardworking men, but is offered equally to women who may have slipped from the virtuous path. As in *My Partner*, western tolerance rejects eastern moral rigidity. In referring to Lena, who was "ruined" and then abandoned by an as yet unrevealed lover who turns out to be the villain Hodgman, the colonel, representing eastern discipline, can only lament, "Too bad, isn't it? She'd 'a' made some chap a good wife." To which Canby "optimistically" replies, "In Arizona, my boy, she's worth a whole hatful of *dead* ones yet" (19). Later, when Tony, a Mexican *vaquero* who works on the ranch, asks to marry Lena despite her past, Canby elaborates further: "That's Arizona. We're a little shy on water, but there's as much charity for a woman as you can round up in the Gospel of St. John" (122).

With Bonham and Canby, Thomas offers a contrast between an eastern civilization that breeds a discipline that is sometimes too rigid, as in the Colonel's attitude toward Lena and his unforgiving demeanor after his wife's possible lapse in discretion,[45] and a western savagery that generates an open-minded pragmatism. While contrasting these two characters and the principles they represent, Thomas is not condemning either, but suggesting the value of both. Setting the play's action at the fort, where the commander Colonel Bonham maintains a tightly disciplined garrison, as well as on Canby's ranch, a location where unrestrained western tolerance holds sway, Thomas implies that Arizona frontier life, and perhaps by extension American life in general, is defined by both civilization and savagery.

This tricky balance of civilization and savagery is vividly embodied, on the one hand, by the play's hero and, on the other, by its heroine. Indeed, the hero and heroine, Lieutenant Denton and Bonita Canby, respectively, are each linked to both eastern civilization and western savagery. Bonita, a native of the southwest, has a "wild Arizona heart" (54), but while she is well adapted to the West, impressing soldiers with her horseback riding skills, she has received a San Francisco education in city ways and refinements and has no intention of spending her life in the western wilderness. When Denton is in danger of being convicted for a crime he did not commit, Bonita is enough of a westerner to defy the law by having the fastest horse on the ranch made ready for his escape even as she submits to the Colonel's careful inquiry into the facts. Her action at this key point in the play epitomizes a balance between spontaneity and discipline.

Denton, who comes from the East and has attended West Point Military Academy, demonstrates a real sympathy with the West after he takes up cowboy work on Canby's ranch midway through the play. According to Canby (124), Denton quickly becomes a cowboy without equal. Having been stifled by the passivity of his army life, Denton loves the "freedom, action, the wide horizon" (104) that he experiences while working on the ranch. At play's end, however, he willingly resubmits himself to military discipline—joining his cavalry comrades as they ride off to bring order to Cuba. Denton's progress through the play represents a movement, which begins as a regression from civilization (cavalry discipline) to savagery (ranch freedom), and is followed by a reinvigorated return to civilization (restoration in the cavalry) at play's end. Denton thus follows a course similar to Frederick Jackson Turner's eastern pioneer who adapts himself to the West to which he has moved, only then to establish a revitalized, freer civilization there. Denton's personal journey also seems to parallel the playwright Thomas's experience of coming to the West, undergoing a revival of energy and then returning east to write this successful play.

In suggesting that the frontier experience can be understood in terms of a Turner-like coming together of civilization and savagery, Thomas appears to offer a very different perspective on the frontier than did Fitch. Nowhere are the differences between the attitudes of the two playwrights more apparent than in the ways they treat the apparently civilized villain who threatens the civilized social order and the apparently savage being who murders him—that is, Mr. Weston and Jim, respectively, in *The Cowboy and the Lady*, and Hodgman and Tony, respectively, in *Arizona*.

While Mr. Weston's inability to restrain his savage lustful desires undermined his civilized veneer—a degradation from which he was redeemed only at his death when he asked for his wife's forgiveness—Hodgman is a more dangerous villain in whom the heat of lust is supplanted only by cold-hearted calculation. Having "ruined" Lena Kellar before the play begins, he very methodically avoids responsibility both for her and for the child he conceived with her. Moreover, his seduction of Estrella is not motivated by uncontrollable sexual desire. He seduces her to acquire her jewels, which will provide him with the financial wherewithal to escape the western wilderness he so adamantly disdains. Indeed, Hodgman is a narrow-minded hypocrite whose primary objective is to return to "God's country," which in his mind is "down East, just between the Mohawk River and Long Island" (41), or at least he hopes to go as far east as New Orleans. His artful pragmatism may suggest something similar to the practical freewheeling freedom represented by Canby, but his intolerant attitude toward the West suggests the worst aspects of eastern civilization. Like Fitch's Weston, he is hateful, but unlike Weston, he is unredeemed even in death. As he dies, he utters a mean-spirited, vindictive lie, accusing Denton of his murder.

While Fitch reclaimed Weston and placed the burden of the play's villainy on his murderer, Jim, who, in an overtly racist fashion, is presented as the "half-breed" exemplar of the kind of dangerous savagery that must be overcome by white civilization, Thomas presents Hodgman's murderer, Tony, a Mexican *vaquero*, in a much more positive light. Again, there is a degree of racism here, as Tony is presented as a wildly passionate man, whose love for Lena prompts him to threaten any man—including her father—that he finds with her. To be sure, Tony, who lacks the ability to restrain any of his impulses, embodies western savage instincts. He is, nevertheless, accepted by Canby. Motivated by an openness to the savage side of experience, the rancher, albeit condescendingly, embraces Tony, claiming that "he's a Mexican, but a pretty good one" (120). Tony's overly passionate nature may be the source of some humor in the play, but his unquestioning love for Lena, despite his knowledge of her past indiscretions, and his loyalty to Denton make him a sympathetic character.

Thomas's guarded approval of Tony and the savage sensibility he embodies is most apparent at the play's end. Like *The Cowboy and the Lady*, *Arizona* concludes with the trial of the hero falsely accused of the murder of the white villain who was, in fact, done in by a nonwhite embodiment of savagery. Here, however, the trial, even though it is conducted by Colonel Bonham, does not give a disciplined, rigorously logical tone to the play's final act. On the contrary, Colonel Bonham's attempt to bring order to the court is tempered by the improvisational nature of the proceedings, which are rushed because of his regiment's imminent departure. References to Denton's revolver as "exhibit A" (141) and the bullet that killed Hodgman as "exhibit B" (146) are obviously forced—especially given the court officer's lack of material to tag the items, a dilemma that is only remedied by the frustrated Colonel Bonham's ripping up the pasteboard back of a writing tablet and throwing the pieces on the table before the officer.

More important, the conclusion of the trial is characterized by the kind of balance of western savagery and eastern civilization that the play seems to advocate. While the disciplined trial procedure of interviewing witnesses and examining evidence finally establishes Denton's innocence and thus paves the way for his return to the cavalry, the court's justice gives way to something in the order of vigilante justice with regard to the real murderer, Tony. After admitting his responsibility for the murder, Tony rushes from the courtyard in which the trial is being held and, much to the joy of his cowboy friends, escapes on Bonita's speedy horse, Cochise. As Canby suggests that no "Arizona jury" would convict Tony and as the ranch cowboys passively prevent anyone from chasing Tony, it seems pretty clear that he rides off to freedom. With both Denton and Tony free, a poetic justice based on a synthesis of restrained eastern legal principles and impulsive western tolerance is attained.

While Clyde Fitch may have put his faith unquestionably in the kind of eastern and civilized inflexible order and discipline that Teddy ultimately embodied in *The Cowboy and the Lady*, Thomas seems to offer an ideal synthesis or marriage of eastern civilized discipline and western savage spontaneity. One caveat regarding this conclusion, however, needs to be offered. Thomas may have embraced western savagery in a way that Fitch never would or could, but in fact the savagery offered is very carefully circumscribed. While Canby may be linked to certain aspects of the savage West, and while he demonstrates a strong sympathy for the nonwhite, non-European natives of Arizona, who embodied this savagery to turn-of-the-century viewers, his egalitarianism is limited. Indeed, his ranch may seem an abode of freedom when compared with fort discipline, but there is still a clear hierarchy in place on the ranch. Canby is the boss, and not only the cowboys, but also Tony and the other non-European character, the Chinese servant Sam, who is presented as a comic stereotype, are clearly subservient to him. Canby and his wife make easy use of derogative terms like "greasers" (18) and "nigger" (18) to refer to members of other races. Even as Canby sympathizes with what he sees as the wild, passionate nature of nonwhite races, he takes for granted his superiority over what he sees as inferior "others." Savagery is acceptable as long as it remains noble, and it is for this reason that Tony, who is willing to give all for Lena, is presented positively, not because of but despite his passionate nature.

There is even more evidence of a Fitch-like perspective in *Arizona*. The description of the ranch that appears in the play's stage directions is very similar to the description of the Hooker ranch Thomas described in *The Print of My Remembrance*. Thomas writes in his autobiography:

> This doby hacienda was a quadrangle about one hundred feet square, with blank walls some eighteen feet high outside. Three sides of the inner court were made up of little rooms one-story high, with roofs sloping to the center and rising to somewhat less than the height of the outer walls, whose superior margin served as parapet in case of attack. A fourth side of the quadrangle, besides having a room or two and a shed for vehicles, had a large reinforced double gate that could be thrown to and fashioned with heavy bars and staples. In the centre of the court thus formed there was a well, so that the colony might have water to withstand a siege.[46]

The scene of the first and last act of *Arizona* are set in "an adobe courtyard" (7) very much like this—even to the extent of including a well upstage in front of "a large gateway, which may be closed by two massive wooden gates" (7). In short, this abode of western freedom, like the cavalry fort, is a fortress (Plate 1). While within the play, Canby and his ranch may be seen as antithetical to the rigid discipline represented by Bonham and the cavalry, this ranch is a bulwark protecting its residents from the

Plate 1 A 1900 poster for Augustus Thomas's *Arizona* representing the Act IV court-martial scene. Note the fortresslike gates enclosing Henry Canby's ranch house, stables, and courtyard. (Library of Congress Prints and Photographs Division, Washington, D.C. 20540)

dangerous savagery of the surrounding desert. Framing Thomas's vision of the frontier as a location where a synthesis of civilization and savagery is possible—a synthesis that may give birth to a more balanced civilization—is a vision very similar to that belonging to Fitch. This similarity is further apparent in the imperialist implications of the play's end—after all, the cavalry is riding off to fight in the Spanish-American War. They hope to bring freedom and order to nonwhite inferiors in Cuba, but what is the nature of this freedom and this order? Is it, in the end, discipline that they offer the Cubans? Are they simply continuing the triumphant march of civilization over savagery?

This ambivalence belonged not only to Thomas. Indeed, Roosevelt and Remington celebrated the outbreak of the Spanish-American War as a great opportunity for Americans to extend themselves into new frontiers—to civilize new and distant savage lands. But they also saw the savagery of war as a way of invigorating their own somewhat decadent civilization.[47] Still more ironic in this regard is that in an earlier draft of the play, Thomas had his cavalry march off to fight Indians.[48] The connection between Indian fighting and foreign imperialist war was very much a part of the frontier discourse of the turn of the century. Foreign conquest was deemed a way of extending the frontier, which seemed to be disappearing in the American West. In fact, this connection was very much a part of popular culture. Even in Buffalo Bill's Wild West Show after 1898, vignettes celebrating the conquest of the West were interchangeable with scenes presenting the victory of civilization over savagery in Cuba.[49]

The distinction between the frontier process presented in Fitch's *The Cowboy and the Lady* and that offered by Thomas in *Arizona* is not absolute; nevertheless, there is a difference. While both playwrights in the end may be subject to similar Euro-American prejudices, Thomas, much more than Fitch, presents a vision of the frontier that is in tune with dominant elements of the developing turn-of-the-century frontier discourse. Moreover, this distinction is in keeping with Montrose Moses's attempt to differentiate the two playwrights by associating Fitch with a feminine and Thomas with a more masculine approach. In fully trusting civilization to restrain the wildness of the frontier, the always-urbane Fitch ran the risk of being viewed as the overcivilized, feminized male, who in the eyes of a robust Teddy Roosevelt, put the nation at risk. Thomas, on the other hand, would have been viewed as the more virile proponent of the kind of masculine vigor and openness that Teddy Roosevelt and other late-nineteenth- and early-twentieth-century commentators sought in the West. In fact, the New York critics commenting on *Arizona* noted the conventional melodramatic underpinning, but praised the "ingenious and virile" things Thomas had his characters do,[50] the "vigor and adroitness" with which he manipulated his characters,[51] and "the stamp of verity," which "is more or less strong on almost every personage."[52] In William Dean Howells's review of Thomas's play, one hears the great American realist praise Thomas's sharp-edged virile style:

> In its intense distinctness the local color has a peculiar charm; the picturesqueness of the life is extraordinarily vivid, and there is no shadow of uncertainty in the action; it is sharp and rapid, as if it were the nervous response of human nature keyed to sympathy with the moistureless air of the region, and unclogged by the vapors of misgiving that burden it in other climes.[53]

Thomas's presentation of the western frontier experience was characterized by a masculine quality not seen in Fitch. In this regard, Thomas was closer to the vision of Turner than Fitch. Much more than Fitch, Thomas captured the marriage of romance and realism that was to characterize many late-nineteenth- and early-twentieth-century representations of the frontier experience. This turn-of-the-century view would be even more obviously present in frontier plays that were soon to appear in New York's first-class theaters. Three seasons after Thomas's presentation of the frontier appeared in New York, two other plays, *John Ermine of the Yellowstone* and *The Virginian*, also shaped by and shaping the turn-of-the-century frontier discourse, appeared on Broadway. It is the examination of these two works, one inspired by Thomas's good friend Frederic Remington and the other by Owen Wister, two authors associated with the Wild West much more than they were with the theater, that will be the focus of the next chapter.

4. Drama from Novels: *John Ermine of the Yellowstone* and *The Virginian*

During the 1903–1904 theater season, New York audiences had the opportunity to see plays based on novels by two of the best-known contributors to the turn-of-the-century frontier discourse: Owen Wister and Frederic Remington. *John Ermine of the Yellowstone*, adapted from Remington's novel of the same name by Louis Evan Shipman, opened on November 2, 1903, and *The Virginian*, dramatized by Wister and Kirke La Shelle, on January 5, 1904. Both plays began their New York theater life at the very prestigious Manhattan Theatre, which Harrison Grey Fiske had sublet and renovated in 1901 for the use by his highly respected and talented actor-wife, Minnie Maddern Fiske, and her performing company.[1] While the Fiskes produced neither of these plays, the very presence of these plays in the Manhattan Theatre suggests the degree to which Wild West material had become attractive to fashionable New York theater audiences.

After Thomas's *Arizona* demonstrated the commercial value of Wild West frontier drama for producers and managers of first-class Broadway theaters, it was inevitable that theater entrepreneurs would be drawn to the work of Owen Wister. A Philadelphia gentleman, Wister had earned a degree in music at Harvard and spent several months working in the Boston financial world before his health gave way and a trip out west seemed the appropriate remedy. Arriving in Wyoming in July 1885, he both recovered his health and found artistic inspiration in the West.[2] During the 1890s, Wister published several volumes of short stories and a novel, *Lin McLean* (1897), dealing with western subject matter, but it was the novel *The Virginian* that firmly established his place as a writer of Westerns. Wister's novel was stunningly successful after it was published in April 1902. Reviews were extremely positive. Claiming that *The Virginian* was "worthy of gratitude, a clean simple, straightforward tale.... and something more," H.W. Boynton of the *Atlantic Monthly* added, "Mr. Wister may be said to have given us a final apotheosis of the cowboy."[3] The *Nation*'s book reviewer wrote, "*The Virginian* has... been one of the most popular books of the season; it deserves to endure through many seasons."[4] Indeed, by the end of August, one hundred thousand copies of the novel had been printed[5]; it was, in fact, a national best seller, receiving kudos even from such reputable authors as Henry James.[6]

Frederic Remington's *John Ermine of the Yellowstone*, also published in 1902, would have looked almost as attractive to potential stage adapters. Though not known as a novelist, Remington was associated with the West through his work as an illustrator and an artist/sculptor. Like Wister, he was eastern bred (although he matriculated at Yale, not Harvard), but only came into his own after wandering West in the early 1880s.[7] As an illustrator, he was closely connected with other contributors to turn-of-the-century frontier literature. He had illustrated Theodore Roosevelt's *Ranch Life and the Hunting Trail* (1888), and during the 1890s, Wister and Remington frequently collaborated. Remington provided illustrations for Wister's stories and essays when they appeared in magazines like *Harper's Monthly* and *Harper's Weekly*, as well as for Wister's first volume of short stories, *Red Men and White* (1895), and his first novel, *Lin McLean*. In his own right, Remington provided articles and short stories for magazines, including *Harper's*, *The Cosmopolitan*, and *Century*. Spurred on by the success of Wister and hoping to capitalize on the same eastern fascination with the West that had made *The Virginian* a success, Remington decided to write his own novel. Five months after the publication of *The Virginian*, Macmillan brought out Remington's *John Ermine of the Yellowstone*. Remington's novel may not have been as successful as Wister's, but it nevertheless earned its share of praise from contemporary critics.[8]

Given the close association of the two authors and the fact that the two novels appeared within half a year of each other, critics could not help but note the kinship between the two works. In his review of *John Ermine and the Yellowstone*, the *New York Times* critic wrote, "The story itself makes one think of *The Virginian*, and yet it is *The Virginian* with a thousand differences, and a much nearer approach to the reality of life on the Western prairies than was to be found in Mr. Wister's entirely satisfying presentation of it from the romantic point of view."[9] Indeed, these two novels of the frontier West complement each other. It is as if Remington's work was meant as a conscious response to Wister's overly idealized portrait of the West.

While the plots of both novels revolve around the relationship of a man who is well adapted to the savage condition of life in the West, and a woman who embodies the conventions and concerns of eastern civilization, the conclusions of the two novels represent diametrically opposite perspectives on the significance of the frontier for the American future. Wister's vision, in keeping with the optimism of a large number of turn-of-the-century contributors to frontier discourse, was in the vein of comedy as defined by Northrop Frye in his discussion of the "mythos of spring."[10] Wister's novel ends with his westerner, the Virginian of the title, and his easterner, Molly Wood, a Vermont schoolteacher, marrying and living prosperously. Here, eastern civilization and western savagery join to form "a new society" embodying a uniquely American destiny. Remington, however, had become increasingly skeptical about the possibility of such a hopeful resolution to the frontier process. Distressed by the degenerate mediocrity, which he viewed as the natural result of industrial civilization's supplanting the heroic life of the Old West, Remington came to see the relationship of East and West in tragic terms. His protagonist, John Ermine, a white man who had been brought up by Crow Indians, is not only rejected by the easterner Katherine Searles, but also is finally murdered by a hot-blooded Indian youth—further underlining the futile dream of reconciling two such opposed cultural traditions. Remington sought to offer an antidote to Wister's extremely unrealistic historical romance, but it would seem that turn-of-the-century audiences were more attracted to Wister's presentation. Given the relative obscurity to which Remington's novel has been condemned in the years since its publication, it appears that later generations of readers concurred.

It is ironic, then, that despite the greater enthusiasm with which Wister's novel was met, it was Remington's novel that was first dramatized for Broadway audiences. This incongruity is somewhat offset by the fact that Louis Evan Shipman's version of *John Ermine of the Yellowstone* borrows the optimistic ending of *The Virginian*—thus turning Remington's tragedy into comedy. Even with an ending that New York playwright Shipman, known primarily for his minor 1901 comedy *D'Arcy of the Guards*, believed more suitable to his audience's taste than the original's sad ending,[11] the play was only a modest success, closing after a run of twenty-four performances.

Opening two months after *John Ermine of the Yellowstone*, the dramatization of *The Virginian* met with a much more enthusiastic response. Originally, it had been the theater producer and architect of the Syndicate, Charles Frohman, who had hoped to produce a play based on Wister's novel; however, Frohman and Wister had a falling out. Perhaps with Thomas's successful *Arizona* in mind, Wister then turned to Thomas to help with the dramatization of the novel. When Thomas backed out, Wister was able to enlist the aid of Kirke La Shelle, who had produced *Arizona*.[12] La Shelle functioned as the production's director, but when he was stricken with appendicitis, Wister, who had no professional theater experience, took responsibility for rehearsals. The production weathered this and other normal theater crises to become a New York success.[13] While critics were somewhat reticent in their praise, audiences embraced the play, and it had a lengthy run of 138 performances, making it one of the biggest hits of the 1903–1904 New York theater season. The play then went on the road, touring for more than a decade and bringing to Wister weekly royalties of $200 to $300, and sometimes even more.[14]

The success of the stage version of *The Virginian* and the more modest response elicited by the play based on *John Ermine of the Yellowstone* reveal much about how first-class theater audiences viewed the frontier. Indeed, a careful examination of how Wister's and Remington's novels were adopted to the theater will provide insight into the ways in which the different expectations established by turn-of-the-century frontier western discourse, on the one hand, and turn-of-the-century theater practice, on the other, could be negotiated.

* * *

The program for the November 2, 1903, Manhattan Theatre production of *John Ermine of the Yellowstone* announces the play as Louis Evan Shipman's "American Drama," which was "suggested by Frederic Remington's 'Sketches of Frontier Life,'"[15] rather than by the novel of the same name as the play; nevertheless, there is little question that the play, which consists of four acts and a prologue, is based on the novel that appeared the year before. Even so, "suggested by" implies a greater distance from the original source than "adapted from," and such an implication is not entirely out of order. After all, not only did the novel's tragic ending give way to a happy resolution, but also other subtle shifts in focus mark the transformation of the novel into a play. Some of these are the inevitable effects of translating a novel into an artistic medium that depends on action rather than narrative, and that requires a concentration of plot, because the play must take place in a shorter time period than that necessary to read the novel. Other modifications, like the changed ending, were meant to make the play fit the expectations of a particular audience at a particular time. The latter changes resulted in a hopeful resolution of the tension between eastern civilization and western savagery; they also temper Remington's contrast between eastern civilization and western savagery. Despite these alterations, Shipman's play, like Remington's novel, remains focused on "the meeting point between savagery and civilization."

In the novel, savagery and civilization meet, but they do not mix. In general, an impassable line is drawn between savagery and civilization—the crossing of which can lead only to tragedy. Although White Weasel, later called John Ermine, is, as his name implies, white, he finds himself on the Indian savagery side of the line. Having lived since infancy with the Absaroke, known as the Crow Indians by whites, White Weasel is fully adapted to their culture—a culture in tune with nature. As in the case of the Indians around him, "the birds and the wild animals talked to the boy, and he understood."[16] White Weasel is content with his Indian existence, but how this white boy came to live with the Crow in the first place is left unclear. Even though Remington often reminds the reader of White Weasel's racial heritage, he provides little information about White Weasel's past connections with white civilization, thus allowing him to be unquestionably associated with primitive savagery—both that belonging to the white race's distant past and that attributed to the Indians of the western present.

A "savage" he may be, but he is white, and given the early-twentieth-century understanding of race, especially the way in which race theory incorporated biological evolution and a racial hierarchy, it is no surprise that White Weasel would seem to have a civilized potential unknown to Indians. When White Weasel reaches adolescence, his foster father—acknowledging the young boy's distinctiveness—conveys him to the white hermit, Crooked Bear, who becomes White Weasel's mentor. Crooked Bear begins educating White Weasel in the ways of the whites, but Remington makes it clear that White Weasel, to whom Crooked Bear gives the white name John Ermine, never loses his spiritual connection with Indian savagery. By teaching him the ways of white civilization, including the English language and Christianity, Crooked Bear hopes to discipline Ermine's wildness, his "White Weasel" self; nevertheless, Crooked Bear fails to root out the savage spirit Ermine has acquired. Whenever Ermine confronts a crisis, he reverts to the "wild gutturals"[17] of the Indian language and the rituals of Indian religion.

Believing that Ermine's assimilation into white civilization would be facilitated by contact with the U.S. army, Crooked Bear urges him to join the half-breed Wolf-Voice, who is traveling to the white soldiers' camp to become an army scout. As Ermine and Wolf-Voice range across the wilderness, Remington sharply distinguishes them from the whites with whom they intend to serve:

> These two figures, crawling, sliding, turning, and twisting through the sunlight on the rugged mountains, were grotesque but harmonious. America will

never produce their like again. Her wheels will turn and her chimneys smoke, and the things she makes will be carried around the world in ships, but she never can make two figures which will bear even a remote resemblance to Wolf-Voice and John Ermine. The wheels and chimneys and the white men have crowded them off the earth.[18]

Remington presents white civilization as a large industrial machine in which individual whites function merely as replaceable parts. On the other hand, the rich vigorous individualism of the Indian is irreplaceable: "If all these white men were dead, it would make no difference; if that Indian on the far-off hill was dead, he could never be replaced."[19] Paradoxically, it is the vast impersonal nature of white man's civilization that initially fascinates Remington's Ermine. He follows Crooked Bear's advice about enlisting in the U.S. army because he wants "to associate with the people who lost 'ten thousand men' in a single battle and who did not regard it as wonderful."[20] He is fascinated by the awesome, unrelenting, machine-like power of civilization—the very aspect of it that would lead to the inevitable destruction of the Indians with whom he spent his youth.

It is this destruction that most disturbed Remington. While drawing a sharp line between the uniquely individual Indian savage and the industrial mass-man of white civilization, his primary focus is on the disastrous interaction of these opposites. Wolf-Voice and Ermine exemplify certain Indian traits and thus stand out from the white civilization they seek to join, but, ironically, both also demonstrate—each in his own way—the consequences of the fatal meeting of savagery and civilization. Although associated with the Indians, Wolf-Voice is a half-breed who is mixed "like that soup the company cook makes,"[21] and, consequently, he lacks not only a true place in white civilization but also a clear tribal connection. He is a perpetual outsider whose only allegiance is to whiskey and money.[22] In short, unlike the relatively innocent Absaroke, whom Ermine knew in his youth, Wolf-Voice is an example of the kind of Indian degradation that follows from contact with whites.

John Ermine is also in an untenable situation vis-à-vis white civilization. A savage in spirit but with a white skin and the superficial understanding of white civilization fostered by Crooked Bear, he appears to bridge the unbridgeable. As a result, he functions for the white soldiers and women he meets as an intermediary in what is actually a futile cultural exchange. Remington writes:

> [Ermine] had thought out the proposition that the Indians were just as strange to the white people as the white people were to them, consequently he saw a

social opening. He would mix these people up so that they could stare at each other in mutual perplexity and bore one another with irrelevant remarks and questions.[23]

Although Ermine is aware of the cultural chasm separating Indian and white—even finding it a source of humor—he himself tumbles into it. Socialized as an Indian, he cannot understand the seemingly arbitrary conventions that circumscribe the behavior of whites. He is especially confused by the rules of "civilized" courtship. Ermine falls in love with Katherine Searles, the daughter of his commanding officer, and cannot see why it is that even if Katherine were attracted to him, which Remington suggests may be the case, she still must reject his proposal of marriage because he lacks the polish of an appropriate suitor. In short, Ermine's savage simplicity and directness conflict with civilized complexity and artifice, and this conflict leads to his tragic demise. Rejected by Katherine when he proposes marriage to her, rebuked by her father and Captain Lewis for his rash proposal, and challenged by her respectable suitor, Lieutenant Butler, Ermine finally explodes, shooting and wounding Butler. He escapes the U.S. army camp, but later, when he tries to return in order to kill Butler and abduct Katherine, he is shot dead by an Indian he had insulted earlier in the novel. Caught between civilization and savagery, he is rejected by both.

For Remington, savagery is inevitably doomed by the relentless evolutionary process that brings civilization to the West. While Crooked Bear had hoped to provide a future for the boy White Weasel by teaching him Christian restraint and sending him off to join the whites, he inadvertently initiates the sequence of events that destroys the "savage" Ermine.[24] In his novel, then, Remington's concern is with the unfortunate results of the kind of discipline that Fitch and, to a lesser extent, Thomas had offered as the virtue of civilization.[25] In the original *John Ermine of the Yellowstone*, Remington draws the contrast between the savage individual who is in tune with nature—both his own and that of the natural world—and the disciplined spiritless slave of machines and social conventions who will replace him. He laments the fact that the natural simplicity of uncorrupted savagery will inevitably be supplanted by modern industrial civilization.

At the start of the play "suggested by" Remington's novel, Louis Evan Shipman highlights the contrast between Indian savagery and white civilization that Remington developed in the original novel. In the play's prologue, Captain Lewis comes to Crooked Bear's hut in the hope of recruiting Ermine into his corps of scouts. When he asks Crooked Bear if Ermine has been affected by civilization, Crooked Bear responds: "No; he's honest and knows nothing of liquor."[26] The implication here is that civilization consists of lies and alcohol—that is, it represents a movement away from pure, simple nature toward artifice and degeneration. This contrast is further developed later in the prologue when Crooked Bear warns Ermine that he must come to know the people with whom he is biologically related—he must learn more about the whites whose lust for material gain in the form of "gold fever" will sweep away anything in their way.

Although Shipman indicates that his John Ermine is untouched by civilization, he does not anchor him as firmly in the savage Indian world as Remington had. In Remington's novel, chapters two and three (from a total of twenty chapters) focus on Ermine's early life among the Absaroke. Shipman, however, begins his play with the prologue set in Crooked Bear's mountain camp. The John Ermine who appears in the prologue has already begun his education in the ways and means of white civilization. Beginning the play with Ermine already Crooked Bear's protégé is an expedient way of concentrating the lengthy time span covered by Remington's novel, but in taking this late point of attack to Remington's story, Shipman—perhaps inadvertently—isolated his hero from the Indian savagery with which he is to be so closely associated.

To a certain extent, Remington had also detached Ermine from the Indians around him in the early chapters of the novel by frequently calling attention to his racial heritage, but at least he had set Ermine within a positive picture of Indian life in those chapters. In Shipman's play, the only non-white character to appear is Wolf-Voice, and he is presented in a demeaning manner. The attitude of Shipman's contemporaries to this stage character is perhaps conveyed by the *New York Times* reviewer when he writes of the performance of the actor playing the role in the Manhattan Theatre production: "As the half-breed Wolf Voice, Albert Perry has all the yellow-dog shrewdness, superstition, and shiftiness of Mr. Remington's original."[27] In addition to employing the bastardized English dialect that Remington gave him, Shipman uses an especially telling incident in Act I, Scene 1, which depicts an attack on a wagon train that Ermine and Wolf-Voice accompany, to further demonstrate Wolf-Voice's inferior Indian nature. When Major Searles asks Ermine and Wolf-Voice to slip through the Sioux siege with orders for reinforcements, Wolf-Voice only agrees after negotiating a fifty-dollar fee, while Ermine agrees to go for nothing. In the novel, this incident suggests the degeneration of Indian nature that results from the meeting of Indian savagery and white civilization. In the play, because the half-breed Wolf-Voice is the only Indian who appears, his action reflects back on Indians in general—suggesting how much less honorable they are than the noble Ermine. Again, as in Thomas's *Arizona*, the white hero may exhibit the attributes inculcated by the savage wilderness, but the hero is clearly distinguished from the natives by an innate virtue. The savagery of the hero is circumscribed in a way that would make it palatable to fashionable turn-of-the-century audiences who were not only familiar with old noble savage stereotypes, but also swayed by racist assumptions regarding the superiority of white Europeans.

The way in which Shipman modifies Remington's protagonist is further demonstrated in the play's prologue when he allows Ermine to explain his motivation for joining the U.S. army. Remington's savage-spirited Ermine had been drawn to the U.S. army out of awe for its war machine—a military might and commitment to victory with which he wants to be associated. In the play, Ermine's primary incentive has a very different source. The decision of Shipman's Ermine to join Captain Lewis's scouts is prompted by his infatuation with the Katherine Searles, who appears in a photograph that Lieutenant Butler had accidentally lost and that Ermine had been fortunate enough to find alongside a wilderness trail. His attraction to the Katherine he sees in the photograph inspires in him a desire to behold the real thing. To fulfill this end, Ermine enters the civilized world of the whites. In other words, Shipman employs a conventional theatrical device—the conveniently appearing stage prop—to prompt Ermine's journey into the whites' civilized world. Insofar as this prop, a photograph of the beautiful Katherine, lures Ermine toward civilization, Shipman conflates feminine beauty and civilization. He depends on the traditional gender construction, whereby the feminine is associated with culture and civilization, as a way of suggesting the powerful attraction of civilization for the savage Ermine.

Remington had also used this device—in fact, Shipman lifted the photograph subplot from the novel. Remington's Ermine likewise found a photograph of Katherine, and this picture whet his appetite for the real thing; however, Remington's Ermine found the picture while on the way to join the whites. It was not his initial motivation for seeking them out. On the other hand, in omitting what Remington presented as Ermine's primary motivation, the fascination with the white man's war machine, Shipman excised what in the novel became a powerful irony: Ermine is attracted by the very same industrial power of white civilization that will destroy the lifestyle he has known.

In displacing this irony, Shipman moves the play in the direction of sentimental romance. The impact of melodrama with its requisite binding love between hero and heroine comes to the fore here, but Shipman does not settle for simple affection between hero and heroine. He reaches for a more intriguing romantic connection. His John Ermine is an idealized romantic hero who easily captures the love of Katherine once he meets her. He brings into her narrow realm of experience a touch of the exotic. He speaks to her of the miracles of nature, and she melts. Indeed, Mrs. Searles is concerned that her daughter is being seduced by Ermine's tales of "the clouds, and the stars" (II, 8). While Remington's Ermine struggles to articulate his interests and needs, Shipman offers a protagonist who expresses himself in an unnaturally poetic fashion. In proposing to Katherine in Act II he employs a richly entrancing language: "You were not made to live the still frozen life of these people. Come with me, and ride with the wind; I'll show you what no white man has ever seen, teach you what the night says—" (II, 18). His allure for Katherine is similar to Othello's for his Desdemona, but in a play that seems to aim at capturing a sense of the real frontier, this dimension of Ermine's character is out of place. As the reviewer for the *New York Dramatic Mirror* wrote: "[I]n the dialogue [Shipman] proves himself more familiar with the novels of Cooper and the poems of Longfellow than with the Indians of Wyoming."[28] To be sure, Shipman's protagonist has more in common with the clichéd "noble savage" than he has with a realistically depicted western Native American.

Shipman's Ermine is more articulate and more sentimentalized than Remington's original, but, in addition, the plot in which he is set is full of the kind of conventional melodramatic incidents that allow him to evidence these traits. It is true, however, that some of these incidents are drawn from the novel. For instance, in Act I, Shipman uses a scene from the novel in which Ermine arrives in the "nick of time" with reinforcements for a troop of soldiers besieged by Sioux warriors. In the play, however, the threatened wagon train includes not only Major Searles and his legion, but also his wife and his daughter, the play's heroine Katherine. In what was even at that time somewhat of a cliché, Ermine arrives at the last minute with reinforcements to save the embattled soldiers and the heroine. Dashing on stage in the midst of what looks to be the bloody demise of Searles and his family, Ermine announces, "The cavalry are here!" (I, 19), and the Act I curtain is dropped amid general jubilation.[29]

Other obvious melodramatic elements of the play are additions to or changes in the novel's plot. This is especially true with regard to the series of events that follow Ermine's proposal of marriage to a stunned Katherine. The rejection of a similar proposal in the novel leads inevitably to Ermine's humiliation, his violent response, and his tragic death. The action of the play moves in a different direction. Shipman shifts the novel's focus from Ermine's futile pursuit of Katherine to Ermine's virtuous efforts to rescue Katherine, his damsel in distress, from various threats to her good name.

As in the novel, Ermine's proposal to Katherine is followed by a scene in which Major Searles and Captain Lewis, having heard about the proposal, confront Ermine that night to inform him of the inappropriateness of his actions. Unlike the novel, this scene in the play is followed by a scene in which Katherine secretly comes to Ermine's quarters to reassure him that Searles and Lewis had spoken to him against her wishes. The fact that she would come alone at night to visit Ermine is extraordinary—such an action would offend the Victorian sense of decency, prized by many in the audience. That she was willing to violate the rules of proper decorum to apologize privately to him for her father's actions—and to do so under the most compromising of circumstances—demonstrates the extent of her devotion to Ermine.

After Ermine again proposes to Katherine and she rejects him, he determines in savage fashion to force her to go with him to the forest. At this point, Katherine, the gentle tamer, civilizes the savage Ermine, reminding him that "the men of your blood—white men—are kind to women, their strength, and courage make them *gentle* with those who are *not* strong" (III, 11). He learns his lesson well: he withdraws his threat, and when Lieutenant Butler knocks on his door, Ermine protects the vulnerable Katherine from disgrace by hiding her so Butler will not discover her in Ermine's room.

Interestingly, Butler, who was Katherine's somewhat tedious but victorious suitor in the novel, is transformed by Shipman into a traditional villain. As in the novel, Butler pursues Katherine, but in the play he does so against her will. Even the all-important photograph of Katherine that Butler at one time had in his possession had been stolen from her, and he refused to return it when she demanded that he do so. Furthermore, it is that photograph that brings Butler to Ermine's quarters in Act III. As in the novel, it is his demand that Ermine return the photograph that leads to harsh words and finally to gunplay. Here, however, Ermine kills Butler in self-defense. Ermine is aware that Katherine has overheard the quarrel and could testify on his behalf, but to testify she would have to admit that she had been alone with Ermine in his room before Butler arrived. To protect her from having to make that disgraceful confession, Ermine flees to the mountains. He similarly escaped in the novel after shooting Butler, but there he had done so to protect himself and not the virtue of the beleaguered heroine.

In the final act, Ermine returns having received a letter from Katherine pleading for him to come back. To Crooked Bear, in whose mountain camp he had sought refuge, he confesses: When Katherine "wants me,...I go" (IV, 9). Even after he secretly returns to the U.S. army camp as a wanted man, Ermine primarily strives to protect Katherine from public humiliation. Katherine confesses to her parents that she was in Ermine's quarters when Ermine and Butler had quarreled and that she knows that Ermine had shot Butler in self-defense, but Ermine reassures her horrified parents, "[T]here will be no trial. What you have heard need never be known outside this room. I will step out that door and walk across the parade. I wouldn't get twenty feet" (IV, 17). At this point, Katherine insists that she wants to save his life because she loves him and is now willing to be his wife. Rather than Ermine going to his death, he and Katherine are finally joined together with the blessing of Major Searles, who reassures his wife, "[T]here, there, Sally; worse things could happen to one's[*sic*] daughter than to have her marry a real man" (IV, 17).

The question as to what is a "real man," in this context, is perhaps more open than Shipman might have meant it to be. Is Searles commending Ermine's independent, wild spirit as it contrasts with that of the tame soldiers around him? Or is the Major calling attention to how well Ermine has appropriated the white man's heroic and chivalrous attitude toward damsels in distress? Is it Ermine's instinctive virility or his ability to restrain and control his virility on behalf of a woman that impresses Searles? Is Searles praising Ermine for illustrating what Gail Bederman described as the savage masculinity so highly prized in the late nineteenth century, or is he applauding Ermine for exemplifying what Bederman wrote of as the more refined manliness that restrained animal urges and that characterized heroic males earlier in the century before the wilderness cult and primal man had gained cultural power?[30] To comprehend fully what this play is saying about the frontier experience, uncertainties like these need to be resolved, and yet at play's end these questions are upstaged by the general celebration that marks the play's final curtain—a celebration that is totally in keeping with the happy ending typical of melodrama.

Certainly, the intensity of the frontier clash of civilization and savagery as it was presented in Remington's novel has been softened in the play to oblige the expectations of audiences bred on melodramas. Ironically, the play's dependence on various sentimental ploys and melodramatic devices that were meant to please turn-of-the-century theater audiences was treated rather disdainfully by some critics. As the *New York Times* reviewer wrote, the play at times slips into the "flimiest [sic] sort of situation-seeking melodrama."[31] More salient is the rebuke offered by the reviewer for the *Sun*. He writes:

> [I]s it not curious that Remington the very apostle of the realistic in the delineation of Indian types and Western life generally, should be transposed to such

a shallow, artificial and theatrical key on the boards!...Again the conventions of the footlights put in claims."[32]

And yet while melodramatic elements stand out, they have not completely displaced the dialectic of discipline and spontaneity that characterized the presentation of the frontier in plays like Fitch's *The Cowboy and the Lady* or Thomas's *Arizona*.

In keeping with melodramatic conventions, the hero in Shipman's adaptation of Remington's novel wins the prize, the hand of the heroine, after a series of heroic actions; however, before his final victory John Ermine undergoes a kind of transformation whereby his savage spontaneity is disciplined. John Ermine is tamed during the course of the action. He moves from what appears to be a primal masculinity to a more refined manliness.

Interestingly, the primitive dimensions of his character as he first appears seem to have been well served by James K. Hackett, the actor who originated the role of Ermine in 1903. Hackett emphasized the character's energetic dimensions by bringing a melodramatic fire to his performance. In his appearance, he was described as "straight as the proverbial arrow, tall as the pine of allegory, sombre, slim, taciturn, handsome"[33] by one reviewer, and as presenting a very "gallant and handsome figure"[34] by another. Critics, however, also agreed that Hackett's performance even in his love scenes was marked by a "vigorous display of tempestuous passion,"[35] a "romantic ardor and melodramatic vigor,"[36] and "a boisterous vehemence which is not the manner or the language of passion,"[37] and that he "spouted like a volcano all the old time poetic jargon."[38] Shipman provided Hackett with the kind of explosive role that would allow him to demonstrate his skill as a hot-blooded melodramatic hero, one whose intensity, according to the *New York Times*, would "no doubt bring down the house when he controls it sufficiently to avoid danger of bringing down the scenery."[39]

Hackett may have been at his best with the more violent aspects of this role, but the text does suggest a transformation in his character, and it is Katherine who plays the largest role in this change. She becomes something of a "schoolmarm" to Ermine, literally providing him with the tools of civilization, "books and...papers" (II, 15). More important is the way she affects his conduct with respect to the opposite sex. As discussed above, Katherine withstands Ermine's almost violent wooing of her with a reminder of the importance of learning to be "*gentle* with those who are *not* strong" (III, 11). Katherine teaches Ermine what in this play seems to be the great lesson of white civilization; she teaches him the Victorian code of behavior, a code central to turn-of-the-century melodrama. As Crooked Bear admits to Ermine when Ermine seeks asylum with him after killing Butler, "[Y]ou have learned what I could never teach you, my son, it is the great heritage of our race; our care for our women..." (IV, 5).[40] During the play, Shipman's Ermine succeeds where Remington's Ermine failed: he fully assimilates the artificial norms of white civilization, which is understood here in terms of chivalry and restraint. During the course of the play, Ermine's primal masculinity is shaped into something akin to Victorian manliness. This process is visualized for audiences by the changes in Ermine's coif. Initially, Ermine appears with "thick tawny hair braided in two plaits behind" (prologue, 4); in Act I, after first joining the white soldiers, his mass of tawny hair is left unplaited and hanging on his shoulders, forming a vivid contrast with the more carefully groomed cavalry men. Later, after the Sioux battle, he appears with his hair cut off in the style of the whites. Shipman's Ermine very agilely adjusts to the civilized world, and, consequently, at play's end his future is guaranteed.

The significance of Ermine's transformation to the play's plot development indicates that this character is, the subject-center of the play—a proposition that is not entirely surprising given the fact that he is the title character. Moreover, Hackett's energetic performance of this role would further emphasize the place of the heroic male at the center of the drama, while the heroine, originally played by Charlotte Walker to mediocre reviews,[41] is relegated, in accordance with Victorian expectations, to a more passive role. According to this reading of the play, Katherine may influence a change in Ermine, but she remains the unchanging vessel of honor for which he strives. In this regard, the play supports and is supported by the kinds of gender construction and hierarchy that were dominant at the turn of the century, and yet Ermine's transformation is not the whole story.

Shipman wasn't content with a Fitch-like affirmation of restraint at the expense of individual freedom and spontaneity. Even as Hackett sought to turn *John Ermine* into a vehicle for himself, the play's gender dynamics are orchestrated in such a manner as to suggest more balanced relations between freedom and restraint, between savagery and civilization, and between hero and heroine. In other words, even as Shipman refashioned Remington's tragic dénouement into a melodramatic happy ending, he shaped his play into what appears to be a triumphal celebration of a frontier synthesis. The balance of East and West, civilization and savagery, and heroine and hero lends itself to a positive marriage of opposites. To this end, Shipman's heroine is not merely the passive object of the hero's desire. Indeed, this Katherine is more similar to Wister's well-meaning, moral schoolmarm, Molly Wood, than to Remington's Katherine, a flirtatious, egocentric slave to eastern fashion. Shipman's Katherine, the embodiment of eastern civilization, and his Ermine, a representative of western savagery—albeit, a somewhat sanitized western savagery—are not only brought together, but during the play they also act on each other and transform each other just as Turner's savage wilderness transformed the civilized eastern pioneer, who in turn transformed the wilderness.

Ermine's wild spirits are disciplined and refashioned in the mold of Victorian manliness, but his frontier independence, his savage spontaneity, in its turn, has a positive affect on Katherine. She may teach him about the virtues of white civilization, but he teaches her about savage freedom. Under the influence of Ermine, Katherine liberates herself from some of the restraints of civilization. In this regard, she seems to fulfill her father's hope for her. Early in the play he had assured his wife, "A little roughing it will...do her good. Too much so called civilization is the ruination of half the young men and women in the East today" (I, 6). Shipman invests Searles with ideas very much in keeping with the late-nineteenth-century wilderness cult—ideas that are vindicated within the context of the play's action. Away from eastern civilization, Katherine begins to free herself from the social conventions that undermine strong individualism. At the end of the play, she is no longer afraid to give herself to Ermine, nor is she afraid to stand up for him publicly, even if doing so may cost her the esteem of narrow-minded easterners who would frown on her illicit visit to Ermine's quarters. Katherine and Ermine's relationship is a two-way street in which the rigid definitions of gender underlying traditional melodrama are loosened—but not overcome. More than Bartley Campbell's Mary Brandon, who exemplified civilization in a marriage of civilization and savagery at the conclusion of *My Partner* (1879), Katherine seems to take on an active role in the play. She is not simply the embodiment of a fixed ideal; she evolves—coming to appreciate, and assuming in her own right, the freedom and spontaneity that connects her hero to the savage West.

It would seem, then, that to create a theater success, Shipman was willing to accommodate himself to the devices and structure of nineteenth-century melodrama, and in doing so he abandoned Remington's pessimistic frontier vision and reshaped the play to suit the new hopes for the frontier laid out by the likes of Turner. The stage version of *John Ermine of the Yellowstone* that resulted, ironically, moved in the direction of Wister's more optimistic view of frontier process. Wister's novel, which had a more "comedic" structure than Remington's, may have been more suitable to melodramatic adaptation than Remington's novel, but even as Shipman assimilated melodramatic conventions in his adaptation of Remington's novel, he also appeared to widen the melodramatic characterizations and the gender assumptions that underlay them. How far he went in this regard is a question we will return to later in the chapter, but what is interesting here—if not entirely surprising, given the way in which the Remington's original novel was twisted to suit ends not entirely its own—is the unfortunate truth that Shipman and James K. Hackett, who not only played the lead but also produced the play, did not come up with a hit. In fact, their play—seemingly "suggested" by Remington's *John Ermine of the Yellowstone* but greatly transformed by the melodramatic conventions of the day and heavily indebted to Wister's novel—was not nearly as profitable as the play version of *The Virginian* that opened in the same theater several months later.

* * *

Wister's novel version of *The Virginian* had its roots in a series of short stories written over a period of ten years. In fact, the Virginian first appeared as a character in Wister's "Balaam and Pedro," which was published in *Harper's Monthly* in December 1893. When he finally got around to composing the novel, Wister basically just gathered many of these stories together. Even though he pulled these stories into a single narrative line, the seams between them are still apparent.[42] To be sure, Wister's initial subtitle, *A Tale of Sundry Adventures*,[43] recalls the novel's origin as a collection of diverse tales. It is not surprising, then, that in adapting the play to the stage, Wister and his collaborator, Kirke La Shelle, created a play with a rather loosely structured plot line[44]—a fact that was consistently noted by the New York reviewers even as they praised the play's vividness of detail and atmosphere.[45]

Although loose in structure, the play brings into sharp relief two of what Christine Bold has called the novel's "three most sustained strands."[46] The drama downplays the novel's framing "strand," which focuses on the tenderfoot-narrator's education in western ways of life, by dispensing with the narrative function and merging this character with one of the novel's minor characters, the New York visitor to the West, Mr. Ogden.[47] The play tightens the lines of action associated with the conflicts between the Virginian and "Bad Man" Trampas, on the one hand, and the Virginian and his love interest, Molly Wood, on the other. Certainly, the latter two strands are closely linked—especially in the play. In fact, together they form the play's melodramatic spine. To a great extent, the struggle between the Virginian and Trampas, the good cowboy and the rustler (a conflict that fits neatly into the conventional melodramatic formula for a hero-villain contest), functions as a catalyst leading to the resolution of the play's Virginian-Molly or hero-heroine romance plot. Indeed, Trampas becomes even more villainous in the play than in the novel, because it is he who cowardly shoots the Virginian in the back (and not, as in the novel, renegade Indians) in a key scene that forces the Virginian under the care of Molly—a turn of events that leads directly to her accepting him for her husband.

While the Virginian-Trampas conflict is perhaps more carefully interwoven into the Virginian-Molly plot in the play than in the novel, it is clearly the latter plot strand that provides coherence for both the novel and the play. In the contrast between the Virginian, a Wyoming cowboy, and Molly Wood, a Vermont schoolmarm, Wister, like Remington and other late-nineteenth- and early-twentieth-century American authors, utilized traditional gender constructions to reinforce the East-West contrast that was his primary focus in both the play and the novel.[48] In fact, the series of binary oppositions—female/male, civilization/savagery, East/West, and Vermont/Wyoming—provide the context within which the action of both the novel and the play develops.

Interestingly, however, Molly Wood is not mentioned until the fifth of the novel's thirty-six chapters and does not appear until the eighth chapter, whereas she appears in the very first act of the play. In this way, the contrast between the New England Molly Wood and the westerners among whom she lives is established from the very start. The first act, set in Uncle Hughey's ranch house, represents a party celebrating the christening of Hughey's twins. The tension between East and West is established early in the act when the cowboys, Skipio, Lin, Steve, and Nebraska, discuss the fact that Molly Wood has refused to dance with any of them. As Lin announces, "Its[*sic*] Wyoming against Vermont" (5). The inability of the cowboys, even the Virginian, to break through Molly's resistance becomes a repeating motif throughout the act. Lamenting the fact that they continually suffer "the Vermont turn-down" (Skipio, 12; Lin, 17), Lin finally concedes, "Vermont is too much for Wyoming" (16). Defeat in the realm of courtship prompts most of the boys to retreat into the "drink room," where they hope to assuage their injured egos. Rejected by Molly, the embodiment of eastern civil society, they return to less tame diversions. As Mrs. Hughey laments, "Its Vermont. The School Teacher has turned the heads of all them cowboys.... All Vermont. Every cowpuncher in Wyoming mooning round her and when she wont look at em its—whisky" (5–6).

Of course, the Virginian, who appears as something of a teetotaler in the play—although it is clear in the novel that he has sown his wild oats—refuses to give up. Disconcerted by Molly's willingness to dance only with married men, the Virginian with his buddy Lin slip into the room where the babies are sleeping and switch babies and clothes, causing no end of confusion and worry among the parents who suddenly realize that the children they have gathered upon leaving are not their own. This scene, one of the more well-known in the novel, is followed by the closing scene of Act I—also taken from the novel—in which the Virginian confronts Molly and promises her that she will love him. And it is apparent, even in Act I, that the Virginian's prophecy will be fulfilled. Earlier in the act, Molly had already revealed a fascination with the Virginian. She had vividly recounted to Mrs. Hughey how when she had first arrived in Wyoming, the Virginian had rescued her from a stagecoach accident. Her lengthy report of his saving her, a damsel in distress, as well as her confession to the Virginian at the end of the first act that she does "like" him (27), are Molly's first steps toward the Act IV union that will prompt the cowboy, Honey, to applaud their imminent marriage with the cry "Vermont and Wyoming—joinin' hands—great!" (81).

East and West come together in this play, and yet, to fully grasp the significance of this union, the nature of the West, of savagery, as it functions in this play needs further elucidation. In this regard, a peculiar irony lies in the fact that the western life of Wyoming is represented in this play (and in the novel) by a character called the Virginian. Wister provides this character with no other name in either play or novel; he is merely designated as the Virginian, which clearly associates him with the East, albeit the *South*east, from where he has come. More specifically, as a Virginian with a gentle drawl, this character seems to be linked to the tradition of southern gentlemanliness. Wister and La Shelle emphasize this connection in the play as Wister did in the novel (chapter ten). In the play's first act, Molly rebukes the Virginian for asking her to dance without being properly introduced—an action that she assumes "Southerners [who] have such good manners" (16), would hardly approve. The Virginian asks her pardon and seeks out Judge Henry, who can make the proper introduction.

Though apparently from the East, Wister's cowboy hero is unlike Fitch's cowboy hero, Teddy North. He is not simply an eastern gentleman—from South or North—in cowboy clothes. Despite his roots in the East, the Virginian's eastern background is not Wister's concern. In fact, very little is offered in either novel or play about the Virginian's eastern past. As in the case of Remington's John Ermine, the Virginian is primarily associated with his western present, and in his western present the Virginian can be viewed as the product of a wilderness process that has stripped him of all of civilization's artificial conventions.

In representing a return to a state of savage vitality, the Virginian embodies some of the ideals that motivated the turn-of-the-century wilderness cult. Perhaps describing what he believed to have been his own experience in the West,[49] Wister wrote of this wilderness process in "The Evolution of the Cow-Puncher," an essay published in the September 1895 issue of *Harper's Monthly*:

> Destiny tried her latest experiment upon the Saxon, and plucking him from the library, the haystack, and the gutter, set him upon his horse; then it was that, face to face with the eternal simplicity of death, his modern guise fell away and showed once again the mediaeval man. It was no new type, no product of the frontier, but just the original kernel of the nut with the shell broken.[50]

In an essay, "Concerning 'Bad Men,'" published in the April 1901, issue of *Everybody's*, Wister wrote even more explicitly:

> Now when people left cities and went to live in the Rocky Mountains, they could not pack the policeman with them; and so they had to take a club. You looked out for yourself; there was nobody else to do it for you. And soon, very soon, your primitive nature, that nature which the cradle of convention at best can never do more than lull into a sleep so light as to be scarcely deeper than a doze, waked up with something like a shout of joy.... It was so good to carry your life in your hand once more, instead of having it grow stale in the policeman's pocket! So you and your heart and your brain leaped straight from the nineteenth century back to the days of Charlemagne and the Paladins. They used spears, and you a revolver; but this was the only difference. It needed scarce one season to shake you out of your shell of civilization.[51]

For Wister, western frontier life meant "taking the bridle off and leaving poor human nature to keep the road by itself."[52] On the western frontier, policemen and lawyers did not mediate between individuals, but individuals acted directly on their own behalves. Moreover, as Wister pointed out in an essay entitled "The Open-Air Education," published in the *Saturday Evening Post* in late 1902, a life in the wild developed in the westerner the skills necessary to live on his own. The open air not only nurtured "muscular strength," but also "brains and quickness"; that is, it taught the able westerner the "perfect coordination between thought and act." In short, the wilderness fostered an "unconscious and absolute independence" in the westerner.[53]

This independence of spirit is very much on display in Wister's Virginian. The Virginian's freedom from eastern restraints is manifested in the frankness of his speech and thought and the unbridled nature of his humor—evidenced, for instance, by the practical joke he plays on the overly anxious parents at Hughey's party.[54] Moreover, his heroic and sometimes violent actions are to be seen as western in kind. To be sure, the Virginian does not hide behind inefficient policemen and lawyers, as Wister suggests eastern gentlemen do. The Virginian takes direct, unmediated action on behalf of justice. When at the close of the play's second act, Molly rebukes him for considering participation in vigilantism, he confesses to her: "I belong to the West. I must do its work" (53).

Wister's Virginian, then, is the product of a revitalizing, liberating process similar to that described by Turner.[55] The savagery that he comes to exemplify, however, has less in common with the savagery defined by Turner as Indian life and practice than it does with a romanticized premodern or medieval European life as references to "the days of Charlemagne and the Paladins" suggest. Indeed, the name "the Virginian" might be intended less as an allusion to the actual American South than as a reminder of a preoccupation with medieval chivalry that stamped itself on southern culture.[56] Wister conflates savage vitality with a knightly code of conduct drawn from romantic literature and stage melodramas. For Wister, medieval knights and wild westerners not only shared a freedom from the artificial conventions of modern civilization, but also a natural sense of honor. As the embodiment of the true western spirit, the Virginian's deference to appropriate etiquette and his chivalrous attitude toward Molly and others are, thus, less related to his being a "southern gentleman" than they are traits of a "noble savage" or, more accurately, a "natural gentleman."

While his gentlemanly ways are attributed less to his southern heritage than to a natural instinct for appropriate behavior, this conduct seems to elevate the Virginian above other cowboys in the play—especially above dangerous cowboys like Trampas. The Trampas of the play, even more than the Trampas of the novel, is motivated by unadulterated self-interest. He is driven by his appetites. To the extent that appetites are primitive, they may be connected with a savage or animal nature; however, Trampas's problem is that what may in another context have been healthy desires have here been corrupted by civilization. In a scene not presented in the novel, Trampas tells his rustler cronies that they will use the money they make from stealing cattle to head for Paris, where they will "tackle their French restaurants and feed rich" (57). In Trampas, both savage purity and civilized culture are degraded; his savage appetite has become civilized greed and hedonism.

The Virginian asserts his innate sense of a higher morality by rejecting Trampas's willful self-indulgence. Whereas Trampas's natural savagery has been corrupted by the temptations of a Parisian or overcivilized decadence,

Wister's Virginian, like Turner's pioneer, has been purged of such degenerate symptoms of civilization, and has been restored to a simpler, more natural state—a state that puts him in tune with a sense of the higher good to be found in self-sacrifice. In this respect, Wister implies that social virtues are not antithetical to western life; the simple savage state is one in which it is natural to feel a loyalty and connection to the larger community. Wister seems to see the synthesis of nature and gentleman that the Virginian embodies less as a synthesis to be constructed than as an unsullied preindustrial state to which we all should return. Interestingly, this synthesis is actually a prototype of the larger synthesis of western savage freedom and eastern civilized restraint that Wister consciously puts in place through the final union of the Virginian and Molly—the primary goal of the play, as evidenced by the recurring refrain that juxtaposes Vermont and Wyoming.

The Virginian represents the best of the West, and as an "original kernel of the nut with the shell broken," a being in touch with savage purity, his natural gentlemanliness functions significantly in the play. To begin with, the qualities of natural gentlemanliness serve to circumscribe the kind of savagery he represents—making it more acceptable to white, middle-class audiences. As in the case of Shipman's John Ermine, Wister's Virginian remains in the tradition of the noble savage; however, he is clearly a white or Saxon savage. His natural gentlemanliness, his natural ability to act with the appropriate decorum may be seen as an aspect of his whiteness. In this regard, it is interesting that in the play Wister has Steve, the Virginian's friend, tell him that he deserves his promotion to foreman because he is "the whitest man on the ranch" (36), where "whitest" implies fairest not only in skin tone but also in sense of justice.[57] In short, the Virginian is the kind of "stage savage" with whom refined eastern tastes would feel comfortable.

In fact, Wister's chivalrous natural gentleman might be more palatable to genteel eastern audiences than was Remington's or even Shipman's noble savage, John Ermine. For the latter, chivalry was the province of civilization and had to be learned from Katherine. For Wister, whose natural gentleman is both a product of the savage, uncivilized West and is imbued with elements of medieval romance, chivalry is part and parcel of the "purest savagery." Here is a savagery that, through an intriguing play of ideas, maintains a connection to what Gail Bederman referred to as the Victorian ideal of manliness, characterized by self-restraint, even as it manifests the early-twentieth-century fascination with a more aggressive masculinity[58]—that is, it is a savage masculinity that perhaps paradoxically includes a natural and instinctual chivalry.

Plate 2 Dustin Farnum as the Virginian in the play of that name by Owen Wister and Kirke La Shelle (1904). (The Billy Rose Theatre Division, the New York Public Library for the Performing Arts)

This strange combination of unpolished naturalness and chivalry was apparently conveyed by Dustin Farnum (Plate 2), who originated the role of the Virginian at the Manhattan Theatre. His work was generally well received by New York reviewers—gaining high praise from the *New York Times*, *Evening Post*, *New York Herald*, *Sun*, and *New York Dramatic Mirror*.[59] The critics seemed to agree that in outward appearance he corresponded well to Wister's frontier hero. As the *New York Dramatic Mirror* reviewer writes, "[I]n appearance, he was an ideal Westerner—stalwart, strong and with the bearing, almost slouch, that is characteristic of men who live in Mexican saddles. His manner of speech was no less characteristic; he was sincere at every moment, and never was he other than manly."[60] The *Evening Post* reviewer praised "his portrayal of deep but sternly repressed emotion," claiming that Farnum was extremely successful in suggesting "latent strength and energy and innate refinement beneath the outer resemblance of roughness and indolence."[61] The *New York Daily Tribune*'s William Winter, who was unimpressed with Farnum's interpretation, described how he acted the role "maintaining a calm, firm manner, and seeming to mean that an inveterate, barbaric purpose should be latent in it,—though this was not made clear."[62] For Winter, "feeling, too much repressed," became, "in effect stolidity."[63] Though a man of great natural feeling, Farnum's Virginian was controlled—maybe even too controlled. Although turn-of-the-century easterners were drawn to the wilderness cult and the savage freedom that cult embraced, the prosperous eastern audiences who made *The Virginian* a popular hit at the Manhattan Theater wanted a western savagery that was indistinguishable from the natural gentlemanliness they attributed to themselves by virtue of their Saxon racial heritage.

The Virginian's status as a natural gentleman places savagery within a romanticized medieval context—a context that is defined by its distance from modern civilization and yet one with which contemporary middle-class audiences could feel comfortable—but this notion of "natural gentleman" also suggests the possibility of a natural aristocracy. Being the "original kernel of the nut with the shell broken," the natural gentleman may rise above the rest of us by virtue of his natural ability and intelligence. In this respect, one might view the Virginian as the product of both de-evolutionary and evolutionary processes. He is the kind of natural aristocrat who can develop in a West that is free of artificial class structures and social conventions. If the western environment makes the easterner into a westerner by stripping him of all inessential and artificial props (de-evolution), it also creates an even playing field where the westerner best adapted to the savage conditions will rise to the top (evolution). A kind of Darwinian dimension thus enters into Wister's presentation of the Virginian. He is a natural aristocrat in the "jungle" represented by the western savage environment.

To be sure, Wister's sense of a natural aristocracy is based on his belief in the superiority of unfettered individualism over democratic egalitarianism—a point of view clearly conveyed in both the novel and play. In the latter, the Judge explains to Ogden:

> By the declaration of Independence we Americans acknowledge the Eternal *Inequality* of man. For by it we abolished a cut and dried aristocracy.... Therefore we agreed that every man should henceforth have equal liberty to find his own level. By this very decree we acknowledged and gave freedom to aristocracy saying—"Let the best man win, whoever he is"[*sic*] Let the best man win, that is America's word, that is true democracy, and true democracy and true aristocracy are one and the same thing. (30)

Wister thus denounced any devices or institutions that curbed the free development of the truly vital individual. His natural aristocrat, a man in touch with his savage core, was not to be propped up by false institutions and inherited titles, nor was he to be restrained by egalitarian social concerns.

Following this logic, Wister condemned not only traditional European class structures upheld by archaic social prejudices, but also unionism and socialism insofar as they limited the possibilities of the "superior" individual who followed the demands of his de-civilized, pure savage heart. Viewing property as an extension of the individual, Wister attacked working-class revolutionary politics. This social dimension of *The Virginian* is perhaps more fully developed in the play than in the novel. In the play, the villainous Trampas justifies rustling by means of working-class revolutionary rhetoric:

> Who says it's stealing? Why should Judge Henry make a pile out of the work you and me do for him? Who does the work? You and me, and how are the proceeds divided? You get $40 and the Judge 5000. Out 'what? Cattle. Did God make the cattle for Judge Henry? There [*sic*] as much yours and mine as his aren't they? Then why shouldn't we take what's our own? (11)

Steve, who eventually joins Trampas's gang but remains the Virginian's friend, answers Trampas's questions bluntly: "You're all out in your reasoning, Trampas" (11). Here, he speaks for both Wister and the Virginian, who defends the sanctity of private property by leading the vigilantes when they hang two rustlers—one being Steve. Certainly, Wister's sense of the natural aristocrat strikes us in the early twenty-first century as classist as well as racist, but the fact that readers and audiences embraced the Virginian suggests that Wister's vision was not idiosyncratic, and, more specifically in the case of the play version of *The Virginian*, it seems to have been shared by the prosperous white audiences who attended productions of the piece. To be sure, the Virginian embodied the ideas of the growing managerial elite, which might enjoy seeing itself as cowboy/savage aristocrats who broke strikes to protect the frontier spirit of American pioneer individualism.

A natural aristocrat and the play's hero, the Virginian is eventually united with the play's heroine, Molly Wood. While the easterner Molly initially rejects western independent action as lawless and is thus associated with civilization's negative restraints, she also exemplifies from the beginning the most positive elements of eastern civilization. A schoolmarm, Molly carries the eastern cultural and artistic traditions into the West. In matching the Virginian and Molly together, Wister appears to bring together the best of the West with the best of the East. As Vermont and Wyoming join hands, East and West, civilization and savagery, are united in a marriage that symbolizes a new healthy, revitalized, and prosperous nation.

The union of Molly Wood and the Virginian is, however, not a union of characters embodying unchanging ideals, nor is it a simple case of the melodramatic heroic male winning the beautiful bride as a prize for honorable and brave actions. Molly Wood may represent the best of the East, the best of civilization, but she is no more static a character than is the Virginian. Not merely the *object* of the hero's aspiration, she is herself also a *subject*. Like Katherine in Shipman's *John Ermine of the Yellowstone*, but even more so, Molly is an active agent of change even as she herself evolves through the play. As in Shipman's *John Ermine of the Yellowstone*, the dynamic interactions of hero and heroine seem to follow the pattern defined by Frederick Jackson Turner in his 1893 speech and essay, "The Significance of the Frontier in American History." The embodiment of civilization, Molly adapts to the savage wilderness only in turn to transform that savage wilderness embodied in the Virginian. Just as Turner had traced the complex interaction of civilization and savagery in his essay, so Wister traces that interaction in his novel and, with La Shelle's assistance, in his play. National evolution is here presented via character evolution, and melodrama's static idealized approach to characterization is therefore somewhat tempered. As Shipman had done in *John Ermine of the Yellowstone*, so too do Wister and La Shelle: they incorporate the late-nineteenth-century preoccupation with historical evolution and change in their presentation of the lead characters.

By the end of the play, both Molly and the Virginian have been transformed from what they first were—they are, in short, not characters who "are," but characters who "become."

Lacking the expansive descriptions that are possible in novels and as a result of the temporal requirements of the theater, the play must dispense with subtlety in the presentation of Molly's transformation. Indeed, the play, more explicitly than the novel, traces the progress of Molly's adaptation to the Virginian's savage West. At the start of the play she has difficulties accepting the untamed world in which she finds herself. This is apparent in her early rejection of the Virginian as a prospective lover. On this score he offers her the challenge:

> I *am* the sort of man you want. Only you don't know it—yet. You see me—just like you see all us Westerners. Through your New England eyes. You can't picture me in Bennington, Vermont. You can't think of the smell of the stables alongside your lavender scented linen without disgust. In your mind you set me alongside some of your New England dudes and I don't show up well. No-seh! But strip us both naked and set us in the wilderness same as Adam was and which would you turn to to build you a fire? (47)

Not long after this challenge, midway through Act II, Molly demonstrates that she has begun to feel comfortable with the western wilderness. To think through her relationship with the Virginian, the Molly of the play makes a decision that the Molly of the novel does not make—she determines to take an extended trip into the wilderness on her own:

> I am going to have my first experience of Western travelling. I'm taking the pony you trained for me, and I am going to look to myself. I am going to see your world without a guide. In the dawn I shall hear "the song of the meadow lark like beaded drops of music in the silence"—alone. Over the range to the foothills, over the foothills to the mountains, through the passes thick with the sentinel pines and down the slopes with the eagle and the rippling torrents for my companions. And so in the silences, alone, I shall fight my battle—and yours. (48)

On this journey she meets up with the Virginian, who has been seriously wounded by Trampas. Having led the vigilantes who have pursued, captured, and lynched two members of Trampas's rustler gang, the Virginian stays "behind to guard the back trail" (63), when Trampas, attempting to even the score with the Virginian, shoots him in the back. In bringing the wounded Virginian to safety, Molly does "a man's work as well as a woman's"

(66). Her independent action proves that she is able to withstand the challenges of savage wilderness life; nevertheless, Molly's greatest difficulty in coming to grips with the West is learning to accept its morality.

Wister and La Shelle seem to structure the acts of the play around the various stages in Molly's progression toward an acceptance of western morality—a progression that culminates in her final embrace of the Virginian. The seeds of their eventual union are laid in Act I. In Act II, Molly learns of the preparations for a vigilante action and condemns the western acceptance of such questionable justice. Act II moves to a climax when in its closing scene, which does not appear in the novel, Molly warns the Virginian that she would never want to see him again if he were to participate in the lynching of rustlers.[64] In Act III, her attitude toward vigilante justice is mollified after the Judge explains to her that vigilantism is the only alternative in Wyoming, where the law courts are controlled by the criminals. Given the corruption of the courts, the Judge claims vigilante hangings are "proof that Wyoming is determined to become civilized" (70).[65] In a Turner-like twist, a higher civilization with a more complete sense of justice is a result of embracing savagery. Certainly, we are far from Fitch's understanding of the relationship of courtroom justice and savagery, but it takes more than intellectual arguments to sway Molly's affections in the direction of the Virginian. Nursing him to health after he is shot by Trampas enables Molly to come to grips with the Virginian's basic humanity. She sees how he suffers over his having had to hang his good friend Steve. The act ends with the union of the Virginian and Molly apparently certain.

Molly's final test arrives in Act IV when she becomes aware that the Virginian and Trampas are to confront each other in a duel to the death. While she had come to accept vigilante justice as having a kind of public legitimacy, she has difficulty accepting one-to-one combat as justified:

> When I first knew about the killing of those cattle thieves, I kept saying to myself: "He had to do it—it was a public duty". And lying sleepless, I got used to Wyoming being different to New England. But this—When I think of tomorrow, of you and me and of—If you do this—there can be no to-morrow for you and me. (97)

The Virginian, however, will not back down, and several moments later the showdown occurs. The Virginian is victorious, and despite her last ultimatum, Molly "bursts through those on the Hotel verandah to Virginian" and "falls into his arms," crying, "Thank God!" (99). The last act's curtain comes down on their embrace—an embrace suggestive of the completeness of their final union.

Molly adapts to the world of western savagery, but as an active agent of change, she also has an important impact on the Virginian. During the course of the play (as in the novel), the Virginian, the embodiment of heroic savagery, begins to take up eastern culture under the civilized schoolmarm Molly's tutelage. The Virginian's friend Ogden notes that Molly lends him books and corrects his grammar (33). Ogden informs Molly:

> Sometimes he studies away into the night, and I don't believe he ever goes out on the range without one of your books... One day I came upon him. He was lying full length under a cottonwood tree, his horse was beside him, and all was silence except for the rustling of the grazing cattle and his voice.... He was reciting Shakespeare. Not bad for a cowboy.(33)

To please Molly, the Virginian is willing to read Shakespeare to become an educated man. In a sense, then, Molly tames the Virginian, but for his part, he invigorates her culture. The Virginian brings a fresh perspective to the literary works she provides him. Impressed with characters who strike him as robust and alive, he speaks highly of the Queen Elizabeth of *Kenilworth* and Falstaff and Prince Hal in Shakespeare's *Henry IV*. The Virginian is especially taken with Shakespeare, whom he claims "makes men talk the way they do in life" (40). In short, the Virginian may absorb some of the schoolmarm's European culture, but he will not be softened by it. In fact, one might say, in Turner's words, with respect to the Virginian's culture: "[T]he outcome is not the old Europe.... The fact is, that here is a new product that is American."[66]

In the mutual transformation and union of the Virginian and Molly Wood, the play can be seen as a ritualized embodiment of a process similar to that which Turner described in his famous essay. It also embodies historical themes developed by Teddy Roosevelt. In presenting the marriage of civilization and savagery, Wister integrates Roosevelt's focus on a healthy savage violence into his vision of a Turner-like union of civilization and savagery. Like the two historians, Wister seems to have been interested in exploring the larger significance of the western experience on the nation as a whole. Moreover, this had been an interest of Wister's for some time. Even before publishing his first book of short stories, *Red Men and White* (1895), Wister had planned a major work, "The Course of Empire," dealing with the role of the West in the development of civilization. This work had been sidetracked when *Harper's* editor convinced him to focus on adventure stories before delving into history. Wister's interest in the larger patterns of history surfaced in essays like "The Evolution of the Cow-Puncher" and in

The Virginian,[67] which he called a "historical novel" in the novel's preface.[68] Not only does Wister set the action of the novel in a historical context by means of this preface, but also, at the very end of the novel, Wister connects the historical past represented in the novel with his reader's historical present. He traces the marriage of the Virginian and Molly Wood forward: outlining the Virginian's successes in the years following his marriage to Molly, Wister notes the Virginian's development from successful rancher to captain of industry. Wister thus closes his novel with an affirmation of the American historical process. Given the necessity of condensing the novel's action to accommodate the theater's temporal demands, it is not surprising that the play lacks the historical projection into the audience's present. Concluding simply with the Virginian and Molly Wood in each other's arms following the Virginian's gunfight with Trampas, the play ends with an allegorical presentation of the kind of union of civilization and savagery that Wister advocated. Inherent in this dramatization is a sense of character which exemplifies the late-nineteenth-century transformation described by Vernon Lewis Parrington when he wrote that the "individual, ... conceived of socially and politically, is no longer an isolated, self-determining entity, but a vehicle through which is carried the stream of life, with a past behind and a future before."[69]

Despite the historical evolution that resonates in the triumphant conclusion of *The Virginian*, the play is nevertheless marked by various cultural assumptions that frame and qualify the surface balance expressed by Honey's celebratory cry: "Vermont and Wyoming—joinin' hands—great!" (81). Indeed, the integration of an allegorical presentation of a historical process into theater performance necessitated a negotiation with aspects of popular melodrama. To a certain extent, the modes of characterization and the gender construction that underlay melodrama were transformed, as they were in Shipman's *John Ermine of the Yellowstone*—transformed but not entirely overthrown. Neither Shipman nor Wister and La Shelle finally depart from melodramatic conventions. Both Shipman and the Wister-La Shelle team were, after all, writing for audiences with fixed expectations—which, in all likelihood, they themselves shared—of right and wrong and of male and female. Underlying the apparent synthesis of civilization and savagery, and the unions of Katherine and John and of Molly and the Virginian, a very definite set of hierarchical relationships prevail—even if they seem to be deemphasized in both plays.

That turn-of-the-century gender constructions are not entirely overcome and, consequently, subvert the appearance of balanced mutuality in the relationship of the Virginian and Molly Wood is amply demonstrated.

As in the case of *John Ermine of the Yellowstone*, the title of novel and play focuses attention on the hero as the center of the work. Moreover, the Virginian clearly upstages Molly Wood. While both hero and heroine assert themselves as subject-actors, the Virginian remains the driving force of the play's action. He changes under the influence of Molly—he even begins to adopt the cultural style of the East; however, this change is largely superficial. As Ogden tells Molly, the Virginian will not be made a better man by the education that Molly is giving him. Ogden goes on to say that "it's good to know he's getting it" (33), but it is not clear why it is "good."

Just as the Virginian is only modestly transformed by Molly, the depth of the change Molly undergoes may also be questioned. At the play's end, when Molly seems to accept the necessity of the Virginian's violent confrontation with Trampas, it appears as if Molly has been truly transformed by the West—that she finally accepts the western way of doing things; however, given the abruptness of her transformation, it may be more realistic to interpret this change as her attempt to accommodate herself to the Virginian—that is, she surrenders her values for love of the Virginian. From this perspective, the play may be seen as similar to other nineteenth-century melodramas in which the hero's actions win him the acquiescent heroine as a prize. Underlying the marriage of civilization and savagery and what may appear to be a balanced interaction of the two key characters of this play are the typical melodramatic plot structure and gender assumptions.

Inasmuch as gender differences are used in *The Virginian* to embody the oppositions of savagery/civilization and West/East, the gender dynamics exemplified in the play affect the resolution of these oppositions. As in Shipman's *John Ermine of the Yellowstone*, the binary oppositions of this play are not finally balanced—despite what appears as a surface symmetry—but are reducible to a series of socially constructed hierarchies. The male remains subject; the female, though taking on a role of subject, also remains the object-prize. As the male is dominant, so accordingly, the West is valued over the East, which is viewed as inefficient and dangerous insofar as eastern institutions hamper and limit the possibilities of real men. And finally, in the same vein, civilization is subordinated to savagery, defined here as the spontaneous, unrestrained, unmediated love of action manifested by white men who have not been corrupted by civilization. Indeed, both Shipman's and Wister-La Shelle's plays may be viewed as attacks on a civilization that had become too effeminate. In short, the plays may appear to suggest a view of the frontier where civilization and savagery are balanced and reconciled, but ultimately what is offered in both plays is a version of the frontier myth that speaks most directly to the needs and interests of white males. What

Jane Tompkins has written of the Western novel and of *The Virginian*, in particular, is certainly true of Wister and La Shelle's play version of the novel as well as Shipman's version of Remington's novel: at their cores, both not only represent a "revolt, historically, against a female-dominated culture," but also, psychologically speaking, "a moment in the psychosocial development of the male that requires that he demonstrate his independence from and superiority to women, specifically to his mother."[70] Overwhelmed by a new emasculating industrial-urban life, the male strikes back.

Augustus Thomas's *Arizona* might have represented a somewhat more "masculine" approach to the frontier western experience than did Clyde Fitch's *The Cowboy and the Lady*, but Wister and La Shelle's *The Virginian* as well as Shipman's *John Ermine of the Yellowstone* go further in this direction. The shift can be seen clearly in the way in which courtroom justice associated with the civilized East gives way to the vigilante justice associated with the savage West. Using courtroom rituals and practices as a metaphor for the civilized discipline that had to be imposed on savagery wherever it existed, Fitch utilized a final-act trial to bring resolution to his action. In *Arizona*, Thomas challenged the perspective offered by Fitch, suggesting a more balanced approach to the opposition of savagery and civilization. The action of his play is resolved by means of a rather perfunctory trial, which exonerates the hero. Moreover, the play offers a nod toward the West's unmediated vigilante justice, in that the villain's true murderer is able to go free without trial. In *The Virginian*, courtroom justice is entirely dispensed with and vigilante justice affirmed. Initially, the case for vigilante justice is made in novel and play by the Judge. More important, it is determined that no trial will be necessary after the Virginian kills Trampas. Here, masculine, or perhaps the wished-for masculine, freedom from a feminine civilization is vindicated even as it is presented as laying the groundwork for a more vital American civilization.

Wister and La Shelle's *The Virginian*, like Shipman's version of *John Ermine of the Yellowstone*, suggests the same kind of affirmative frontier myth that Turner and others offered the nation during the 1890s and in the following decade. Here, however, we see a melding of Turner's sense of frontier process with Roosevelt's glorification of the heroic "strenuous life" as it was lived on a frontier where violent conflict was usual but also necessary for the health of the race. Certainly, Turner's analysis provides a way of looking at the plot structures and characters of these two plays, but in their dependence on melodramatic sensationalism, both plays recall Roosevelt's boyish enthusiasm for thrilling confrontations. In short, a more analytic and a more nuanced or realistic approach to plot and characterization—an approach associated with the growing fixation on historical process and evolution—is contained within a predominantly melodramatic theater form. As in other manifestations of the turn-of-the-century frontier myth, scientific realism and romantic idealism are uncomfortably bound together, but here romance in the form of melodrama seems to be in the ascendant.

The particular blend of realism and romanticism that we find in Shipman's *John Ermine of the Yellowstone* and Wister and La Shelle's *The Virginian* had its foundations in the gender, race, and class assumptions that not only characterized the general cultural discourse of affluent white society at the turn of the century, but also pervaded the melodramatic form through which most playwrights spoke at the time. This is not to say that all subsequent contributions to this frontier discourse, which appeared in the fashionable Broadway theaters patronized by the affluent, repeated an identical pattern as that presented in Wister and La Shelle's play as well as that of Shipman. On the contrary, two very successful frontier plays from the 1905–1906 season, Edwin Milton Royle's *The Squaw Man* and David Belasco's *The Girl of the Golden West*, offered interesting variations on this frontier pattern. While still functioning within the parameters made explicit by Turner and others like Roosevelt, these plays represent significant contributions to the turn-of-the-century frontier discourse and will be the focus of the next chapter.

5. Variations on the Frontier Myth: Edwin Milton Royle's *The Squaw Man* and David Belasco's *The Girl of the Golden West*

Edwin Milton Royle's *The Squaw Man*, which opened at Wallack's Theatre on October 23, 1905, and David Belasco's *The Girl of the Golden West*, which opened at the Belasco Theatre on November 14, 1905, were among the most successful Broadway-style plays of the 1905–1906 theater season. According to the information on New York productions for that theater season, compiled by Garrison P. Sherwood for Burns Mantle's *The Best Plays of 1899–1909*, *The Squaw Man*, which had an initial run of 222 performances,[1] and *The Girl of the Golden West*, which had an initial run of 224 performances,[2] were among the five longest-running productions in a season that included over a hundred entries. The other three long-running shows were Charles Klein's incredibly successful four-act play *The Lion and the Mouse* (686 performances), the Hippodrome musical extravaganza *A Society Circus* (596 performances), and the legendary production of J.M. Barrie's *Peter Pan*, starring Maude Adams (223 performances).[3] Of the five, Royle's and Belasco's plays—both frontier plays—had the most in common. The success of these two works indicates not only their authors' skills but also the general appeal of the frontier play for 1905 Broadway theater audiences.

Moreover, if parody is the highest form of praise, then these two productions were the recipients of high praise indeed. The popularity of these plays and the frontier drama they represented was demonstrated by the fact that there was a market for Edgar Smith's burlesque, *The Squawman's Girl of the Golden West*, which opened at Joe Weber's Music Hall on February 26, 1906. The burlesque, which was described in the *New York Dramatic Mirror* as "by far the best thing Edgar Smith has done in all the years he has been writing for this house,"[4] was certainly offered in good-spirited fun. To be sure, the March 6, 1906, matinee of the burlesque was attended by William Faversham, who played Royle's title character, and Blanche Bates, who played Belasco's Girl, as well as Royle and Belasco themselves. These celebrity audience members apparently heartily enjoyed the parody.[5]

Of course, there was no reason why Royle and Belasco would not enjoy themselves at Joe Weber's Music Hall. The plays that were the subject of the burlesque were raking in great profits and would continue to do so for some time. Both plays ran through the 1905–1906 season and reopened for short runs during the 1906–1907 seasons, and then in early 1908 both plays had brief runs at the Academy of Music in New York. According to Burns Mantle, after *The Squaw Man* was produced in London as *A White Man* in 1908, it was "played around the world under one title or the other."[6] Mantle thought highly enough of Royle's drama to include it as the representative play for the 1905–1906 season in *The Best Plays of 1899–1909*.[7] Cecil B. DeMille turned to *The Squaw Man* when making his debut as a screen director in 1914. A six-reel film version of Royle's play, this was one of the first Hollywood feature-length movies and starred Dustin Farnum, the actor who had been the first to play the title character of *The Virginian* on stage in 1904. DeMille returned to *The Squaw Man* on two other occasions, remaking the film in 1918 and again in 1931.[8] Belasco's play, one of the prolific author's most successful works, continued to run in New York and appeared throughout the country over the next three years, only then to be recycled into Puccini's opera *La Fanciulla del West*, which received its American premiere in 1910. Belasco's play, like Royle's, first came to the big screen under Cecil B. DeMille's direction in 1914 and was remade as a film in 1923, 1930, and again in 1938.

Certainly, these two plays were popular and critical successes, and as such they not only helped to disseminate the turn-of-the-century frontier discourse, but also contributed substantially to it. Insofar as they were shaped by the prevailing frontier discourse, both works represent the frontier as "the meeting point between savagery and civilization," but in tracing the interaction of civilization and savagery, both diverge somewhat from the basic pattern that manifests itself in Turner's frontier analysis and that provided the overarching structure for Shipman's dramatization of Frederic Remington's *John Ermine of the Yellowstone* and Wister and La Shelle's adaptation of Wister's novel *The Virginian*. In short, while both Royle's *The Squaw Man* and Belasco's *The Girl of the Golden West* belong to the melodramatic tradition that included earlier plays like Shipman's *John Ermine of the Yellowstone* and Wister and La Shelle's *The Virginian*, they offer intriguing variations on the melodramatic presentation of the East/West, civilization/savagery interaction.

* * *

The Squaw Man was unquestionably Edwin Milton Royle's best-received play. Born in Missouri and educated at Princeton, Edinburgh, and Columbia Law School, Royle was, in fact, a one-hit playwright.[9] *The Squaw Man* earned very positive reviews from New York critics who seemed to be especially impressed by the fact that although the play undeniably belonged to the tradition of stage melodrama, Royle had succeeded in creating well-rounded characters who were developed with a kind of restraint rarely seen in melodrama. As the *New York Herald* reviewer wrote, it was a "success because the play is melodrama without being overdone, and because its author has depicted human beings instead of mannikins."[10]

Royle crafted characters with depth and substance, but in tracing their relations, he also presented audiences with a moving dramatic action, on the one hand, and a thoughtful exploration and commentary on the interaction of civilization and savagery, on the other.[11] In his presentation of civilization and savagery, however, Royle, unlike the playwrights examined in the previous two chapters, did not identify "civilization" with the eastern section of the United States. For Royle, "civilization was much more accurately associated with the Old World, specifically England, than with the American East. In a sense, he traced eastern civilization back to its roots. In his play, then, he dramatized the meeting point between the world of age-old English traditions and the new untamed world of America's Wild West. To convey the magnitude of this contrast, Royle allows the audience to enter into both worlds: he sets the first act on the ancestral estate of the Earl of Kerhill at Maudsley Towers in England, and moves the action of the later acts to Wyoming and Utah. In a 1906 printed version of the play,[12] Royle describes the Act I scene as "[a] court at Maudsley Towers," which looks out on "a typical English park, ... in the distance is a ruined castle. The house on the L. is one of the timber edifices of the sixteenth and seventeenth centuries.... across back and on R. the ruins of an abbey of a much older date" (11). Together the various structures suggest England's long history—a rich past that, at least from the Euro-American perspective, the American West did not have. To make the contrast perfectly clear, Royle explicitly requests that the scenic designer accentuate the differences separating the Kerhill estate in England from the hero's Utah ranch. He concludes his description of the Act I set: "It is moonlight night in summer, and the scene should represent the English landscape at its beautiful best, and form a striking contrast to the desolation of the ranch in the third act" (11). When the desolate Green River ranch does appear in Act III, it is not to be veiled in the moon's half-light, but to be viewed at the end of a long day during which "the alkali plains have crackled under the withering sun" (57). Amid "adobe stables," "a straggling adobe dwelling," and "a decrepit wagon" (57), the "solitary tribute to civilization" is a "disreputable towel" (58) that hangs on a nail by a bucket of water. There is no history, no life here. "Across the river to the west," the stage directions read, "even the sage brush and scrub-oak have given up in despair, and the Red Lands stretch lifeless to the foot-hills of the snow-capped Uinta peaks" (58).

The movement from the romantically defined English estate to the harsh reality of the western ranch is not incidental, but is a key aspect of the play's dynamics. Such a shift from an idealized world to a world of hard facts was a device often used by Royle's British contemporary George Bernard Shaw, but as the *New York Times* reviewer wrote, "the Squawman is not the Shawman."[13] In a very unShavian fashion, Royle never relinquishes his allegiance to the idealized world of the play's first act. Unlike Shipman or Wister and La Shelle, who embrace a kind of idealized western savagery through their protagonists, Royle and his protagonist, James Wynnegate, aka "Jim Carston," completely reject the western savage life at play's end.

Given the play's final outcome, it may appear somewhat ironic that the *New York Times* critic found the first act set in England to be plagued by a "dullness so dense,"[14] a complaint reiterated by the *Evening Post* reviewer who lamented "some deadly dull minutes with the British aristocracy,"[15] and the *Theatre Magazine* critic who claimed that the act was "not only technically clumsy, but weak."[16] Along similar lines, Arthur Hobson Quinn wrote some years later that "the first Act, laid in England, is conventional melodrama, whose only excuse is the transfer of Captain James Wynnegate from his ancestral halls, through an act of self-sacrifice, to the plains of Wyoming."[17] The dullness and the conventionality of the first act may result from Royle's stereotypic presentation of English aristocratic social life. In this regard, the play's opening act is overburdened with melodramatic clichés that convey his characters' exaggerated sense of their class duties and responsibilities.

The generally positive response to the play suggests that audiences and critics were willing to forgive these distortions, and this seems to be true even of English audiences. At least the critic for the *Times* appeared to indicate as much in his review of the London production of the play, called *A White Man* for English audiences. After making a series of sardonic references to how Royle views his fictitious aristocratic Kerhill family as a "part of the history of England," he wrote in general of the play:

> Such a story as this, if told by an Englishman, would be quite intolerable; but fortunately it is told by an American, Mr. Edwin Milton Royle, who secures your forgiveness for the absurdity of the English part by the freshness, raciness, and "snap" of the Western-American details. Whether these details are true or not, authentically "part of the history of America," we cannot say; the point is that an English audience is quite ready to accept them as true, and to enjoy the novelty and fun of them.[18]

In the same vein, one may suppose that American audiences were willing to accept the play's presentation of the "details" of British life as true, whether they were or not.

Audiences may have been forgiving, but Royle himself seems to have been troubled by the first act. Between the production represented in the 1906 prompt-book version of the play and the version of the play described in Mantle and Sherwood's *The Best Plays of 1899–1909*, Act I may have undergone some revisions.[19] Primarily it would seem that efforts were made to smooth out some of the roughest melodramatic edges and to make James Wynnegate even more clearly a heroic paragon of civilization. It is in the later version that we hear from the Kerhill family friend, Sir John Applegate, that James is "a thundering good sort" and "a white man," and from a fellow officer that he is "the most popular officer we have."[20]

Whatever the extent of his heroic nature, James finds himself in a similarly unpleasant predicament in both first acts. In the English society that Royle offers us, individual action is circumscribed by historical obligations to family and class. This is certainly the case for James Wynnegate, who is the poor cousin in a very well-to-do aristocratic family. While he is generally presented as a man of integrity and described by his cousin-in-law, Diana, as the kind of man who though "too idealistic.... will always have the love of women" (21),[21] he remains in the shadow of his cousin, Diana's husband, Henry, the Earl of Kerhill. Jim has always subordinated his own interests to those of the Earl, who, as the family head, must stand before the public as the embodiment of the Wynnegate's long and honorable heritage. In turning his back on his own hopes and expectations, Jim confesses in both versions of Act I to having rejected "a brilliant offer to go into commercial life because it would not lend dignity to 'Henry and the family'" (16),[22] and he has even sacrificed his longtime love for Diana, which is clearly mutual, for the benefit of "Henry and the family." In setting family honor and tradition over personal interest, James illustrates the kind of nobility defined by the play's Dean of Trentham when this reverend elder proclaims at the start of the Mantle version of Act I that "the noblest deeds of history have sprung from pride of birth, pride of name, the pride of family, pride of race!"[23]

During the course of the first act, Jim makes one more significant sacrifice for his cousin. After Jim learns that Henry has illicitly appropriated a large sum from a charity fund and that he then lost this money in a bad speculation, Jim chooses to take the blame for Henry's misdeeds to protect the family name from the disgrace that it would suffer if it were known that the Earl had been the true miscreant. He decides to run off to America, thus exciting suspicion that he is the embezzler. He hopes to save the family from shame, but in a chivalrous vein he also desires more specifically to spare Diana the scandal she would suffer if her husband's deeds were brought to light. While La Shelle and Wister saw chivalry as an instinctual attribute of the "natural gentleman," here, as in Shipman's *John Ermine of the Yellowstone*, chivalry is associated with civilized restraint.

For Jim, duty to family and love of Diana are closely linked. In fact, they represent two sides of the civilization from which he flees. If Jim's duty to his family epitomizes the restraints on individualism imposed by the aristocratic sense of the sanctity of tradition, then Diana represents the beauty and refinement for which civilization's advocates strive and for which they make sacrifices. Again, as in Shipman's *John Ermine of the Yellowstone*, Wister and La Shelle's *The Virginian*, and many other turn-of-the-century plays, the virtuous romantic heroine, on the one hand, and civilized ideals, on the other, are conflated so that she embodies those ideals within the play. Jim remains true to Diana and the ideals of civilization, and he requires the same of the Earl; Jim is willing to assume the Earl's guilt as long as the Earl promises to be loyal and true to Diana and, by extension, to civilized ideals in the future.[24]

As the first act ends, Jim suffers a self-imposed banishment from the civilized world he knows and permanent estrangement from the woman he loves. As painful as his departure is, it represents nonetheless a kind of liberation for Jim. He has found his ancestral home to be a prison. Bound by obligations to kin, he has paid excessively for "the glory and privilege of belonging to a great family" (16),[25] but once in America he will apparently be free from the artificial restraints imposed on him by English aristocratic civilization. On the other hand, to survive he will have to adapt to the savage world into which he enters. In fact, Jim appears to experience the kind of pioneer process described by Turner. Jim finds that on the western frontier, "the environment is at first too strong for the man," and that "he must accept the conditions which it furnishes, or perish...."[26] Like Turner's pioneer, Jim is gradually stripped of all civilization's accoutrements.

Jim's descent into the world of western American savagery occurs during Acts II and III, each act articulating a separate stage in the adaptation process. The play's second act, which occurs two years after the first, is set in Wyoming, in the Long Horn saloon of Maverick, "a cow town on the U.P.R.R.A. [Union Pacific Railroad]."[27] Through the double doors at the back of the saloon can be seen a railroad platform and a recently arrived train. Within the context of the play's development, the Maverick location represents, both literally and figuratively, a "station" in Jim's journey into the heart of western savage existence—a journey that is not completed until Act III. This first station exemplifies Jim's exposure to the wild-and-woolly western town life.

When he appears in Act II, Jim has been deprived of name and rank. He is no longer Captain James Wynnegate, cousin to the Earl of Kerhill, but simply Jim Carston, would-be rancher. His English background is of no use to him in the American West. If he is respected by his cowhands, it is because he has proven himself in deed. During the act, Jim is able to hold his own against the rustler and dangerous "gun-man" Cash Hawkins. He successfully stands up to Cash on two separate occasions. First he prevents Cash from duping the Indian Taby-wana out of his cattle and from sexually abusing Taby-wana's daughter Nat-u-ritch. Then, when Cash Hawkens pulls his gun and harasses the Earl of Kerhill, Diana, and their friends, who are all passing through Maverick on their way back east after a trip to Yellowstone, Jim intervenes once again, getting the drop on Cash and forcing him to back down.

The Act II scenes in which the Wynnegate party briefly appears suggests how far removed Jim is from his civilized past. When Diana's cousin, Sir John, recognizes him, Jim denies that he is James Wynnegate. Henry maintains the deceit by rejecting the notion that Jim is his cousin, though admitting that there is a more than striking resemblance. After a brief scene in which Diana and Jim are alone and she acknowledges him and confesses to him that she knows he never stole from the charity fund, the English tourists board the train and continue east. Jim is a permanent exile from the world of luxury and ease symbolized by the parlor car to which the Wynnegates retreat. The world of the West in which Jim remains is a savage world where might makes right. It is the wild world in which, as Wister wrote, individuals are on their own without the benefit of the mediating institutions of law and order. Here desperados like Cash Hawkens are free to publicly harass and humiliate others. Moreover, as Jim's loyal cowpuncher foreman, Big Bill, warns him, the county sheriff, Bud Hardy, is pretty tight with Cash Hawkens (45). In this western community, the line between lawman and "bad man" is very blurry indeed. In fact, given their equally malevolent behaviors, Royle's western lawman and his western bad man are equally related to the melodramatic stage villain tradition, but neither has the dramatic weight that villains had in the frontier plays by Fitch, Thomas, Shipman, or Wister and La Shelle. Hawkens and Hardy do not serve the play as Jim's antagonists as much as they help to establish the general western savage context in which he finds himself.

While savage violence is the norm in Maverick, certain aspects of civilization still remain. There is, in fact, a very definite social structure or hierarchy. It may not be as elaborate as the hierarchy and social structure that Jim left behind in England when he abandoned the society of earls and their ladies, but Royle's white westerners clearly acknowledge a distinction between whites and Indians. A savage villain like Cash Hawkens claims that Nat-u-ritch "ain't a woman, she's a squaw" (43), and even Jim's cowboys have difficulty understanding why their boss would take the time to defend Indians:

> SHORTY:.... Say, boss, what did you let him make it a matter of Injins fer? You got the sentiment of the kummunity agin' and right from the jump. Looks like fightin' fer trifles.
> GROUCHY:.... Yes, it's some dignified to fight over cattle, but Injins—Pshaw! (44)

Indians are on the very bottom of the frontier social ladder; they are the "untouchables" of this Wild West.

Indians are ostracized from the white social order because for western whites they represent the true savage other. In other words, while western Americans in *The Squaw Man* may seem wild and even savage to the English characters of the play, Anglo-Saxon westerners do not see themselves as savages, but distinguish themselves from Indians, whom they view as the real savages. On a continuum of cultural progress from savagery to civilization, the Indians represent savagery, the aristocratic English civilization, and the westerners of Maverick something in between. Given the low regard for Indians in *The Squaw Man*, the "civilized" and "savage" categories designate more than just social/cultural developmental distinctions. As in Turner's analysis, Indians here don't appear to be capable of development; they merely exemplify the savage environment that white pioneers confront.

Representing the fullest embodiment of frontier savagery, Royle's Indians are not romantically conceived noble savages, but neither are they to be viewed as degenerate subhuman demons. Indeed, it would seem that Royle wanted to represent "real" Indians and not clichés. To this end, he actually hired the Ute Indian Baco White to play himself in the role of Indian interpreter and to coach the actors playing the other Indians in appropriate Ute dialect. In fact, neither of the two major Indian characters—Nat-u-ritch and her father, Taby-wana—speak English. For the most part, Nat-u-ritch and Taby-wana depend on either gestural language or Baco White's translations to be understood by others. This may be a realistic touch, but in depriving these characters of the language that others speak within the play, Royle reduces them to a prelingual inarticulateness; they are objects, not subjects, of discourse.

While these Indian characters are presented in a somewhat balanced fashion—with virtues as well as vices—the common denominator linking all three Indian characters is their basic primitiveness. Nat-u-ritch and Taby-wana may be sympathetic insofar as they demonstrate passions that Royle suggests are universal, but these passions are always painted in primary colors. Nat-u-ritch is presented as a loyal wife and mother, but as a "helpless child-mother" (84),[28] it is clear that she would never fit into the civilized world of English society. She demonstrates absolute loyalty to Jim after he defends her in Act II, but completely lacks the subtlety of the civilized lady. Her father, Chief Taby-wana, is similarly characterized in bold strokes. He first appears drunk, having been plied with liquor by Cash Hawkins, but he is not without dignity and demonstrates a heartfelt loyalty to his child—even threatening war in order to protect her from being arrested by Bud Hardy for the murder of Cash Hawkens; however, his love of his daughter has limits. Like Shipman's Indian half-breed, Wolf-Voice, who recommends that recalcitrant women be violently punished, Taby-wana claims that if Nat-u-ritch does not obey her husband, she should be punished, and if she "disobeys again—kill her!" (84).[29] The suggestion, here as in Shipman's play, is that while whites demonstrate their civilization by treating the "weaker sex" with delicacy, Indian males demonstrate their primitive savage nature by behaving harshly toward their women.

Together Nat-u-ritch and Taby-wana represent the savage bottom of the social hierarchy as presented in this play, and during the course of his "journey" into the savage West, Jim becomes closely linked with these two characters. In short, he appears to cross the lines separating civilization from savagery, on the one hand, and White from Indian, on the other. Jim seems to enter into the Indian world. Not only does he defend Indians from brutal white treatment, but between Acts II and III, Jim marries Nat-u-ritch—thus becoming a "squaw man."

Jim does not, however, marry Nat-u-ritch out of love but from gratitude for her having saved his life on two separate occasions. First, she saves him from Cash Hawkens. At the end of Act II, after the British tourists depart, Hawkens returns to the Long Horn Saloon and finds Jim distressed over his interview with Diana and seated at a table with his head buried in his arms (51). Cash determines to take advantage of Jim's apparent vulnerability to avenge previous humiliations. Before he can shoot the unsuspecting Jim, Nat-u-ritch shoots and kills him. While this episode provides a dramatic curtain to close Act II, the second occasion when Nat-u-ritch rescues Jim occurs offstage between Acts II and III. We learn in Act III that after he had been incapacitated while gathering cattle in winter, she trudged through a winter storm to find him when others had given him up for dead, and then nursed him through several bouts of a life-threatening fever that he contracted after his exposure. As his wife, Nat-u-ritch continues to offer Jim devotion and love, but he cannot offer her the same. His marriage to her is less an act of love than a lonely man's effort to reconcile himself to the savage world in which he finds himself.

In embracing savagery as he does in marrying Nat-u-ritch, Jim consciously disregards the norms of appropriate conduct as defined not only by the English civilization that he has left behind, but also by whites on the western frontier. During a conversation with Petrie, a British visitor, Jim acknowledges this:

JIM: ... Even here I am a "squaw-man"—that means socially ostracized. You see we have social distinctions even out here.
PETRIE: How absurd!
JIM: Social distinctions usually are. (69)

In plunging into the world of western savagery, Jim has lost his name and English aristocratic rank, but, in addition, he has surrendered all social standing—even that available in nonaristocratic America.[30]

Jim's immersion into the savage western world climaxes in Act III, which takes place some five years after the action of Act II and is set on his ranch that is in "a state of partial dilapidation."[31] Not only has he married Nat-u-ritch, thus alienating himself from the civilized world, but he has also lost all physical evidence of his previous connection to white society. An unfavorable turn in western economic and climatic conditions even forces Jim to give up his ranch. In this regard, he is less the victim of human maliciousness than of environmental circumstances. Jim may belong to the melodramatic hero family, but unlike other such heroes, his major problems arise more from an intransigent geographic and economic environment[32] than from human villainy. The play's action depends less on the clash of hero and villain than on something similar to the environmentalism that underlies Turner's historical analysis. In telling his Turner-like tale, Royle moves melodrama toward a closer scrutiny of characters within socioeconomic contexts.

Confessing to his cowboy hands that his attempts at ranching have failed, Jim offers his employees whatever odds and ends he possesses in the hope that the townspeople might purchase these objects and provide the cowboys with cash. Not only must he relinquish the last remaining worldly goods that he had been able to carry with him from England—a package of "trinkets" (59) to Andy, a "jewel case" (86) to Shorty, and a repeating rifle to Grouchy—but he must also send away his former cowboy foreman and friend, Big Bill. In thus cutting himself off from white America, Jim is deprived of everything but his wife, Nat-u-ritch, and an infant son, Hal. Having no choice but to "sell out, move on, begin all over again" (61), he is reduced to the most primitive circumstances.

While Turner viewed the stripping away of civilization and the adopting of Indian ways as the first phase in a process whereby the wilderness remakes the pioneer into a new kind of democratic individual, Royle traced a similar descent into savagery, but drew very different conclusions. Jim may divest himself of all physical connections to his civilized past, but in doing so he is not finally and irrevocably liberated from a corrupting tradition of arbitrary social conventions. Jim may associate himself with a world of Indian savagery, but, Royle suggests, as a white man he can never finally become an Indian. His racial/cultural heritage will always assert itself. In short, unlike Turner's pioneer and Wister's cowboy, Jim is never completely integrated into the savage environment in which he lives, nor is he really remade on the frontier.

In fact, Jim actually changes very little because of his frontier experiences. He may be divested of his title and worldly connections to civilization, but he remains at heart a "civilized man." What prompts him to defend Tabywana and Nat-u-ritch from Cash Hawkens is a sense of fair play, or more exactly, a noblesse oblige, which he brings over from England. Moreover, as he admits, it is a sense of obligation and not love that prompts him to marry Nat-u-ritch. In thus accepting the power of obligation over individual desires and independent action, Jim imposes on himself restraints similar to those imposed on him by England's aristocratic society.

That Jim is fundamentally unchanged by his western experience is evident from the fact that he never stops missing England. When Mr. Petrie arrives from England with the news that Jim's cousin, Henry, has died and Jim can now return to England as the new Earl of Kerhill, he is initially ecstatic:

> I love old England—as only an exile can. I love the English way of doing things, even when they're wrong; the little ceremonies, the respectful servants, the hundred little customs that pad your comfort and nurse your self-respect. Home, eh? And I love old London. I think I'm prepared even to like the fogs. Do you know what I'll do when I get back?... I'll ride a week at a time on top of the 'busses up and down the Strand, Piccadilly Circus, Regent street, Oxford street. And the crowds! How I love the crowds! The endless crowds! And, Petrie, my boy, I'll go every night to the music halls, and what's left over of the night to the clubs, and, by Jove! I'll come into my own at last. (66)[33]

For Jim, civilization is not just artificial social restrictions and conventions; it has its own particular delights that more than compensate for its unpleasant aspects. As Diana, who has come to America to bring Jim back, admits, "Civilization has bred in people like you and me many needs and interests—we have books, Nature, music and art..." (84).[34] Nature, understood here as a tame garden, and the other refined pleasures of civilization, epitomized by Diana herself, can neither be forgotten by those who have been bred among them nor outweighed by the oppressive obligations that civilization imposes on its members.

And yet for the truly civilized man, social and moral obligations cannot be ignored. Despite, his initial enthusiasm, Jim finds himself as trapped by his sense of duty to Nat-u-ritch as he had been by his sense of duty to the Wynnegate family name. The depth of this obligation is made clear in a conversation with Petrie:

> JIM: Petrie, I would not desert a dog who had been faithful to me. That wouldn't be English, would it? The man who tries to sneak out of the consequences of his own acts? Oh, no; I couldn't do that, could I?
> PETRIE: Believe me, I would advise nothing unbecoming to a gentleman, but aren't you idealizing Nat-u-ritch a little?
> JIM: On the contrary; we never do these primitive races justice. I know the grief of the ordinary woman; it doesn't prevent her from looking into the mirror to see if her bonnet is on straight, but Nat-u-ritch would throw herself into the river out there, and I would be a murderer as much as if I pushed her in. (68-69)[35]

Because Jim is still bound by a civilized sense of responsibility, one that he associates with being "English," he determines not to return to his English homeland. At the same time that he feels obliged to remain in America with Nat-u-ritch, he feels equally obliged to send his son, Hal, who someday will be the Earl of Kerhill, back to England. In a strangely ironic use of the term "manifest destiny," Petrie convinces Jim that not allowing Hal to be educated as a gentleman and exposed to a world of culture and refinement would be tantamount to robbing him of his manifest destiny (70).

Rather than end *The Squaw Man* with Hal's departure, Royle ends the play with what appears to be the same kind of marriage of civilization and savagery that had marked the conclusions of plays like Shipman's *John Ermine of the Yellowstone* and Wister and La Shelle's *The Virginian*: the white male, in this case Jim, who has journeyed into the savage world is to be allowed to marry the eastern, civilized heroine. To achieve this resolution, Nat-u-ritch has to be eliminated, and this is expeditiously accomplished. Taking pity on her brokenhearted husband, whom she worships with an elemental, animal-like loyalty, Nat-u-ritch commits suicide, thus making it possible for him to rejoin his son, return to England, and most probably marry Diana. The closing image showing Jim carrying the dead Nat-u-ritch into the house may suggest a tragic curtain, but the play's subtitle, *A Comedy Drama*,[36] indicates that we are to also be hopeful for Jim. The play ends on what was to be the morning set for Hal's departure, but turns out to be the morning of a new day for Jim, now liberated from the harsh circumstances of his western life.

Returning from the savage frontier, Jim may marry the refined Diana, but his future marriage to Diana has only the semblance of a marriage of civilization and savagery, for while Diana clearly epitomizes the virtues of civilization, Jim, who is reduced to rather meager circumstances, never becomes one with the savage world. In this regard, the prospective union of Diana and Jim bears some similarity to that of Teddy and Mrs. Weston in Fitch's *The Cowboy and the Lady*. Both plays conclude with what is more of a marriage of East and East than East and West; that is, for both the Amherst-educated Fitch and the Ivy Leaguer Royle, the eastern prerogative holds sway. However, while Fitch seemed to use the exotic frontier setting to add color to a rather straightforward case for the necessity of civilized restraint, Royle enters more fully into the frontier discourse. Rather than depend solely on melodramatic conflicts between heroes and villains to put forward his brief for civilization, Royle explores the interaction and impact of the western environment on his civilized hero. The result is a more complex, more nuanced, and consequently, more "realistic" play than Fitch's.

Royle utilizes the frontier setting for its adventurous associations and, more important, to offer what turns out to be a very strong retort to those who subscribed to the wilderness cult.

Presenting the frontier in terms of a meeting of civilization and savagery—and consequently remaining within the parameters of the turn-of-the-century frontier discourse—Royle nonetheless suggests that the easterner maintains his basic eastern identity, his connection to civilization, no matter what his experiences in the West. Royle's pioneer is not remade but simply brings his civilized sensibility to bear on whatever he encounters in the West. While Royle examines the meeting point between civilization and savagery, he seems to imply that civilization and savagery never really interact. The West may seem to loosen the bonds of rigid civilized conventions and deprive pioneers of civilization's material benefits, but immigrants coming from the East are never entirely stripped of their civilized pretensions and beliefs. Consequently, they are never entirely returned to the savage condition, as Turner would have it. On the other hand, Indians, who have never experienced the advantages or the artificial restraints of civilization, remain in a primitive savage state. Whether Royle believed that savage Indians could someday be assimilated into civilization is not completely clear. For Nat-u-ritch, Jim bluntly declares that it is too late for such an education or socialization (83), and yet for Hal, the offspring of Jim's interracial marriage, there appears to be some hope.[37]

The prospective marriage of Jim and Diana is, then, not to be seen as a reconciliation of opposites, but the culmination of Jim's struggle against circumstances threatening the value system he espouses from the start. As the titles of Shipman's play and Wister and La Shelle's play indicate, so Royle's title also indicates the focus and subject of the play—the white male hero. Jim's marriage to Diana should thus be viewed as his just reward for all of the sacrifices he has made for others. The acceptance of obligations and duties—no matter how seemingly arbitrary these obligations and duties appear—allowed him to triumph over his desolate western environment and paved the way for the joy that marriage to Diana promises. In presenting this ultimate victory of the "virtuous" hero, *The Squaw Man* reestablishes its connection with the plot conventions of traditional melodrama. Sacrifice prepares the hero Jim for ultimate reward, but, of course, the irony here is that it was Nat-u-ritch's final sacrifice—for which she earns no reward—that enabled the hero to receive his "just reward" and retake his rightful place within a civilization that he had at least emotionally never actually left.

For Jim, and apparently for Royle, white civilization, which had its advantages and its drawbacks, represented a higher form of human life than did Indian savagery, and for better or worse there was no going back on this evolutionary process. Like Turner's, Royle's understanding of the frontier takes shape in a context dominated by evolutionary modes of thought, but rejecting the romantic elements in Turner's interpretation, Royle placed his faith in eastern civilization. While lamenting the artificiality and repressiveness of class and family obligations in civilized society, Royle ultimately justified them as the means to the refinement and beauty of civilization and naturalized them as necessary instruments of an inevitable evolutionary process.

Unlike Shipman or Wister and La Shelle, who seemed to suggest that savage vigor would reinvigorate what was becoming an overcivilized America, Royle seems to imply that the pursuit of civilized norms and ideals is enough to engender the vitality necessary not only to overcome savagery, but also any threat that civilized peoples might face. While Shipman and especially Wister and La Shelle tried to qualify "savagery" enough to make it acceptable to successful bourgeois audiences, Royle, with a certain honesty, rejected savagery as a lower stage of development. This shift in focus is exemplified most concretely by the fact that the male protagonists of Shipman's and Wister and La Shelle's plays were presented as emanating from the West: their backgrounds and connections to white civilized societies are obscured in mystery. On the other hand, Jim's connections to white civilization are explicit from the start. The first act of *The Squaw Man* provides important information about Jim and his background, informing the viewers who he is and why he embraces the virtues of manly restraint over the vigor of masculine aggressiveness. In a sense, Turner's kind of environmentalism is vindicated, for here the impact of Jim's original civilized environment—and, perhaps, his race—can not be overcome or forgotten.

Offering a less colorful perspective than that presented in Shipman's *John Ermine of the Yellowstone* and Wister and La Shelle's *The Virginian*, Royle, like those earlier playwrights, accommodated a basic melodramatic structure and sensibility to a vision of the frontier process, albeit a vision less sympathetic to frontier savagery. His play was, however, not any less popular with well-to-do audiences attending New York's first-class theaters. If Shipman, Wister, and La Shelle romanticized the West on the way to presenting a theatrical affirmation of American exceptionalism—an affirmation that would celebrate the source of the new managerial elite's success—Royle's more fatalistic approach reassured the prosperous audience members of the appropriateness of their place atop the social hierarchy and the validity of their culture. Although the view of the frontier process offered in *The Squaw Man* is fundamentally different from that presented in *John Ermine of the Yellowstone* and *The Virginian*, all three plays worked within the parameters of the late-nineteenth-century frontier discourse, and all three fulfilled needs and interests of prosperous audience members while also speaking to those who wished to be associated with the elite attending the play at Wallack's Theatre and elsewhere.

* * *

While Royle's *The Squaw Man* ostensibly moves toward a conclusion similar to those offered in Shipman's *John Ermine of the Yellowstone* and Wister/La Shelle's *The Virginian*, both of which climax in a marriage of a white male hero whose frontier experience associates him with western savagery and a heroine who embodies the best aspects of civilization, it becomes clear on close examination that Royle's play diverges from this model. On the other hand, David Belasco's *The Girl of the Golden West*, with its focus on a frontier girl who seems to have little in common with the heroines of *John Ermine of the Yellowstone* and *The Virginian*, appears to move in an entirely different direction from these plays, and yet, in the end, it has much in common with them.[38]

David Belasco had deep roots in the West—even deeper than those of Remington and Wister. Unlike them he was born there, in San Francisco on July 25, 1853. He completed his stage apprenticeship working in the San Francisco theater and with touring companies in California and Oregon. By the late 1870s, Belasco had established himself as a writer and director at San Francisco's Baldwin Theatre, but in 1882 he moved to New York, where his career blossomed on a national level. Still, the impact of his early California years[39] can be seen in plays like *The Girl of the Golden West* and *The Rose of the Rancho* (1906). While the latter actually had a longer initial Broadway run,[40] the script was not entirely Belasco's work. *The Rose of the Rancho*, dealing with the ways in which Spanish landowners in California were displaced by Anglo land-grabbers in the years following the Treaty of Guadalupe Hidalgo, which ended the Mexican-American War, is actually an adaptation with Richard Walter Tully of Tully's earlier play *Juanita*. *The Girl of the Golden West* is completely his own. More important in this context, *The Rose of the Rancho* focuses less on the frontier process, the meeting of civilization and savagery, than does *The Girl if the Golden West*. Certainly the former play captures a moment in California history, but the play revolves around the confrontation of two civilized cultures—the colorful Spanish-Mexican and the commercial Yankee cultures. The effect of wilderness on the pioneer is more directly explored in *The Girl of the Golden West*. The commercial success of *The Girl of the Golden West* can be partially traced to vintage Belasco features, such as his inimitable scenic wizardry,[41] but what most distinguishes this play is that it represents a climactic reiteration of various popular motifs and formulas developed in earlier frontier melodramas, including Shipman's and Wister and La Shelle's. Indeed, the success of *The Girl of the Golden West* may be attributed largely to Belasco's skillful interweaving of contradictory elements drawn from late-nineteenth-century frontier discourse. As a native westerner and experienced theater director, producer, and playwright, Belasco demonstrated mastery in this regard with his creation of the play's colorful title character, Minnie. Representing an engaging if somewhat enigmatic blend of lively frontier traits—or what went for frontier traits—and traditional feminine characteristics, Minnie recalls both the frontier savage and the frontier civilizer stereotypes.

In discussing the play's first production in his biography of David Belasco, William Winter wrote that "in Belasco's drama the *Girl* is the play, and with Miss [Blanche] Bates as the *Girl* there was little more to be desired."[42] According to Winter, Belasco claimed that the role as he wrote it fit Bates "from her head to her feet,"[43] but Belasco himself also wrote in the "Description of Characters" accompanying the published play that the Girl "is rather complex."[44] Discrepancies in the reviews to the 1905 New York premiere suggest that Minnie's complexity may have troubled some critics. For instance, the *New York Dramatic Mirror* reviewer noted: "[R]eared to the customs [of rugged California]...the Girl carried the rough exterior of the people about her."[45] Conversely, an unsigned article appearing in the *New York Times* on November 19 praised the play, but, referring to a "girlishness...at times too saccharine," observed that "the Girl, as written, is invested with qualities a little inconsistent with the experiences incident to her rough-and-ready environment."[46] While the appearance of a "rough exterior" might presage, as Daniel Gerould has recently claimed, the twentieth-century's independent "new woman,"[47] a saccharine and girlish demeanor suggests a more conventional nineteenth-century melodramatic heroine. Perhaps both reviewers were right. In fact, Minnie is a double-natured character, functioning simultaneously in two separate semantic systems or texts, which intersect in *The Girl of the Golden West*.

On the one hand, Minnie figures in a local color comedy. In this regard, she is reminiscent of the kind of rustic heroine made popular by Bret Harte when he created the frontier waif M'liss in the story "M'liss: An Idyl of

Red Mountain" (1863), which Clay Greene successfully adapted for the stage in 1873. Stuart Wallace Hyde has described this character type as coarse and uneducated but often seeking education, impulsive and fearless but motivated by common sense and morality, and skilled in the practices necessary for and typical of life in a savage West.[48] The popularity of the rustic heroine in the late nineteenth century may stem from the fact that she provided the predominately eastern audiences with both a vicarious release from a rigid Victorian sensibility and the pleasure of a complacent superiority as they witnessed the heroine, symbolizing the frontier West as a whole, struggling to be more like themselves—that is, to become more civilized. The connection of Belasco's Minnie to this type of character was noted by William Winter in his *New York Daily Tribune* review of the play,[49] and was discussed by later critics and historians, such as Belasco biographer Craig Timberlake, who connected Minnie to Harte's saloon owner, Miggles,[50] and Stuart Wallace Hyde, who wrote that she had much in common with the rustic heroines who appeared in a series of late-nineteenth-century frontier plays. Among those dramatic antecedents, Hyde noted Carrots, from Joaquin Miller's *Forty-Nine* (1881), and Possy Burroughs, the heroine of Henry C. DeMille and Charles Barnard's *The Main Line* (1886).[51]

Underlying the M'liss-like guise, however, is a Minnie who shares traits with a second character type: the traditional western schoolmarm—that is, despite the surface coarseness, Minnie has much in common with Wister's schoolmarm, Molly Wood. Appearing in countless films and stories throughout the twentieth century, this western character type, like the M'liss character, had its roots in Harte's writings of the 1870s; more specifically, this character type appeared as Miss Mary in the story "The Idyl of Red Gulch" (1869) and then in Harte's play *Two Men of Sandy Bar* (1876).[52] It was Wister, however, who, in the novel *The Virginian*, assimilated this character into an allegorical representation of the late-nineteenth-century frontier myth. Insofar as Minnie manifests certain schoolmarm characteristics, she too figures in a more complex allegorical presentation of the late-nineteenth-century frontier myth than that embodied in the play's local color comedy. On this allegorical level, *The Girl of the Golden West* shares certain structural elements with other frontier plays of the period, such as *John Ermine of the Yellowstone* and *The Virginian*, and consequently, like these plays it must be seen within the context of the Turner thesis and other turn-of-the-century frontier analyses.

Minnie appears as the untamed protagonist of a local color comedy in the Bret Harte vein, but she also figures as a gentle tamer bringing civilization to the Wild West in an allegorical Turner-like representation of the frontier. Paradoxically, both aspects of Minnie's character are brought into sharp relief as a result of the contrast between her character and that of the man she loves, the Dick Johnson-Ramerrez character. Indeed, this play—again, like *John Ermine of the Yellowstone* and *The Virginian*, as well as earlier frontier plays like Campbell's *My Partner*—is structured around a romance of contrasting characters that represent civilization and savagery. What distinguishes *The Girl of the Golden West* as local color comedy from Shipman's play, Wister and La Shelle's play, and even from Campbell's play is that the genders usually associated with the two categories have been reversed, or at least at first sight appear to have been. In this regard, Daniel Gerould claims that it is the "freshness and unconventionality in the Girl's nature that captivated the suave, Eastern-educated, European-traveled hero of the play, Johnson/Ramerrez."[53]

On the surface a very different kind of character than either Shipman's Katherine or Wister and La Shelle's Molly, Minnie runs the Polka Saloon and is a self-supporting, self-reliant woman. In the "Description of Characters" accompanying the play, Belasco describes her in terms suggesting a contradictory combination of what his audiences may have understood as traditional feminine innocence and masculine worldliness:

> Her utter frankness takes away all suggestion of vice—showing her to be unsmirched, happy, careless, untouched by the life about her. Yet she has a thorough knowledge of what the men of her world generally want. She is used to flattery—knows exactly how to deal with men—is very shrewd—but quite capable of being a good friend to the camp boys. (8)

Unencumbered by either feminine refinement or delicacy, Minnie has made a home for herself in the rough-and-tumble West. Dealing with the camp boys on their own terms, which includes carrying a weapon to protect herself if things get out of hand, Minnie seems to manifest the characteristics of the M'liss-like or rustic western heroine.[54] Unquestionably, she has both the respect and affection of the various raw miners who patronize the Polka saloon.

Into the unpretentious world of Minnie's Polka Saloon comes Dick Johnson, a man with whom Minnie fell in love when she met him briefly during a visit to Sacramento and Monterey before the start of the play. In the "Description of Characters" at the start of the play, Belasco describes Johnson as

> a young man of about thirty—smooth-faced, tall. His clothing is bought in fashionable Sacramento. He is the one man in the place who has the air of

a gentleman. At first acquaintance, he bears himself easily but modestly, yet at certain moments there is a devil-may-care recklessness about him. He is, however, the last man in the world one would suspect of being the road-agent, Ramerrez. (9)

While appearances do turn out to be deceptive insofar as Johnson is indeed Ramerrez, Johnson as he first appears seems to belong to a cultivated world well above Minnie's. A worldly and erudite man, he makes easy reference to cultural figures like Dante, whose name Minnie mispronounces as "Dant—Dantee" (72) in her attempt to impress Johnson. Aware of Johnson's refinement and her own unschooled, western manner, Minnie concedes in an Act II scene set in her cabin, where Johnson and she share an intimate repast: "I know I ain't good enough for you, but I'll try hard. If you see anything better in me, why don't you bring it out?" (77).

Minnie's uncultivated style contrasts with Johnson's urbane manner, and unlike Shipman's Katherine and Wister and La Shelle's Molly, who ultimately are spectators to the heroic actions taken on their behalf by the title characters of those plays, throughout most of Belasco's play it is Minnie's ability to deal with the dangers of the savage West that protects Johnson. Such a divergence from the stereotypic melodramatic passive heroine is especially visible in Act II after Minnie learns that Johnson is in reality the "road-agent" Ramerrez. This new knowledge brings their intimate dinner to a sudden end when, in anger over his deception, she sends him from her cabin into a raging blizzard. Moments later, he returns, having been wounded by the posse that pursues him. At first, Minnie hides him in her loft. Then, after the sheriff—her former suitor, Jack Rance—discovers Johnson's whereabouts, Minnie lures Rance into a game of poker with the stakes being Johnson's freedom if she wins and herself in marriage if Rance wins. Drawing aces from her stocking when Rance is not looking, she prevails. A gambler and cheater, Minnie stops at nothing to protect the vulnerable man she loves.[55]

While Minnie's relation to this more colorful, savage side of western life recalls Bret Harte's M'liss, she is, in the end, not reducible to the M'liss model. Like Harte's character, Minnie seems to lack traditional feminine traits, and also like Harte's M'liss, she seems to have gained a practical, earthy common sense from her experience living in a mining camp. Harte offers a gender reversal of the usual savage pioneer and civilized schoolteacher pattern, but his M'liss nevertheless begins to take on a more conventionally feminine persona after she becomes acquainted with the young male schoolteacher. On the other hand, it turns out that Belasco's Minnie needs to make no such transformation. Minnie is not a savage in need of civilized manners and values. She already has the major attributes of the civilized heroine. From the play's start, Minnie demonstrates that, despite an outward coarseness suited to her circumstances, she possesses the feminine attributes that Barbara Welter had associated with the mid-nineteenth-century "cult of true womanhood." In short, Minnie manifests "piety, purity, domesticity, and submissiveness," the "four cardinal virtues" of "true womanhood,"[56] and, in doing so, she exemplifies the best of civilization. As focus is shifted toward this dimension of Minnie's character, her place in an action pattern similar to that underlying Shipman's *John Ermine of the Yellowstone* and Wister and La Shelle's *The Virginian* becomes more visible.

Minnie's purity goes unquestioned by the miners around her. Contrary to expectations about most female saloon keepers, Minnie is known as "the one decent woman in Cloudy.... A lady, damn it!" (26). Living alone, she has never even had a male visitor in her cabin (66) until Johnson arrives in Act II. Almost immediately, Johnson makes sexual advances, but Minnie resists—only yielding him a single kiss, her first kiss, because as she eventually confesses: "I've loved you ever since I saw you first—'cause I knowed that you was the right man" (77). Both her purity and her piety are demonstrated after the quickly developing blizzard prompts her to suggest that Johnson, whose criminal career she is yet to discover, stay the night in her cabin. Offering Johnson her bed, Minnie plans to make herself comfortable on a rug by the fire. As they prepare for sleep, Minnie says "a brief prayer" (83). Even when the posse suddenly intrudes, a naive Minnie demonstrates no concern about the awkwardness of Johnson's presence. In an effort to protect both himself from capture and Minnie from humiliation, he warns her to ignore the posse members who knock on her door. A stage direction informs the reader that "it never occurs to [Minnie] that the situation is compromising" (84).

Minnie's devotion to domesticity and her concomitant submissiveness to the male are also amply evidenced throughout the play. Minnie nostalgically recalls the happy family life she experienced in her youth. Undaunted by the fact that these memories are set within a saloon and gambling hall, she fondly remembers her mother "fussin' over Father an' pettin' him, an' Father dealin' faro.... Talk about married life! That was a little Heaven" (37). Despite her present circumstances, Minnie dreams of finding a similar "Heaven" for herself, and after exchanging vows of love with Johnson, she confesses:

> Well, show me the girl who would want to go to Heaven alone.... I'll sell out the saloon. I'll go anywhere with you—you bet!... They's a little Spanish Mission Church here—I pass it 'most every day.... I often thought: What'd they think if I was to walk right in to be made—well, some man's wife? That's

a great word, ain't it—wife? It makes your blood like pin-points thinkin' about it. There's somethin' kind o' holy about love, ain't there? (81)

Minnie makes this confession before discovering Johnson's true identity— Ramerrez, the outlaw; however, despite momentary jealousy when she believes Johnson-Ramerrez is bound to another woman, she remains loyal to him notwithstanding his questionable past. Hoping that her actions— which include cheating the Sheriff—have made it possible for Johnson to escape, she reassures him, "[Y]ou was the first—there'll never be any one but you. All that Mother was to Father, *I'm* goin' to be to you. ... you must get through safe—and, well, think of me here jes' waitin'—jes' waitin'— jes' waitin'..." (128).

In fact, Minnie's loyalty to Johnson helps to bring civilized order to his unsettled life. If the apparently unrefined Minnie actually embodies the virtues of eastern civilization, the apparently refined Johnson is actually associated with the more savage aspects of the California mining frontier. As Ramerrez, he is a dangerous outlaw: a robber, "a vagabond by birth," and "a cheat and a swindler by profession" (91). After Minnie discovers his true identity, Johnson-Ramerrez admits to her:

> I'm all that—and my father was all that before me. I was born, brought up, educated, thrived on thieves' money—but until six months ago, when he died, I didn't know it. ... I only learned the truth when he died and left me with a rancho and a band of thieves—nothing else—nothing for us all—and I—I was my father's son—no excuse—it was in me—in the blood—I took to the road. I didn't mind much after—the first time. I only drew the line at killing. (91)

Johnson-Ramerrez seems to be modeled on the notorious bandit Joaquin Murieta, who, according to John Rollin Ridge's popular account of the outlaw published in 1854, was a similarly gallant "Robin Hood" surrounded by vicious cutthroats.[57] Like Murieta, Belasco's Johnson-Ramerrez was a law-abiding citizen forced into a savage way of life as a response to the greed and racial violence typifying the California mining frontier.

While Johnson-Ramerrez is associated with a Mexican gang, he appears, however, not to be Mexican. From the start of the play, Belasco attempts to disassociate Johnson from Ramerrez—that is, from what appears to be a Spanish or Mexican heritage:

> RANCE: Is this Ramerrez a Spaniard?
> ASHBY: No, can't prove it. Heads a crew of greasers and Spaniards. His name's assumed. (28)

For Belasco and his audiences, who seemed to accept the Turner frontier myth, which marginalized nonwhite races, this distancing of Johnson-Ramerrez from "the crew of greasers and Spaniards" is important. Insofar as Johnson is Ramerrez and is linked with the violent Murieta, he embodied a most dangerous western savagery to early-twentieth-century audiences. Insofar as Ramerrez is an assumed name and Johnson's Mexican roots are denied, he can be joined with the civilizer, Minnie, in a marriage celebrating the emergence of a healthy new American democratic society, albeit a white American democratic society. In other words, Johnson becomes another white hero who is forced to adapt to and become an embodiment of the savage West in which he finds himself, and Minnie, as an emissary of civilization, allays the effects of Johnson's savage past. A dutiful wife-to-be, she nurses the wounds he receives from his pursuers and offers him the possibility of a peaceful and contented future.

Minnie's role as an agent of civilization is apparent both in relation to Johnson and to all of the other western characters of the play. Shortly after her first entrance, she is already imposing civilized standards on the Indian Billy Jackrabbit: she insists that Billy marry the Indian woman whose "papoose six months old" (31) he apparently fathered. Moreover, as it turns out, the Polka Saloon provides the closest approximation to a traditional domestic situation for the single men living in the mining town of Cloudy; it is, as a sign above the bar reads, "A REAL HOME FOR THE BOYS!" (15). Not only is the Polka Saloon a home away from home, but in the winter when the mines close down, the Polka also serves as the "Academy" where Minnie conducts a school for the miners. As she admits, "I learn m'self... an' the boys at the same time" (71). In a comic interlude during Act III, Minnie is presented teaching her fully grown students. As a teacher, Minnie demands that her students polish their boots, wash their hands, and leave their whiskey behind. While her attempt to teach reading and writing seems futile, all of the miners enthusiastically agree when one of their number confesses: "I look upon this place as somethin' more than a place to set around an' spit on the stove. I claim they's culture in the air of California—an' we're here to buck up again' it an' hook on" (114). Unlike M'liss, who was a struggling pupil, Minnie is the teacher, and thus like Molly Wood, the schoolmarm heroine in Wister's *The Virginian*, Minnie is a standard-bearer of frontier civilization.[58]

Minnie's efforts are not without effect. Despite her attempting to prevent his being caught, the boys capture her beloved Johnson in Act III and plan to hang him without trial; however, after they witness his brief "last" interview with Minnie, which takes place in the same space as the Academy and shortly after the Academy scene, they decide as a group to relent. The purity of Minnie's love for Johnson and the moral lessons she has labored to impart to her students inspire them to act compassionately. Rather than hang Johnson in a savage act of frontier vigilante justice, they allow him to escape to the East with Minnie.[59] The liberated frontier bandit Dick Johnson and the self-taught schoolmarm Minnie are thus joined in a union like that between the Virginian and Molly Wood—one that, by suggestion, promises a happy future for all.

The tableau-like Act IV of *The Girl of the Golden West* functions as a kind of coda presenting in summary form the entire movement of the play. The climactic union of civilization and savagery as it was presented on the stage here and in other plays like *John Ermine of the Yellowstone* and *The Virginian* is reiterated. Set on "the boundless prairies of the West" (131), the curtain rises with Johnson "lying on the grass and leaning against saddle, smoking a cigarette. The GIRL now appears...having formerly not been seen, being in the tepee" (132). Johnson, the product of frontier savagery now tamed, appears as the free, natural male, at ease lounging under the sky, and Minnie, the civilizer coarsened by frontier life, is initially domiciled safely within the tepee—a domestic structure albeit a rather rough one. She comes forth to join Johnson, and together as the sun rises they bid farewell to the past and to the golden West (Plate 3).

Johnson and Minnie may be leaving the frontier West for the settled East, but as Frederick Jackson Turner wrote, the frontier West was itself becoming more like the settled East. Turner, however, could console his readers that "the outcome is not the old Europe," but rather "a new product that is American."[60] In the eyes of Turner's contemporaries, like the popular playwright David Belasco, this new American product could perhaps be understood in terms of the marriage of characters like the civilized savage Johnson and the savage civilizer Minnie. However, even as these characters begin to bridge the gap between savagery and civilization, neither is entirely freed from the tyranny of old gender assumptions; Johnson remains primarily associated with the outside material world ("lying on the grass") and Minnie with the inside domestic sphere ("being in the tepee").

The frontier experience presented in *The Girl of the Golden West* may seem to suggest the possibility of an understanding of gender roles very different from that circulating at the close of the nineteenth and the start of the twentieth centuries, but the theater language that conveyed this suggestion remained the language of traditional gender difference. The categories West/savage/male and East/civilization/female are harmonized at play's

Variations on the Frontier Myth 165

Plate 3 Act IV of David Belasco's *The Girl of the Golden West* with Blanche Bates as Minnie, the Girl, and Robert Hilliard as Dick Johnson (aka Ramerrez). (The Billy Rose Theatre Division, the New York Public Library for the Performing Arts)

end but not finally transcended. Indeed, Minnie embraces her subordinate female role when she sacrifices her California life to follow Johnson east. Her last line and gesture clearly establish the hierarchy of values that motivate her conduct:

> Oh, my mountains—I'm leaving you—Oh, my California, I'm leaving you—Oh, my lovely West...my Sierras!—I'm leaving you!—Oh my- *(Turning to Johnson, going to him and resting in his arms.)*—my home.
>
> Curtain. (133)

Despite Minnie's achievements as a standard-bearer of eastern civilization in the Sierras, her submission to Johnson-Ramerrez represents subservience to the male western savagery that, according to the Turner frontier myth, had made for the uniqueness of American democracy. In other words, in this context, western savagery receives the final nod over eastern civilization, and consequently, reading the play in this fashion leads to the impression that Belasco reverses the hierarchical relationship of civilization and savagery, East and West, offered by Royle in *The Squaw Man*. Still, Belasco's savage hero is rather tame. Johnson's frontier wildness is disguised under his demure and charming, gentlemanly facade. He is a savage westerner who would in no way alienate the sympathies of staid white, middle-class audiences, and consequently, while savagery is dominant in this reading, it is not a threatening savagery but a relatively wholesome, masculine one.

In Minnie's last speech, however, there is another lingering note—one that recalls her connection to a M'liss-like character rather than the role of gentle civilizer. Indeed, her last speech represents what might be viewed as the final taming of a M'liss-like Minnie. In bidding farewell to "my lovely West—My Sierras," Minnie abandons the colorful West made popular in the East by Bret Harte; that is, she bids farewell to her own savage self. The independent western frontier woman and saloon keeper accepts the role of wife and finds a home within the arms of her man. She thus embraces the kind of traditional civilization that was foreign to her as a M'liss-like character. Just as Minnie had tried to impose civilization on the Indians and "boys" who wandered through the Polka Saloon, so it is imposed on her. Again, Belasco offers a frontier allegory; here, however, the allegory, catering to what appears to be an eastern sense of cultural superiority, represents a simple victory of eastern civilized values over western savagery. With this reading of the play, Belasco validates Royle's interpretation of the frontier experience.

In his tableau-like Act IV, as in his entire play, Belasco intertwines two distinctly different views of frontier development, but he covers the contradictions inherent in such disparate views with a veneer of romanticism. It is here that Belasco's well-documented genius for theatrical staging came to the fore. For instance, in his New York production, the action of the brief Act IV was accompanied by a series of carefully orchestrated light cues, which were meant to establish a uniquely Californian sunrise, and by almost continuous music, including pieces like "Old Dog Tray" and "Oh, My Sierras!," which were certainly meant to tug at audience members' hearts. Moreover, the entire act was set behind a gauze or scrim (132).[61] As Lise-Lone Marker has written, this scrim enhanced "the soft, far-away quality of the picture."[62] Even as Belasco seemed to highlight the contradictory implications of the frontier discourse underlying the play's action, he literally veils them behind a romantic gauze. There was, however, no sleight of hand here. Audience members and reviewers patronizing Belasco's theaters looked forward to the romantic effects of his staging more than the profundity of the dramas that graced his stages. As the New York *Sun* reviewer wrote, *The Girl of the Golden West* represented a "concoction of long familiar material redeemed by Mr. Belasco's incomparably artistic stagecraft."[63]

In *The Girl of the Golden West*, and especially his "girl" of "the Golden West," David Belasco thus was able to successfully package what is, in fact, a complex portrayal of the contradictory American attitudes about the frontier at the turn of the century. While the native westerner Belasco claimed that "there are things in my *The Girl of the Golden West* truer than many of the incidents in Bret Harte!,"[64] what really distinguished the pattern of action underlying this play from what one might find in Bret Harte was the intrusion of the kind of frontier western discourse most prevalent at the end of the nineteenth and during the first decade of the twentieth century. In balancing a colorful Bret-Harte-like representation of the mining West with a dramatic representation of the turn-of-the-century version of the frontier myth, which itself is the product of the intersection of Turner's frontier analysis and accepted gender ideology, Belasco was able to give frontier melodrama dimensions it had not had before.

Not only did Belasco combine different frontier "texts," different frontier interpretations, but in doing so, he also created a play with all the spectacle and excitement of past melodramas and with a complexity of character and action not seen in *The Cowboy and the Lady*, *Arizona*, *John Ermine of the Yellowstone*, and *The Virginian*. The two-sided aspects of both Minnie and Johnson-Ramerrez give these characters a depth not apparent in the other plays, and in focusing the action so fully around their developing relationship, Belasco moves away from the formulaic melodramatic struggle between hero and villain. Indeed, while Royle had de-emphasized the role of stage villains in *Squaw Man*, there is no villain in this play at all. Johnson's rival for Minnie's affections, Rance, has a sense of honor that makes him entirely sympathetic especially at play's end when he forcefully contributes to the couple's escape eastward. In Belasco's play melodramatic tension is internalized as hero and heroine each strive to come to terms with his or her own divided consciousness. The dramatic world of this play becomes more complex, more realistic, without ever sacrificing melodramatic romance. In short, here was an innovative melodrama that successfully delighted Belasco's wealthy eastern audiences even as it incorporated their conflicting hopes and ideals.

In *The Girl of the Golden West*, Belasco effectively made use of frontier material, as had Royle in *The Squaw Man* and Wister and La Shelle in *The Virginian*. All three of these plays had very successful runs in first-class New York theaters. They clearly indicate the interest in frontier western matters that characterized the elite eastern culture of the early twentieth century.

What is also interesting is that all three plays take on the kinds of ideas and attitudes that dominate the frontier analyses offered by the likes of Turner and Roosevelt, and yet each offers a somewhat different perspective on the significance of the frontier in American development. The three frontier melodramas all move within the same field of discourse, but they move in different directions. In studying these three plays we are left with a sense of both the range and limitations that governed early-twentieth-century attempts to assimilate the very dramatic frontier western experience. Still, further variations can be viewed with William Vaughn Moody's *The Great Divide* and Rachel Crothers's *The Three of Us*, the plays to be examined in the next chapter. It is in these last plays that the union of a hard-nosed seemingly empirical scientific objectivity and a sentimental romantic sensibility, of realism and idealism—a union that had been so instrumental in winning the minds and hearts of several generations of Americans to Frederick Jackson Turner's analysis—attains its most balanced theatrical form.

6. From Melodrama to Realism: William Vaughn Moody's *The Great Divide* and Rachel Crothers's *The Three of Us*

The appeal of plays dealing with frontier western materials for first-class New York theater audiences—an appeal that was evidenced in the 1905–1906 theater season by the outstanding successes of Royle's *The Squaw Man* and Belasco's *The Girl of the Golden West*—continued into the 1906–1907 season. Burns Mantle and Garrison Sherwood list more than one hundred productions for the 1906–1907 season, and of these, four of the seven longest-running productions dealt with the frontier West. The four include: William Vaughn Moody's *The Great Divide*, which opened at the Princess Theatre on October 3, 1906, and ran for 238 performances; Rachel Crothers's *The Three of Us*, which opened at the Madison Square Theatre on October 17, 1906, and had a run of 227 performances; David Belasco and Richard Walton Tully's *The Rose of the Rancho*, another of Belasco's spectacularly mounted productions, which opened at the Belasco Theatre on November 27, 1906, and ran for 240 performances; and *Pioneer Days*, "a spectacular drama in three scenes by Carroll Fleming," which opened at the New York Hippodrome on November 28, 1906, for a run of 288 performances.[1] *The Rose of the Rancho* was not meant to be as broad a spectacle as *Pioneer Days*, but Belasco's play abounded in the theatrical wizardry that made him such a success at the turn of the century. Despite their differences, these two plays stood out especially for their stagecraft. *The Great Divide* and *The Three of Us*, however, seemed to contemporaries to be striking out in new directions. Both were praised by critics for rising above the level of popular melodrama and establishing the foundations for a new, more modern and realistic drama.[2] Indeed, writing some thirty years later, Arthur Hobson Quinn claimed that 1906 was significant in the development of a "new dramatic generation." More specifically, Quinn cited Moody's and Crothers's plays along with Langdon Mitchell's *The New York Idea* and Percy MacKaye's *Jeanne D'Arc* as evidence that the 1906–1907 theater season witnessed the arrival of "the advance guard of the new drama."[3] As a herald of a new drama, *The Great Divide* has been especially exalted, often described as "the first modern American play."[4]

Whether or not one agrees that Moody's and Crothers's plays represent a new direction in American theater and drama, it is difficult to deny the significance of the response both plays elicited from contemporary audiences. Not only did *The Great Divide* have a long and prosperous run in New York, but, as in the case of *The Squaw Man* and *The Girl of the Golden West*, the positive reception to Moody's play is demonstrated by the fact that it became the subject of a popular burlesque, Joseph Herbert's *The Great Decide*, which was produced by Lew Fields at the Herald Square Theatre on November 15, 1906, and ran for a respectable fifty-three performances. In addition to its New York triumph, *The Great Divide* toured successfully across the country during the next several years, and then in the fall of 1909 opened in London, where it was also a hit.[5] Rachel Crothers's *The Three of Us* also toured across the United States and made it to London, and for that London production of the play, none other than Ethel Barrymore played the lead role.[6]

The popularity of *The Great Divide* and *The Three of Us*—both examples of the mining frontier drama—evidence the continuing interest in plays dealing with frontier western motifs, but even more intriguing is the fact that these two plays offer two very different perspectives on the western frontier experience. As critics past and present suggest, Moody's play represents what could be called the culmination of turn-of-the-century frontier drama. Here, a Turner-like vision of the frontier experience receives its most potent dramatic expression. Crothers, however, entering the turn-of-the-century frontier discourse with a protofeminist perspective, provides an interesting variation on the Turner-like interpretation. In short, while Moody's play epitomizes many of the features of the Turner turn-of-the-century frontier myth, Crothers suggested a new approach to material that had been traditionally viewed as belonging to the male domain.

* * *

Born in Spencer, Indiana, in 1869, William Vaughn Moody demonstrated an artistic temperament early on. He studied painting at Pritchett Institute of Design in Louisville, but eventually made his way to Harvard, where as an undergraduate he became the class poet.[7] With the publication of a book of poetry in 1901, this skilled man of letters established himself as a successful author of verse. Nevertheless, in writing *The Great Divide* (1906) five years later, Moody would depend on more than poetic fancy. His sense of the West was molded by several trips there—one with Hamlin Garland to the Rocky Mountains in 1901[8] and a second to the Arizona desert in 1904.

Despite the apparent realism of both the play script and its 1906 production, for which Moody made another brief trip to New Mexico to gather appropriate stage props, his ambitions were somewhat larger than a realistic portrayal of life in the far West. More than any other of the playwrights treating the frontier at the turn of the century, Moody seems to have intentionally molded his materials with a mythic perspective in mind. Indeed, his predilection for cosmic dramas is apparent in the two plays he wrote prior to *The Great Divide*, namely *The Masque of Judgment* (1900) and *The Fire Bringer* (1904). An erudite poet and a professor at the University of Chicago while working on these verse dramas in the early 1900s, Moody envisioned them as the first two parts of a trilogy dealing with "the unity of God and man."[9] Based on biblical and Greek mythological materials, these plays were stylistically speaking a far cry from the kind of realism for which Moody was praised in *The Great Divide*.

In adapting what one reviewer referred to as the "utmost austerity of realism"[10] for the latter play, Moody was not repudiating the concern with universal themes that motivated the earlier works. The play, which focuses on the evolving relationship of the New Englander Ruth Jordan and the western ruffian turned successful miner Stephen Ghent, is driven not so much by the characters' carefully drawn psychological motivations—the hallmark of his new realistic style—as by the broad cultural-social ideas Moody wished to convey, and this explains why critics, like the *New York Times* reviewer who praised the play's characterizations as "splendidly real,"[11] were at times troubled by improbabilities in plot development.[12] In short, while Moody might have distanced himself from some melodramatic devices in his effort to develop complex rounded characters for *The Great Divide*, character was subordinate to philosophy in this play.

The philosophical dimensions of the play were duly noted by the New York reviewers. The "great divide" of the play's title was easily understood not only as the continental divide separating rivers flowing eastward from those flowing westward, but also as the line separating the easterner Ruth Jordan and the westerner Stephen Ghent. The New York *Sun* reviewer put it succinctly: "The great divide of his title is the barrier which exists between the rigor and dry formality of old civilization and the larger and freer, if more brutal, impulses of the frontier."[13] In tracing Stephen's and Ruth's progress in dealing with the social and ethical differences that threatened their relationship, Moody focused on what the reviewer of the *Evening Telegram* called "spiritual issues."[14] The New York reviewers pointed out that under the influence of the refined easterner Ruth, the savage western qualities of Stephen were mollified, while Stephen's liberated western manner enabled Ruth to free herself from the rigidity of her eastern moral scruples. In other words, New York reviewers noted that the play's action records how Ruth and Stephen mutually transform each other and, at play's end, arrive at a happy marriage, which optimistically suggests a synthesis of the larger principles they represent—a synthesis indicative of the new spiritual order brought into existence as a result of the American frontier experience.

Even if Turner's name did not appear in the reviews, the New York critics seemed to have been aware that they were viewing a play representing "the meeting point between savagery and civilization." To be sure, the more recent critic Jerry V. Pickering has noted the similarities between Turner's understanding of the tensions between East and West, on the one hand, and the East/West conflict of Ruth and Stephen, on the other[15]; however, the extent of this parallel and the degree to which a Turner-like paradigm governs the action of this play has not been fully explored.

While the meeting between civilization and savagery, between East and West, is presented in *The Great Divide* primarily as it had been in other turn-of-the-century frontier plays as a meeting between a heroine embodying the virtues of the civilized East and a hero embodying the best of the savage West, Moody deepens his presentation of this encounter—shaping the play's action along lines more closely parallel to Turner's analysis than was the case in other frontier plays of the decade. Turner had described the meeting of civilization and savagery in terms of the eastern pioneer's movement into savage wilderness land—that is, Turner had not presented the meeting of savagery and civilization as an interaction of individuals, but as a confrontation of civilized individual and savage environment.[16] This Turner-like way of explicating the meeting of civilization and savagery is very evident in Moody's play, especially in the relationship of the New England born and bred Ruth Jordan to the savage western desert environment.[17] Ruth has traveled from her home in Milford Corners, Massachusetts, to southern Arizona with her brother[18] to develop a cactus fiber business that will salvage the family fortune. Unlike her sister-in-law, Polly, who misses civilized amenities and looks forward to returning to a rich urban social and cultural life, Ruth finds the limitless possibilities of the western wilderness irresistibly alluring.

In establishing Ruth's overpowering attraction to the western wilderness, Moody goes a long way toward assimilating the play's romantic plot focused on the interaction between the easterner Ruth and the play's western hero into a more strictly conceived Turner-like analysis of the interaction between eastern pioneer and western environment. This particular intersection of a Turner-like historical analysis, a Turner "text," and a melodramatic romantic plot, a melodramatic "text," becomes readily apparent in Act I when Ruth tries to explain to Polly why she does not want to marry her eastern friend, the somewhat sentimental doctor Winthrop Newbury:

> RUTH:...Poor dear Win! He's so good, so gentle and chivalrous. But—[*With a movement of lifted arms, as if for air*] ah me, he's—finished! I want one that isn't finished!
> POLLY: Are you out of your head, you poor thing?
> RUTH: You know what I mean well enough. Winthrop is all rounded off, a completed product. But the man I sometimes see in my dreams is—[*pausing for a simile*]—well like this country out here, don't you know—?
> *She breaks off, searching for words, and makes a vague outline in the air, to indicate bigness and incompletion.*
> POLLY: [*Drily*] Yes, thank you. I do know! Heaven send you joy of him!
> RUTH: Heaven won't, because, alas, he doesn't exist! I am talking of a sublime abstraction—of the glorious unfulfilled—of the West—the Desert.[19]

Ruth's wished-for love interest is equated with the wild western environment, and consequently, her sense of the western environment is somewhat romanticized.[20] It is based on the kind of western desert scene that she (and the audience) can see through the "long low window at the back" (728) of her and her brother's Arizona cabin, which is the setting for Act I: "[T]he desert is seen, intensely colored, and covered with the uncouth shapes of giant cacti, dotted with bunches of gorgeous bloom" (728). While enjoying this idealized desert vista, Ruth has yet to experience the harsher, more violent side of the western desert environment—a dimension of the desert environment that she first confronts shortly after the above-quoted confession to Polly when Stephen and his desperado friends make their entrance.

Significantly, Stephen manifests stereotypic western character traits, such as an unconstrained violent individualism, and, at least at the start of the play, he is closely associated with the savage wilderness environment that surrounds Ruth as she tries to make a life in the West. Indeed, Stephen has all the unfulfilled, unfinished qualities of the desert environment that so excites Ruth. Moreover, Moody directly connects Stephen to the landscape, for it is out of it that he and his friends come—both literally, as one of them first appears outside the window revealing the desert landscape, and then all three enter the Act I cabin set from the desert, and figuratively, as they are products of the harsh struggle for survival that takes place in the desert wilderness.

Like Turner's pioneers who find their civilization has ill prepared them for the savage environment, Ruth finds herself unprepared when she is confronted with the harshness of the savage wilderness.[21] Toward the end of Act I, Ruth is left alone in the isolated family cabin: her brother Philip has taken Polly to the railroad depot so she can catch a train to San Francisco, while family friend and doctor Winthrop has been suddenly called away to tend to an injured foreman. It is at this point that Stephen Ghent and his two companions, the half-breed Mexican Shorty and the sadistic Dutch, break into the cabin. Ruth finds herself gravely threatened. "Blind-drunk and sun-crazy, and looking for damnation the nearest way" (735), these three intruders overcome Ruth's attempt to defend herself by disarming her of her gun and then of a knife. Initially, Moody describes these desperados in homogeneous terms. In the stage directions, he writes: "All three are dressed in rude frontier fashion.... All are intoxicated, but not sufficiently so to incapacitate them from rapid action" (733). Individually and collectively, they give form to the threatening material reality of the western desert environment. Only as they interact with Ruth does each of the three begin to take on uniquely individual characteristics.[22]

In her attempt to deal with the savage danger represented by these three desperados, Ruth singles out Stephen, the least aggressive and the most awed by her, as the most sympathetic of the intruders. While Shorty and Dutch try to determine who will rape Ruth first, she pleads with Stephen to defend her. She promises to give herself to him if he will protect her from the others, and he accepts the bargain, bribing Shorty with a necklace of gold nuggets and shooting Dutch in a gunfight. Ruth's arrangement with Stephen may have struck some viewers—as it did Ruth's mother (754)—as a clear breach of appropriate behavior in that, according to

Victorian moral standards, Ruth should have chosen to die rather than accept Stephen under such unseemly circumstances.[23] What is significant in this context, however, is that Ruth protects herself from physical violence by adapting herself to the conditions in which she finds herself. Just as Turner's pioneers find civilized conventions and conduct useless to them in the wilderness, so Ruth finds civilized conventions and conduct ineffective against the savage circumstances that invade her cabin and overwhelm her. In keeping herself from more severe injury, Ruth, like the able pioneer Turner describes, demonstrates an ability to adjust to the savage western environment (Plate 4).

The arrangement she makes with Stephen is, however, only the first stage in the process of adaptation that Ruth undergoes. While retaining enough of her New England sensibility that she feels compelled to keep her word and depart with Stephen at the end of the act, she continues the process of stripping herself of the accoutrements of civilization. Like Jim in *The Squaw Man*, Ruth not only relinquishes her family ties and connections, but in taking only a few items with her, she also deprives herself of most of the worldly goods that connect her to civilization.

Again, as in the case of Jim's journey into the savage sphere of experience, Ruth's journey into savagery is visually expressed by means of stage scenery.

Plate 4 Act I of William Vaughn Moody's *The Great Divide* with Henry Miller as Stephen Ghent and Margaret Anglin as Ruth Jordan. (The Billy Rose Theatre Division, the New York Public Library for the Performing Arts)

176   Early-Twentieth-Century Frontier Dramas

Plate 5   Act II of William Vaughn Moody's *The Great Divide* with Henry Miller as Stephen Ghent and Margaret Anglin as Ruth Jordan. (The Billy Rose Theatre Division, the New York Public Library for the Performing Arts)

When Ruth flees with Stephen at the end of Act I, she leaves the safety of the cabin for the desert outside. The scene for Act II is an exterior, and Moody's stage directions describe a dramatic southwestern vista (Plate 5). On one side of the stage is Stephen and Ruth's cabin, which is set on the wall of a canyon. In the background is the other side of the canyon, "of which the distant wall and upper reaches are crimsoned by the afternoon light" (737). In Act II, the illusion of protection from the savage world that the Act I cabin walls seemed to offer—but, in fact, didn't—is gone, and yet Ruth survives, which is more than can be said of her brother, whose cactus fiber business fails after Ruth's sudden departure.

Just as Turner maintained that the pioneer must adopt Indian practices, so too are the modes of adaptation to the savage environment of both Jim in *The Squaw Man* and Ruth in this play characterized by a growing association with western Indians. Again, as in the case of Jim, it is Ruth's eastern sensibility that prompts her to deepen her connection to the Indian world. While Jim's sense of obligation prompted him to marry the Indian Nat-u-ritch, Ruth's eastern pride and dignity motivate her to learn Navajo Indian handicrafts as a means of regaining control of her life. She weaves blankets and baskets, which she then sells to tourists without Stephen's knowledge to earn enough money on her own to purchase back the necklace of gold nuggets that Stephen used to buy off Shorty. In returning this necklace to Stephen, she intends to buy herself out of the compromising arrangement she made with him.

Ruth does more than regain control of her life. Just as Turner's pioneer first accepts the conditions offered by the frontier environment, and then "little by little he transforms the wilderness,"[24] so does Ruth transform the wilderness in which she finds herself. Moody hoped to suggest as much with the scenery he called for in Act II. A creative sensibility pervades the foreground space, which represents an open area adjacent to Stephen and Ruth's cabin. The plain adobe walls of the cabin are covered by "vines loaded with purple bloom" (737). Describing the crude stone furniture to be found in the open space, Moody wrote: "In the level space before the rocky terrace is a stone table and seats, made of natural rocks roughly worked with the chisel. The rude materials have manifestly been touched by a refined and artistic hand, bent on making the most of the glorious natural background" (737). This "refined and artistic hand" is Ruth's. Trying to remind Ruth that they have shared some pleasant times, Stephen recalls "the day we made the table; the day we planted the vines" (746). In these shared past recollections, Ruth's impact on the environment and her impact on Stephen are conflated: she transforms the wild western environment, but, significantly, she also transforms Stephen from the coarse, rough force of nature he was when he invaded the Act I cabin to a socially productive individual.

Even as Ruth simultaneously affects both environment and Stephen—suggesting the connection between the two—this connection is gradually severed as a result of that very impact. From the moment he first sees Ruth, Stephen begins to separate himself from the rough desert desperados with whom he initially appeared. Moreover, when Ruth accepts the terms of their agreement, she provides him with the motivation to rise above his wild, savage nature. In his quest to please his wife-to-be, Stephen promises at the end of the first act, "I'll put you where you can look down on the proudest. I'll give you the kingdoms of the world and all the glory of 'em" (736). In other words, Ruth's arrangement with Stephen motivates him to live up to what he believes are her expectations. Stephen thus ceases to be a mere embodiment of the savage desert from which he and his desperado friends had come; he also begins to act upon that environment. Between Acts I and II, Stephen is transformed from desert drifter to successful mine owner.

Ghent's accomplishments demonstrate his character's superior skills as an engineer/entrepreneur and deepen the play's mythic dimension—that is, his mercurial rise is mythic in scale. Indeed, such a socioeconomic success story was no mean trick. It was, in fact, a historical rarity. As "new western historian" Patricia Limerick points out in her study of the American western past, *The Legacy of Conquest*, very few miners really rose up the social ladder. Most found themselves dreaming about striking it rich while having to accept salaried labor in mining operations that were underwritten by distant owners. After the short-lived, individualistic placer mining phase, mining rapidly entered a corporate phase of development, one in which the independent miner gave way to large business enterprises.[25]

Despite Stephen's extraordinary financial and managerial achievements, his ultimate transformation is nevertheless far from complete at the end of Act II. He has been tamed only insofar as his natural energy is focused toward the amoral, materialistic accumulation of wealth. Stephen is still unable to fully understand the depth of Ruth's remorse over having betrayed her civilized heritage. As Martin Halpern writes, Stephen in Act II is "the prosperous entrepreneur, sure of his money-making gifts and dedicated to the proposition that bigger-and-better gold mines and larger and more sumptuous mansions are the key to the good life."[26] Because Stephen's savage energy is directed toward the accumulation of the kind of wealth he wrongly hopes will impress the refined Ruth, he becomes a conqueror of nature, but even as he does so he remains a force of nature. At the start of Act III, Polly suggests that he has not yet transcended the natural into the spiritual, the savage into the civilized. In a peculiarly incongruous passage given the realistic everyday nature of the play's dialogue and characters, the somewhat frivolous Polly suddenly offers a deeply poetic insight. She tells her mother-in-law: "O, he's *good!* so is a volcano between eruptions. And commonplace, too, until you happen to get a glimpse down one of the old volcanic rifts in his surface, and see—far below—underneath the cold lava-beds—fire, fire, the molten heart of a continent!" (751). Driven by natural and material forces, Stephen has yet to become a moral, spiritual individual.

Early in Act III, Polly describes him as a force of nature, but by the end of Act III, Stephen appears to have undergone a final moral transformation. Stephen surreptitiously followed Ruth across country, when, having purchased her freedom from him, she returned to the safety of her mother's Milford Corners home. While in New England, he loyally but secretly provides Ruth with necessary financial support through her mother. Having literally traveled thousands of miles from the western desert, and having willingly sacrificed his Arizona mine and the fortune he had built out of the desert in the hope of acquiring Ruth's love, Stephen can no longer be seen as either the simple embodiment of the harsh western desert environment or as a mere suggestion of the power of that environment turning on itself in the form of a crass materialism. The extent of Stephen's metamorphosis becomes most apparent when he appears before Ruth late in the act. Finally understanding the source of Ruth's pain and guilt, he now suffers greatly at the possibility of losing Ruth. He confesses to her:

> You ask me to suffer for my wrong. Since you left me I *have* suffered—God knows! You ask me to make some sacrifice. Well—how would the mine do? Since I've been away they've [his business partners have] as good as stolen it from me. I could get it back easy enough by fighting; but supposing I don't fight. Then we'll start all over again, just as we stand in our shoes, and make another fortune—for our boy. (755)

In short, Stephen has become a complex combination of western individualism and eastern humanism; he is an individual motivated not only by material but by spiritual forces.

Even as Stephen completes his transformation under Ruth's influence, she completes her transformation under his influence. Like Royle's Jim Carston, Ruth experienced life in the savage West but willingly returned to the civilized East when the opportunity arose. Unlike Jim, however, Ruth has been changed by the West and is no longer satisfied in the East. Having sought refuge in the protective warmth of her mother's old-fashioned New England home—scenically represented here by her mother's sitting room, with its portraits of her distinguished ancestors—Ruth is nonetheless unhappy. She is trapped in what Polly calls "a state of divided feeling" (750), both attracted to and repulsed by Stephen and the western life he lives. Depressed, she feels alienated even from her and Stephen's son to whom she has given birth since her return east. Only by liberating herself from the repressive eastern heritage symbolized by the family portraits that surround her in the Jordan family sitting room can she complete the metamorphosis begun in the West. In Act II she demonstrated her ability to adapt to the physical environment of the West, but in the play's last act, Ruth finally acknowledges the transformation that the western environment had prompted in her moral and spiritual sensibilities.

When Stephen confronts Ruth at the act's end, his sacrifices and suffering become clear to her. In terms of her eastern moral sense, he has expiated his sin, but even more significantly, Ruth sees that while Stephen has undergone a change, he has not become another "finished" Winthrop. Maintaining a faith born of the West, Stephen still asserts that "[o]ur law is joy, and selfishness.... What does the past matter, when we've got the future..." (755). Affirming the kind of freedom and independence from past civilization that Turner claimed was the product of the frontier, Stephen inspires Ruth to break free of the last psychological and moral bonds that hold her to the old eastern way of looking at the world. Ruth finally concedes, "You have taken the good of our life and grown strong. I have taken the evil and grown weak, weak unto death. Teach me to live as you do!" (756). Royle's Jim Carston could never cut those ties; therefore, despite his journey into a savage environment, he always remained a civilized European. Ruth, on the other hand, breaks free of unnecessary eastern moral restraints and fully embraces western independence at the play's end.

In their various interactions, Stephen and Ruth capture the complexity of a troubled human relationship, but they also function on an allegorical level, representing the unfolding frontier interaction of civilized pioneer and savage wilderness. Turner's frontier process, which their interaction parallels, is not complete until the end of the play. Just as the mutual transformation of pioneer and wilderness described by Turner culminates in something new—something that he claimed to be distinctly American—the mutual transformation of Ruth and Stephen, or what Martin Halpern called their "double reversal,"[27] enables these characters to place their relationship on a new healthy foundation at the play's end. In so doing, they embody the promise of a new dawn for American life and culture—a dawn that is heralded in the play by Stephen's reference to their son, ironically, as the "little rooster."

Interestingly, Moody's first version of this play under the title *A Sabine Woman* ended much more ambiguously than the successful New York revision. The earlier version was presented as a Chicago tryout in April 1906. In its last act, Ruth is willing to accept Stephen as in the later version, but in this draft it is unclear whether they will finally be united. Stephen has been seriously wounded by Ruth's angry brother, and at play's end his survival is not certain. In rewriting this original conclusion, Moody brought more definite closure to the play.[28] He thus seemed to stumble onto a formula that provided the play with an artificial coherence—a resolution that seemed, even if unintentionally, to give Turner's thesis lucid theatrical form.

In fusing allegory and psychological complexity to represent a marriage of civilization and savagery, Moody appears to bridge multiple oppositions in much the same way as Turner did. Indeed, despite the evidence to the contrary offered by the first Chicago ending, the tendency to overcome the distance between supposed opposites runs deep in Moody's play. With his understanding of effective theater and his careful observation of specific detail, Moody synthesizes melodrama and realism, consequently helping to establish what was viewed at the time as a new American drama. More than the other playwrights we have examined, he assimilates the new, seemingly scientific sensibility into his romantic drama, thus taking drama in the direction described by Vernon Lewis Parrington in his analysis of the new realistic literature.[29] Moreover, in balancing the melodramatic emphasis on larger-than-life individuals with the realistic preoccupation on the environment that molds individuals, Moody, like Turner, binds a romantic faith in an Emersonian individualism with a Darwinian understanding of environment. This convergence of key, often-opposing elements in the American cultural matrix functioned as it did in Turner's historical analysis to capture the hearts and souls of early-twentieth-century American audience members who hungered for a national affirmation as a way to offset doubts and fears brought on by rapid social change.[30]

The resolution of opposites offered here is, however, not as harmonious as it may first appear. The Turner-like nature of the conclusion that Moody developed for *The Great Divide* is not without contradictions. In fact, the play's action and resolution are plagued by some of the same discrepancies and limitations that haunted Turner. As in Turner's analysis, the apparent balance of East and West, civilization and savagery, disguises a western bias. Moreover, this imbalance in Moody's play is linked not only to the kind of gender bias that characterized Turner's analysis, but also to the kind of gender bias that pervaded nineteenth-century melodrama. The play's union of Ruth/East/civilization/pioneer and Stephen/West/savagery/wilderness may appear to be a synthesis in which both groups of terms have an equal weight, but such is not entirely the case.[31] Based on stage time, one might argue that Ruth is the focus of the play—in short, that it is her play. Nevertheless, Moody clearly viewed Stephen and the West as a healthy antidote for an enervated eastern culture. It is, in fact, Stephen's resources that in the end rescue Mrs. Jordan and her children. Not only does Stephen prevent the Jordans from losing their home when Philip fails in business, but he also buys Philip's cactus fiber business, oversees its prosperity, and then hands it back over to Philip. In the end, Stephen is very much a hero in the melodramatic vein. Certainly, the primary villain he must overcome during the course of the play is the dangerous, godless part of himself. He is, consequently, a complex hero embodying elements of heroism as well as villainy, but he is still the dominating man of action on whom all finally depend.

Furthermore, Moody's apparent acceptance of Victorian melodramatic conventions reduces Ruth to a relatively inactive role in the working out of the play's action. In a sense, Moody follows the typical melodramatic pattern by awarding Ruth to Stephen after he proves himself worthy of her—that is, after he proves himself appropriately chivalrous. Stephen's potential in this regard is demonstrated in Act I, when he protects Ruth from Dutch and Shorty. It is further demonstrated in Act I after Stephen has chased away the other intruders when he places his weapon on the table within Ruth's reach as a way of providing her with an opportunity of freeing herself from him—an opportunity that she rejects.

The melodramatic nature of the play's plot, however, does not always support the Turner-like bias toward the West that informs the play's action. *The Great Divide* is occasionally marked by a tension between the melodrama form and the Turner "text" that meet within it. Indeed, melodrama's morality—based on clear distinctions between right and wrong—is closely associated with the kind of moral absolutism that is identified in this play with the puritan East. This moral sensibility, on the one hand, directs the action of the play insofar as it is a melodrama, but, on the other, is overcome within the play at its conclusion. This contradiction is most clearly seen in Stephen. At play's end, this melodramatic hero wins his prize, the heroine Ruth, when he demonstrates his virtue by speaking on behalf of the kind of moral sensibility that underlies melodrama in general, and Ruth's thinking throughout the play in particular. In this regard, his transformation seems to go beyond that required of the Turner text. For a moment, Stephen appears to assume not only the best attributes of civilization, but also those that in the world of this play are understood as the worst, most repressive attributes of eastern civilization—the rigidly absolutist moral sense. In his last speech before Ruth's final acquiescence to him, Stephen suggests, in what appears to be a contradiction of his advocacy for the "law of joy, of selfishness," that he has learned the difference between an unconditional right and an unconditional wrong:

> I know what you're saying there to yourself, and I guess you're right. Wrong is wrong, from the moment it happens till the crack of doom, and all the angels in Heaven, working overtime, can't make it less or different by a hair. That seems to be the law. I've learned it hard, but I guess I've learned it. I've seen it written in mountain letters across the continent of this life.—Done is done, and lost is lost, and smashed to hell is smashed to hell. We fuss and potter and patch up. You might as well try to batter down the Rocky Mountains with a rabbit's heart-beat!...You've fought hard for me, God bless you for it.—But it's been a losing game with you from the first!—You belong here, and I belong out yonder—beyond the Rockies, beyond—the Great Divide! (755–56)

With this speech Stephen finally wins Ruth. After hearing him express this newly acquired understanding of the sharp line between good and evil, Ruth gives herself up to him.

The irony here, of course, is the fact that Ruth wants Stephen to carry her across the Great Divide into the West, where they will try to bring up their son free of the kinds of conventions that have enabled Stephen to win her. In short, melodramatic morality is simultaneously vindicated and challenged. In this regard, the melodrama text and the Turner text make uncomfortable bedfellows. The melodramatic structure serves to support the male hegemony over the action of this play, yet, paradoxically, the morality of melodrama is overturned at play's end even as male hegemony is guaranteed. Associated with the new law of joy and selfishness that characterizes the western savage domain, male hegemony is vindicated despite the fact that melodramatic absolutism is overturned. Moody may reject the melodramatic sensibility at play's end, but he remains loyal to the traditional gender hierarchy.

Just as Moody submits to the gender hierarchy prevailing among the late-nineteenth-century bourgeois elite, he also works with the same kind of racial assumptions that characterize the culture of that elite and that are manifested in Turner's historical analysis. *The Great Divide* emphasizes the value of western individualism, but the western individualism validated here is an Anglo-Saxon individualism. Moody's vision of the frontier process is one in which non-Anglo-Saxons are marginalized or, in the case of the half-breed Shorty, even demonized. The only nonwhite character in the play, Shorty is the most savage of the Act I intruders. As James John Koldenhoven has written of these desperados, "the nearer you are to Anglo-Saxon blood, the more is the likelihood that you are not savage."[32] Clearly, Shorty's venality and his inarticulate, poorly spoken English was meant to demonstrate his distance not only from Anglo-Saxon, but also from conventionally accepted civilized behavior.

While there are no Indians in Moody's play, Indian culture is treated with only a modest sympathy. When Ruth takes up Indian weaving, she is lowering herself to the humble level of her savage environment. Indeed, without the presence of Indian characters to suggest the human origin of these cultural activities, Indian crafts are reduced to being merely manifestations of the rough western environment. Moody, like Turner, depersonalizes Indians and Indian culture, interpreting them as nothing more than abstract signifiers of savagery.

Certainly, from the perspective of the twenty-first century, Moody's play shares some of the same racial and gender subtexts that inform Turner's essay. This is not, however, a matter of Turner influencing Moody as much as it a result of both Moody's play's and Turner's essay's being informed by the racial and gender constructions prevalent at the turn of the nineteenth into the twentieth century. Both Moody and Turner were molded by and were disseminators of structures of thought that were prevalent among the American Anglo-Saxon elite. In upholding these structures of thought, however, neither Moody nor Turner had an unqualified optimism regarding the future of the heroic Anglo-Saxon male. Both struggled with certain contradictions that undermined the faith each held in the historical significance of western rugged individualism. Most significant here were the ways in which both Turner and Moody dealt with the tensions developing between the rugged individualism they advocated and the corporate society in which they lived.

In this regard, Turner's thesis offered hope, on the one hand, by stressing how the frontier had fostered the development of rugged individuals, and demonstrated anxiety, on the other, insofar as Turner reiterated the claim made by the superintendent of the 1890 census that the frontier that fostered this individualism was closed. While Turner asked what would replace the now closed frontier as a crucible for American individualism—and he would continue to ask this question and offer various answers through later essays[33]—this question seemed to be outweighed by the assertion of identity that his thesis seemed to offer his fellow Americans. In other words, the celebration of the frontier past overshadowed the dread of a frontierless future in Turner's analysis, or at least in the way that analysis was received by many turn-of-the-century Americans.

Similarly, Moody in *The Great Divide* focused more on the frontier past, which was a source of rugged individualism, than on the western present or future, in which rugged individualism was on the wane. While the uncertain resolution of the original version of the play may have captured some of his apprehensions about the future of rugged individualism in a frontierless society, the version of *The Great Divide* that appeared on the Princess Theatre stage downplayed such ambiguities. Nevertheless, the action of the revised script is not without an undertone—perhaps unintended—of concern. In this version of the play, Stephen Ghent may be viewed as the kind of rugged individual made possible by the frontier, but even as he extends himself on the frontier, he helps to close the very frontier that produced individuals like himself. More specifically, even as Stephen proves himself a truly rugged individual by developing his successful mine, he opens the door to the kind of corporate infighting that steals the mine from him and eventually will dominate the West; that is, Ghent paves the way for a civilization, which in practice puts little value on individualism—a civilization marred by a repressiveness not entirely unlike the one from which Stephen liberates Ruth.

At play's end, Ghent confidently asserts that he could win his mine back if he were willing to fight for it. The logic of the play's melodramatic structure may appear to substantiate Ghent's assertion; however, one must wonder to what extent such a claim is mere bravado—a product of Moody's wishful thinking. Moody's attempt to represent the real socioeconomic environment of the West is significant here. On several occasions in the play, he calls attention to Ghent's dependence on capital to develop his mine and to Ghent's anxiety over the corporate maneuvers that ultimately oust him from its management.[34] These passing references to business realities suggest that Ghent will not have an easy time if he tries to reinstate himself in the financial hierarchy of the West. An old aristocratic civilization may be replaced by a new corporate, industrial civilization, but the individual will again find him- or herself constrained by civilization all the same.

Interestingly, the production history of *The Great Divide* is marked by a similar ambiguity with respect to the power of the rugged individual to withstand the tide of corporate America. The financial success of this play—a play that so positively affirmed the ruggedly independent American—is directly related to the fact that advanced technology (for instance, the growth of the railroad) and the consolidation of the American theater under the Syndicate and later the Shuberts (what Alfred Bernheim had called the "industrial revolution in the theatre"[35]) made nationwide touring of the full production of new plays possible. Indeed, the individual as a force in the American theater was rapidly losing ground to large commercial corporate interests.

More specifically, *The Great Divide* was produced by the Shuberts, who in 1906 were engaged in a theater war with the monopolistic Syndicate headed by Charles Frohman. In the early years of the twentieth century, the Shuberts were able to rally to their side independent producers like David Belasco and the Fiskes, who all saw themselves as rugged individualists fighting the monolithic Syndicate. The Shubert production of *The Great Divide* may be seen as Moody's contribution to this struggle, and in fact he did view the Syndicate as a dangerous enemy to his play. For instance, in a letter to his wife-to-be, Harriet Brainerd, postmarked September 18, 1906, Moody accused the Syndicate of trying "to stab us in the back"[36] by hiring a critic to write a brutal review of the play for the *Washington Star* during its out-of-town tryout. The irony, of course, is that whatever Moody may have felt about his alliance with the Shuberts and whatever virtue he attributed to them, they eventually won their theater war with the Syndicate and proceeded to exercise the same kind of dictatorial control over the American theater as their predecessors had.[37]

It would appear that the celebration of the rugged individual offered in a play like *The Great Divide* merely diverted the playwright and his audiences from the fact that such an entity—if it ever had existed, which is an open question[38]—was less and less significant in American life. Whatever the reality, larger corporate interests seemed to hide behind the mask of rugged individualism, and the well-to-do audiences who attended performances of *The Great Divide* at the Princess Theatre seemed to find the myth of American rugged individualism enticing. To be sure, the success of Moody's play supports the latter assumption, and businesses advertising in the program for *The Great Divide* sought to capitalize on this allure of rugged individualism. For instance, among the various advertisements for luxury items (such as pianos, candies, restaurants, champagnes and other alcoholic beverages, facial creams, and furs) that might have attracted the interest of the relatively wealthy audiences who came to the Princess Theatre during the week beginning December 17, 1906, were advertisements placed by two mining investment brokerage houses: "THE THREE OF US: Patrick, Elliott and Camp: Goldfield, Nevada, and 6 Wall Street, New York" and "J.J. BAMBERBER & CO. BROKERS: Mines and Mining Stocks, 44-46 Broadway (Second Floor), New York City."[39]

Trying to take advantage of the excitement in mining generated not only by *The Great Divide*, but also by plays like Crothers's *The Three of Us*, these advertisers hoped to entice investments from audience members who wanted to experience the thrill of western rugged individualism from the safety of their New York homes. Explicit in this regard is the following excerpt from the advertisement for Patrick, Elliott, and Camp that appeared in the Princess Theatre program for the week beginning March 4, 1907:

> The whole world has gone wild over the enormous possibilities for making money in Nevada. The oldest Wall Street operators have never known such excitement. It is of such importance that our great American playwrights are devoting their most earnest attention to it, and have presented the New York public with five new mining plays within the past season, namely: "THE THREE OF US," "THE GIRL OF THE GOLDEN WEST," " THE GREAT DIVIDE," "BEDFORD'S HOPE," and the "HEIR TO THE HOORAH." Just think of it. *ARE YOU AWAKE TO THE TRUE FACTS?*
>
> Nevada has the confidence of the investing public, and here leading mining operators insist that that confidence be made secure. We are PIONEERS

IN NEVADA. We have made more successful mines than any other promotion house in the great State. We gave to the American investor FIVE OF THE GREATEST MINES IN NEVADA.... You should keep posted on our offerings, as we make a success of EVERY PROPOSITION WE PUT OUT.[40]

The author of the copy for this advertisement conflates Nevada pioneering with successful mine promotion. Rugged individualism and business acumen are brought into an accord that the reader can share—if he or she is willing to invest. Like Moody's play, this advertisement suggests that there is no tension between rugged individualism and corporate capitalism and that they both flourish on the western frontier. In short, Turner's frontier analysis, Moody's *The Great Divide*, and this advertisement all manifest a similar faith in the historical possibilities that the western frontier opened to the Anglo-Saxon male—a faith that masked its own contradictions. True or false, this faith pervaded the early-twentieth-century frontier discourse that America's ruling elite embraced and disseminated and that other Americans simply absorbed uncritically.

* * *

Two weeks after the triumphant New York opening of Moody's *The Great Divide*, another Western mining-region play, Rachel Crothers's *The Three of Us* opened at the Madison Square Theatre. Born into an affluent Illinois family[41] in 1878, Crothers had moved east after graduating from the State Normal School in 1892 to study for the stage in Boston and New York. With *The Three of Us*, Crothers the playwright introduced herself to New York audiences. The play, which provided the Patrick, Elliott, and Camp firm with a headline for its advertisement in *The Great Divide* program, was the author's first major New York success. It launched a playwriting career that would last for more than thirty years. Described by Judith Barlow as "by far the most successful American woman playwright in the early part of this century,"[42] Crothers created a string of New York hits between 1906 and 1938. While demonstrating mastery of the skills necessary for writing conventionally popular, "safe" plays, she also exhibited a willingness to explore controversial subjects. Especially in her early plays, such as *A Man's World* (1908) and *He and She* (1911), Crothers treated women's issues and, more significantly, brought a feminist perspective to the drama—a perspective that was certainly not common in the turn-of-the-century theater.[43]

Given Crothers's interest in the place of women in American society, it may appear peculiar that she began her long Broadway career with a play set in the frontier western environment of a Nevada mining town—a typically male domain. Even though she set the play in a frontier environment, she was very careful nonetheless to avoid the Wild West clichés of earlier frontier dramas, including *The Great Divide*. In fact, New York critics commented favorably on the lack of traditional frontier western theatrical paraphernalia. Reviewers noted that the play did without the "sombrero, pick, shovel...flannel shirt" and even "gun play" (*New York Herald*)[44]; the "red shirts" and whiskey (except for an eastern highball) typical of mining camp dramas (New York *Sun*)[45]; and, in general, "the coarse exaggeration usually characteristic of plays relative to life in the Far West" (*New York Daily Tribune*).[46] As the *New York Dramatic Mirror* critic wrote:

> Here is a Western drama stripped of conventional accessories and dealing with people alone; plain human beings, fighting against ordinary evils.... It has none of the romance so energetically striven for by other playwrights of Western inclination, and there are none of the types so familiar in dramas of this locality.[47]

Not only does Crothers dispense with the familiar frontier accessories and character types, but in *The Three of Us* she also makes light of the kinds of perspectives that led to the use of these theatrical devices in other frontier dramas. Her attitude toward frontier clichés is perhaps most apparent during the second-act dinner party arranged by Mrs. Tweed Bix, a disenchanted mining camp resident. Mrs. Bix hopes to use this party to convince her guest of honor, the easterner Lorimer Trenholm, to buy her mine, thus providing her the funds necessary to move back to New York. In response to a question from Trenholm about one of the many Indian artifacts with which she decorates her living room, Mrs. Bix, or Bixie, as her friends call her, confesses to a rather idealized notion of Indians and their culture. Her overly romantic view of the Indian is undermined by her husband Tweed's humorous interjection:

> MRS. BIX: Tweed says I'm silly about the Indians. I'm always looking for romance in them. I did find one perfect Hiawatha.
> TWEED: Yes, and he gave you the Minne-ha-ha, too.[48]

The juxtaposition of Bixie's romantic idealizing and Tweed's deflating commentary is reiterated to greater effect a few moments later when Tweed playfully assumes the costume and behavior of a stereotypic savage Indian even as Bixie waxes poetically on Indian culture:

> MRS. BIX: They really have beautiful traits of character, Mr. Trenholm, and a strong artistic sense. See this blanket?
> (MRS. BIX *and* MR. TRENHOLM *rise and take up blanket from couch at L. of fire.* TWEED *snaps his fingers, and beckons, calls* RHY. *She goes to him and they go behind the piano, wher*e RHY *assists* TWEED *in putting the Indian blanket about him which is on the piano. He takes also a savage looking weapon on the wall.* MR. TRENHOLM *and* MRS. BIX *stand with their backs to* RHY *and* TWEED....)
> ...
> MRS. BIX: Aren't those colors stunning? They are done with the vegetable dyes. I'm particularly fond of this blanket, because it was woven by the last of the tribe. I wish you would have seen him. Really a gentle poetic creature. I always said he *looked very much* like Tweed.
> (MAGGIE [a servant] *enters L. with coffee on tray—stands an instant for orders, then advances to C.* RHY *gives* TWEED *a push, and he bounds into the C. of stage with a war whoop.*)
> MAGGIE: Lord God Almighty! (*Terribly frightened, she holds onto the tray, but the cups shake violently as* TWEED *circles about her in a wild dance*...). (55)

On cue, Tweed interrupts his wife's Cooperesque homage to Indian life and culture with his caricature of the villainous savage Indian. In this sudden transition from the subtle satire of the overly romanticized view of the noble savage, on the one hand, to the overt parody of the portrayal of the Indian as demon-devil, on the other, Crothers both calls attention to the falseness of both perspectives and suggests the kinship between them—each representing a different side of the same coin, each defined as the reversal of the other. Despite these implications, the *New York Times* reviewer condemned this scene, claiming that "one could spare the bit of Indian masquerading in the second act. It makes the cheapest sort of a bid for laughter."[49] This scene does, however, clearly position Crothers with respect to some of the traditional attitudes on which frontier plays were built.

Rejecting theatrically exaggerated Western character types, Crothers nonetheless does not entirely break free of the East/West, civilization/savagery, binary oppositions that informed other turn-of-the-century plays set in the American West. Indeed, these oppositions give shape to the action in Crothers's play, only they do so in a less overt fashion than in a play like Moody's *The Great Divide*. As the reviewer for the *New York Dramatic Mirror* claimed, Crothers rejected Western stereotypes for "plain human beings,"[50] but undergirding this "plainness" are subtle reminders of the Turner East/civilization-West/savagery opposition.

As "plain" as Crothers' characters in *The Three of Us* may have appeared to the generally well-to-do audiences who attended the production at the Madison Square Theatre, these characters—not surprisingly, given Crothers's own social background—for the most part, either are or once were associated with the white Anglo-Saxon upper class.[51] In the latter category is the Macchesney family, who are the focus of the play. Holding this family together is the young woman Rhy Macchesney. She is responsible for bringing up her two younger brothers, nineteen-year-old Clem and thirteen-year-old "Sonnie," the three having been orphaned well before the start of the play. Rhy and her two brothers jointly own the Three of Us mine and eke out their livelihood from the interest on a sum of money inherited from their father. They may be struggling against poverty in the present, but as Rhy comments in Act I when showing her brothers daguerreotype images of their mother and father, their father was "a gentleman of the old school" (13) and their mother was a lady. The stage directions suggest that the "general effect" of their living room "is that of the remains of some old-fashioned elegance which have fallen at last into very poor surroundings" (6). Some residue of former prosperity is still to be found in their home. Rhy willingly lends Bixie items inherited from better days, including china and chairs, to help her create the proper setting for her party, and Rhy wears one of her mother's old stylish New York gowns for the dinner. Moreover, while Rhy runs the household, she does so with the assistance of a servant, Maggie.

As Rhy struggles to maintain the family's integrity and respectability against both internal and external pressures, she is amorously pursued by two young men, Louis Berrisford and Stephen Townley. It is primarily through these suitors for Rhy's hand that the East/civilization-West/savagery opposition is established in the play. In that Crothers primarily represents this opposition by means of these two male characters, she parts company from other turn-of-the-century playwrights, who, like William Vaughn Moody, used period gender constructions to sharpen the civilization/savagery opposition. While these other playwrights resorted to what Joan Wallach Scott described as "the legitimizing function of gender"[52] to reinforce the civilization/savagery opposition, Crothers does not, and consequently, her presentation of this opposition is less emphatic. Moreover, in avoiding obvious regional characteristics and by providing both suitors with enough social skills to maintain the play's overall upper-class ambience, she further tempers traditional East/West, civilization/savagery distinctions. From the perspective of an easterner like Bixie, what primarily distinguishes these two characters is the fact that Berrisford has money and Townley does not.

Even so, Crothers's construction of these two characters brings into relief Berrisford's connection with the East and Townley's connection with the West. When Mrs. Bix argues that Rhy should consider Berresford as a husband because he is "a man of the world" with "social position in New York," Rhy, who is favorably disposed toward Steve, responds, "Steve had social position in Kansas City" (24). Both may have or have had "social position," but Rhy's defense of Steve suggests a predilection for the West, with its less refined—and therefore perhaps more democratic—social sensibility.

Crothers's stage directions elaborate on this distinction. On his first entrance, Steve Townley is described as "a tall strong fellow about thirty, clean shaven and well bronzed, with the freedom of fresh air of the west, the unmistakable stamp of the gentleman, and a half shy boyishness. His clothes show hard wear and are splashed with mud" (28). On the other hand, the New Yorker Berresford is described several pages later as "a tall, dark, lithe fellow about thirty-five with great charm of manner and distinction of personality. Extremely well dressed in riding clothes" (34). As described in these directions, the two young men represent two very different types. Steve is a wholesome outdoorsman, a product of the "fresh air of the west." He may appear awkward, as suggested by his "shy boyishness" and his shabby dress, but he is to be seen as a man of honor and integrity. Steve, as described in the stage directions, recalls the kind of natural gentleman offered in Kirke La Shelle and Owen Wister's *The Virginian*. On the other hand, the litheness, "charm," "distinction of personality," and fine clothes attributed to Berresford[53] in the above-cited stage directions suggest a polish that is only skin deep. Indeed, his actions throughout the play indicate a questionable moral character.

A "man of the world," Berresford is no true gentleman; he is a careful and sly schemer. Maintaining a calm, controlled exterior, Berresford selfishly attempts to manipulate the play's other characters. He takes advantage of Clem's youthful restlessness and his boredom with life in this small mining town to draw key information from him. Berresford learns of Steve's discovery of a rich gold vein, which runs through Steve's stake as well as Bixie's and maybe even that belonging to the Macchesney children, from Clem, who, unbeknownst to Steve and Rhy, overheard Steve tell Rhy of his strike. Berresford then cunningly purchases Bixie's mine while it is still cheap, and before Trenholm, who represents larger economic interests, can. Moreover, Berresford convinces Trenholm not to do business with Steve. Finally, he puts Rhy in a position in which she, and not her brother, appears to have betrayed Steve, causing a rift between Rhy and Steve. A smooth Machiavellian, Berresford comes close to assuming the role of melodramatic villain. He is the corrupt, overrefined, egoistic product of a too worldly civilization.

Steve, on the other hand, may have attributes in common with the heroic natural gentleman, but throughout the play he also evidences a tendency toward impulsive judgment and action. In this regard, he embodies the spontaneity, the untamed, unrestrained quality of the wild frontier. This aspect of his character colors the sequence of events that led to his discovery of gold. As he relates these occurrences to Rhy, it becomes clear that chance and impetuousness contributed equally to his success. Having stumbled on an old trail he had never seen before, he followed it and came upon the abandoned mine, "a black, ugly looking hole" (29), into which he descended by means of an old rotten ladder that he found in the shaft. When Rhy scolds him for his foolhardy adventurousness ["Oh—how could you? That was terribly dangerous" (29)], he simply responds "I *had* to" (29), before going on to describe the actual discovery. Steve is a doer, not a thinker.

While his impulsiveness propels him toward the rich vein of ore, it also threatens his relationship with Rhy. Unlike the always controlled Berresford, Steve jumps to conclusions with regard to Rhy's connection to his rival. Seeing Rhy shake Berresford's hand during a brief tête-à-tête at Mrs. Bix's dinner party, Steve rashly assumes that Rhy has agreed to marry Berresford. After she rebukes Steve for his silly accusation, he responds with the confession, "Don't tease me, Rhy. I can't keep up with that sort of thing. I'm too slow. Tell me how it is—Have I got any chance or not?" (47). Seeking to cut through the "civilized" social games that characterize courtship in this society, Steve is easily misled by ambiguous appearances. When toward the end of Bixie's dinner party Steve learns of Berresford's machinations regarding Bixie's mine, he quickly concludes that Rhy has betrayed him by informing Berresford of his discovery of gold, and again later that evening when he finds Rhy in Berresford's room, he hastily determines that Rhy's honor requires that she marry Berresford. He may mean well toward Rhy, but his unrestrained rashness leads him astray. The directness of his style, while appropriate to life in the western wilderness, becomes problematic when applied in more civilized contexts.

During the course of the play, Rhy finds herself caught between the worldly and cunning easterner Berresford and the frank and impulsive westerner Steve. Indeed, the play's major line of action follows her as she works through the various complications resulting from the rivalry of these two suitors. While it is clear from the beginning that Rhy's heart is with Steve and that she is drawn to his western spirit, their union is only certain at the play's end. In fact, her connection to the westerner Steve can be understood as the culmination of a process that recalls Turner's frontier process—a process during which Rhy, whose roots are in the East, has freed herself of vestigial eastern ties to completely fulfill her western identity.

Rhy's parents, who were wealthy members of a refined social world, were apparently easterners. Nevertheless, her family's past prosperity in the civilized East is outweighed by present adversity in the West. Unfortunately for Rhy, her parents lost most of the family fortune long before the start of the play. As she confesses to Mrs. Bix, "They did have lots of beautiful things, but we moved so often and things were sold so much that there wasn't much left by the time we got here" (23). The Macchesney family's loss of material comfort parallels the kinds of losses experienced by Turner's pioneers, who, upon moving to the West, very soon found themselves reduced to primitive circumstances. For Rhy and her brothers, the stripping away of connections to the East was not complete, however, until their parents died: their mother died the year before the family arrived in the Nevada mining camp in which the play is set, and their father the year after. Deprived of most of their worldly goods and without the parents who could provide them with a sense of the social and cultural continuity so important to "civilized" life, Rhy and her brothers found themselves isolated in a relatively primitive frontier environment. Like Turner's pioneer settlers, they had to adapt to this new environment. In this effort, Rhy seems to have been very skillful.

Rhy's success in this regard is apparent from the very start of the play. She first enters in rather unladylike fashion, carrying—with Maggie's help—a heavy trunk. On this occasion the stage direction describing her reads:

RHY MACCHESNEY, *a girl of twenty-five, is forceful and fearless as a young Amazon, with the courage of belief in herself—the audacity and innocence of youth which has never known anything but freedom—the lovableness of a big nature and sunniness of an undying sense of humor. What she wears is very far from the fashion, but has charm and individuality and leaves her as free and unconscious of her strength and beauty as an animal.* (11)

As a "forceful," "fearless," and "young Amazon" who "has never known anything but freedom," whose "sunniness" suggests a big-hearted optimism, and whose freedom from fashion manifests itself in an individuality of style, Rhy has many of the traits that Turner attributed to frontier existence.[54]

Rhy's successful adaptation to life in the West is apparent in her upbeat responses to those who show distaste for the West. When her brother Clem, feeling trapped in the small mining community in which they live, complains, "There's not a damned thing here but hope," Rhy answers, "That's a good deal" (18). Several minutes later, when Rhy's neighbor and friend Bixie laments, "I'm so tired of this hope to-day—and despair to-morrow. How I hate, hate, hate this wretched hole!" again Rhy offers positively, "I *love* it" (21). What is most important is the positive effect of Rhy's boundless energy—she and her brothers have survived; Rhy has successfully kept her family from disintegrating.

Rhy is, in the words of Arthur Hobson Quinn, "an active force"[55] in this play. As such, she represents a challenge to the traditional gender constructions that had informed character development especially as it appeared in nineteenth-century melodrama. No mere passive "vessel of virtue" that the melodramatic hero is awarded in recompense for his chivalrous actions, Rhy transcends narrow gender definitions. While feminine enough to attract two gallant suitors, she is also described as boyish on several occasions.[56] Rhy is, in short, an able, self-reliant individual. Crothers's feminism comes to the fore in this western woman character, but interestingly, the playwright's feminism is somewhat allayed for eastern audiences because Rhy's independence can be understood as a product of her western context. Indeed, Rhy very subtlety manifests some of the tomboy attributes that one could see more boldly presented in Bret Harte's M'liss, Joaquin Miller's Carrots, DeMille and Barnard's Possy Burroughs, and Belasco's "Girl."

The complex symbiosis of feminism and Turner-like analysis that underlies the play is extremely apparent in what was perhaps its most crucial scene: the Act III scene when Rhy comes unattended to Berresford's rooms late at night. After Mrs. Bix's dinner party, Rhy goes to Berresford's cabin to ask him to release her from an oath that he challenged her to take while they were alone at Mrs. Bix's party—an oath that bound her to keep secret the information he then confessed to her about purchasing Mrs. Bix's mine. Sworn to silence, she is unable to defend herself when Steve becomes suspicious that she betrayed his discovery of the possible value of the Bix mine to his rival Berresford.

Regardless of the motivation, a young woman's visiting a young man's private quarters late at night was deemed highly inappropriate by Victorian traditionalists. Such a view had been pivotal in Louis Shipman's dramatization of Remington's *John Ermine of the Yellowstone*. In that play, produced three years earlier, Ermine exhibited sensitivity to Katherine's precarious situation when their illicit interview was suddenly interrupted by the arrival of his rival for Katherine's hand. Ermine's actions demonstrated his right to the title of "natural gentleman," as well as his growing awareness of civilized values, and consequently, made it possible for audiences to accept the savage westerner Ermine as a proper mate for a daughter of the civilized East at play's end. In short, that play's final resolution hinged on the fact that characters and audiences alike were troubled by Katherine's conduct, which was problematic not because her motives were without virtue, but because it was an unacceptable breech of gender decorum.

In Crothers's play, Rhy rejects Berresford's assessment that she has compromised herself by coming to his cabin:

> It's true then—all women must be afraid. I haven't believed it. I've thought we could do anything that was *right* in *itself.* I *still* think it! I *know* it! A good woman hasn't anything to be afraid of. Nothing can make a thing wrong that's really right. I'm not afraid of the *world*—it's *you*—*you* who can't understand. (77)

Refusing to be circumscribed by appearance and rejecting the hypocrisy that mediates or manipulates appearance, Rhy believes in frank, unmediated actions. A western disdain for eastern conventions and machinations blends here with a feminist repudiation of the double standard. Rhy's belief that her truth outweighs appearance is tested a moment later when Steve knocks on Berresford's door. Unlike Katherine, who hid behind a door in *John Ermine of the Yellowstone*, Rhy refuses to hide. When Berresford tries to change her mind, she challenges Berresford: "Open the door, or I will" (78).

Unfortunately, Steve interprets Rhy's presence in Berresford's room as evidence that Berresford and Rhy are intimately involved. Hoping to protect her honor, he insists that she agree to marry Berresford. Rhy's response to this demand is a demand of her own—that she be allowed to defend her own honor: "Don't you dare to speak of my honor and my good name!... Don't you dare to say you'll 'take care of it.' My honor! Do you think it's in your hands? It's in my own and I'll take care of it, and of everyone who *belongs* to me. I don't need you—either of you. 'Love—protection—trust!' Why I have to fight you both" (81). Here, western independence and feminism converge in an attack on the traditional moral sensibility, which had been at the heart of melodramas like Shipman's *John Ermine of the Yellowstone*. What is most interesting about this declaration of independence is that it had the full support of New York theater critics, like the *New York Times* reviewer who wrote that this was "a fresh and interesting scene, in which the young woman, for once, dominates the situation."[57] Other New York critics expressed similar relief that Crothers had departed from the old tired conventions that determined the outcomes of similar scenes in the past.[58] More important, these endorsements suggest that the moral assumptions that underlay conventional melodramas of the period were no longer the moral assumptions held by the elite audiences of the Broadway theater.

It is, however, possible that Rhy's assertiveness at the end of Act III was acceptable to audiences and critics because, in Act IV, taking place the next morning, she seems to retreat from it. She reclaims Clem by convincing him not to run off to Salt Lake City, but to stay and defend her from the ugly gossip that will result from her late-night visit to Berresford's cabin. While she may not truly need Clem's protection any more than she needed Berresford's or Steve's at the end of Act III, she is willing to act the role of the needy woman to keep Clem on the straight and narrow path. A further retreat comes when Steve arrives shortly thereafter. Having declared her independence from Steve at the end of Act III, Rhy acquiesces in Act IV. She confesses her heartfelt love for him and demands his trusting love in return, and Steve relents—only to be rewarded for his new unquestioning devotion by hearing from Clem that it was Clem and not Rhy who had betrayed him.

Despite Rhy's declaration of independence at the end of Act III, at the end of Act IV she and Steve are brought together. Again, as in other turn-of-the-century frontier plays, the marriage of hero and heroine represents the promise for a hopeful future. The marriage here, however, is not a marriage of characters clearly representing East and West (as in *The Virginian* or *The Great Divide*), nor is it a marriage of two characters deeply rooted in the East (as in the case of *The Cowboy and the Lady* or *The Squaw Man*). At the start of the play, Rhy has already broken free of her eastern roots to manifest all the positive traits that Turner attributed to the western experience, and Steve, who may be at ease among easterners, is still a Westerner—even if the Kansas City from which he comes is not a wild frontier. In short, here is a marriage of two characters closely associated with the West. In the end, Rhy's protofeminist perspective is absorbed within the play's presentation of frontier process; it is a natural corollary of a healthy western sensibility. Rhy is no "man-woman," but merely a western woman who ultimately finds joy with a western man. Both characters come from Anglo-Saxon stock, and while both characters have roots in civilization, both have been reinvigorated by life in the frontier West and now fully identify with that region.

In focusing on the westernness of her heroine and her hero, Crothers's play represents the reversal of Fitch's *The Cowboy and the Lady*. In that play, the final marriage of two eastern characters heralded the ultimate triumph of eastern order over western spontaneity. In Crothers's play, the western characters to a certain extent liberate themselves from the archaic repressive structures that dominate eastern social life. In this regard, Rhy, despite her retreat in Act IV, frees herself from the tyranny of antiquated social conventions that force women into passive roles. Steve, by embracing Rhy in a trusting love at play's end, also demonstrates a freedom from outdated prejudices.

While Rhy and Steve rise above restrictive eastern social conventions and prejudices, their ability to free themselves from an economic dependency on eastern financial structures is not certain. Rhy and Steve's union at play's end sweeps away all other concerns, including what had been a recurring if considerably downplayed preoccupation throughout the play with eastern capital. To be sure, Bixie had hoped to sell her mine to Trenholm's eastern syndicate so she could return to the East, but Steve too had hoped to convince Trenholm to invest in his mine. He was aware that the low grade of ore he discovered would require eastern financial investments to make his mine viable.[59] At play's end, no capital seems forthcoming, and Trenholn, who had been looking for good investment possibilities in the West, has gone home empty-handed. In other words, the union of Rhy and Steve may represent a victory of western individualism and tolerance over eastern conventions and restraint, but the certainty of this victory is somewhat in question. Steve and Rhy will need eastern capital to put their marriage on a stable footing.

Here, then, is an ambivalence similar to that which underlies Moody's play. Western individualism is celebrated only by ignoring the complex eastern socioeconomic structures on which it is built. As in the case of Moody's play, this blindness in the script has a strange parallel in the play's production history. Just as Moody had sought to avoid the power of the monopolistic theater Syndicate, so did Crothers. As Lois Gottlieb points out, "Crothers seems to have consciously avoided the Syndicate" by turning to "the independently owned Madison Square Theater."[60] As in Moody's case, Crothers's gesture on behalf of individual freedom had less of an impact in the real world than did western individualism in the fictitious world of *The Three of Us*, but even in Crothers's fictitious world, independent, individual action was severely limited. In short, Crothers's gesture on behalf of the theater artist's struggle against theater monopolies would no more change the mode of theater production than Rhy and Steve's stance against eastern social conventions would free them from a dependence on eastern capital.

Despite these ironies, wishful thinking held sway among the prosperous audiences attending Crothers's play, and consequently, spectators could enjoy the assertion of independence on which Crothers's play ends. After all, for audiences attending New York City's first-class Broadway theaters in 1906, the accomplishments of the rising managerial elite were understandable in terms of individual self-expression and merit. For these generally well-to-do viewers, who were largely a part of that new managerial class, the economic achievements of this class exemplified the positive possibilities of an unfettered—or at least only slightly fettered—but inherently moral individualism. From the perspective of the twenty-first century, this conflation of individual success and corporate success may appear naive, but it was not deemed so in the early twentieth century. To be sure, one might make the claim that glorifying the rugged frontier hero was a way of masking the true socioeconomic forces driving American industrial expansion.

In the ruggedly individualistic protagonists of Moody's *The Great Divide* and Crothers's *The Three of Us*, we see amalgams of romantic idealism and pragmatic realism. Yet these characters are unlike many of the idealized heroes and heroines of early-nineteenth-century melodramas. The characters of these earlier melodramas were self-determining entities defined by moral attitudes and largely unaffected by their social environments; however, Moody and Crothers give us heroic characters who not only lack the moral purity and definition of earlier melodramatic heroes and heroines, but also are complexly tied to their environments, and as such are in a constant process of becoming. Like Wister and La Shelle, Royle, and Belasco before them, Moody and Crothers offer us characters who are products of a combination of romance and science, and plays that blend old-style melodrama and realism, but here the balance more fully embraces the kind of scientific realism described by Vernon Lewis Parrington.[61] Both Moody and Crothers adhere more emphatically to this scientific realism than did their predecessors, but neither yields up the climactic romantic assertion of optimism that characterized the earlier plays. Moody's *The Great Divide* and Crothers's *The Three of Us* represent a truth about experience that is indistinguishable from ideology, but this ideological dimension was not apparent to viewers who celebrated these plays as key transitions from melodrama to the new realism. Indeed, it is because these plays more successfully created the illusion of objective reality that the truth they represented seemed to hold so much more weight for 1906 Broadway audiences than did Thomas's, Wister/La Shelle's, Royle's, and Belasco's apparently less believable if also popular frontier melodramas.

Conclusion

William Vaughn Moody in *The Great Divide* and Rachel Crothers in *The Three of Us* have much in common with respect to how they envisioned the impact of the frontier experience on U.S. culture and society. To be sure, there are differences in how these two playwrights represented the western frontier process. Moody's vision, like that of Frederick Jackson Turner, revolves around the heroic actions of the white male. Crothers, on the other hand, merges a Turner-like frontier analysis with a protofeminist perspective. Despite this significant difference, the reliance on a Turner-like perspective links the two plays. In fact, a vision of the western experience, which shares a conceptual foundation with a Turner-like perspective, underlies all eight plays treated in this study. As in Turner's classic essay "The Significance of the Frontier in American History," oppositions such as East/West, civilization/savagery, masculine/feminine, freedom/constraint, and individual/community define the parameters within which turn-of-the-century playwrights treated the "western experience."

As Fitch, Thomas, Shipman, La Shelle/Wister, Royle, Belasco, Moody, and Crothers tried to come to grips with the frontier experience, by necessity they took up Turner's language, the language of the turn-of-the-century frontier discourse. After all, the frontier experience at the time these playwrights wrote was defined and primarily existed in terms of the language of this discourse. Consequently, in writing frontier dramas for New York's first-class theater, all of these playwrights entered into a discursive field that had a certain regularity. This is true even though the binaries that are so significant to this field are not always understood in identical fashions. The meaning of especially key concepts like "civilization" and "savagery" slip and slide from one play to the next. In short, the regularity of the field on which all eight plays emerge was flexible enough to allow each playwright to have some impact on the exact parameters of the field as it developed in time—that is, each of the eight frontier plays discussed in this study was not only molded by the frontier western discursive field, but also contributed to the shaping of that discursive field.

One aspect of the regularity circumscribing all eight plays is the fact that all envision frontier experience as a temporal evolutionary process.[1] In each play, the presentation of this process culminates with a concluding marriage or union of hero and heroine, a union that symbolizes some resolution of the opposition of eastern civilization and western savagery. Sometimes the culminating marriage of hero and heroine represents a union in which two representatives of eastern civilization are joined, a union celebrating the positive future that results from the victory of civilized discipline over the dangers of western savagery. Sometimes this marriage is a more narrowly Turner-like marriage of East and West, civilization and savagery, a marriage that represents the climax of an historical process tracing the eastern pioneers' gradual adaptation to the rigors of the West while simultaneously imposing civilized order on that savage wilderness. Sometimes it is a marriage of two characters associated with the West, a marriage celebrating a future in which the weaknesses of an overrefined eastern civilization have been overcome. What is important here is that all three variations offer interpretations of the frontier experience in which a higher form of American identity arises from the confrontation of civilization and savagery. To be sure, in each of the plays the concluding "marriage" is meant to actualize a future that promises a more fulfilling level of existence than was available in the past.

Just as Turner employed a language similar to that utilized by natural scientists to describe an evolutionary development in time, so these playwrights arranged their plots to represent action that can be understood as analogous to evolutionary process. The actual plot structures of these plays are significant in the sense that they provide audiences with patterns by which they might understand and order their own more random experiences of the world. These patterns of actions or events are, then, suggestive of larger historical patterns of action/events. Consequently, the characters of these plays may appear to be real, but they also take on allegorical significance. The heroes and heroines of these plays epitomize what Vernon Lewis Parrington described in the late 1920s when he wrote that in the "new realistic" writing, "the individual, thus conceived of socially and politically, is no longer an isolated, self-determining entity, but a vehicle through which is carried the stream of life, with a past behind and a future before. He is a portion of the total scheme of things, tied by a thousand invisible threads to the encompassing whole."[2] In short, the characters, who appear like specific, everyday individuals, are not only molded by their environments, but also subsumed within larger social, historical processes. In fact, they embody these processes. To the extent that they function on both realistic and allegorical plains, these characters represent historical dimensions not seen in earlier melodramas. The larger-than-life, self-reliant autonomous characters of melodrama no longer stand outside history as rarified embodiments of good and evil, but are integrated into larger historical evolutionary transformations.

Still, all eight plays were originally conceived within the parameters of a theater, which in 1900 continued to be dominated by a melodramatic sensibility. The different ways in which these plays negotiate the demands of melodrama, however, significantly distinguishes them from each other. While the first four plays depended more heavily on melodramatic devices, Royle and Belasco edged away from melodrama. Neither Royle's *The Squaw Man* nor Belasco's *The Girl of the Golden West* focused primarily on the hero-villain conflict as a means of pushing the action forward. In fact, both do without traditional villains, focusing primarily on the interactions of more complex, multifaceted characters to move the plot. In both plays, the title characters, Royle's Squaw Man and Belasco's Girl, respond more to their social/cultural contexts than they do to the actions of specific antagonists. In this regard, both plays focus more fully than the earlier plays on setting characters within their particular environments—albeit in Belasco's case, this environment, in typical Belasco fashion, is more romanticized than in Royle's play. In these plays characters lose their independence from the environment; the setting is carefully manipulated to suggest its impact on the characters. Setting is, therefore, less a colorful background that provides the occasion for exotic costumes than it is an important force molding the actions of the characters. This shift is in line with the tendency of late-nineteenth- and early-twentieth-century theater practitioners to embrace what they may have thought of as "realistic," "naturalistic," and "scientific" approaches to experience.

Moody's *The Great Divide* and Crothers's *The Three of Us* offer even more nuanced characters, as well as simpler and more recognizably matter-of-fact plots than do Royle in *The Squaw Man* and Belasco in *The Girl of the Golden West*. Moody's and Crothers's characters more fully assimilate historical process and geographical background than was the case in Belasco's and Royle's plays; that is, character is even more clearly defined as the intersection of temporal and spatial variables, and these variables are more instrumental in pushing action forward than the conflict of good and evil, heroism and villainy, of earlier melodramas. This focus on the careful development of temporal and spatial variables contributes to the specificity of environment and setting, which is the hallmark of turn-of-the-century realism. Consequently, these last two plays more than the other six discussed in this study are meant to be viewed as seamless representations of reality. While contemporary critics commented on the overly theatrical devices marking the first six plays, this is much less the case with reviewers of Moody's and Crothers's two plays. Rather than impose a shape on action that highlights the distinction between hero and villain, these plays, even more than Royle's and Belasco's, call attention to the ambivalence and uncertainty of the main characters. Moral complexity underlies characters like Moody's Ghent and Ruth as well as Crothers's Rhy and Steve, and this moral complexity helps to make them more personable and lifelike to audience members who can see their own ambivalence mirrored in these characters.

In *The Great Divide* and *The Three of Us*, more than in the earlier works, the power of the "fourth wall" is manifested. This separation lent validity to the illusion that viewers were to observe events occurring onstage as if they were looking at an exact mirror image of happenings in the world outside the theater. Here, the machinery of theater was for the most part hidden, and audiences were to witness realistic looking events with the objectivity, if not the lack of passion, of scientists observing experiments.[3] In such a representational approach to theater, there is increasingly less space (in the theater or in the play) from which passively viewing audiences can challenge the mirror representation offered by the play. Insofar as their plays approach what was to appear as a "seamless representation of the real world," Moody and Crothers naturalize the happenings and characters presented. Because what is represented is to look real—a representation with the subtlety of life in which moral oppositions are muted—it may be perceived by audiences as the equivalent to life. In this regard, these theater events can take on an undeserved authority for audiences and can consequently become significant tools for the socialization of audience members. These plays can provide a means by which audience members shape their own experiences of the real world. In other words, these frontier plays facilitate the incorporation of audience members into the turn-of-the-century frontier western discursive field; that is, these plays make it easy for audience members to assimilate the parameters of this discursive field, and to utilize it as a grid by which they might interpret their own experiences.

The shift in form that brought *The Great Divide* and *The Three of Us* especially close to the new realistic dramaturgy appropriately corresponds with the content of turn-of-the-century frontier plays. The evolutionary progress represented by the action of each of the eight plays treated in this study is seemingly evidenced by the development within the group of what has come to be seen as formal realism—that is, the plays each represent an evolutionary historical development even as they as a group manifest an evolutionary development. More specifically, the movement from a representation that was melodramatic in nature to one that has been described in terms of a more realistic modern drama could be seen as exemplifying for audiences the kind of evolutionary progress that drives the action of each of the eight plays. Evolution as a scientific truth and as a cultural ideal is highlighted by the content of these plays, as well as by the shift in form that these plays as a group illustrate. In this regard, the fact that both Moody's *The Great Divide* and Crothers's *The Three of Us* represent a challenge to and the historical transcendence of melodrama suggests why these two plays may be understood as especially culminating works. In these plays, form and content are closely integrated to offer dramatizations of the kind of evolutionary progress that epitomized the turn-of-the-century approach to the western frontier. These two plays not only offer action that dramatizes the kind of shift that Parrington described, but also in their appropriation of new realistic elements, these plays exemplified the kind of evolutionary development that early-twentieth-century audiences celebrated.

Twenty-first-century audiences, however, may not be as convinced that evolutionary change in theatrical and dramaturgical conventions is inevitable. For these contemporary viewers, there is no guarantee that one dramaturgy is a higher form than the one that historically precedes it. To be sure, both Moody's and Crothers's plays offered enthusiastically confident pictures of the development of American culture and society. In both plays, particularly Moody's, optimism is based on an unquestioned faith in the proposition that the flux and flow of life can be understood as an evolution from lesser to higher forms. Although this proposition is not so readily affirmed in the twenty-first century, it was taken as a truism in the late nineteenth and early twentieth centuries. In embracing and conveying this truism, both Moody, with his cosmic and religious interests, and Crothers, who espoused a proto-feminist perspective, transcended their individual preoccupations to create dramas that were extremely successful with audiences who were anything but nonconventional. One might conclude that *The Great Divide* and *The Three of Us* succeeded because they skirted hard truths regarding tensions between the individual and society, as well as between differing gender, class, and racial ideologies. Such truths had no place in the turn-of-the-century frontier discourse. These plays spoke to their times, offering the kind of affirmation that affluent Broadway audiences sought in the decade after the Spanish-American War, a decade during which Turner's thesis provided a blueprint for progressive prosperity even as President Theodore Roosevelt led the march toward a grandiose future. Indeed, these two plays do something very similar to what Turner did in his famous 1893 thesis. They represent a convergence of nineteenth-century American idealism—an idealism that exalted the exceptional nature of the American individual and American institutions—with the popular late-nineteenth and early-twentieth-century pseudoscientific assumptions of social Darwinism; that is, these plays seemed to ground optimism in the certainty of science. For Crothers and especially Moody, this marriage of an American idealism and a Darwinian scientific approach can be seen as a surprisingly unproblematic marriage of melodramatic absolutism and realistic empiricism.

* * *

Ironically, plays like *The Great Divide* and *The Three of Us* appeared on New York City stages even as their place in the theater disappeared. With the coming of film and its meteoric rise as a major medium of representation throughout America, frontier melodrama on the stage began to give way to screen Westerns. The screen, after all, offered certain advantages over the stage in the presentation of the frontier. For one, the scenic flexibility of film made it possible to capture the size and wonder of the western environment. The West's panoramic vistas, the vast spaces, could be captured on the screen more easily than they could ever be on stage. Signature Western movie locations gave a feel for the wide-open spaces that the stage could only suggest. While the stage veered away from the spectacular action scenes that could be more masterfully presented in film, these sequences would be the hallmark of cinematic directors of Westerns like John Ford, who almost single-handedly created the full-length Western feature film. Moreover, movies could do for Westerns what the stage could never do—vividly examine the relationship of individual to environment. In the theater, this tension had been transformed into an interrelationship of living characters. Even if the human presence of live actors was lost, the Western movie could treat the tension between individual pioneer and wilderness setting in a literal fashion that was not possible on the stage.

The stage representation of the confrontation of civilization and savagery as a conflict between characters did not, however, disappear in the cinema. The way in which Moody, Wister, and others used gender to convey the conflict of civilization and savagery was carried into the movies as many of their plays, including *Arizona*, *The Girl of the Golden West*, *Squaw Man*, and *The Great Divide* moved from stage to screen. Even in a mid-twentieth-century movie classic like *High Noon* (1952), the tension between savagery and civilization is carried through the gender tensions that arise between a realistic lawman and his idealistic Quaker wife, as well as between the wife and the whole male-dominated town that is the site of the action. The cinema might have borrowed the plot lines and characters of the stage, but the inexpensiveness with which the movies could disseminate the Western tale made it difficult for frontier stage melodramas to compete with movie Westerns. To be sure, in the late twentieth and early twenty-first centuries, even the Western movie seems to have lost much of its cultural power. The golden age of the movie Western may indeed be past, but the genre has not died. Every few years a new successful Western will recall the past glory years.

While the Western film genre lives on even if in a massively revised form, it is interesting that the frontier western discourse out of which it originated has been challenged. Over the past quarter-century, a new approach, a new discursive field dealing with the western past has been opened up: the "New Western History" of Patricia Limerick, Richard White, Donald Worster, William Cronon, and many others.[4] While revisionists appeared on the scene well before this new generation of historians, they generally remained on the same field as the old frontier western writers and artists. The focus was less on changing the parameters of the old frontier discourse than it was in rereading the hierarchical alignments. The white pioneers still confronted a wilderness West, but in films like *Little Big Man* (1970), *Soldier Blue* (1970), and even the more recent *Dances with Wolves* (1990), as well as the "sci-fi Western" 3-D epic *Avatar* (2009), these white pioneers become the dangerous savages recklessly destroying a more humanely civilized Indian world.

With the New Western Historians, things change. The West is no longer seen as the wild Old West, and the very notion of frontier loses its significance as a governing concept. One can see the discursive shift exemplified by New Western Historians and their fellow travelers as a shift from frontier studies to regional studies. The frame of reference that had been linear, progressive, evolutionary history gave way to an analysis that in many ways was much more spatial than temporal. The focus is less on whites supplanting Native Americans as they move westward across the continent than on the continuous and complex interactions of divergent populations in the trans-Mississippi continental United States. The East-West axis of frontier studies is obliterated as participants on this new field of discourse not only study the migration of Euro-Americans westward, but also of Asian-Americans eastward to "gold mountain," Latin-Americans northward to "el norte," and Native Americans who moved east, west, north, and south within the region described as the American West. In this multiracial, multiethnic complex, heterogeneous regional discourse, concepts like frontier, frontier development, and civilization and savagery lose their earlier meanings.

Despite this discursive shift, old ways of seeing and knowing hold on. Controversies such as that surrounding the 1991 Smithsonian "The West as America" exhibit suggest that a conflict of discourses, with the participants in the respective discourses totally unable to engage each other for lack of a common language, were opened on the academic and institutional level. No such conflict, however, undermines the popular cultural view of the frontier. Films like *Dances with Wolves* and *Avatar* shift the weight of the terms, but the power of "frontier" and "civilization and savagery" remain potent in popular culture. These terms still hold sway in American perceptions of themselves—at least as they manifest themselves in domestic politics and foreign affairs. Whether we fight in Vietnam or Iraq or Afghanistan, we still partially justify our actions as a struggle of civilization with savagery. Many of us still believe that the victory will be ours, because while we are "civilized," we also have the frontier-born savage vigor that our enemies lack. We can beat the lowly "savages" at their own game.[5] In the early years of the twenty-first century, we have yet to free ourselves of a way of seeing the world, which very well might spell disaster for our national hopes and dreams.

Notes

INTRODUCTION

1. See Elliott West, "Selling of the Myth: Western Images in Advertising," *Wanted Dead or Alive: The American West in Popular Culture*, ed. Richard Aquila (Urbana: University of Illinois Press, 1996), 283.
2. Regarding this campaign, see, for instance, Loren Stein, "How to Fight Big Tobacco and Win," A Healthy Me, 2001 Consumer Health Interactive, June 10, 2009, http://www.ahealthyme.com/topic/bigtobacco.
3. See Henry Nash Smith, *Virgin Land: The American West as Symbol and Myth* (1950; Cambridge, MA: Harvard University Press, 1978); Leslie Fiedler, *The Return of the Vanishing American* (New York: Stein and Day, 1968); Richard Slotkin, *Regeneration Through Violence: The Mythology of the American Frontier, 1600–1860* (Middletown, CT: Wesleyan University Press, 1973); Slotkin, *The Fatal Environment: The Myth of the Frontier in the Age of Industrialization, 1800–1890* (Middletown, CT: Wesleyan University Press, 1985); Slotkin, *Gunfighter Nation: The Myth of the Frontier in Twentieth-Century America* (New York: Atheneum, 1992); Annette Kolodny, *The Lay of the Land: Metaphor as Experience and History in American Life and Letters* (Chapel Hill: University of North Carolina Press, 1975); John G. Cawelti, *The Six-Gun Mystique*, 2nd ed. (Bowling Green, OH: Bowling Green State University Popular Press, 1984); Jane Tompkins, *West of Everything: The Inner Life of Westerns* (New York: Oxford University Press, 1992).
4. For instance, see Smith; Fiedler; Slotkin, *Regeneration Through Violence*; Kolodny.
5. For instance, see Smith again; Cawelti; Tompkins; Slotkin, *Gunfighter Nation*.
6. Stuart Wallace Hyde, "The Representation of the West in American Drama from 1849 to 1917," diss., Stanford, 1954.
7. Rosemarie Katherine Bank, "Rhetorical, Dramatic, Theatrical, and Social Contexts of Selected American Frontier Plays, 1871 to 1906," diss., University of Iowa, 1972.

8. Bank, 6.
9. Roger A. Hall, *Performing the American Frontier, 1870–1906* (Cambridge: Cambridge University Press, 2001).
10. Discussing this turn-of-the-century popular melodrama, especially of "the 10. 20. 30." variety, Montrose J. Moses referred specifically to the American Theatre on Eighth Avenue and the Thalia Theatre in the Bowery. See, *The American Dramatist* (Boston: Little, 1925; New York: Benjamin Blom, 1964), 298.
11. See Hall, Chapter 6, "Dominance: 1899–1906," 186–225.
12. For instance, see Patricia Nelson Limerick, *The Legacy of Conquest: The Unbroken Past of the American West* (New York: Norton, 1987), and Richard White, *"It's Your Misfortune and None of My Own": A New History of the American West* (Norman: University of Oklahoma Press, 1991).
13. Robert Rogers, *Ponteach: Or the Savages of America, A Tragedy*, with an introduction and a biography of the author by Allan Nevins (Chicago: Caxton Club, 1914), 201.
14. Slotkin, *Regeneration Through Violence*, 235.
15. The significance of Pocahontas for the early American sense of national identity is explored in Susan Scheckel, "Domesticating the Drama of Conquest: Pocahontas on the Popular Stage," in *The Insistence of the Indian: Race and Nationalism in Nineteenth-Century American Culture* (Princeton, NJ: Princeton University Press, 1998), 41–69.
16. Richard Moody, *America Takes the Stage: Romanticism in American Drama and Theatre, 1750–1900* (Bloomington: Indiana University Press, 1955), 105.
17. The complex relation between the representation of the Native American in Euro-American culture and the "true nature" of Native Americans is the subject of landmark studies like Roy Harvey Pearce, *Savagism and Civilization: A Study of the Indian and the American Mind* (Baltimore: John Hopkins Press, 1953, 1965) and Robert F. Berkhofer, Jr., *The White Man's Indian: Images of the American Indian from Columbus to the Present* (New York: Vintage Books, 1979). In this regard, also see Rosemary K. Bank, "Staging the 'Native': Making History in American Theatre Culture, 1828–1838," *Theatre Journal* 45.4 (1993), 461–486, and Bank, "Representing History: Performing the Columbian Exposition," *Theatre Journal* 54.4 (2002), 589–606.
18. Pearce suggests that playwrights like Stone were actually caught between two traditions. On the one hand, his Metamora embodied elements of the Noble Savage, the product of the romantic "primitivistic literary tradition"; on the other, Stone incorporated into his play elements of the savagism tradition, which held that the Indian was the product of an inferior stage in the development of the human race (176–78).
19. For instance, see Arthur Hobson Quinn, *A History of the American Drama: From the Civil War to the Present Day*, vol. I (New York: Appleton-Century-Crofts, Inc., 1936), 105; Moody, 174.

20. At least this was the view of audiences in the 1830s. In this regard, see James Tidwell's introduction to James Kirke Paulding, *The Lion of the West*, revised by John Augustus Stone and William Bayle Bernard and edited by James N. Tidwell (Stanford, CA: Stanford University Press, 1954), 7–8.
21. Hyde, 29.
22. In "The Representation of the West in American Drama from 1849 to 1917," Stuart Wallace Hyde has documented the increase of Western plays in the years after 1870 by charting the number of Western plays written each year between 1849 and 1917 (see Chart #1, p. 433). Hyde discusses the increase of Western plays after 1870 on pages 186–89. Also see Bank, "Rhetorical, Dramatic, Theatrical, and Social Contexts," 2, 105–06, 148–50, and Hall, 16–20.
23. In this regard, see Rosemarie Bank, "Frontier Melodrama," in *Theatre West: Image and Impact, Dutch Quarterly Review Studies in Literature 7*, ed. Dunbar H. Ogden with Douglas McDermott and Robert K. Sarlós (Amsterdam: Rodopi, 1990), 152, and Bank, "Historical, Dramatic, Theatrical, and Social Contexts," 105–6.
24. Regarding "dry land farming," see Frieda Knobloch, *The Culture of Wilderness: Agriculture as Colonization in the American West* (Chapel Hill: University of North Carolina Press, 1996), 62–66.
25. See Samuel Eliot Morison and Henry Steele Commager, *The Growth of the American Republic*, vol. II, 5th ed. (New York: Oxford University, 1962), 133–35, 152–58. For another and somewhat more recent discussion of Western migration in the nineteenth century, see Richard White, 183–211.
26. This fact not only is noted by Frederick Jackson Turner, but also inspired his famous essay "The Significance of the Frontier in American History," in *The Frontier in American History* (Tucson: University of Arizona Press, 1986), 1.
27. In *The Fatal Environment*, Richard Slotkin discusses the way in which frontier events were communicated by the new popular media, especially how frontier events could be appropriated for the political agenda of a new managerial class (477-98).
28. Hyde concluded his study of frontier plays in 1917, and in "Rhetorical, Dramatic, Theatrical, and Social Contexts," Bank wrote that "frontier plays... continued to be written in numbers until the vogue for them died out in the legitimate theatre about 1920" (3).
29. In regard to the unity of a discourse, Michel Foucault writes: "[I]f there really is a unity, it does not lie in the visible, horizontal coherence of the elements formed; it resides, well anterior to their formation, in the system that makes possible and governs that formation.... By system of formation, then, I mean a complex group of relations that function as a rule: it lays down what must be related, in a particular discursive practice, for such and such an enunciation to be made, for such and such a concept to be used, for such and such a strategy to be organized" [*The Archeology of Knowledge*, trans. by A.M. Sheridan Smith

(New York: Pantheon, 1972), 72–4]. Foucault's analysis of discourse in *The Archeology of Knowledge* has been very significant for the discussion of discourse set forth here.
30. Foucault, 125.
31. Foucault, 209.
32. Is a "frontier" to be seen as the margin or edge of a positive center, or is it to be seen as the area or line between two states, as in the case of Europe? Is it a place or a process? Patricia Limerick pursues such conceptual problems. See, for instance, Limerick, 23–7.
33. Frederick Jackson Turner, 3.
34. In this regard, Turner wrote in a letter to Merle Curti that "[A]s you know, the 'West,' with which I dealt, was a process rather than a fixed geographical region: it began with the Atlantic Coast; and it emphasized the way in which the East colonized the West, and how the 'West,' as it stood at any given period affected the development and ideas of the older areas of the East...." [quoted by Wilbur Jacobs in "Frederick Jackson Turner," *The American West Magazine* 1.1 (1964), 32].
35. Various scholars have explored the significance of the fact that both Turner and Buffalo Bill were associated with the Columbian Exposition in Chicago. See Ann Fabian, "History of the Masses: Commercializing the Western Past," in *Under an Open Sky: Rethinking America's Western Past*, eds. William Cronon, George Miles, Jay Gitlin (New York: Norton, 1992), 223–238; Richard White, "Frederick Jackson Turner and Buffalo Bill," in *The Frontier in American Culture*, ed. James R. Grossman (Berkeley: University of California Press, 1994), 6–65; and Bank, "Representing History: Performing the Columbian Exposition."
36. Regarding Turner's reviews of Roosevelt's *Winning of the West*, see Ray Allen Billington, *Frederick Jackson Turner: Historian, Scholar, Teacher* (New York: Oxford University Press, 1973), 83–84 and 176–77, and Allan G. Bogue, *Frederick Jackson Turner: Strange Roads Going Down* (Norman: University of Oklahoma Press, 1998), 87–88 and 137–39.
37. Augustus Thomas, *The Print of My Remembrance* (New York: Scribner's, 1922), 336, 344.
38. Darwin Payne, *Owen Wister: Chronicler of the West, Gentleman of the West* (Dallas: Southern Methodist University Press, 1985), 163–4.
39. Frank P. Morse, *Backstage with Henry Miller* (New York: Dutton, 1938), 277.
40. In describing discourse as a "field," Foucault, in his historical analysis of discourse, which he calls "archeology," may seem to be substituting a spatial order for the temporal one that had previously dominated the history of ideas and culture. Consequently, he could be accused of applying a synchronic structuralist methodology to historical study—a claim that he rejected. In fact, Foucault called attention to the ways in which his analysis of discourse

allowed for and depended on a temporal dimension. He accepted the fact that discourse is marked by "temporal vectors of derivation" (169)—that is, that some ideas derive from others in a chronological sequence— and additionally maintained that discourse engages "external" events, which in turn impose their temporality on discourse. See Foucault, 167–69.
41. Foucault, 68.
42. Foucault challenged dichotomies like cause and effect, internal and external, and base and superstructure (where the second terms are construed as the discursive products of the first nondiscursive agents or sources). More important in this context, Foucault dispensed with the dualism ideology/truth—suggesting that "ideology" is a useless concept if it refers only to that which isn't "true." In this regard, in "Truth and Power," in *Power/Knowledge: Selected Interviews and Other Writings 1972–1977*, ed. Colin Gordon, trans. Colin Gordon, Leo Marshall, John Mepham, Kate Soper (New York: Pantheon, 1980), he wrote: "I believe that the problem does not consist in drawing the line between that in a discourse which falls under the category of scientificity or truth, and that which comes under some other category, but in seeing historically how effects of truth are produced within discourses which in themselves are neither true nor false" (118).
43. While Gramsci does not abandon Marxist materialistic determinism, he uses the concept of "hegemony" to explain and explore the problematics of "political consciousness" and "progressive self-consciousness." For instance, see Antonio Gramsci, "The Study of Philosophy and of Historical Materialism," in *The Modern Prince and Other Writings*, trans. Louis Marks (New York: International Publishers, 1957), 66–67.
44. The shift from late-nineteenth-/early-twentieth-century frontier discourse to late-twentieth-/early-twenty-first-century frontier discourse is exemplified by the tension between the "old triumphal frontier history" and the "New Western History" expressed by the likes of Patricia Limerick and Richard White in *Trails: Toward a New Western History*, ed. Patricia Nelson Limerick, Clyde A. Milner II, and Charles E. Ranken (Lawrence: University Press of Kansas, 1992). The way in which the "New Western Historians" restructured the field of Western history is most obvious in how they address the concept of "frontier," which Limerick humorously called the "F-word" ("The Adventures of the Frontier in the Twentieth Century," in *The Frontier in American Culture*, 72). Understanding Turner's "frontier" as a process, Limerick changes the parameters of the field by "choosing to stress place more than process" (Limerick, *The Legacy of Conquest*, 26). Replacing the term "frontier" with a term like "region" only begins to suggest the paradigm shift underlying the new discourse. Also see Richard White, *"It's Your Misfortune and None of My Own": A History of the American West* (Norman: University of Oklahoma Press, 1991). For a discussion of various aspects—both pro and con—of New

Western History, see *The New Western History: The Territory Ahead*, ed. Forrest G. Robinson (Tucson: University of Arizona Press, 1997).
45. Richard Slotkin, "Myth and the Production of History," in *Ideology and Classic American Literature*, ed. Sacvan Bercovitch and Myra Jehlen (Cambridge: Cambridge University Press, 1986), 82.
46. Slotkin, "Myth and the Production of History," 82.
47. Stephen Greenblatt, *Shakespearean Negotiations: The Circulation of Social Energy in Renaissance England* (Berkeley: University of California Press, 1988), 8.
48. Greenblatt's comments on Hamlet's dictum seem relevant in this regard. Citing Hamlet's words, "To hold, as 'twere, the mirror up to nature: to show virtue her feature, scorn her own image, and the vary age and body of the time his form and pressure," Greenblatt writes: "Yet even in Hamlet's familiar account, the word *pressure*—that is, impression, as with a seal or signet ring—should signal to us that for the Renaissance more is at stake in mirrors than an abstract and bodiless reflection. Both optics and mirror lore in the period suggest that something was actively passing back and forth in the production of mirror images, that accurate representation depended upon material emanation and exchange" (8).
49. Bruce McConachie, *Melodramatic Formations: American Theatre and Society, 1820–1870* (Iowa City: University of Iowa Press, 1992), xii.
50. McConachie, xii.

1 FRONTIER WESTERN DISCOURSE AT THE TURN OF THE NINETEENTH TO THE TWENTIETH CENTURY

1. See Mary Rowlandson's captivity narrative, "The Sovereignty and Goodness of God," in *Puritans among the Indians: Accounts of Captivity and Redemption, 1674–1724*, ed. Alden T. Vaughan and Edward W. Clark (Cambridge, MA: Belknap, 1981), 29–75. On the cultural function of "captivity narratives," including that of Rowlandson, see Christopher Castiglia, *Bound and Determined: Captivity, Culture-Crossing, and White Womanhood from Mary Rowlandson to Patty Hearst* (Chicago: University of Chicago Press, 1996); Kathryn Zabelle Derounian-Stodola and James Arthur Levernier, *The Indian Captivity Narratives, 1550–1900* (New York: Twayne, 1993); Gary L. Ebersole, *Captured by Texts: Puritan to Postmodern Images of Indian Captivity* (Charlottesville: University Press of Virginia, 1995); Annette Kolodny, "Among the Indians: The Uses of Captivity," *New York Times Book Review*, Jan 31, 1993, 1, 26–9; June Namais, *White Captives: Gender and Ethnicity on the American Frontier* (Chapel Hill: University of North Carolina Press, 1995).

2. On the post-structuralist analysis of polar oppositions, see, for instance, Jacques Derrida, "Positions: Interview with Jean-Louis Houdebine and Guy Scarpetta," *Positions*, trans. Alan Bass (Chicago: University of Chicago Press, 1981) 41–42.
3. Certainly this process has been the object of much critical commentary. In describing the spread of agriculture through the American West, Frieda Knobloch speaks of this "civilizing" process as a "colonization in the American West" [see *The Culture of Wilderness: Agriculture as Colonization in the American West* (Chapel Hill: University of North Carolina Press, 1996)]. The way this "process" was used to conceptualize, or perhaps more accurately, rationalize, white relations with Indians during the nineteenth century has been examined by many. See Roy Harvey Pearce, *Savagism and Civilization: A Study of the Indian and the American Mind* (Baltimore: Johns Hopkins Press, 1953, 1967), 105–134; Robert F. Berkhofer, Jr., *The White Man's Indian: Images of the American Indian from Columbus to the Present* (New York: Vintage, 1979), 49–55; Curtis M. Hinsley, *The Smithsonian and the American Indian: Making a Moral Anthropology in Victorian America* (Washington, DC: Smithsonian Institute, 1981), 125–144; Michael Elliott, *The Culture Concept: Writing and Difference in the Age of Realism* (Minneapolis: University of Minnesota Press, 2002), 89–123.
4. Regarding the use of the Indian as the other in early-nineteenth-century American literature, see Pearce, 169–236, and Berkhofer, 86–96.
5. On the ways in which the conquest of savagery informed the technical and scientific thought on western agriculture, see Knobloch (for instance, 57–78). The triumph of civilization over savagery structured much of the written material dealing with the frontier and the American West in general, and this motif received expression in various images disseminated for popular consumption. See, for instance, John Gast's "American Progress" (1872), which was used to illustrate the popular guide book *New Overland Tourist and Pacific Coast Guide*. This illustration can be seen in Berkhofer, Plate 8, and in *The Oxford History of the American West*, ed. Clyde A. Milner II, Carol A. O'Connor, Martha A. Sandweiss (Oxford: Oxford University Press, 1994), 194.
6. Fittingly, the first chapter of Alan Trachtenberg's *The Incorporation of America: Culture and Society in the Gilded Age* (New York: Hill & Wang, 1982) "deals with the West as land, national resource, and also as myth, especially 'civilization' wrested from its perceived opposite, the 'savage' culture of Indians" (8). Trachtenberg goes on to explore the primary social and cultural transformations that characterize the United States during the last decades of the nineteenth century. His analysis informs the assumptions made here about the rising bourgeois elite. Also relevant in this context is Robert Wiebe's discussion of the United States' late-nineteenth-century social and cultural transformation—a transformation that he outlines in the first half of *The*

Search for Order: 1877–1920 (New York: Hill & Wang, 1967)—as well as analyses of late-nineteenth-century socioeconomic transformations by Jack Beatty in *Age of Betrayal: The Triumph of Money in America, 1865–1900* (New York: Vintage, 2008), and Maury Klein in *The Genesis of Industrial America, 1870–1920* (New York: Cambridge University Press, 2007), and T. J. Jackson Lears's discussion of shifting cultural sensibilities in Chapter 2, "The Mysterious Power of Money," in *Rebirth of a Nation: The Making of Modern America, 1877–1920* (New York: Harper, 2009), 51–91.

7. In drawing this conclusion, the superintendent of the census defined the frontier as a line beyond which the population did not exceed two persons per square mile. Whatever one may think of this definition, according to it, as Duncan Dayton points out, there was still a frontier one hundred years after the superintendent of the census's announcement. Dayton writes that in the 1990 census, "132 counties within 15 western states in the Lower 48…still had fewer than two persons per square mile"—that is, "13 percent of the nation's contiguous landmass" [*Miles from Nowhere: In Search of the American Frontier* (New York: Penguin, 1993), 7].

8. David M. Wrobel, *The End of American Exceptionalism: Frontier Anxiety from the Old West to the New Deal* (Lawrence: University Press of Kansas, 1993), 98. Klein summarizes the significant demographic shifts in the United States with the following facts and numbers: "The population grew at an unprecedented rate. Between 1850 and 1900 it more than tripled from 23 million to 76 million; by 1920 it had increased another 39 percent to 106 million. It was also moving steadily from the country into cities and towns. In 1850 only about 15 percent of Americans lived in urban territory (defined as places with 2,500 or more people). The United States had become a predominantly urban nation, thanks in large measure to industrialization and the enormous flow of immigrants into the country. Between 1850 and 1920 an astounding 31.7 million people migrated to the United States, nearly half of them after 1900" (136).

9. See Wrobel, 18–20, 52.

10. Certainly, industrial culture was never monolithic. The new managerial elite did not impose its ideas and art on all below in a unidirectional flow. In fact, marginal groups and classes have continued to evolve cultural forms, but by the time these forms receive a national audience, they have often been tamed. Given the power to disseminate culture that belongs to the managerial elite in modern and postmodern America, it is not surprising that forms with potential commercial value would be taken up and "domesticated" to meet its concerns. Kathy Peiss notes this kind of co-optation in *Cheap Amusements: Working Women and Leisure in Turn-of-the-Century New York* (Philadelphia: Temple University Press, 1986). Peiss writes that turn-of-the-century working-class culture "made its way into the entertainment of the middle class. Entrepreneurs and promoters scoured the city's 'low' dance halls

and variety theaters for songs and dance steps and observed street culture for new fads and fashions. Introducing novelties into nightclubs, amusement parks, and the movies, they transformed them into safe, controllable activities that could be sold to all classes" (187). This does not mean that such cultural transpositions stripped popular artistic expression of all subversive resonances. As Jim Cullen argues in his book *The Art of Democracy: A Concise History of Popular Culture in the United States* (New York: Monthly Review Press, 1996), to emphasize "popular culture's hegemonic qualities and narcotic effects... is a perspective that tends to ignore those elements of a working people's worldview that survive commodification, as well as the subversive elements within it that defy control or price tags" (95).

11. Gunther Barth, *City People: The Rise of Modern City Culture in Nineteenth-Century America* (Oxford: Oxford University Press, 1980), 233. In this regard, see also Trachtenberg, especially Chapters 4, "Mysteries of the Great City," and 5, "The Politics of Culture," (101–181), and George Cotkin, *Reluctant Modernism: American Thought and Culture, 1880–1900* (New York: Twayne, 1992), Chapter 5, "A Consuming Culture," (101–129).

12. See Sven Beckert, *The Monied Metropolis: New York City and the Consolidation of the American Bourgeoisie, 1850–1896* (New York: Cambridge University Press, 2001). Beckert's account of the shift in power from a predominately mercantile to a predominately industrial elite, and "the broadening gap between bourgeois New Yorkers and other social groups, and the economic elite's... unprecedented hold over the American economy, society, and politics" (323) are relevant here.

13. John Higham, "The Reorientation of American Culture in the 1890s," in *Writing American History: Essays on Modern Scholarship* (Bloomington: Indiana University Press, 1970), 79.

14. Higham, 80. Turning to untamed nature was only one way that the intellectual elite responded to the impersonal modern environment. As T.J. Jackson Lears relates in *No Place of Grace: Antimodernism and the Transformation of American Culture, 1880–1920* (Chicago: University of Chicago Press, 1981), the revolt against modern, industrial culture took multiple forms, such as religious revivalism, medievalism, and "arts and crafts" aestheticism. Ironically, as Lears tells us, these interests laid the groundwork for the transition from nineteenth-century production-oriented culture to twentieth-century consumer-oriented modernism. On this trend, see also Cotkin, 116–129.

15. For more discussion of this "wilderness cult," see Roderick Nash, *Wilderness in the American Mind*, 3rd ed. (New Haven, CT: Yale University Press, 1982) 141–60.

16. Renato Rosaldo, *Culture and Truth: The Remaking of Social Analysis* (Boston: Beacon, 1993), 68–87.

17. The railroad is, of course, the master metaphor that Leo Marx explores in his exploration of the impact of industrial growth on nineteenth-century American

culture in his study *The Machine in the Garden: Technology and the Pastoral Ideal in America* (Oxford: Oxford University Press, 1964). Interestingly, in *Organizing America: Wealth, Power, and the Origins of Corporate Capitalism* (Princeton: Princeton University Press, 2002), Charles Perrow argues that railroads were key to the development of the "giant organizations at the end of the century" (223), and that they launched our corporate culture, our "society of organizations" (227). In short, it was the way railroads were organized that led us into the modern era of corporate capitalism. Similarly, Beatty described the railroads as the driving force behind the corporate capitalism of the "Gilded Age" in his analysis of post–Civil War America (3–17).

18. United States Bureau of the Census, *Historical Statistics of the United States, Colonial Times to 1970*, Part 1, Bicentennial ed. (Washington: U.S. Dept. of Commerce, Bureau of the Census, 1975), 322. On train ticket prices, see Earl Pomeroy, *In Search of the Golden West: The Tourist in Western America* (1957; Lincoln: University of Nebraska Press, 1990). He notes that schoolteachers in this period made $200 per year—two-thirds of what it would cost to travel by train from coast to coast (7). In *Devil's Bargains: Tourism in the Twentieth-Century American West* (Lawrence: University Press of Kansas, 1998), Hal K. Rothman restates these numbers (38).

19. For information on transcontinental Pullman car accommodations and Raymond and Whitcomb tours, see Earl Pomeroy, 7–17; G. Edward White, *The Eastern Establishment and the Western Experience: The West of Frederic Remington, Theodore Roosevelt, and Owen Wister* (New Haven, CT: Yale University Press, 1968), 47; and Anne Farrar Hyde, *An American Vision: Far Western Landscape and National Culture, 1820–1920* (New York: New York University Press, 1990), 107–46; Rothman, 38–39.

20. Pomeroy, 31–34; Anne Farrar Hyde, 69, 129, 137.

21. Anne Farrar Hyde, 190.

22. Regarding late-nineteenth-century western hotels and resorts, see Pomeroy, 17–28; Anne Farrar Hyde, 147–90; G. Edward White, 47–48.

23. Anne Farrar Hyde, 295. For more information regarding the "log palaces," see Anne Farrar Hyde, 244–295. Rothman claims that these "palaces" never lacked amenities for their wealthy patrons, and that a railroad resort like Fred Harvey's El Tovar Hotel controlled the scenic Grand Canyon site—dominating local competitors and packaging an "authentic" western experience that might in the end have had little connection to the original setting (55–80).

24. Pomeroy, 122–3.

25. Pomeroy, 7, 59–60.

26. Anne Farrar Hyde, 246, 253, 267.

27. Barth, 84. In this regard, see also Cullen, 115.

28. Richard Slotkin notes that subtle messages about the frontier experience and its larger significance were conveyed in newspapers through the juxtaposition and layout of articles. In the late nineteenth century, connections between

stories dealing with Indian troubles and labor conflicts were established by such techniques. The Indian War paradigm was thus applied to both Indians and striking workers, who were viewed as different forms of "red" threat. See Slotkin, *The Fatal Environment: The Myth of the Frontier in the Age of Industrialization, 1800–1890* (Middletown, CT: Wesleyan University Press, 1986), 338–345.
29. Higham, 79.
30. The rush toward professionalization in the late nineteenth century affected not only law and medicine, but also acting. See Benjamin McArthur, *Actors and American Culture, 1880–1920* (Philadelphia: Temple University Press, 1984), 85–112.
31. Burton Bledstein, *The Culture of Professionalism: The Middle Class and the Development of Higher Education in America* (New York: Norton, 1976), 121.
32. Johns Hopkins University, founded in 1876 primarily as a center for graduate study, became the nation's leading producer of PhDs in the 1880s and 1890s. On the new professional academic world into which Turner entered, see Allan G. Bogue, *Frederick Jackson Turner: Strange Roads Going Down* (Norman: University of Oklahoma Press, 1998), 145–48.
33. Regarding these predecessors, see Herman Clarence Nixon, "Precursors of Turner in the Interpretation of the American Frontier," *South Atlantic Quarterly* 28 (1929), 83–89; Henry Nash Smith, *Virgin Land: The American West as Symbol and Myth* (1950; Cambridge, MA: Harvard University Press, 1978); and Wrobel, 3–35.
34. Quoted in Frederick Jackson Turner, "The Significance of the Frontier in American History," *The Frontier in American History* (Tucson: University of Arizona Press, 1986), 1.
35. Turner, 1.
36. See Richard Hofstadter, *The Progressive Historians: Turner, Beard, Parrington* (New York: Alfred A. Knopf, 1969), 54–61; and Bogue, 99–102.
37. Turner, 3.
38. In the spirit of Turner's thesis, I use the third person masculine pronoun intentionally—not to delineate a generic pioneer, but to refer to the male pioneers who function as the protagonists of Turner's analysis.
39. Turner, 3–4.
40. Turner, 4.
41. Turner, 37.
42. See Ronald H. Carpenter, *The Eloquence of Frederick Jackson Turner* (San Marino, CA: Huntington Library, 1983), 47-70; William Cronon, "Turner's First Stand: The Significance of Significance in American History," in *Writing Western History: Essays on Major Western Historians*, ed. Richard W. Etulain (Albuquerque: University of New Mexico Press, 1991), 82–86; Harold Simonson, *Beyond the Frontier: Writers, Western*

Regionalism, and a Sense of Place (Fort Worth: Texas Christian University Press, 1989), 16–27.
43. Carpenter, 8, 18, 21, 49-50. Bogue has also commented on Turner's skill with "antithesis and parallel constructions" (97–98).
44. Hofstadter, 75–6.
45. See Billington, *Frederick Jackson Turner: Historian, Scholar, Teacher* (New York: Oxford University Press, 1973), 30–1, 58–62; Jacobs, *On Turner's Trail: 100 Years of Writing Western History* (Lawrence: University Press of Kansas, 1994), 35–57; Bogue, 43–53.
46. See Herbert Spencer, "The Social Organism" [first published in *The Westminister Review* (January 1860)], in *The Man Versus the State with Four Essays on Politics and Society* (Baltimore: Penguin, 1969), 215.
47. While there is no record of Turner's having read Morgan's volume, he would probably have heard about Morgan's work from his University of Wisconsin teacher William Francis Allen. According to Wilbur Jacobs, Allen made reference to Morgan in his personal lecture notes: "Attempting to answer the formidable question, 'What is civilization?' Allen assured his students that they should read three of his most trusted sources, Henry Thomas Buckle, Lewis Henry Morgan, and Herbert Spencer" (44). The impact of Morgan on the national science scene, specifically on the developing concern with ethnology at the Smithsonian and Bureau of Ethnology, is described by Hinsley, 125–44.
48. Lewis H. Morgan, *Ancient Society* (1877; Cambridge, MA: Belknap Press, 1964). Morgan claims "the invention of the art of pottery" denotes the shift from savagery to barbarism, and "the invention of a phonetic alphabet, with the use of writing" denotes the shift from barbarism to civilization (18).
49. Morgan, 18.
50. Morgan, 41.
51. Morgan, 40.
52. See, for instance, Ray Allen Billington, 62–66, 111–112; or Wilbur R. Jacobs, 49–50.
53. Turner, "The Problem of the West," in *The Frontier in American History*, 205–6.
54. See, for instance, Billington, 435–37; Jacobs, 54–55; Bogue, 185–86.
55. See Wrobel, 50.
56. Jacobs, 55, 164–6.
57. Regarding Turner's critics' presentation of his approach to Indians, see, for instance, Patricia Nelson Limerick, *The Legacy of Conquest: The Unbroken Past of the American West* (New York: Norton, 1987), 21, 179–222; or Patricia Nelson Limerick, Clyde A. Milner II, and Charles E. Rankin, *Trails: Toward a New Western History* (Lawrence: University Press of Kansas, 1991), in which Turner's (mis)understanding of Indians is a theme that runs throughout. With respect to supporters, see Billington, 453–4; Jacobs, 164–6; Bogue, 377–78.

58. Turner, "The Significance of the Frontier," 11.
59. Turner, "The Significance of the Frontier," 13.
60. Turner, "The Significance of the Frontier," 2–3.
61. Billington, 10, 24.
62. Quoted in Billington, 433.
63. Billington, 433. Regarding Turner's sense of the outdoors as a restorative for body and soul, see Bogue, 32–33, 63, 193, 273–76. This wilderness cure recalls the late-nineteenth-century discourse on neurasthenia. Often the West was offered as a remedy for the physiological symptoms of the stress resulting from modern urban life. See Tom Lutz, *American Nervousness, 1903: An Anecdotal History* (Ithaca, NY: Cornell University Press, 1991), 1–30; Lears, *No Place of Grace*, 49–58; and *Rebirth of a Nation*, 63–71.
64. John Muir, *The Story of My Boyhood and Youth* (1913; Madison: University of Wisconsin Press, 1965), 228.
65. Gretel Ehrlich, forward to John Muir, *The Mountains of California* (1894; San Francisco: Sierra Club, 1988), viii.
66. Muir, *The Mountains of California*, 46.
67. Muir, *The Mountains of California*, 55.
68. Muir, *The Mountains of California*, 192.
69. John Muir, *Our National Parks* (1901; Madison: University of Wisconsin Press, 1981), 1.
70. Muir, *The Story of My Boyhood and Youth*, 145.
71. Muir, *The Story of My Boyhood and Youth*, 26–28. See also Simonson, 28–43.
72. Turner may have had more in common with President Theodore Roosevelt's head of the Division of Forestry, Gifford Pinchot, who worked on behalf of conservation rather than preservation. In this regard, see Bogue, who writes that Turner "appears to have been more sympathetic to the Progressive ideal of wise and efficient use of resources found in the thought of Gifford Pinchot and [Charles] Van Hise than to John Muir's commitment to pure wilderness" (414). Still, with respect to the impact of the frontier experience on American character, Roosevelt and Turner shared many ideas. It's no great leap to maintain that Roosevelt may have preceded Turner in his condemnation of the "germ" theory of American development and in the claim that American exceptionalism was a product of the interaction of pioneer and wilderness environment. Michael Collins makes this argument in *That Damned Cowboy: Theodore Roosevelt and the American West, 1883–1898* (New York: Peter Lang, 1989), 105–09.
73. See Pomeroy, 94–104; G. Edward White, 60–67.
74. Pomeroy, 101–02.
75. One receives a somewhat different sense of Roosevelt's relation to the West in Collins's presentation of his cowboy experiences. Collins suggests: "Just as President Roosevelt considered himself a Westerner in spirit, so too did the people of the American West embrace him, in the words of one commentator,

as 'our own Teddy'" (159). Still, as Collins describes Roosevelt's back-and-forth traveling between the East Coast and his North Dakota ranch in the 1890s, one gets the feeling that Roosevelt's western hunting excursions and the periods of hard work on his ranch "furnished him a perfect refuge from the political arena" (159) and an escape from career and familial responsibilities.
76. Roosevelt spoke directly of "the strenuous life" in the title essay of *The Strenuous Life: Essays and Addresses* (New York: Century, 1900), 1–21.
77. Theodore Roosevelt, "Biological Analogies in History," in *History as Literature and Other Essays* (1913; Port Washington, NY: Kennikat Press, 1967), 45.
78. Theodore Roosevelt, "The World Movement," in *History as Literature and Other Essays*, 120.
79. Regarding Roosevelt's understanding of these aspects of the wilderness legacy, see Nash, 149–53.
80. 1893 Boone and Crockett publication quoted in Nash, 152.
81. See Gail Bederman, *Manliness & Civilization: A Cultural History of Gender and Race in the United States, 1880–1917* (Chicago: University of Chicago Press, 1995), 1–44.
82. G. Edward White, 152–55. Also see Theodore Roosevelt, *The Rough Riders* (1899; New York: Modern Library, 1996), 8–20; and Dale L. Walker, *The Boys of '98* (New York: Tom Doherty Associates, 1998), 100–22.
83. Robert Hine, *The American West: An Interpretive History* (Boston: Little, Brown, 1973), 186.
84. Nash, 138–39.
85. Richard Slotkin, *Gunfighter Nation: The Myth of the Frontier in Twentieth-Century America* (New York: Atheneum, 1992), 33. Slotkin makes a number of salient points in his comparison of Turner's and Roosevelt's frontier visions (see 29–63).
86. See Billington, 438, 111–12; Hofstadter, 47–61.
87. Hamlin Garland, *Crumbling Idols* (1894; Gainesville, FL: Scholars' Facsimiles & Reprints, 1957), 155–6.
88. Garland, 178.
89. See G. Edward White, 77–144.
90. Jane Tompkins, *West of Everything: The Inner Life of Westerns* (New York: Oxford University Press, 1992), 39.
91. Tompkins, 42.
92. Working within the parameters of nineteenth-century frontier western discourse, dime novel authors employed the savagery/civilization dichotomy to offer working-class youths entertainment that seemed to represent resistance to the ideals of the management elite even as it encouraged support for these ideals. Thus, the masters of publishing houses disseminating dime novels used frontier materials to practice the co-optation—sometimes conscious, sometimes unconscious—that Antonio Gramsci's understanding of "hegemony" has prompted contemporary cultural critics to explore. In short, in

pulp novels that glorify antiestablishment outlaws such as Deadwood Dick, the underlying tone may not really be oppositional. For instance, in the first of Edward J. Wheeler's Deadwood Dick novels, *Deadwood Dick, The Prince of the Road* (1877), a distinction is made between the "bad" capitalists, the deceitful urban Filmores, Senior and Junior, who relentlessly pursue Dick, and the healthy, hard-working capitalists who successfully develop the mining possibilities of Flower Pocket, a hidden mountain valley. The good capitalist Harry Redburn and his friends bring industrial progress into the isolated, idealized mountain valley, and in doing so they benefit both themselves and members of the Ute tribe, who work in the mine and consequently are "now utilized to a better occupation than in the dark and bloody days of the past" [Edward J. Wheeler, *Deadwood Dick, The Prince of the Road*, in *Reading the West: An Anthology of Dime Westerns*, ed. Bill Brown (Boston: Bedford, 1997), 326]. Selfish capitalists are punished, but individual free entrepreneurs bring prosperity and a more civilized way of life to all. Such may be the dominant message of mass-produced pulp fiction. In this way, class resentments could be reconstituted to benefit the new managerial elite. Christine Bold offers a more open reading of the impact of dime novels. See "Malaeska's Revenge; or, The Dime Novel Tradition in Popular Fiction," in *Wanted Dead or Alive: The American West in Popular Culture*, ed. Richard Aquila (Urbana: University of Illinois Press, 1996), 21–42.

93. See Cody's autobiography, *The Life of Buffalo Bill* (1879; London: Senate, 1994), and his sister Helen Cody Wetmore's biography, *Buffalo Bill: Last of the Great Scouts* (1899; Lincoln, NE: Bison, 1965). For a more dispassionate account of his early life, see Louis S. Warren, *Buffalo Bill's America: William Cody and the Wild West Show* (New York: Alfred A. Knopf, 2005).

94. See Richard White, "Frederick Jackson Turner and Buffalo Bill," in *The Frontier in American Culture: An Exhibition at the Newberry Library, August 26, 1994–January 7, 1995* (Berkeley: University of California Press, 1994), 29–34. For a brief but insightful exploration of the complex interrelationship of fact and legend in the history of the West, see Ann Fabian, "History for the Masses: Commercializing the Western Past," in *Under an Open Sky: Rethinking America's Western Past*, ed. William Cronon, George Miles, and Jay Gitlin (New York: Norton, 1992), 223–38. For a succinct history of the Buffalo Bill–Yellow Hand affair and how Cody employed it for theatrical effect, see Joy S. Kasson, *Buffalo Bill's Wild West: Celebrity, Memory, and Popular History* (New York: Hill and Wang, 2000), 34–41; Warren, 117–22.

95. Nate Salsbury, quoted in *Buffalo Bill's Wild West: Historical Sketches & Programme*, ca. 1901, 3. This and other Wild West program material cited here are in the Billy Rose Theatre Division of the New York Public Library for the Performing Arts at Lincoln Center.

96. Sarah J. Blackstone, *Buckskins, Bullets, and Business: A History of Buffalo Bill's Wild West* (New York: Greenwood, 1986), 1.

97. Blackstone, 109.
98. Col. Dodge, *Thirty Years Among the Indians*, quoted in *Buffalo Bill's Wild West: Historical Sketches & Programme*, 1895, 10.
99. *Buffalo Bill's Wild West: Historical Sketches and Programme*, 1895, 8.
100. Phil Sheridan quoted in *Buffalo Bill's Wild West: Historical Sketches and Programme*, 1895, 45. For discussion of how the Wild West Show souvenir program might have informed the opinions of audience members, see Kasson, 105–112.
101. Regarding Cody's ambivalence vis-à-vis Indians, see Warren, 190–204.
102. Regarding the degree to which Turner's thesis is concerned with temporal process, see Turner's 1928 letter to Merle Curti, quoted in the introduction of this book, note 34.
103. This regeneration theme is developed throughout Richard Slotkin's three volumes dealing with the myth of the frontier: the two volumes cited above (*The Fatal Environment* and *Gunfighter Nation*) and *Regeneration Through Violence: The Mythology of the American Frontier, 1600–1860* (Middleton, CT: Wesleyan University Press, 1973).
104. See for instance, Charles Darwin, *The Origin of Species* (New York: New American Library, 1958), 129–30.
105. Turner, "The Significance of the Frontier," 12, 14–5. Bogue explores Turner's dependence on organic metaphors (77–118).
106. Limerick, *The Legacy of Conquest*, 21.
107. Richard White, "Trashing the Trails," in *Trails: Toward a New Western History*, 31.
108. Limerick, *The Legacy of Conquest*, 322–23.
109. Northrop Frye, *Anatomy of Criticism: Four Essays* (Princeton: Princeton University Press, 1957), 163.
110. This gendering of the frontier is at the heart of Annette Kolodny's fascinating analysis of nineteenth- and twentieth-century American literature in *The Lay of the Land: Metaphor as Experience and History in American Life and Letters* (Chapel Hill: University of North Carolina Press, 1975). Especially interesting in this context is Kolodny's discussion of how Turner presents western land as both mother and mistress for the male pioneer conqueror (136–37).
111. Frye, 40, 167.

2 THE TURN-OF-THE-CENTURY AMERICAN THEATER CONTEXT

1. Stephen Greenblatt, *Shakespearean Negotiations: The Circulation of Social Energy in Renaissance England* (Berkeley: University of California Press, 1988), 8.

2. This theme, of course, has been explored by Richard Slotkin at length in his three volumes: *Regeneration Through Violence: The Mythology of the American Frontier, 1600–1860* (Middleton, CT: Wesleyan University Press, 1973); *The Fatal Environment: The Myth of the Frontier in the Age of Industrialization, 1800–1890* (Middleton, CT: Wesleyan University Press, 1986); and *Gunfighter Nation: The Myth of the Frontier in Twentieth-Century America* (New York: Harper Perennial, 1993).
3. A good analysis of George II's contribution to the role of scenography in the theater is still to be found in Lee Simonson's *The Stage is Set* (New York: Harcourt, Brace, 1932; New York: Theatre Arts Books, 1963), in Part III, Chapter II, "Royal Innovations: George II, Duke of Saxe-Meiningen" (272–308). As Simonson says, it was George II who claimed that "the fundamental problem to be answered by the scene-designer is not, What will my setting look like and how will the actor look in it? but, What will my setting make the actor do?" (272).
4. In discussing the kind of social interaction that comprises "theatrical formations," Bruce McConachie writes: "[G]roups of spectators and theater performers produce each other from the inside out as artists-to-be-experienced and audiences-to-be-entertained in a given historical period. The result is what may be termed a theatrical formation, the mutual elaboration over time of historically specific audience groups and theatre practitioners participating in certain shared patterns of dramatic and theatrical action," *Melodramatic Formations: American Theatre and Society, 1820–1870* (Iowa City: University of Iowa Press, 1992), xii.
5. McConachie, 40.
6. Robertson Davies, *The Mirror of Nature: The Alexander Lectures, 1982* (Toronto: University of Toronto Press, 1983), 9–13.
7. The melodramatic forms cited here are drawn from McConachie's study, *Melodramatic Formations*.
8. Daniel C. Gerould, "The Americanization of Melodrama," in *American Melodrama*, ed. Daniel C. Gerould (New York: Performing Arts Journal Publications, 1983), 7.
9. Gerould 9.
10. Alan Trachtenberg explores a similar contradiction when he speaks about the conflict between the ethical ideal and business ethics in the pursuit of success during the Gilded Age. See *The Incorporation of America: Culture & Society in the Gilded Age* (New York: Hill and Wang, 1982), 80–81.
11. Jeffrey D. Mason, *Melodrama and the Myth of America* (Bloomington: Indiana University Press, 1993), 18.
12. McConachie refers to "Manicheanism" as "an appropriate framework for analyzing modern melodrama," but notes that "it does not "structure the plays of Pixérécourt and his imitators" (note 15, 265–66).
13. Grimsted, *Melodrama Unveiled: American Theater and Culture, 1800–1850* (Chicago: University of Chicago Press, 1968), 215–18.

14. Grimsted, 217.
15. Grimsted, 217.
16. Grimsted, 217–18.
17. See Richard Moody, *America Takes the Stage: Romanticism in American Drama and Theatre, 1750–1900* (Bloomington: Indiana University Press, 1955), 105–107.
18. James Kirke Paulding's *The Lion of the West* (1830) was written for popular comic actor James Hackett, who took advantage of Davy Crockett's notoriety as a tall-tale humorist.
19. In regard to the change in perspective on frontier heroes, Henry Nash Smith describes "how slowly the Western hunter gained sufficient social standing to be allowed to marry the heroine. This fictional emancipation of the Wild Westerner was not clearly worked out before the late 1870s," in *Virgin Land: The American West as Symbol and Myth* (1950; Cambridge, MA: Harvard University Press, 1978), 211.
20. With regard to the interconnectedness of race and gender within the civilization/savagery dichotomy, see Gail Bederman, *Manliness & Civilization: A Cultural History of Gender and Race in the United States*, 1880–1917 (Chicago: University of Chicago Press, 1995).
21. Barbara Welter, "The Cult of True Womanhood: 1820–1860," *American Quarterly* 18 (1966), 151.
22. Welter, 152.
23. Welter, 152.
24. The effect of this hierarchy on males is the focus of studies about male gender construction in America—studies like E. Anthony Rotundo, *American Manhood: Transformations in Masculinity from the Revolution to the Modern Era* (New York: Basic, 1993); Michael Kimmel, *Manhood in America: A Cultural History* (New York: Free Press, 1996), 43–188; Bederman 1–44.
25. Kathy Peiss discusses how the subculture of young working women at the turn of the century was instrumental in this change. This is a case of a marginalized subculture impacting the broader culture even if the members of this subculture remain substantially powerless. See Peiss, *Cheap Amusements: Working Women and Leisure in Turn-of-the-Century New York* (Philadelphia: Temple University Press, 1986), 185–88.
26. Welter, 173–4. The degree to which these stereotypes—gender constructions that exemplified the domestic values that Victorian bourgeois society sought to maintain—affected the thinking of late-nineteenth-century pioneer women who left the safety of the East for the West has been a source of debate among frontier historians. But even a historian like Sandra Myres, who claimed that frontier women "modified existing norms and adopted flexible attitudes and experimental behavior patterns," still admitted that while "the *reality*" of women's lives on the frontier "changed dramatically…the public *image* remained relatively static. Image, myth, and stereotype were contrary

to what women were actually experiencing and doing" [*Westering Women and the Frontier Experience: 1800–1915* (Albuquerque: University of New Mexico Press, 1982), 269]. Moreover, historians agree that when women went west for employment on the frontier, they often entered professions that could be viewed as extensions of their domestic responsibilities: teaching, health care, and missionary work. In this regard, see Julie Roy Jeffrey, *Frontier Women: The Trans-Mississippi West: 1840–1880* (New York: Hill and Wang, 1979), 11–12, 79–106; Myres, 238–270; Glenda Riley, *The Female Frontier: A Comparative View of Woman on the Prairie and the Plains* (Lawrence: University Press of Kansas, 1988), 102–147. In short, women's role as the guardian of civilized values was upheld on the frontier, only here the realm of action was enlarged from the family to include the entire community. In either case, however, women's role as protector of culture was subordinate to the male role, which revolved around more practical economic concerns.
27. Welter, 174.
28. Rotundo, 227.
29. See Rotundo, 222–284; Kimmel, 81–188; Bederman, 1–44. Bederman's distinction between Victorian "manliness" and the late-nineteenth-century obsession with "masculinity" is especially relevant here. Also see John F. Kasson, *Houdini, Tarzan, and the Perfect Man: The White Male Body and the Challenge of Modernity in America* (New York: Hill and Wang, 2001), 179–83.
30. Joan Wallach Scott, "Gender: A Useful Category of Historical Analysis," in *Gender and the Politics of History* (New York: Columbia University Press, 1988), 45. Scott's discussion of "conceptual language" is useful in the explication of dramatic structure, but it is important to recall that she uses "language" as post-structuralists do—not to "mean words but systems of meaning—symbolic orders—that precede the actual mastery of speech, reading, and writing" (37).
31. See Bartley Campbell, *My Partner*, in *America's Lost Plays*, vol. XIX, *The White Slave and Other Plays*, ed. Napier Wilt (Bloomington: Indiana University Press, 1965), 47–98.
32. Vernon Louis Parrington, *Main Currents in American Thought: An Interpretation of American Literature from the Beginnings to 1920, Vol. III: (1860–1920), The Beginnings of Critical Realism in America* (New York: Harcourt-Brace, 1930), 191–92.
33. While this connection was challenged by those who opposed social Darwinism (for instance, at the turn of the century, social scientists like Franz Boas, who sought to move anthropology from a "diachronic" to a "synchronic" understanding of culture), the tendency to embrace evolutionary development was mainstream thinking until several decades into the twentieth century. Regarding Franz Boas's critique of evolutionary approaches in anthropology, see Michael A. Elliott, *The Culture Concept: Writing and Difference in the Age of Realism* (Minneapolis: University of Minnesota Press, 2002), 1–34. In

Reluctant Modernism: American Thought and Culture, 1880–1900 (New York: Twayne, 1992), George Cotkin also discusses Boas's rejection of overarching delineations of evolutionary progress (59–63).
34. For a thoughtful examination of "realism" in the American theater, see Brenda Murphy, *American Realism and American Drama, 1880–1940* (Cambridge: Cambridge University Press, 1987).
35. Interrogating the concept "objectivity," Lorraine Daston and Peter Galison explore the nineteenth-century understanding of "objectivity" and its relation to a naive faith in the truthfulness of photography and other modes of mechanical reproduction. See "The Image of Objectivity," *Representations* 40 (Fall 1992), 81–128.
36. See Arthur Hobson Quinn, *A History of the American Drama: From the Civil War to the Present Day*, vol. I (New York: Appleton-Century-Crofts, 1927), 108–114; and Richard Moody, 177–84.
37. Quinn, 108. In this context, see also Laurence Hutton's discussion of *Davy Crockett* in *Curiosities of the American Stage* (New York: Harper & Brothers, 1891), 30–35.
38. The analysis of Murdock's *Davy Crockett* as well as the comparison of this play with Campbell's *My Partner* offered here are drawn from my essay "Americanizing Frontier Melodrama: From *Davy Crockett* (1872) to *My Partner* (1879)," *Journal of American Culture* 12.1 (1989), 7–16.
39. Frank Murdock, *Davy Crockett; Or, Be Sure You're Right, Then Go Ahead* in *America's Lost Plays*, vol. IV, *Davy Crockett and Other Plays*, ed. Napier Wilt (Bloomington: Indiana University Press, 1963), 119.
40. All three of these stories appear in Bret Harte, *"The Outcasts of Poker Flat" and Other Tales* (New York: Signet, 1961).
41. "Amusements: Bret Harte's New Drama: *The Two Men of Sandy Bar* at Union Square Theatre," *New York Times*, August 29, 1876, 5. See Bret Harte, *Two Men of Sandy Bar*, in *California Gold-Rush Plays*, ed. Glenn Loney (New York: Performing Arts Journal, 1983), 103–75.
42. "The Amusement Season: Dramatic Events: Union Square Theatre," *New York Times*, Sept. 17, 1879, 5.
43. "Amusements: Union Square Theatre—*My Partner*," *New York Herald*, Sept. 17, 1879, 5.
44. This general turn is described and closely analyzed by Trachtenberg in his study of late-nineteenth-century America, *Incorporating America: Culture and Society in the Gilded Age* (New York: Hill and Wang, 1982). Also relevant here is Charles Perrow's argument regarding the impact of the particular nature of organization pioneered by the monopolistic railroad corporations on how the United States has evolved a "society of organizations" [*Organizing America: Wealth, Power, and the Origins of Corporate Capitalism* (Princeton: Princeton University Press, 2002)].
45. Alfred L. Bernheim, *The Business of the Theatre: An Economic History of the American Theatre, 1750–1932* (1932; New York: Benjamin Blom, 1964),

31–33. For a brief, more recent account of this transformation of the theater, see John Frick, "A Changing Theatre: New York and Beyond," *The Cambridge History of American Theatre: Volume II: 1870–1945* (Cambridge: Cambridge University Press, 1999), 196–20.

46. Bernheim lists the following cities: "Portland, Boston, Providence, New York, Brooklyn, Troy, Albany, Rochester, Buffalo, Philadelphia, Pittsburgh, Baltimore, Richmond, Savannah, Mobile, New Orleans, Memphis, Louisville, Cincinnati, Cleveland, Indianapolis, Chicago, Omaha, Denver, Salt Lake City, Sacramento, San Francisco" (30).

47. Bernheim and others, like Jack Poggi, *Theatre in America: The Impact of Economic Forces, 1870–1967* (Ithaca, NY: Cornell University Press, 1968), tended to view the disappearance of stock companies and the appearance of combination companies as a natural, historical progression. More recent historians have challenged the assumption that combination companies grew out of the old stock companies in a gradual and inevitable way. In this regard, Rosemarie K. Bank, "A Reconsideration of the Death of Nineteenth-Century American Repertory Companies and the Rise of the Combination," *Essays in Theatre* 5.1 (1986), 61–75, questions the assertion of a predetermined connection between the demise of stock companies and the rise of combination companies; and Peter Davis, "From Stock to Combination: The Panic of 1873 and its Effects on the American Theatre Industry," *Theatre History Studies* 8 (1988), 1–9, has explored the impact of the Panic of 1873 on both these trends.

48. Bernheim, 30–31; Jack Poggi, 7.

49. Initially, the term "combination company" may have been more flexibly employed to refer not only to stars traveling with an entire production, but also to stars touring with just a core of supporting actors who took the major secondary roles in a production, with the rest of the casting and production needs being assumed by local stock companies. It would be logically convenient to think of such a truncated company as a transitional form between the stock repertory system and the full company combination—a transitional form that vanished as the disappearance of stock companies forced touring stars to become wholly independent of local resources. Whether one can speak of such a transitional period or not, it is interesting to note the particular case of Arthur McKee Rankin's touring production of Joaquin Miller's *The Danites*. As Levi Damon Phillips's research has disclosed, during the first year of the tour (1877–1878) Rankin's company occasionally was reduced to a core to take advantage of local stock actors. Rankin traveled with a complete company throughout the next three years of the tour (1878–1881). See Levi Damon Phillips, "Arthur McKee Rankin's Touring Production of Joaquin Miller's *The Danites*," diss., University of California, Davis, 1981, note 2, page 13; 48; 78–79; 97.

50. Poggi, 5–6.

51. Bernheim's claim of "nearly one hundred" (30) is drawn from an article in the *New York Dramatic Mirror*; Bank has suggested that there are good reasons to question the reliability of this article ("Reconsideration," 63–4).

230 Notes

52. Bernheim, 30.
53. Poggi, 6.
54. John W. Frick, *New York's First Theatrical Center: The Rialto at Union Square* (Ann Arbor: UMI Research Press, 1985), 1–10.
55. For brief histories of this theater war, see Bernheim, 64–74; Poggi, 15–26.
56. McConachie, 256.
57. Poggi, 5.
58. Poggi, 248.
59. Poggi, 249.
60. Poggi, 253.
61. Frick has argued that it is unfair and inaccurate to blame the Syndicate for a decline in the quality of the American theater. He claims that while this notion has gone as historical fact, it was the by-product of an attack on the Syndicate by late-nineteenth-century scholars and critics, and is based on distortions and inaccuracies ("A Changing Theatre," 215–16). It is true that neither the Syndicate nor the Shuberts after them were entirely responsible for the kinds of drama that are characteristic of this period. Indeed, these organizations were less the cause than a symptom of the "bottom line" preoccupations that drove the theater of the late nineteenth century.
62. Regarding the construction of a "highbrow/lowbrow" cultural hierarchy, see Lawrence W. Levine, *Highbrow/Lowbrow: The Emergence of Cultural Hierarchy in America* (Cambridge, MA: Harvard University Press, 1988), especially 219–242.
63. Mary C. Henderson, *The City and the Theatre: New York Playhouses from Bowling Green to Times Square* (Clifton, NJ: James T. White, 1973), 143. The Union Square Theatre was among the more prestigious of New York theaters—the home of Albert M. Palmer's repertory company, which was highly esteemed for its "artistic and commercial success" (Henderson, 143). Perhaps this play was all the more shocking given the nature of the venue and the expectations that audiences brought to this theater.
64. "The Drama: My Partner," *New York Daily Tribune*, Sept. 17, 1879, 4.
65. "Amusements: Union Square Theatre—*My Partner*," 5.
66. "Mr. Hackett in Role of Scout," *New York Herald*, Nov. 3, 1903, 10.
67. "Belasco's New Theatre Opened," *New York Daily Tribune*, Oct. 24, 1905, 7.
68. Gunther Barth, *City People: The Rise of Modern City Culture in Nineteenth-Century America* (Oxford: Oxford University Press, 1980), 207.
69. "Theatre Prices Will Be Reduced," *Chicago Daily Tribune*, Dec. 30, 1903, 4.
70. Michael M. Davis, *The Exploitation of Pleasure: A Study of Commercial Recreations in New York City* (New York: Department of Child Hygiene of the Russell Sage Foundation, ND), 25–6.
71. United States Bureau of the Census, *Historical Statistics of the United States, Colonial Times to 1970*, Part 1, Bicentennial ed. (Washington: U.S. Department of Commerce, Bureau of the Census, 1975), 321.
72. Michael M. Davis, 29.

73. Michael M. Davis, 37.
74. Theodore Kremer quoted in Montrose J. Moses, *The American Dramatist* (New York: Benjamin Blom, 1939), 302. Ironically but not surprisingly given the cost of admission, productions of spectacular melodramas at "ten-twenty-thirty" theaters were rather spare. Touring versions of "ten-twenty-thirty" melodramas tended to travel without scenery, depending on the stock scenery of the houses in which they performed. See Garrett H. Leverton, "Introduction," in *The Great Diamond Robbery & Other Recent Melodramas, America's Lost Plays*, vol. VIII (Bloomington: Indiana University Press, 1940), viii–ix.
75. Renato Rosaldo, *Culture and Truth: The Remaking of Social Analysis* (Boston: Beacon, 1993), 68–87.
76. Bruce A. McConachie, "Using the Concept of Cultural Hegemony to Write Theatre History," in *Interpreting the Theatrical Past: Essays in the Historiography of Performance*, ed. Thomas Postelwait and Bruce A. McConachie (Iowa City: University of Iowa Press, 1989), 47. McConachie's discussion in this essay (37–58) of how Kenneth Burke provides the rhetorical underpinning for an understanding of how theater communicates and disseminates ideology is very relevant here.
77. Michael M. Davis, 24.
78. Garff B. Wilson, *Three Hundred Years of American Drama and Theatre*, 2nd ed. (Englewood Cliffs, NJ: Prentice-Hall, 1982), 223–224.
79. "At the Theatres: Princess—*The Great Divide*," *New York Dramatic Mirror*, Oct. 13, 1906, 3.
80. Richard Moody, introduction to *The Great Divide*, in *Dramas from the American Theatre: 1762–1909*, ed. Richard Moody (Boston: Houghton Mifflin Co., 1966), 727.

3 DISCIPLINE AND SPONTANEITY: CLYDE FITCH'S *THE COWBOY AND THE LADY* AND AUGUSTUS THOMAS'S *ARIZONA*

1. Mary C. Henderson, *The City and the Theatre: New York Playhouses from Bowling Green to Times Square* (Clifton, NJ: James T. White, 1973), 188.
2. An earlier version of the following discussion of Clyde Fitch's *The Cowboy and the Lady* appeared in my article "Taming the Frontier Myth: Clyde Fitch's *The Cowboy and the Lady*," *Journal of American Culture* 16.2 (1993), 77–84.
3. For a brief critical biography of Fitch, see Arthur Hobson Quinn, *A History of the American Drama: From the Civil War to the Present*, vol. I (New York: Appleton-Century-Crofts, 1936), 265–296.
4. Montrose Moses, *The American Dramatist* (1925; New York: Benjamin Blom, 1964), 319.
5. In this regard, see Thomas Lowell Hellie's very informative dissertation on Clyde Fitch, "Clyde Fitch: Playwright of New York's Leisure Class," diss., University of Missouri–Columbia, 1985.

6. Hellie, 139.
7. "'The Cowboy and the Lady': Mr. Goodwin and Miss Elliot in Mr. Fitch's Mining Camp Drama," *New York Times*, Dec. 26, 1899, 7.
8. Campbell's play was probably the most successful mining camp play or frontier play of any sort in the first-class theaters of New York during the last half of the nineteenth century. Campbell's contemporaries thought very highly of this play. For instance, see "Union Square Theatre," *New York Times*, Sept. 17, 1879, 5; "Union Square Theatre—*My Partner*," *New York Herald*, Sept. 17, 1879, 5; "The Drama—*My Partner*," *New York Daily Tribune*, Sept. 17, 1879, 4–5; and "Fall Opening: The Hit at the Union Square," *New York Mirror*, Sept. 20, 1979. The *Tribune* reviewer was perhaps most adamant, announcing that "it is a better piece, of its class, than has hither to been produced in America" (5). Twentieth-century critics continue to speak well of this play. For instance, Arthur Hobson Quinn called it "the drama of the frontier in its most impressive form" (119–20).
9. For a discussion of the "traditional" way in which women are presented in late-nineteenth-century drama, see Rosemarie K. Bank, "Rhetorical, Dramatic, Theatrical, and Social Contexts of Selected American Frontier Plays, 1871–1906," diss., University of Iowa, 1972, for instance, 191–92. For a fuller discussion here of gender in the nineteenth-century theater, see chapter 2.
10. Henry Nash Smith, *Virgin Land: The American West as Symbol and Myth* (1950; Cambridge, MA: Harvard University Press, 1978), 211.
11. Joe has some awareness of the larger frontier process that the play suggests. He recalls the early days on the frontier—the days before women arrived, when men often turned to violence to solve problems. Describing a past occasion when he and Ned had been involved in a knife fight "down in 'Dead Man's Gulch,'" Joe recollects, "Ah! That was a big day.... Three men killed. Ah! There ain't no such good times in California any more. There were no women in the mines then" [Bartley Campbell, *My Partner* in *The White Slave & Other Plays*, ed. Napier Wilt, *America's Lost Plays*, vol. XIX (1940; Bloomington: Indiana University Press, 1965), 60]. The reference to women in this quotation is significant: the arrival of women meant the arrival of at least a rudimentary form of civilization. Joe's friend, the politician Major Britt, laments the fact that women's "moral influence goes a great way.... once a woman gets her moral influence on a man, he's a goner!" (65). As Britt suggests, the presence of women on the frontier helped to establish a more restrained political and moral atmosphere. For Joe, this change is welcome. While he intermittently reminisces about the past, Joe is pleased that women have arrived. When asked if he was "happier without women," Joe responds, "Lord bless you, no! Why, there ain't no happiness where there ain't no women" (60).

The fact that Campbell presents a movement from savagery toward civilization did not go unnoticed at the time: the *New York Times* reviewer wrote:
> Like Mr. Miller in "The Danites," Mr. Campbell has chosen California as the ground of his story, although, unlike his predecessor and others

who have labored in the same field, he has placed its action within recent years—as late as 1859—when the old harsh, murderous life, once so closely identified with California's "glorious climate" and big trees, was almost entirely a thing of the past. The effect of this is, from a theatrical point of view, exceedingly fresh and unconventional. We catch a glimpse in the play, it is true, of the rough-and-tumble existence led in the mines; the hero, indeed, is one of the old Forty-niners, who has passed from amidst savagery into a more tempered state of civilization. ("Union Square Theatre," 5) As Jeffrey D. Mason claims, early editions of the play set it in 1879, so the reference to 1859 here would seem to be a mistake [*Melodrama and the Myth of America* (Bloomington: Indiana University Press, 1993), note 37, 218].

12. Campbell, 94–95. For a sense of the intensely controversial nature of this tolerant attitude toward a "lost" woman in Victorian-era America, see Napier Wilt, "Alphabetical List of the Plays of Bartley Campbell," in *"The White Slave" and Other Plays*, xlviii–xlix. In this context, it might be valuable to recall what the successful late-nineteenth-century playwright Bronson Howard said about erring women characters in a lecture at Harvard University in 1886: "The death, in an ordinary play, of a woman who is not pure...is perfectly satisfactory, for the reason that it is inevitable....The wife who has once taken the step from purity to impurity can never reinstate herself in the world of art on this side of the grave; and so an audience looks with complacent tears on the death of an erring woman" (quoted in Quinn, 44–45).

13. For a more in-depth discussion of the way in which the frontier myth is dramatized in *My Partner*, please see my article "Americanizing Frontier Melodrama: From *Davy Crockett* (1872) to *My Partner* (1879)," *Journal of American Culture* 12:1 (1989), 7–16.

14. Clyde Fitch, *The Cowboy and the Lady* (New York: Samuel French, 1908), 12. Further references to this play will be cited parenthetically in the text.

15. For instance, see Bederman, Chapter 1, "Remaking Manhood through Race and Civilization," *Manliness & Civilization: A Cultural History of Gender and Race in the United States, 1880–1917* (Chicago: University of Chicago Press, 1995), 1–44.

16. Hellie has also discussed the significance of the courtroom resolution to this play. He claims that Fitch's resolving the play with a courtroom climax as opposed to "a shootout at the OK Corral" is another example of the fact that this play "was not a Western at all, for it retained an attachment to the manners, the customs, the civilization of the East and of Europe" (139). Hellie's point is well taken, but the point here is that the play is about the East, but additionally about the East's transformation of the West. The significance of this court scene as an embodiment of the victory of civilized law and order over the savage West becomes all the more apparent when one compares this play to *My Partner*, which despite the many parallels in structure, keeps the formal court scene offstage.

17. Certainly, a degree of symmetry is apparent in the descriptions of the sets for the first two acts as well as the third-act courtroom scene. Significant here is that symmetry is much more obvious in the Act III set than in the others. For instance, compare Fitch's description of the Act III set (quoted in the text) with the following set description for Act I:
    Teddy's Ranch. Across the stage from R. to C. is the house. It stands on a ledge (evidently) behind it. Beyond the gully rises a mountain in the near distance. There are boulders and small hardy trees about. The sky is very blue, the clouds white and fleecy, the green of the foliage, such as there is, is very bright, all showing a clear, rarified air, high up. A path goes from the porch off L.U. and R.; also one goes extreme R. between house and proscenium arch. The path that leads off L.U. is the principle one, and shows that as it disappears it makes an abrupt descent. The horses are not ridden up to the house, but are left at the foot of this steep porch. There are common kitchen chairs on the porch and the old soap box which also serves as a stool or seat. (5)
    The randomness of nature here gives way to ordered interior design in Act III.
18. Richard Slotkin, *The Fatal Environment: The Myth of the Frontier in the Age of Industrialization, 1800–1890* (Middletown, CN: Wesleyan University Press, 1985), 531.
19. Slotkin, 531.
20. Slotkin, *Gunfighter Nation: The Myth of the Frontier in Twentieth-Century America* (New York: Atheneum, 1992), 18–19.
21. Slotkin, *Fatal Environment*, 332–33.
22. For a handy summary of the original New York reviews, see James J. Murray, "The Contributions of Clyde Fitch to the American Theatre," diss., Boston University, 1950, 175–77.
23. Edward Dithmar, "At the Play and with the Players," *New York Times*, Dec. 31, 1899, II-16.
24. Dithmar, 16.
25. Dithmar, 16.
26. Murray, 172–73.
27. Murray, 173.
28. That *Her Own Way* was a success was at least the opinion of the *New York Times* reviewer who wrote: "Taken all in all, it is the most evenly excellent of Mr. Fitch's social comedy dramas, and it bids fair to be his greatest success" ("Clyde Fitch at His Best," *New York Times*, Sept. 29, 1903, 5).
29. The similarities and differences between Sam Coast and Moody's Stephen Ghent (from *The Great Divide*) are very telling. While starting out as a bandit, Stephen, like Coast, becomes a very rich miner, and also like Coast he eventually comes east to find his wife; however, as a westerner in the East, he is presented in an entirely positive light—a good influence on "stuffy" eastern civilization. See Fitch, *Her Own Way* (London: MacMillan, 1907).

30. *Arizona* was apparently written as early as 1897, but its production was held up, according to Ronald J. Davis, because after "the outbreak of the Spanish-American War in April 1898, theater managers became cautious in staging new productions" [*Augustus Thomas* (Boston: Twayne, 1984), 14]. The play had its world premiere at Chicago's Hamlin's Grand Opera House on June 12, 1899. According to Jack Poggi, the Syndicate kept *Arizona* out of New York for over a year—a practice they would employ when they believed a play was not likely to succeed [*Theater in America: The Impact of Economic Forces, 1870–1967* (Ithaca, NY: Cornell University Press, 1968), 257]. Ironically, given the later conflict between the Shuberts and the Syndicate, when it was finally produced at the Herald Square Theatre, that theater was a Shubert theater—their first in New York. Alfred L. Bernheim writes that it was through productions like the 1900 production of *Arizona* that the Shuberts were able to restore the Herald Square Theatre to the status of a first-class theater [*The Business of the Theatre: An Economic History of the American Theatre, 1750–1932* (1932; New York: Benjamin Blom, 1964), 64].
31. Ronald J. Davis, 14; Poggi, 249.
32. Ronald J. Davis, 1–10; Quinn, 239–42.
33. Moses, 302.
34. For instance, in reviewing and condemning Thomas's *Colorado* (1901), which had a very short run, the *New York Times* critic wrote that in the past, Thomas had "contributed several plays that in reflecting the life of some portion or another of this broad land, has put the people of some other portion of it into touch with what exists elsewhere.... He has presented types of people, not caricatures, and it is the more to be regretted, therefore, that in this latest contribution he has not repeated the success of 'In Mizzoura,' and 'Arizona,' and others of his plays, wherein the name of the State was but an index to the phases of life he succeeded in representing" ("'Colorado' on Stage," *New York Times*, Nov. 19, 1901, 6).
35. See G. Edward White, *The Eastern Establishment and the Western Experience: The West of Frederic Remington, Theodore Roosevelt, and Owen Wister* (New Haven: Yale University Press, 1968), 75–144.
36. Augustus Thomas, *The Print of My Remembrance* (New York: Scribner's, 1922), 342; see also Ronald J. Davis, 13–14.
37. Thomas, *The Print of My Remembrance*, 336.
38. In writing about *Arizona*, some critics, like Quinn (249, 262) and Ronald J. Davis (45), have noted the importance of these contrasts to the play, but they have not probed the connection between these contrasts and the turn-of-the-century frontier myth.
39. Indeed, Thomas was always unusually open about his creative process. As Montrose Moses writes, in prefaces to his plays Thomas often traced "the processes by which these plays came to life, the external incentives, drawn from

his own interests and expediency" (365). In his autobiography, he does that for *Arizona*.
40. Thomas, *The Print of My Remembrance*, 336.
41. Remington was attracted to martial virtues, as Thomas suggests, but it was not iron-fisted military discipline that fascinated him. This was especially true after his experiences as a correspondent during the Spanish-American War. As White writes, "The technological aspects of modern war were most distressing to Remington....The spontananeity and glory of an Indian fight had been replaced by a mass of technological equipment which seemed to dwarf men's deeds and depersonalize their reactions" (115).
42. Thomas, *The Print of My Remembrance*, 351.
43. Thomas, *The Print of My Remembrance*, 351.
44. Augustus Thomas, *Arizona: A Drama in Four Acts* (New York: R.H. Russell, 1899), 8. Further references to this play will appear in text.
45. After his late-night discovery of Denton and Estrella, Colonel Bonham has difficulty trusting his wife. While a sense of duty to Denton's father mollifies his response to Denton, no such circumstance affects his anger toward his wife. Only at the very end of the play, when the whole truth of the Denton-Estrella late-night meeting is revealed, does the Colonel's attitude begin to soften. Perhaps learning some of the tolerance of his western friends and associates, the Colonel gives a sign—the return of a fallen rose to his wife—that he will once again love her as he had before.
46. Thomas, *The Print of My Remembrance*, 351.
47. Just as Roosevelt found savage Dakota frontier life to be an invigorating, transforming experience, so too did he look to war with Spain as a further way of testing his masculine virility and as a way of spreading American democratic civilization among "savage peoples" in the Caribbean and the Pacific. In this regard, see Michael Collins, *That Damned Cowboy: Theodore Roosevelt and the American West, 1883–1998* (New York: Peter Lang, 1989), 140–50. Reawakening the savage in oneself to spread civilization among savages may seem paradoxical, but in the late nineteenth century such an attitude seemed appropriate given the context not only of social Darwinist principle, but also of the new rough-and-tumble masculinity that Bederman describes (1–44). The manner in which the political debates over the war with Spain became entangled with gender politics—how the assertion of masculinity and an aggressive foreign policy were conjoined in the late 1890s—is the focus of Kristin L. Hoganson's *Fighting for American Manhood: How Gender Politics Provoked the Spanish-American and Philippine-American Wars* (New Haven: Yale University Press, 1998). Hoganson notes Roosevelt's hopes that the Spanish-American War and the push for empire would restore the vigor lost to the English-speaking peoples of the overcivilized, modern, industrial era (118–124,138–143).
48. See Thomas, *The Print of My Remembrance*, 356–8.

49. Not only was the fight in Cuba interchangeable with Indian War, but imperial conflicts elsewhere, such as China, also served the same purpose for Buffalo Bill. To develop an understanding of how Buffalo Bill's Wild West and Congress of Rough Riders of the World represented the victory of civilization over savagery in China, one need only look at the show programs. In one such program (located in the Billy Rose Division of the New York Public Library for the Perfoming Arts) from around 1901, "The Battle of Tien-Tsin" is listed as the climactic act of the show. It is in the place that was traditionally held by "Attack on Settlers' Cabin"—a signature vignette that represented Buffalo Bill with his band of cowboys, scouts, and frontiersmen coming to the rescue of a frontier family attacked by Indians. Replacing this act with the Tien-Tsin episode is indeed telling. Especially interesting in this context is the ending of the Tien-Tsin act, which consists of two scenes. The second scene's action is described in the program in the following terms: "The walls of Tien-Tsin. The Royal Standard of Paganism floats proudly defiant of the Christian World. The Alarm, the Attack, the Defense and the STORMING OF THE WALLS. The Royal Standard comes down and the BANNERS OF CIVILIZATION take its place" (*Buffalo Bill's Wild West: Historical Sketches & Programme*, ca. 1901, 3). Here, paganism is to Christianity as savagery is to civilization.
50. "Two More Theatres Open: New Plays Given at the Herald Square and the Bijou," *Sun*, Sept. 11, 1900, 4.
51. "Music and Drama: 'Arizona,'" *Evening Post*, Sept. 11, 1900, 7.
52. "Dramatic and Musical: 'Arizona' by Augustus Thomas Acted Here at Last, " *New York Times*, Sept. 11, 1900, 5.
53. W.D. Howells, "The Recent Dramatic Season," *North American Review* 172.3 (1901), 474

4   DRAMA FROM NOVELS: *JOHN ERMINE OF THE YELLOWSTONE* AND *THE VIRGINIAN*

1. Mary C. Henderson, *The City and the Theatre: New York Playhouses from Bowling Green to Times Square* (Clifton, NJ: James T. White, 1973), 163.
2. Ben Merchant Vorpahl, *My Dear Mr. Wister: The Frederic Remington–Owen Wister Letters* (Palo Alto, CA: American West, 1972), 15–20. Darwin Payne, *Owen Wister: Chronicler of the West, Gentleman of the East* (Dallas: Southern Methodist University Press, 1985), 77–99.
3. H.W. Boynton, "Books New and Old," *Atlantic Monthly*, August 1902, 277.
4. "Recent Novels," *Nation*, Oct. 23, 1902, 331.
5. Vorpahl, 308.
6. Vorpahl, 308; John L. Cobbs, *Owen Wister* (Boston: Twayne, 1984), 24.
7. Vorpahl, 4–12.
8. For instance, the *New York Times* reviewer praised the book, concluding that "Mr. Frederic Remington is certainly to be thanked…for a most entertaining story

that could hardly be improved in the telling" ("Remington's Novel," *New York Times Saturday Review of Books and Art*, Dec. 13, 1902, 897). The brief review in the *Nation* concluded, "The figure of John Ermine is romantic, and his fate tragic. The girl for whom he died is singularly unworthy of sacrifice, but this fact does not detract from the probability of Ermine's character and conduct, which is excellently sustained throughout" ("Recent Novels," *Nation*, March 19, 1903, 233).
 9. "Remington's Novel" 897.
10. Northrop Frye, *Anatomy of Criticism: Four Essays* (Princeton: Princeton University Press, 1957), 163. With regard to how Frye's view of comedy can relate to the frontier myth, see chapter 1.
11. Some critics preferred the original's tragic ending. See "Last Night's New Plays: Hackett as John Ermine," *New York Times*, Nov. 3, 1903, 5.
12. This information on the first production of *The Virginian* is drawn from N. Orwin Rush's introduction to Owen Wister and Kirke La Shelle, *The Virginian: A Play in Four Acts* (Tallahassee, FL: n.p., 1958), ii. Darwin Payne provides some of the same information; however, he claims that the Frohman with whom Wister negotiated was Daniel Frohman. In referring to Daniel Frohman as a "powerful producer" (213), I wonder if he was not really referring to Daniel's brother, Charles.
13. Payne, 221–26.
14. Payne, 226.
15. A copy of the Manhattan Theatre program for the week of November 2–7, 1903, can be found in the Billy Rose Theatre Division, the New York Public Library for the Performing Arts, Lincoln Center.
16. Frederic Remington, *John Ermine of the Yellowstone* (1902; Ridgewood, NJ: Gregg, 1968), 27.
17. Remington, 228.
18. Remington, 87–8.
19. Remington, 114.
20. Remington, 90.
21. Remington, 151. Wolf-Voice's mixed heritage is alluded to by Ermine in a conversation with the Englishman Harding.
22. Much to Ermine's dismay, Wolf-Voice looks forward to buying whiskey with the payment received for delivering military messages (Remington, 91), and when the Sioux attack a wagon train, Wolf-Voice only agrees to seek help for the besieged soldiers when the commander promises him a fee of "feefty doaller" (Remington, 132).
23. Remington, 153.
24. In this regard, Crooked Bear may be seen as the tragic protagonist of Remington's novel. It is his hubris that leads to the play's tragic outcome. His hope of bringing order to John Ermine's life, of giving John Ermine the freedom to succeed in the civilized world that he himself never had, is a tragic

aspiration akin to what has been described as the "enlightenment project" by postmodern critics.
25. While Thomas in *Arizona* seemed to suggest that a balance of civilization and savagery was possible—that a flexibility learned in the savage West could mitigate an inflexible eastern civilized discipline—Remington in his novel *John Ermine of the Yellowstone*, like Fitch in *The Cowboy and the Lady*, seemed to have little faith in such a balance. Unlike Fitch, who viewed civilized discipline as the necessary antidote to dangerous savage passions, Remington laments the displacement of the savage individual by a disciplined, spiritless slave of industry and convention.
26. Louis Evan Shipman, *John Ermine: A Play in a Prologue and Four Acts*, unpublished manuscript in the Billy Rose Theatre Division, the New York Public Library for the Performing Arts, Lincoln Center, prologue, 2. The cover page of this manuscript notes "Windsor, Vermont, 1903." Future references to this play will be to this version of the script and will be cited in the text. Judging from the reviews of the original production, this version of the script, though very close to the one used, may not be exactly the same as that reviewed. For instance, one might note the end of Act III as described in the reviews "Last Night's New Plays: Hackett as John Ermine," *New York Times*, Nov. 3, 1903, 5, and "Manhattan—*John Ermine of the Yellowstone*," *New York Dramatic Mirror*, Nov. 14, 1903, 18. In both reviews, there is mention of Major Searles and Captain Lewis's bursting into Ermine's cabin after Ermine has shot Lieutenant Butler, an action that forces the indiscreetly present Katherine to slip out a secret door. In the Lincoln Center typescript version, there is only reference to "the sound of VOICES" (III, 14), which indicates the approach of Searles and Lewis. Perhaps the actual appearance of the two was a production addition.
27. "Last Night's New Plays: Hackett as John Ermine," 5.
28. "Manhattan—*John Ermine of the Yellowstone*," 18. This reviewer also noted that "Mr. Shipman and Mr. Hackett [who played Ermine], in their work in the play, have not been as fair to the West as have the scene painters, the costumers and the property men" (18). Earlier in the review, the critic wrote, "Mr. Remington knows the outward semblance of the frontier, and by reason of his supervision the production, pictorially, was splendidly accurate" (18). Other critics also spoke well of the stage pictures. For instance, the *New York Herald* critic claimed that the primary value in the production would be found in the stage pictures: "The play would be worth seeing for its excellent and truthful stage pictures and costumes if for nothing else, details which have evidently been studied with care..." ("Mr. Hackett in Role of Scout," *New York Herald* Nov. 3, 1903, 10). The *New York Dramatic Mirror* reviewer was not alone in criticizing Shipman's efforts at poetic dialogue. In "Hackett as 'John Ermine': A Remington Sketch Turned into Stage Pictures," *Sun*, Nov. 3, 1903, 7, the reviewer complained about Shipman's tendency to incorporate

"old home poetic jargon about trees and clouds, and sky and the white man; in a word, Longfellow's 'Hiawatha,' not to mention other faded rhetoric." The reviewer for the *New York Herald* (10) and William Winter in "The Drama: Mr. Hackett as John Ermine: Manhattan Theatre," *New York Daily Tribune*, Nov. 3, 1903, 7, also connected Shipman's language to the tradition of Cooper and Longfellow.

29. In this regard, William Winter wrote: "Mr. Shipman has pressed into the service a goodly number of the old complexities of Indian adventure and the old and tried expedients of stage-effect, so that, as his play unfolds its time-honored narrative of beleaguered whites and murky, stealthy, murderous savages—implicating, of course, the one brave boy who dashes through unnumbered perils to bring the providential relief, and the maiden fair who rewards him at last with the priceless treasure of her celestial love,—the observer fondly recalls his happy youthful days with Big Serpent and Uncas...." (Winter 7).
30. Regarding the distinction between manliness and masculinity, see Gail Bederman, *Manliness and Civilization: A Cultural History of Gender and Race in the United States, 1880–1917* (Chicago: University of Chicago Press, 1995), 1–44.
31. "Last Night's New Plays: Hackett as John Ermine," 5.
32. "Hackett as 'John Ermine': A Remington Sketch Turned into Stage Pictures," 7.
33. "Hackett as 'John Ermine': A Remington Sketch Turned into Stage Pictures," 7.
34. "John Ermine," *Evening Post*, Nov. 3, 1903, 3.
35. "John Ermine," 3.
36. "Last Night's New Plays: Hackett as John Ermine," 5.
37. Winter, 7.
38. "Hackett as 'John Ermine': A Remington Sketch Turned into Stage Pictures," 7.
39. "Last Night's New Plays: Hackett as John Ermine," 5.
40. Shipman's language here suggests that what Ermine has learned with respect to the treatment of women has a racial foundation. This sense is also apparent in Katherine's earlier reference to the fact that "men of your blood—white men—are kind to women" (III, 11). Nevertheless, it would appear that the knowledge he gains is something he had to learn from an outside source and not something he might discover in himself—that is, this knowledge is a product of nurture not nature.
41. William Winter was most harsh in his evaluation of Walker's performance, writing that her "crude acting and careless articulation made the heroine an irrational cause of all the amatory excitement" (Winter, 7).
42. Cobbs, 73; Payne, 135–37, 193.
43. Cobbs writes that this was the "prepublication subtitle for the novel...for which he substituted 'A Horseman of the Plains' for the first edition" (73). Also see Payne, 193.
44. The extent to which each collaborator contributed to this adaptation is hard to determine. According to Wister's daughter: "My father first wrote five acts

and Kirke La Shelle wrote parts of the third act and gave advice" (quoted in Rush, ii). Payne suggests that while the stage version of the play grew out of an agreement between La Shelle and Wister, wherein Wister's responsibility was primarily to assist in the writing of dialogue, the third act, which includes the lynching scene, was largely Wister's contribution (Payne, 216–7, 224–5).

45. In this regard, the *New York Times* reviewer noted that the play, which was "well worth seeing," was "made up of a series of exquisitely real and soundly sentimental pictures of life and character, with little or no bearing on the story, which crops up at irregular intervals" ("Wister's *The Virginian*," *New York Times,* Jan. 6, 1904, 2); William Winter in the *New York Daily Tribune* wrote that the novel was "hampered with trivial episodes" and that the play made "a practical but inexpert use... of salient points of the novel" ("The Drama: New Play at the Manhattan—*The Virginian*," *New York Daily Tribune*, Jan. 6, 1904, 9); the reviewer of the *New York Herald* noted that the play was well received by opening-night audiences, but it "still needs pruning before it can expect lasting favor.... too much unnecessary dialogue and the action lags in the early parts" (*"The Virginian* Now a Live Hero," *New York Herald,* Jan. 6, 1904: 12) and claiming that the play's "accuracy of detail, and the consequent wealth of true atmosphere, is, therefore, the chief value of the play," the reviewer for the *New York Dramatic Mirror* conceded that the play, like "most dramatizations," was "fragmentary" ("At the Theatres: Manhattan—*The Virginian*," *New York Dramatic Mirror*, Jan. 16, 1904, 16).

46. Christine Bold, *Selling the Wild West: Popular Western Fiction, 1860 to 1960* (Bloomington: Indiana University Press, 1987), 41.

47. In the cast list published in the *New York Herald* review (*"The Virginian* Now a Live Hero," 12), Ogden is listed as "of New York." Not surprisingly, in the version published in Tallahassee in 1958, Ogden becomes an English traveler. This version, as editor N. Orwin Rush makes clear, was the version used for the London production (i). There is a typescript version of the play in the Billy Rose Theatre Division of the New York Public Library for the Performing Arts. The script is noted in the catalog as "New York? 1904?," but this version is cut considerably and is much less like the script described in New York reviews than is the London text. The latter version does have a somewhat different Act III than that described in reviews. The version that New York reviewers saw seems to consist of an overburdened single scene. After the Virginian and his posse lynch the Virginian's old friend Steve and another rustler, the reviewer for the *New York Dramatic Mirror* writes, "The schoolmistress [Molly Wood] and Judge Henry suddenly appear in most unplausible fashion. The Virginian apparently forgets all about Trampas [the villain], and stands, off guard, talking with the girl. Trampas, ambushed behind a tree, shoots the hero in the back. He falls, and the schoolmistress, bending over him, confesses, in an agony of emotion, her love for him" ("At the Theatres: Manhattan—*The Virginian*," *New York Dramatic Mirror*, 16). The awkwardness of the arrival of Molly and the Judge is abated in the English version. The

Virginian is shot while watching over the rustler's camp after the hangings have occurred. Molly arrives alone while on an outing she had prepared us for during the second act. She tends to the Virginian here and in a second scene added to the act, which is set at her residence. It is during this second scene that Molly and the convalescing Virginian finally embrace in a love that will be finalized with their presumed wedding at the end of Act IV. Other minor changes seem to have been made in the script between New York and London. For instance, Lin Maclean, who appears in none of the cast lists for the New York production, appears as a character in the London version. Given the overall similarity between this London version and the one that was reviewed in New York in 1904, this version will be used as the basis of the following critical analysis. All further references to this version will be cited parenthetically in the text.

48. Payne speaks of this contrast as one that preoccupied Wister, who was brought up in the East amid genteel prosperity, which included trips to Europe, where he studied music (3–61). As an adult, Wister discovered fulfillment in the wilder West (77–90), to which he returned a number of times. Regarding Wister's understanding of the contrast of East and West, see Payne, 84–85.
49. In regard to the impact on Wister of his Western experience, see G. Edward White, *The Eastern Establishment and the Western Experience: The West of Frederic Remington, Theodore Roosevelt, and Owen Wister* (New Haven, Yale University Press, 1968), 122–44.
50. Owen Wister, "The Evolution of the Cow-Puncher," in Vorpahl, 86. The full text of "The Evolution of the Cow-Puncher" appears in Vorpahl, 77–96.
51. Owen Wister, "Concerning 'Bad Men,'" in *Owen Wister's West*, ed. Robert Murray Davis (Albuquerque: University of New Mexico Press, 1987), 87.
52. Wister, "Concerning 'Bad Men,'" 88.
53. Owen Wister, "The Open-Air Education," in *Owen Wister's West*, 114.
54. In his discussion of *The Virginian* in *Performing the American Frontier* (Cambridge: Cambridge University Press, 2001), Roger A. Hall calls attention to the Virginian's sense of humor. He writes: "His impish humor melds with his sense of honor to produce an utterly charming combination" (195). He also refers to the Virginian's "Will Rogers–like wit" (195).
55. Payne notes the parallels between Turner's and Wister's ideas about the significance of the West. See Payne, 139. Interestingly, Payne suggests that Wister was connected with the 1893 Chicago World's Columbian Exposition at which Turner presented his famous thesis. Wister helped "arrange the Boone and Crockett Club's exhibit" for the exposition (134).
56. In his provocative study of Western novels, *The Return of the Vanishing American* (New York: Stein and Day, 1969), Leslie Fiedler makes connections between *The Virginian* and what he calls its "English prototype," *Ivanhoe*, and both to the Southern literary tradition. With its "Ivanhoe in chaps," *The Virginian* exemplifies what Fiedler refers to as the "southernized Western" (138). The

fascination with medievalism was not limited to the South during this period. See T.J. Jackson Lears's discussion in *No Place of Grace: Antimodernism and the Transformation of American Culture, 1880–1920* (Chicago: University of Chicago Press, 1981), 141–181. As Lears points out, medievalism and the wilderness cult represented two related strategies embraced by late-nineteenth-century intellectuals, who sought to resist what they felt to be the repressive, debilitating impact of late-nineteenth-century producer-oriented industrial culture.

57. In this regard, it is worth recalling how Wister used the term "white man" in his praise of Theodore Roosevelt. He claimed: "Mr. Roosevelt shines, not quite alone, but conspicuous. He takes no mean advantage of an adversary; he stops when 'time' is called; he fights 'on the square;' he is what the West calls a 'white man:' and that is the true cause of him and his great popularity" (Wister, "Theodore Roosevelt: The Sportsman and the Man," in *Owen Wister's West*, 102).
58. Bederman, 1–44.
59. See "Wister's *The Virginian*," 2; "Music and Drama: *The Virginian*," *Evening Post*, Jan. 6, 1904, 7; "*The Virginian* Now a Live Hero," 12; "Nothing Much in Four Acts: *The Virginian* Dramatized Comes Out on Stage," *Sun*, Jan. 6, 1904, 9; and "At the Theatres: Manhattan—*The Virginian*," 16.
60. "At the Theatres: Manhattan—*The Virginian*," 16. The reference to "manly" here seems very apt. It caps a description in which Farnum is presented as embodying both what Bederman referred to as manly and what she spoke of as the new masculinity.
61. "Music and Drama: *The Virginian*," 7.
62. William Winter, "The Drama: New Play at the Manhattan—*The Virginian*," 9.
63. William Winter, "The Drama: New Play at the Manhattan—*The Virginian*," 9.
64. Interestingly, Molly's reservations about lynch justice were shared by many easterners. In fact, La Shelle had originally developed an Act III for the play in which no lynching scene appeared. He was convinced that eastern audiences would find such a scene to be in very poor taste. Indeed, just a few years earlier, Edward Dithmar's response, "At the Play and with the Players," *New York Times*, Dec. 31, 1899, 11–16, to the offstage lynching scene of Fitch's *The Cowboy and the Lady* would seem to justify La Shelle's concerns. After La Shelle's bout with appendicitis temporarily forced him to withdraw from rehearsals, Wister, sensing that the production of *The Virginian* was in need of a dramatic boost, introduced a lynching scene. Audiences seemed to approve and La Shelle agreed to let the scene remain. The lynching scene, which begins Act III, is spare in style and is discrete in how it actually represents the death of the two rustlers who are hanged; it is perhaps the most effective scene in the play. In this regard, see Payne, 213–24.
65. The historical events on which the play's conflict between ranchers and rustlers is based were actually more complex than one would guess from the

presentation here. The conflict was less a struggle of law-abiding ranchers against rustlers than one between big ranchers and little ranchers. Richard Slotkin lays out this background in his discussion of Wister's novel in *Gunfighter Nation: The Myth of the Frontier in Twentieth-Century America* (New York: Atheneum, 1992), 169–183.

66. Frederick Jackson Turner, "The Significance of the Frontier in American History," in *The Frontier in American History* (Tucson: University of Arizona Press, 1986), 4.
67. See Vorpahl, 35–36, and Cobbs, 15–17.
68. Owen Wister, *The Virginian* (1902; New York: Airmont, 1964), 11.
69. Vernon Louis Parrington, *Main Currents in American Thought: An Interpretation of American Literature from the Beginnings to 1920, Vol. III: (1860–1920), The Beginnings of Critical Realism in America* (New York: Harcourt-Brace, 1930), 192. For further discussion on Parrington and the shift toward American dramatic realism, see Chapter 2.
70. Jane Tompkins, *West of Everything: The Inner Life of Westerns* (New York: Oxford University Press, 1992), 144. As a means of exploring Wister's relation to the larger cultural community, Tompkins gives attention in this book's chapter on Wister to his relationship with his mother, a very powerful figure in his life.

5 VARIATIONS ON THE FRONTIER MYTH: EDWIN MILTON ROYLE'S *THE SQUAW MAN* AND DAVID BELASCO'S *THE GIRL OF THE GOLDEN WEST*

1. Burns Mantle, *The Best Plays of 1899–1909*, eds. Burns Mantle and Garrison P. Sherwood (New York: Dodd-Mead, 1947), 207.
2. Mantle, 500.
3. Numbers of performances cited here are drawn from Mantle, 492–515.
4. "Joe Weber's—*The Squawman's Girl of the Golden West*," *New York Dramatic Mirror*, March 10, 1906, 3.
5. See "Weber's Clever Burlesque Makes the Originals Laugh," *New York Telegraph*, March 7, 1906. This article appears in a scrapbook within the Robinson Locke Collection (vol. 481, Joseph Weber, vol. 1, 53), the Billy Rose Theatre Division, the New York Public Library for the Performing Arts, Lincoln Center.
6. Mantle, 208.
7. Mantle, 207–41.
8. John H. Lenihan, "Westbound: Feature Films and the American West," in *Wanted Dead or Alive: The American West in Popular Culture*, ed. Richard Aquila (Urbana: University of Illinois Press, 1996), 111.
9. Roger A. Hall, *Performing the American Frontier* (Cambridge: Cambridge University Press, 2001), 205–6. For a brief discussion of other of his plays, see

Arthur Hobson Quinn, *A History of American Drama: From the Civil War to the Present Day*, vol. II (New York: Appleton-Century-Crofts, 1936), 123–26, and Mantle, 343. Apparently, in 1910, Royle had hoped to premiere a sequel to *The Squaw Man*, a play originally entitled *These Are My People* and then called *The Silent Call*, a work based on his 1910 novel, *The Silent Call*. The play version of the novel was scheduled to open in January 1911, but was held back. See "Change to 'The Squaw Man,'" *New York Times*, Dec. 31, 1910, 4. Nothing more seems to have come of it.

10. "'The Squaw Man' Earns Its Success," *New York Herald*, Oct. 24, 1905, 10. Other reviewers offered similar judgments. The *New York Daily Tribune* critic wrote that "there are suggestions of melodrama in the situations and the effects employed, but the action is well restrained.... and the result was a generally well rounded performance of a play that is sentimental without mawkishness and vivid without sensationalism" ("'The Squaw Man'—Wallack's Theatre," Oct. 24, 1905, 7); the *New York Dramatic Mirror* critic wrote that *The Squaw Man* was a "thoroughly American play, quick beating with the red heart-blood of manly sincerity and self-sacrifice.... It goes far toward satisfying the general hunger for strong and human drama and therefore merits popularity" ("Wallack's—*The Squaw Man*," Nov. 4, 1905, 3); the reviewer for *Theatre Magazine* wrote that in this play, "we have more detail, character and atmosphere than conventionality and theatric trickery. The characters are to the life, numerous as they are.... The details of character, manner and speech are too minute to convey by description, a proof of the genuineness of this very successful, touching and powerful play" ("Wallack's. 'The Squaw Man,'" Dec. 1905, 293).

11. Interestingly, Burns Mantle writes: "In the autobiography on which he was working at the time of his death Edwin Milton Royle recalls that the first thought of 'The Squaw Man' came to him one night when he and Mrs. (Selena Fetter) Royle were playing in vaudeville in Chicago. It kept him awake all night, but when he talked it over with Mrs. Royle in the morning she frankly advised him to forget it. 'Why do you think of these *sad* plays?' she demanded. 'Your forte is comedy.' Edwin Milton thought perhaps she was right" (Mantle, 208).

12. This printed version of the play, catalogued as "'*The Squaw Man,' A Comedy Drama in Four Acts* by Edwin Milton Royle, [New York?] 1906," appears in the New York Public Library at 42nd Street. This version includes promptbook information from the 1905–1906 production. Future references to the play, unless otherwise stated, will be from this version and will be cited parenthetically in the text. There is also a manuscript copy of the play in the Billy Rose Theatre Division, the New York Public Library for the Performing Arts, Lincoln Center. The cover page of this manuscript notes: "New York, 1905." For the most part, this 1905 version seems to be the unpolished prototype for the 1906 version. Both bear the stamp "The Property of Leibler & Co., New York." Leibler and Company was the producer of the original 1905 New York production.

13. "How the Squaw Man Is Not the Shawman," *New York Times*, Oct. 24, 1905, 6. In comparing this play to the work of Shaw, the *New York Times* reviewer writes that *The Squaw Man*, "though conventional to a degree and full of all those appeals to time-worn sentiment at which G. B. Shaw jeers, undoubtedly pleased the company." With regard to Shaw's way of shifting from idealist rhetoric to something more realistic, one might note a play like his *Arms and the Man*, which moves from a romanticized view of war expressed by Major Sergius Saranoff to the practical realism of the Swiss mercenary Captain Bluntschli, or to a play like *Major Barbara*, which moves the audience from Barbara's Salvation Army "spirituality" as it is played out at the religious order's shelter to the hard-nosed realism exhibited in Undershaft's munitions factory.
14. "How the Squaw Man Is Not the Shawman," 6.
15. "Music and Dance: 'The Squaw Man,'" *Evening Post*, Oct. 25, 1905, 9.
16. "Wallack's. 'The Squaw Man,'" 293.
17. Quinn, 123.
18. "Lyric Theatre—'A White Man.' By Edwin Milton Royle," *Times*, Jan. 13, 1908, 7.
19. Changes in the first act may have slightly affected the rest of the play and perhaps clarify the chronological connection between the two New York Public Library versions and that described by Mantle. For instance, in the 1906 version, a letter of confession that Jim demanded of his cousin Henry before he would undertake the sacrifice of accepting the blame for Henry's misdeeds (28–31) reappears in Act III as a crinkled, weather-beaten, "old and faded" document (65) that Jim has kept on his person through all the years of his exile. This letter appears in Act III as a kind of deus ex machina to absolve Jim of any responsibility for his brother's crimes. In neither Act I nor Act III of the Mantle description of the play is such a letter mentioned. Interestingly, to relieve Jim of this clumsily contrived method of proving his innocence, Royle appended a brief scene to the conclusion of the 1905 Act III—a scene that apparently was meant to replace the scene in which Jim reveals the letter to Petrie, the visiting family solicitor. In this new scene, Petrie reveals to Jim that Henry, "a most unhappy man," had made a "complete confession" before passing away. The device not only provides Henry with more depth, but also seems much more plausible. Its presence as a kind of afterthought to the act suggests that this after-the-fact confession was developed after the letter device had been tried and rejected. In any event, this scene does not appear in the 1906 printed version of the play, but it is integrated into the Mantle description of the play's action (231).
20. Mantle, 211.
21. See also Mantle, 215.
22. See also Mantle, 213.
23. Mantle, 211.

24. Mantle, 218.
25. In Mantle, the words are "the honor and glory of belonging to a great family" (214).
26. Frederick Jackson Turner, "The Significance of the Frontier in American History," in *The Frontier in American History* (Tucson: University of Arizona Press, 1986), 4.
27. Mantle, 220.
28. See also Mantle, 239. Her silence in addition to her dedication to husband and child suggest the subservient position that Whites assumed Indian women held within the tribe. With regard to the questionable nature of this assumption, see Rosemarie K. Bank, "Rhetorical, Dramatic, Theatrical, and Social Contexts of Selected American Frontier Plays, 1871–1906," diss., University of Iowa, 1972, note 27, 160.
29. Mantle, 239. Regarding the Indians of this play, see Bank, "Rhetorical, Dramatic, Theatrical, and Social Contexts," 159–61.
30. In the Wild West, the lack of institutions of law and order does not prevent the development of social distinctions; however, for western whites living closer to savagery than their English contemporaries, these distinctions are relatively fluid. Although Jim is stigmatized as a "squaw man," he is, as Big Bill claims in the play's last act, "respected in spite of the fact that he's a squaw-man. He's lived that down" (82). Of course, it is possible that he is so respected because, as will be discussed shortly, despite his connections with savagery, he remains very much a product of white civilization.
31. Mantle, 230.
32. As Bill tells other of Carston's ranch hands, "Oh, it's no use, boys; it's the business that's no good. Nothin' in it. The packers have got us skinned to death. They pay us what they like for cattle and charge the public what they like for beef!" (59).
33. Also see Mantle, 232.
34. Also see Mantle, 239.
35. Also see Mantle, 233.
36. "A Comedy Drama in Four Acts" appears as the subtitle on the cover and title page of the 1906 version of the play. The shortened version that appears in Mantle is subtitled simply "A Drama in Four Acts."
37. Hal's difficulties are explored in *The Squaw Man*'s novel sequel, *The Silent Call* (1910), for which Royle attempted a dramatization that made it to out-of-town try-outs but never to New York.
38. Much of the material on Belasco's *The Girl of the Golden West* presented here appeared in an earlier form in my essay "'Local Colour' Plus 'Frontier Myth': The Belasco Formula in *The Girl of the Golden West*," *Essays in Theatre/Études Théâtrales* 11.1 (1992), 85–97.
39. With respect to Belasco's early years working in the California theater, Arthur Hobson Quinn wrote: "[T]here emerges the figure of a hard-working

actor and playwright, learning his profession in a school which developed Herne, Harrigan, and other dramatists, the highly colored life and theatre of California in the seventies. Of all who worked in that atmosphere, Belasco seems to have been most deeply affected by it, as was perhaps natural since it was his native soil, and while the others saw it from the point of view of the theatre, it had been part of his education" (vol. I, 165).

40. According to Garrison Sherwood's information, *The Rose of the Rancho* opened at New York City's Belasco Theatre on November 27, 1906, and ran for 240 performances during the 1906–1907 and 1907–1908 seasons (Mantle, 527).

41. Especially stunning for audiences and critics was a startlingly effective blizzard in Act II. Belasco's staging received praise from the original New York reviewers. For instance, the *New York Times* reviewer wrote: "In respect to staging, David Belasco has done nothing better than this latest play" ("'Girl of the Golden West' Wins At The Belasco," Nov. 15, 1905, 11). Likewise the reviewer for the *Sun* notes Belasco's "incomparably artistic stagecraft" ("Belasco and Blanche Bates," Nov. 15, 1905, 7). The *Evening Post* reviewer wrote: "The scenery and the stage management were worthy of Mr. Belasco's reputation, and the introductory mountain pictures were beautiful" ("Music and Drama: 'The Girl of the Golden West,'" Nov. 15, 1905, 9). The reviewer for the *New York Dramatic Mirror* also speaks highly of Belasco's "master-artist touch" with which he "realized the picturesque possibilities of the Western mining camp" ("Belasco—*The Girl of the Golden West*," Nov. 25, 1905, 3). For other and more recent discussions of Belasco's scenic effects in this play, see William Winter, *The Life of David Belasco*, vol. II (New York: Moffat, Yard and Co., 1918), 205–208; Craig Timberlake, *The Life and Work of David Belasco: The Bishop of Broadway* (New York: Library Publishers, 1954), 284–85; and Lise-Lone Marker, *David Belasco: Naturalism in the American Theatre* (Princeton: Princeton University Press, 1975), 139–60.

42. Winter, 199. In his biography of Belasco, Winter reiterates what he had written in his original review. At that time he also claimed that "[t]he Girl herself is the play, and Miss Blanche Bates is the Girl" ("The Drama—'The Girl of the Golden West'—Blanche Bates," *New York Daily Tribune*, Nov. 15, 1905, 7).

43. Winter, *The Life of David Belasco*, 200.

44. David Belasco, *The Girl of the Golden West* (New York: Samuel French, 1915, 1933), 8. Future references to this play will be to this version of the script and will be parenthetically cited in the text.

45. "Belasco—*The Girl of the Golden West*," 3.

46. "David Belasco as Dramatist and Stage Manager," *New York Times*, Nov. 19, 1905, X3.

47. In this context, see Daniel Gerould's discussion of Minnie in "The Americanization of Melodrama," in *American Melodrama*, ed. Daniel C. Gerould, (New York: Performing Arts Journal, 1983), 26. Minnie's

combination of "wildness and femininity" has led Gerould to write that this self-reliant heroine is "a specifically American version of the New Woman who appeared in life as in literature around the turn of the century."
48. Stuart Wallace Hyde, "The Representation of the West in American Drama from 1849 to 1917," diss., Stanford, 1954, 276–77.
49. Winter, "The Drama—'The Girl of the Golden West,'" 7.
50. Timberlake, 284.
51. Stuart Wallace Hyde, 260–77.
52. In this regard, see Wallace Stegner, introduction to Bret Harte, *"The Outcasts of Poker Flat" and Other Tales* (New York: Signet, 1961), ix.
53. Gerould, 26.
54. See Stuart Wallace Hyde, 273–4.
55. Minnie's actions in this scene seem strangely to parallel the actions that the westerner Stephen Ghent takes to win the easterner Ruth Jordan in Act I of *The Great Divide*. As Rosemarie Bank has pointed out, Minnie prepares to gamble for the life of Johnson, just as Ghent at first prepares to gamble with his two savage companions for the "ownership" of Ruth, whom they have found alone and unprotected after breaking into her cabin ("Rhetorical, Dramatic, Theatrical, and Social Contexts," 186). Also like Minnie, Ghent resorts to morally questionable means—bribery and gunplay—to assure his victory. At least superficially spurning civilized values, Minnie seems to have more in common with the kind of savage/western/male figure who would appear in Moody's play a year later than with Moody's moralistic, New England heroine.
56. Barbara Welter, "The Cult of the True Womanhood: 1820–1860," *American Quarterly* 18 (1966), 152.
57. See Yellow Bird (John Rollin Ridge), *The Life and Adventures of Joaquin Murieta* (Norman: University of Oklahoma Press, 1955), 13–18, 65, and 105.
58. In this regard, Belasco's Minnie exemplifies the late-nineteenth-century transformation of the ideal of "true womanhood." Welter herself wrote that the ideal of true womanhood she defined for the years 1820–1860 was transformed during the course of the nineteenth century: "But even while the women's magazines and related literature encouraged this ideal of the perfect women, forces were at work in the nineteenth century which impelled woman herself to change, to play a more creative role in society. The movements for social reform, westward migration, missionary activity, utopian communities, industrialism, the Civil War—all called forth responses from women which differed from those she was trained to believe were hers by nature and divine decree" (173–74). Moreover, it is important to remember that the ideal of true womanhood was not the only way in which womanhood was constructed in the nineteenth century. The significance of this cult is that it represented the gender ideology of the dominant interests of the period—interests that were white, male, and bourgeois.

59. In that Minnie's civilizing influence prevents a lynching, this play recalls the response to that form of frontier justice offered in Fitch's *The Cowboy and the Lady*; however, here lynching does not give way to a formal trial as in the earlier play. Again, as in Thomas's *Arizona*, the perpetrator is allowed to escape—a kind of vindication of spontaneous public judgment over mediated court procedure. In short, Belasco's treatment of vigilante justice in this play is marked by the same kind of ambivalence that we will see in his treatment of the allegorical dimensions of Minnie and Ramerrez-Johnson's union.
60. Turner, "The Significance of the Frontier," 4.
61. The specifics of Belasco's staging of Act IV are drawn from the Samuel French version of the play, which was "set up from the acting prompt manuscript of the play" (163).
62. Marker, 159.
63. "Belasco and Blanche Bates," 7.
64. Quoted in Winter, *The Life of Belasco*, 205.

6 FROM MELODRAMA TO REALISM: WILLIAM VAUGHN MOODY'S *THE GREAT DIVIDE* AND RACHEL CROTHERS'S *THE THREE OF US*

1. Burns Mantle and Garrison P. Sherwood, *The Best Plays of 1899–1909* (New York: Dodd, Mead, 1947), 527. Performance numbers are drawn from Mantle, 515–40.
2. Of *The Three of Us*, the *New York Times* critic wrote: "There is some refreshing characterization in Miss Crothers's play, there is easy natural dialogue, and there are some very excellent contrasts of people and of incident" ("Carlotta Nillson in 'The Three Of Us,'" Oct. 18, 1906, 9). The *New York Daily Tribune* reviewer wrote that "the piece is happily free from much of the course exaggeration usually characteristic of plays relative to life in the Far West" ("The Drama—The Madison Square Theatre—'The Three of Us,'" Oct. 18, 1906, 7); the New York *Sun* reviewer wrote that "Mr. Howells, and many of his way of thinking, would, and, it is to be hoped, will delight in the play" ("Realism in 'The Three of Us': Domestic Drama in a Nevada Mining Camp," Oct. 18, 1906, 7); and the reviewer of the *New York Dramatic Mirror* claimed: "Here is a Western drama stripped of conventional accessories and dealing with people alone; plain human beings fighting against ordinary evils" ("Madison Square—*The Three of Us*," Oct. 27, 1906, 3). Moody's play was even more highly praised for its innovative dramaturgy. The *New York Times* reviewer, writing that the play was far above the normal melodrama, praised its characterizations as "splendidly real" ("A Powerful Play Beautifully Acted," Oct. 5, 1906, 9); the *New York Daily Tribune* critic wrote that "there is much human nature in the piece" ("The Drama—Mr. Miller

and Miss Anglin—Princess Theatre," Oct. 4, 1906, 7); the *Evening Telegram* reviewer wrote, "In a day, when undue emphasis is laid on scenery and costumes, it is hard to be moderate in praise of a play such as this, wherein the drama lies in spiritual issues" ("Prompt Aid to the Injured Prompter," Oct. 4, 1906, 10); the *New York Dramatic Mirror* reviewer wrote that the play "rises far above the mere theatric effectiveness of melodrama," and that in its treatment "of the basic principles of things," it "set a new standard for the American drama" ("The Princess—*The Great Divide*," Oct. 13, 1906, 3); and perhaps most explicitly, the review in the New York *Sun* maintained that Moody set "A new mark in American drama" ("Mr. Moody's 'The Great Divide,'" Oct. 4, 1906, 6).
3. Arthur Hobson Quinn, *A History of the American Drama: From the Civil War to the Present Day*, vol. II (New York: Appleton-Century-Crofts, 1936), 4.
4. Richard Moody, introduction to *The Great Divide*, in *Dramas from the American Theatre: 1762–1909* (Boston: Houghton Mifflin, 1969), 727.
5. Maurice F. Brown, *Estranging Dawn: The Life and Works of William Vaughn Moody* (Carbondale: Southern Illinois University Press, 1973), 245–46.
6. Lois C. Gottlieb, *Rachel Crothers* (Boston: Twayne, 1979), 24.
7. Richard Moody, 721.
8. This Moody-Garland trip received different accounts from the two authors. Garland claimed to cut it short due to Moody's suffering lumbago [see Garland, *Companions on the Trail: A Literary Chronicle* (New York: Macmillan, 1931), 92]. On the other hand, Moody wrote in an undated letter from around August 19, 1901, to his future wife, Harriet Brainerd, that the trip was curtailed because of a horse-riding accident in which Garland hurt a foot [William Vaughn Moody, *Letters to Harriet*, ed. Percy Mackaye (Boston: Houghton Mifflin, 1935), 78–79]. It is also interesting to note that there are striking parallels between Garland's Far West novel, *Hesper* (New York: Harper, 1903), and Moody's *The Great Divide*. Both deal with the relationship of a western cowboy turned miner and an eastern woman who has accompanied her brother to the West. While Garland's novel is set in the Colorado Rockies and Moody's play in Arizona, both trace the impact of the two characters on each other. The eastern heroine is liberated by western freedom, and the western hero is "civilized" by the exponent of eastern culture. Both tales end with the promise of a happy marriage between the representatives of East and West.
9. Quoted in Richard Moody, 722. Moody completed only one act of the third play in the trilogy, *The Death of Eve* (1907).
10. "Mr. Moody's 'The Great Divide,'" 6.
11. "A Powerful Play Acted Beautifully," 9.
12. See, for instance, "A Powerful Play Acted Beautifully," *New York Times*, in which the reviewer noted "the employment of coincidence as a means of bringing its several important characters together after a long lapse of time"

(9); the *Evening Post*, in which the reviewer complained that the play was "a little crude in conception" and the central characters a little overdrawn, but still concluded that the play was "a genuine American play, with a strong and vital motive, involving a fierce struggle between widely contrasted human types and treated with marked vigor and originality" ("Music and Drama—'The Great Divide,'" Oct. 4, 1906, 7); and the *New York Dramatic Mirror*, in which the "improbability of the story" is cited and then excused ("Princess—The Great Divide," 3).
13. "Mr. Moody's 'The Great Divide,'" 6.
14. "Prompt Aid to the Injured Prompter," 10.
15. Jerry Pickering, "William Vaughn Moody: The Dramatist as Social Philosopher," *Modern Drama* 14.1 (1971), 98–99, writes: "If one accepts the social milieu in which Moody lived as one undergoing a major historical crisis, torn between the static values of a culturally mature East and a raw and expanding West, then the significance of Turner and his interpretation of the frontier in American history becomes of vital interest when filtered through Moody's dramas.... [In *The Great Divide*] we encounter once again Moody's prevalent theme of 'moral unity,' with Ruth and Stephen dependent on each other if happiness is to be achieved. Furthermore, the image of the West is also revealed in the reconciliation between Stephen and Ruth, who each in their own way, symbolize the promise that the West represents to the American experience. This promise revealed by Moody is the same promise made by both [William] James and Turner...."
16. Even where Turner treated the European/Indian frontier interaction, he always seemed to subsume Indians under the category environment. See Frederick Jackson Turner, "The Significance of the Frontier in American History," in *The Frontier in American History* (Tucson: University of Arizona Press, 1986), 1–38; see chapter 1, note 57.
17. In this regard, Moody's play follows a pattern similar to Royle's play, where Jim leaves his English home and journeys to the American West. Royle explores Jim's relationship to the wild western environment, which is represented by scenery as well as by characters (savage Indians and outlaws) who people this setting. Royle's play, however, moves to a very different conclusion than that of Turner or Moody. The western environment presented by Royle is ultimately conceived in terms of colorful western characters. Moreover, the Act I eastern environment juxtaposed to it is also more idealistically presented.
18. The biblical associations suggested by Ruth Jordan's name obviously indicate continuity between this play and Moody's poetic dramas. Unlike her biblical namesake, who traveled from Moab to Bethlehem with her mother-in-law, this Ruth travels into a new land with her brother.
19. William Vaughn Moody, *The Great Divide*, in Moody, *Dramas from the American Theatre: 1762–1909*, 730. Further references to this script will appear parenthetically in the text. This version of the play is drawn from

William Vaughn Moody, *Poems and Plays*, vol. II (Boston: Houghton Mifflin, 1906).
20. In regard to Ruth's romantic sentimentality at the start of the play, see James John Koldenhoven's unpublished dissertation, "A Structuralist Approach to the Realistic Drama of William Vaughn Moody," diss., University of Minnesota, 1986, 129–32.
21. Turner's analysis of the interaction of eastern civilization and western savagery might have its prototype in the captivity tales that can be traced back to the seventeenth century. In this regard, Moody's *The Great Divide* might be interpreted as a late version of a captivity tale. I offer a detailed analysis of Moody's play in terms of the captivity tale structure in "Reworking the Frontier Captivity Narrative: William Vaughn Moody's *The Great Divide*," *American Drama* 9.2 (2000), 1–28.
22. Koldenhoven makes a similar point. Having claimed that Dutch, Shorty, and Stephen are the "savages" of this play, he writes: "[A]s they burst into the cabin they are of a single mind, to rape this unprotected young woman. On seeing Ruth, however, a transformation takes place. The three 'savages' take on distinguishing characteristics..." (114).
23. In this regard, see, for instance, the review of the play in *Theatre Magazine*. Here the play is described as "wholly unsympathetic" and "unnecessary and unpleasant." More specifically, Ruth's actions are judged to be "illogical and unacceptable" and the play's theme described as "true enough to life in its primitive aspect, but it is one of questionable taste to exploit" ("Princess. 'The Great Divide,'" Nov. 1906, 283–84).
24. Turner, 4.
25. See Patricia Nelson Limerick, *The Legacy of Conquest: The Unbroken Past of the American West* (New York: Norton, 1987), 99–124.
26. Martin Halpern, *William Vaughn Moody* (New Haven, CT: College and University Press, 1964), 124.
27. Halpern, 129–130.
28. Regarding this early version of the play and the revisions Moody made to it, see Brown, 215–17. In a letter dated June 5, 1906, to his eventual wife, Harriet, Moody, explained some of the factors affecting the change: "After hammering at the thing in the back regions of my head for days and weeks, today I had the felicity to see pop into the front regions the right kind of ending for the play. It looks right today anyhow, whatever it may look tomorrow. It seems to me to preserve everything vital in the first, the violent, ending, and it brings the play to a close in an upswinging mood of lightness, going towards comedy—an immense advantage of course. Moreover, it makes Zona [Ruth's original name] herself and not the brute catastrophe the Erlösungselement (such a word?) with only a fillip of the nerves to help her; and it brings in the family again, instead of leaving them hanging in the air with all their yarn unraveling, as in the makeshift Chicago version. Hoopla! Also, it makes

Zona the active petitioner and pleader for the thing she has rejected many times from the hands of the lover, and makes him—through incredulity—the withholder. This last, though it may not be spotless gallantry on the author's part, is good drama" (Quoted in William Vaughn Moody, *Letters to Harriet*, 280).

29. See the Parrington discussion in chapter 2. For the Parrington reference, see Vernon Lewis Parrington, *Main Currents in American Thought: An Interpretation of American Literature from the Beginnings to 1920, Vol. III: (1860–1920), The Beginnings of Critical Realism in America* (New York: Harcourt-Brace, 1980), 192.

30. Thomas Postlewait in his essay "From Melodrama to Realism: The Suspect History of American Drama," in *Melodrama: The Cultural Emergence of a Genre*, ed. Michael Hays and Anastasia Nikolopoulou (New York: St. Martin's Press, 1996), 39–60, pointed out that late-nineteenth-century advocates of realism used a similar kind of blending of "evolutionary" scientific thinking and romantic idealism in making their case for a new drama. On the one hand, they argued that realism was a more sophisticated form than melodrama, and thus embracing it meant accepting an evolution from simple to complex. On the other hand, they argued for a simple, true, more natural American drama in the vein of *Davy Crockett*, *Rip Van Winkle*, and *My Partner* that would free the American theater from "melodrama... identified with an overly complex and decadent European culture" (51).

31. Even this ostensible balance between hero and heroine was difficult for Moody to achieve given the egos of the actors he dealt with. If we can trust Moody's letters to his wife, Harriet, this was especially a problem with Margaret Anglin, who was to play the female lead. In his letter dated May 4, 2006, Moody referred to "Miss A's feverish suggestions... as to how her rôle might be made to dominate the whole play, and herself enabled to snatch the honors of popular sympathy from the brows of the prospective personator of 'Stephen' " (William Vaughn Moody, *Letters to Harriet*, 262). In the same letter, Moody wrote positively of Henry Miller, who was to play Ghent. According to Moody, Miller declared that "his first desire to be to have me make of it a thoroughly well-rounded and self-sufficing piece of dramatic art, without regard to his own *particular rôle*" (William Vaughn Moody, *Letters to Harriet*, 262).

32. Koldenhoven, 114. One could also argue that in Moody's play savagery is associated with the working classes. Indeed, the Jordans and Newberrys are not only the embodiments of civilization, but also seem to be the beneficiaries of old wealth. On the other hand, Stephen's movement away from savagery is paralleled by his increasing wealth.

33. For instance, in his 1914 essay "The West and American Ideals," in *The Frontier in American Society* (Tucson: University of Arizona Press, 1986), 290–311, Turner projected new frontiers into the realm of the spirit, claiming, "As we

turn from the task of the first rough conquest of the continent there lies before us a whole wealth of unexploited resources in the realm of the spirit. Arts and letters, science and better social creation, loyalty and political service to the commonweal,—these and a thousand other directions of activity are open to the men, who formerly... saw success only in material display" (309).
34. In Act II, there are references to a "Dispute about the ownership of the mine" (741), and later Ghent explains to Winthrop that he is only "Part owner... I hadn't the capital to develop with, so I had to dispose of a half-interest" (743). In Act III, Ghent tells Mrs. Jordan that he is having "Trouble at the mine.... [his business partner]'s competent to steal the whole outfit. In fact, is doing it, or has done it already" (751), and later in the act, he tells Ruth, "Since I've been away they've as good as stolen it from me. I could get it back easy enough by fighting..." (755).
35. Alfred L. Bernheim, *The Business of the Theatre: An Economic History of the American Theatre, 1750–1932* (1932; New York: Benjamin Blom, 1964), 31–33.
36. See this letter in William Vaughn Moody, *Letters to Harriet*, 300. Several days later Moody expressed doubts as to whether the unpleasant review was actually a Syndicate ploy (William Vaughn Moody, *Letters to Harriet*, 303–04). The first letter is also quoted in Richard Moody, 726.
37. See, Bernheim, 64–75; and Jack Poggi, *Theater in America: The Impact of Economic Forces, 1870–1967* (Ithaca, NY: Cornell University Press, 1968), 15–26.
38. For instance, see Limerick, 78–96.
39. From the program for the Princess Theatre production of *The Great Divide*, week beginning December 17, 1906, located in *The Great Divide* materials housed in the Billy Rose Theatre Division, the New York Public Library for the Performing Arts at Lincoln Center.
40. From the program for the Princess Theatre production of *The Great Divide*, week beginning March 4, 1907, located in *The Great Divide* materials housed in the Billy Rose Theatre Division, the New York Public Library for the Performing Arts at Lincoln Center.
41. Both of Crothers's parents were doctors, and connections between her father's family and Abe Lincoln suggest a relatively affluent background (Quinn, 50–51).
42. Judith E. Barlow, introduction, *Plays by American Women: 1900–1930*, ed. Judith E. Barlow (New York: Applause, 1985), xiv.
43. In this regard, see Gottlieb, 146–51; Barlow, xiv–xviii; Yvonne B. Shafer, "The Liberated Woman in American Plays of the Past," *Players* 49.3–4 (1974), 95–97; Doris Abramson, "Rachel Crothers: Broadway Feminist," in *Modern American Drama: The Female Canon*, ed. June Schlueter (Rutherford: Fairleigh Dickinson University Press, 1990), 55–65; Brenda Murphy, "Feminism and the Marketplace: The Career of Rachel Crothers," in *The*

256 *Notes*

    Cambridge Companion to American Women Playwrights, ed. Brenda Murphy (Cambridge: Cambridge University Press, 1999), 82–97. Also interesting here is Eleanor Flexner's late 1930s evaluation of Crothers's plays. Flexner praised the promise of the playwright's early plays—a promise Flexner believed Crothers had failed to live up to in her later plays. Flexner believed that Crothers, like most other American playwrights of the early twentieth century, was never able to integrate a critique of the larger social context into her dramatic action. See Eleanor Flexner, *American Playwrights: 1918–1938* (New York: Simon, 1938), 239–48.

44. "'Three of Us' is a 'Lucky Strike,'" *New York Herald*, Oct. 18, 1906, 11.
45. "Realism in 'Three of Us': Domestic Drama in a Nevada Mining Camp," 7.
46. "The Drama—The Madison Square Theatre—'The Three of Us,'" 7.
47. "Madison Square—*The Three of Us*," 3.
48. Rachel Crothers, *The Three of Us: A Play in Four Acts* (New York: Samuel French, 1916), 54–55. All further references to the play will be from this version and cited parenthetically in the text. This version is described as a revision of the play, but scenic and lighting information as well as the included cast list would seem to refer to the 1906 production. In the Billy Rose Theatre Division, the New York Public Library for the Performing Arts, there is a typescript version of the play dated 1906. This latter version has the same scenic directions and appended prop list and light information as in the 1916 Samuel French version. Generally the action and dialogue are identical. There are a few phrases added to the 1916 version that do not appear in the 1906 version. More significant is the fact that the Act I and Act IV scenes between Rhy and Steve and the Act II, III, and IV scenes between Rhy and Berresford are much tighter in the later version. It would seem that the revisions were meant to eliminate redundant passages in the above-noted scenes—sharpening but not changing the actions represented. A third version of the play can be found in the Lawrence and Lee Theatre Research Institute, The Ohio State University Thompson Library. This typescript version of the play originally came from the Grand Opera House in Canton, Ohio, and is dated 1906 (though that date may have been appended after the fact--that is, when this version was catalogued). This version has much of the material of the 1906 Lincoln Center version that was cut in the 1916 Samuel French version, but other details and word choices are more similar to the 1916 version.
49. "Carlotta Nillson in 'The Three of Us,'" 9.
50. "Madison Square—*The Three of Us*," 3.
51. Interestingly, Crothers's character list in this play include a Chinese servant, Hop Wing, who is very much in the tradition of the Chinese cook/servant that so frequently appears in Western melodramas, films, and even television series like *Bonanza*. Treated brutally by Berresford—the closest thing to a villain in this play—Hop Wong functions primarily as a device clarifying Berresford's character.

52. Joan Wallach Scott, "Gender: A Useful Category of Historical Analysis," in *Gender and the Politics of History* (New York: Columbia University Press, 1988), 45.
53. It is interesting that Berresford is referred to in the script by his last name while Steve is referred to by his first name. Such a distinction suggests that Steve is the more personable and less formal of the two.
54. In his "The Significance of the Frontier," Turner claimed: "That coarseness and strength combined with acuteness and inquisitiveness; that practical, inventive turn of mind, quick to find expedients; that masterful grasp of material things, lacking in the artistic but powerful to effect great ends; that restless, nervous energy; that dominant individualism, working for good and evil, and withal that buoyancy and exuberance which comes with freedom— these are traits of the frontier, or traits called out elsewhere because of the existence of the frontier" (37). Rhy embodies much of this.
55. Quinn, 51.
56. For example, when Clem tosses the keys to the trunk to Rhy, the stage directions state that she "catches the keys like a boy" (11). As another example, at the end of the play, when Berresford asks Sonnie if, when he does something wrong, does Rhy forgive him, Sonnie replies: "Yes—she's kind of a boy herself. She knows a fella can't be good all the time" (96). Regarding how Crothers integrates these boyish features into Rhy without reducing her to a comic tomboy, see Gottlieb, 25.
57. "Carlotta Nillson in 'The Three of Us,'" 9.
58. The critic of the *Sun* praised this scene for its "originality and strength," claiming that it deserved the applause that it received (7). The reviewer of the *Evening Post* claimed that this scene was "uncommonly strong and ingenious" ("Music and Drama: 'The Three of Us,'" Oct. 18, 1906, 9). The reviewer in *Theatre Magazine* wrote of this scene that "the situation is conventional, but it is handled and acted with discretion and untheatrically" ("Madison Square; 'The Three of Us,'" Dec. 1906, 316).
59. Of his gold strike, Steve tells Rhy, "It's only low grade—nothing like yours, but *it's all right*" (30), and of Trenholm he says, "[H]e's the best man we've ever had here, represents the biggest kind of a syndicate;... I'll *give* him a share in *my* claim if he'll put up the money to work that when he opens Bixie's. See? And I'm *pretty sure* he'll listen to my proposition. Trenholm's the man, but he's got to be handled" (31–32). When an angry Trenholm turns his back on Steve, Rhy feels she may have inadvertently "taken away the chance of his life for success. I've made Mr. Trenholm think Steve's done a contemptible thing. He had his chance in his hand, and I took it away" (76).
60. Gottlieb, 24.
61. For instance, see Parrington, 192. Certainly, in developing their approach to realism, neither Moody nor Crothers were as self-consciously scientific in their approaches as was the French theorist of naturalism and author Emile Zola.

In regard to Zola's naturalism, see Emile Zola, *The Experimental Novel and Other Essays*, trans. Belle M. Sherman (New York: Haskell House, 1964).

7 CONCLUSION

1. The preoccupation with temporal development or evolution was, as discussed in chapter 1, a major aspect of the late-nineteenth-century American intellectual and cultural scene. Interestingly, this concern was imported directly into theater criticism. As Thomas Postlewait has written in his essay "From Melodrama to Realism: The Suspect History of American Drama," in *Melodrama: The Cultural Emergence of a Genre*, ed. Michael Hays and Anastasia Nikolopoulou (New York: St. Martin's Press, 1996), late-nineteenth-century and early-twentieth-century writers like William Dean Howells and Hamlin Garland adopted an evolutionary language in their campaigns on behalf of their literary ideals. Postlewait points out that historians of twentieth-century theater and drama accepted this evolutionary framework without question, hence the tendency to place realistic drama on a higher artistic level than melodrama that still manifests itself in American theater scholarship. Postlewait notes the irony in the fact that critics dealing with American theater history from 1880 to 1920 often describe the movement from melodrama to realism in the melodramatic terms of a battle between good and evil (49). Even more intriguing is the failure of these critics to see beyond the evolutionary thesis that imprisons their thought.
2. Vernon Lewis Parrington, *Main Currents in American Thought: An Interpretation of American Literature from the Beginnings to 1920, Vol. III: (1860–1920), The Beginnings of Critical Realism in America* (New York: Harcourt-Brace, 1930), 192.
3. Certainly there is a paradox here. Audiences are separated from, made distant from, theatre events by the proscenium arch, and yet they are to enter emotionally into and vicariously live through these events. This contradiction was challenged by later twentieth-century playwrights like Bertolt Brecht.
4. Regarding "New Western History," see introduction, note 44.
5. This interpretation of the frontier myth as an Indian war has received its most thorough analysis from Richard Slotkin in his massive three-volume study of the myth: *Regeneration Through Violence: The Mythology of the American Frontier, 1600–1860* (Middletown, CT: Wesleyan University Press, 1973); *The Fatal Environment: The Myth of the Frontier in the Age of Industrialization, 1800–1890* (Middletown, CT: Wesleyan University Press, 1985); *Gunfighter Nation: The Myth of the Frontier* (New York: Atheneum, 1992).

Index

Note: Page numbers in **bold** face denote illustrations.

Adams, Herbert Baxter, 35
Adams, Maude, 141
Anglin, Margaret, 251 (n 2),
  254 (n 31), **175**, **176**
Appalachian Mountain Club, 27

Baldwin Theatre, 156
Bank, Rosemarie, 2, 7, 211 (n 23), 229
  (nn 47 & 51), 249 (n 55)
Barker, John Nelson, 5
  *Indian Princess, or La Belle Savage,
  The* (1808), 5
Barrie, J.M., 141
  Peter Pan (1905), 141
Bates, Blanche, 142, 157, **165**
Beadle & Adams, 46, 48
Belasco, David, 3, 5, 11, 16, 17, 62, 71,
  73, 74, 78, 140–142, 156–168,
  169, 185, 194, 198, 199, 200,
  203–204, 247–248 (n 39)
  Girl of the Golden West, The (1905),
  3, 11, 16, 17, 62, 73, 78, 79, 140,
  141, 142, 156–168, 169, 170, 186,
  203, 206, 248 (n 41); compared
  with *The Cowboy and the Lady*
  and *Arizona*, 250 (n 59), **165**
  Rose of the Rancho, The (1906), 156,
  169, 248 (n 40)
Belasco Theatre, 78, 141, 169, 248 (n 40)
Bird, Robert Montgomery, 6
  Nick of the Woods (novel, 1837), 6
Boone and Crockett Club, 27, 41, 242
  (n 55)

Boucicault, Dion, 70, 72
Boy Scouts of America, 27
Brand, Max, 45
Brougham, John, 6, 59
  *Metamora, or The Last of the
  Pollywogs* (1847), 6
  *Po-Ca-Hon-Tas, or The Gentle
  Savage* (1855), 6
Bryan, William Jennings, 43
Bush, George W., 1

Campbell, Bartley, 8, 60, 63–64, 67,
  68, 73, 86–87, 94, 97, 123, 159,
  232 (n 8), 232–233 (n 11)
  My Partner (1879), 8, 60, 63–64,
  67, 68, 73, 83, 86–87, 92, 95,
  100, 123, 159, 232 (n 8), 232–233
  (n 11), 233 (n 16), 254 (n 30)
Campfire Club, 27
"captivity narratives" or "captivity
  tales," 22, 23, 253 (n 21)
Cawelti, John, 2
Chicago World's Columbian
  Exposition (1893), 3, 10, 30, 44,
  242 (n 55)
class conflict, 93, 218–219 (n 28)
  in *The Great Divide*, 254 (n 32)
  in *Her Own Way*, 94
  in *The Virginian* (play), 132–133
Cody, William (aka Buffalo Bill), 10,
  22, 46–48, 50, 237 (n 49)
combination company, 69–70, 72, 229
  (n 49)

Cooper, James Fenimore, 5, 6, 22, 23, 46, 59, 118, 189
  Last of the Mohicans, The (1826), 59
Crockett, Davy, 6, 60, 66, 226 (n 18)
Cronon, William, 207
Crothers, Rachel, 3, 5, 16, 17, 168, 169–170, 186, 187–199, 201, 203–206, 255 (n 42), 255–256 (n 43), 257 (n 61)
  He and She (1911), 187
  Man's World, A (1909), 187
  Three of Us, The (1906), 3, 16, 17, 168, 169–170, 186, 187–199, 201, 203–206, 250 (n 2), 256 (nn 48 & 51), 257 (nn 53, 54, 56, 58, 59)
"cult of true womanhood," 61, 161
Custis, George Washington Parke, 5
  Indian Prophecy, The (1827), 5

Daly, Augustin, 8, 67, 69
  Horizon (1871), 8, 67
Darwin, Charles, 34, 35, 39, 49
  Origin of Species, On the (1859), 34
Darwinian social thought (social Darwinism), 23, 33–34, 35, 36, 38, 39, 41, 49, 54, 63, 65, 131–132, 181, 206, 227–228 (n 33), 236 (n 47)
Delano, Alonzo, 7
  Live Woman in the Mines, A (1857), 7
DeMille, Cecil B., 142
Demille, Henry C. and Charles Bernard, 62, 158, 194
  Main Line; Or, Rawson's Y, The (1886), 62, 158, 194

Emerson, Ralph Waldo, 25, 37, 38, 181

Farnum, Dustin, 131, 142, 243 (n 60), **130**
Faversham, William, 142

Fiedler, Leslie, 2, 242–243 (n 56)
Fields, Lew, 170
Fiske, Harrison Grey, 74, 109, 185
Fiske, Minnie Maddern, 71, 109, 185
Fitch, Clyde, 4, 5, 17, 74, 83–96, 100, 102, 103–104, 105, 106–107, 115, 122, 126, 135, 139, 148, 153, 197, 201, 234 (n 28)
  Barbara Frietchie (1899), 85
  Captain Jinks of the Horse Marines (1901), 85
  Climbers, The (1901), 85, 90
  Cowboy and the Lady, The (1899), 4, 17, 83–86, 87–96, 233 (n 16), 234 (n 17); compared with *Arizona*, 97, 100, 102, 103–104, 105, 106, 139; with *The Girl of the Golden West*, 167, 250 (n 59); with *Her Own Way* (1903), 94–95, 234 (n 28); with *John Ermine of the Yellowstone* (novel), 115, 239 (n 25); with *John Ermine of the Yellowstone* (play), 121, 122; with *The Squaw Man*, 148, 153; with *The Three of Us*, 196, 197; with *The Virginian* (play), 126, 135, 139, 243 (n 64)
  Lovers' Lane (1901), 85
  Moth and the Flame, The (1898), 90
Fleming, Carroll, 169
  Pioneer Days (1906), 169
Ford, John, 206
Forrest, Edwin, 5
Foucault, Michel, 9, 12, 13, 14, 211–212 (n 29), 212–213 (n 40), 213 (n 42)
Frye, Northrop, 51, 52, 87, 111

Garland, Hamlin, 11, 42–44, 48, 93, 171, 251 (n 8), 258 (n 1)
  Crumbling Idols (1894), 11, 44
  Hesper (1903), 251 (n 8)

gender construction, 13, 36, 45, 60–64, 96, 206–207, 224 (n 116), 226 (n 26) 236 (n 47)
  in *Arizona*, 97
  in *The Cowboy and the Lady*, 88–89, 90
  in *The Girl of the Golden West*, 159–160, 164–166, 249 (n 58)
  in *The Great Divide*, 181, 183–184
  in *John Ermine of the Yellowstone* (play), 117, 122, 123, 124, 137–140
  in *My Partner*, 86
  in *The Squaw Man*, 146
  in *The Three of Us*, 187–188, 190–191, 194–196
  in *The Virginian* (play), 125, 137–140
Georg II, Duke of Saxe-Meiningen, 54
Goethe, Johann Wolfgang, 56
Gramsci, Antonio, 13, 77, 213 (n 43), 222 (n 92)
Grey, Zane, 45
  Riders of the Purple Sage (1912), 45

Hackett, James K., 121–122, 124
Hall, Roger A., 2–3, 7, 242 (n 54)
Harte, Bret, 44, 62, 66–68, 73, 157, 158, 160, 166, 167, 194
  "Idyl of Red Gulch, The" (1869), 158
  "M'liss: An Idyl of Red Mountain" (story, 1863), 62, 157–158, 159, 160, 163, 166, 194
  Two Man of Sandy Bar, The (1876), 67–68, 73
Herald Square Theatre, 78, 95, 170, 235 (n 30)
Herbert, Joseph, 170
  Great Decide, The (with music by Gustav Kerker and A. Baldwin Sloane, 1906), 3, 170
Hilliard, Robert, **165**

Howard, Bronson, 72, 233 (n 12)
Howells, William Dean, 106, 250 (n 2), 258 (n 1)
Hudson River School, 25
Hugo, Victor, 56
Hyde, Stuart Wallace, 2, 6–7, 158, 211 (n 22 & 28)

imperialism, 105–106, 237 (n 49)
"imperialist nostalgia" (Rosaldo), 26, 37, 76
"Indian Plays," 5–6, 23, 59–60, 210 (n 18)
Indian represented in literature and theatre, 21–24, 59–60
  in Buffalo Bill's Wild West Show, 47
  in captivity narratives, 21–22
  in *The Cowboy and the Lady*, 91
  in *The Girl of the Golden West,* 163, 166
  in *The Great Divide*, 176–177, 183
  in "Indian Plays", 5–6, 59–60, 210 (n 18)
  in *John Ermine of the Yellowstone* (novel), 113–115
  in *John Ermine of the Yellowstone* (play), 115–118, 120–121, 149, 240 (n 29)
  in *The Squaw Man*, 147, 148–150, 152–153, 155, 176
  in *The Three of Us*, 188–189
  in Turner Frontier Thesis, 31, 36, 50, 176, 183
  in *The Virginian* (play), 128
Indian-White conflict, 5, 7, 8, 22, 24, 47, 59, 93, 94, 105–106, 218–219 (n 28), 236 (n 41), 237 (n 49), 258 (n 5)
industrial-managerial elite class, 4, 11, 24–25, 29, 38, 52, 65, 68, 71, 77, 133, 155, 198, 211 (n 27), 216–217 (n 10), 222–223 (n 92)

"job actors," 72
Joe Weber's Music Hall, 141–142
Judson, E.Z.C. (aka Ned Buntline), 46, 48

Klein, Charles, 141
   Lion and the Mouse, The (1905), 141
Knickerbocker Theatre, 93
Kolodny, Annette, 2, 51, 224 (n 110)

La Shelle, Kirke, 3, 5, 11, 16, 17, 74, 78, 83, 109, 111–112, 124–140, 142, 144, 146, 148, 157, 159, 160, 167, 198–199, 201, 240–241 (n 44), 243 (n 64)
   Virginian, The (play with Owen Wister, 1904), *see under* Wister, Owen
Limerick, Patricia Nelson, 5, 50, 51, 178, 207, 212 (n 32), 213 (n 44)
"line of business," 71
"log palaces," 28
Longacre Square (Times Square), *see* Times Square
Longfellow, Henry Wadsworth, 6, 23, 118, 239–240 (n 28)
   Song of Hiawatha, The (1855), 6, 23, 188, 239–240 (n 28)
lynching, *see* vigilante justice

MacKaye, Percy, 170
   Jeanne D'Arc (1906), 170
Madison Square Theatre, 167, 187, 190
Manhattan Theatre, 78, 109, 112, 116, 131
Marlboro Man, 1
Mazamas, 27
McCloskey, James J., 8
   Across the Continent (1870), 8
McKinley, William, 43
Medina, Louisa, 6
   Nick of the Woods (adaptation of Bird novel, 1838), 6

Melodrama (in general), 46, 55–68, 73, 74–76, 76–79, 84, 203, 205–206, 207, 254 (n 30), 258 (n 1)
   in *Arizona*, 96, 97, 106
   in *The Cowboy and the Lady*, 86, 89, 90, 93, 96
   in *The Girl of the Golden West*, 142–143, 157, 160, 167
   in *The Great Divide*, 169, 171, 173, 180–185, 198–199, 250–251 (n 2)
   in *John Ermine of the Yellowstone* (play), 117, 118, 120–124, 139–140
   in *My Partner*, 86
   in *The Squaw Man*, 142–143, 144, 145, 148, 151, 153, 154, 155, 245 (n 10)
   in *The Three of Us*, 169, 192, 194, 196, 198–199, 250–251 (n 2)
   in *The Virginian* (play), 128, 133, 137, 138, 139–140
Miller, Henry, 11, 254 (n 31), **175, 176**
Miller, Joaquin, 8, 44, 67, 158, 194, 229 (n 49)
   Danites in the Sierras, The (1877), 8, 229 (n 49)
   Forty-Nine (1881), 67, 158
mining frontier, 7, 44, 66–67, 160, 162, 163, 167, 177–178, 186, 188, 191, 193, 194, 223 (n 92), 248 (n 41)
mining frontier drama, 2, 53, 86, 167, 170, 186, 187, 188, 232 (n 8), 248 (n 41)
Mitchell, Langdon, 170
   New York Idea, The (1906), 17
Moody, William Vaughn, 3, 5, 11, 16, 17, 78–79, 168, 169–187, 190, 197–199, 201, 203–206, 251 (nn 8 & 9), 252 (nn 15 & 18), 253 (n 21), 253–254 (n 28), 254 (n 31), 255 (n 36), 257 (n 61)

Index

Death of Eve, The (1907), 251 (n 9)
Fire Bringer, The (1904), 171
Great Divide, The (1906), 3, 11, 16, 17, 78–79, 168, 169–187, 175, 176, 188, 190, 196, 197–199, 201, 203–206, 249 (n 55), 250–251 (n 2), 251 (n 8), 251–252 (n 12), 252 (nn 15 & 18), 253 (nn 21, 22, 23), 253–254 (n 28), 254 (n 32), 255 (n 34); compared with *The Girl of the Golden West*, 249 (n 55); with *Her Own Way*, 234 (n 29); with *The Squaw Man*, 252 (n 17); with *The Three of Us*, 188, 190, 196
Masque of Judgment, The (1900), 171
Morgan, Lewis H., 34–35, 36, 41, 50, 220 (nn 47 & 48)
 Ancient Society (1877), 34, 35, 220 (n 48)
movie westerns, 1, 2, 3, 78, 79, 142, 206–207, 217–218 (n 10)
 3:10 to Yuma (2007), 1
 Appaloosa (2008), 1
 Arizona (1918), 206
 Avatar (2009), 207, 208
 Dances with Wolves (1990), 1
 Girl of the Golden West, The (1914, 1923, 1930, 1938), 142, 206
 Great Divide, The (1915, 1925, 1929), 206
 Great Train Robbery, The (1903), 45, 78
 High Noon (1952), 201
 Little Big Man (1970), 207
 Open Range (2003), 1
 Soldier Blue (1970), 207
 Squaw Man, The (1914, 1918, 1931), 142, 206
 Tombstone (1993), 1
 True Grit (2010), 1
 Unforgiven, The (1992), 1
 Wyatt Earp (1994), 1

Muir, John, 38–40, 41, 42, 43, 48, 50, 221 (n 72)
 Mountains of California (1894), 38, 39
 Story of My Boyhood and Youth, The (1913), 40
Murdock, Frank, 8, 60, 64, 66, 67
 Davy Crockett (1872), 8, 60, 64, 66, 67, 254 (n 30)
Murieta, Joaquin, 162, 163
myth, 14
 "frontier myth," 1, 3, 14–15, 17, 47, 51–52, 79, 215 (n 6), 258 (n 5); in *Arizona*, 103–104; in *The Cowboy and the Lady*, 85, 93–94, 95; In *The Girl of the Golden West*, 158, 163, 165, 167; in *The Great Divide*, 170, 171, 177–178, 186; in *Her Own Way*, 94–95; in *John Ermine of the Yellowstone* (play), 138–140; in *My Partner*, 87; in *The Squaw Man*, 154–155, in *The Virginian* (play), 111, 139–140
 "mythos of spring" (Frye), 51, 87, 111

national parks, 27–28, 37, 39, 42
neurasthenia, 221 (n 63)
"New Western History," 207–208, 213–214 (n 44)
"noble savage," 5–6, 59, 60, 87, 117, 118, 128, 129, 149, 189, 210 (n 18)

Panic of 1873, 69, 70, 229 (n 47)
Panic of 1893, 25, 32, 52, 84
Parrington, Vernon Lewis, 65, 137, 181, 198, 202, 205
 Main Currents in American Thought (1927, 1930), 65
Paulding, James Kirke, 6, 60, 226 (n 18)
 Lion of the West, The (1830), 6, 60, 83, 226 (n 18)

Payne, John, 56
Pixérécourt, Guilbert de, 56, 225 (n 12)
Populists, 25, 43
Princess Theatre, 78, 169, 184, 186
Puccini, Giacomo, 142
 La Fanciulla del West (1910), 142
Pullman Car (Pullman Company), 26, 28

race, 13, 34–36, 41–42, 50–51, 58, 59–60, 218 (n 18)
 in *Arizona*, 102–103, 104
 in *The Cowboy and the Lady*, 91, 102
 in *The Girl of the Golden West*, 162–163
 in *The Great Divide*, 183–184
 in *John Ermine of the Yellowstone* (play), 113, 116–117, 122, 140, 240 (n 40)
 in *The Squaw Man*, 146, 148–151, 152, 154, 155
 in *The Three of Us*, 190, 197
 in *The Virginian* (play), 131, 132–133, 139, 140
railroads, 7, 8, 24, 25, 26, 27–28, 31, 61, 66, 70, 147, 174, 185, 217–218 (n 17), 218 (n 23), 228 (n 44)
 Transcontinental Railroad, 7, 26, 28
Raymond and Whitcomb tours, 26
Reagan, Ronald, 1
realism, 17, 48, 49, 54, 55, 64–65, 67–68, 76, 79, 91, 106, 120, 140, 149, 151, 153, 167, 168, 169, 171, 178, 180–181, 198–199, 202–206, 254 (n 30), 257–258 (n 61), 258 (n 1)
Remington, Frederic, 4, 11, 17, 45, 48, 83–84, 95, 105, 107, 109–124, 125, 126, 129, 139, 142, 156
 Friendship with Thomas, 11, 96, 98–99, 236 (n 41)

John Ermine of the Yellowstone (novel, 1902), 4, 17, 98, 110–111, 112–115, 116, 117–118, 120–121, 122, 123–124, 126, 129, 237–238 (n 8), 238 (n 22), 238–239 (n 24), 239 (n 25)
John Ermine of the Yellowstone (play, 1903), *see under* Shipman, Louis Evans
"Rialto," 70
Ridge, John Rollin, *see* Yellow Bird
Rogers, Major Robert, 5
 Ponteach, or The Savages of America (1766), 5
romanticism, 6, 23, 33, 36, 37, 38, 42, 45, 48, 49, 55–56, 65, 66, 68, 76, 110, 118, 121, 128, 131, 140, 144, 146, 149, 155, 166, 168, 173, 181, 188, 189, 198, 203, 210 (n 18), 237–238 (n 8), 246 (n 13), 253 (n 20), 254 (n 30)
Roosevelt, Theodore, 10, 11, 40–43, 45, 47, 48, 49, 50, 63, 83, 87, 88, 95, 96, 98, 105, 106, 110, 136, 139, 140, 168, 205, 221 (n 72), 221–222 (n 75), 222 (nn 76, 79, 85), 236 (n 47), 243 (n 57)
 "Biological Analogies in History" (1910), 41
 Ranch Life and the Hunting Trail (1888), 11, 40, 110
 Winning of the West, The (1889–1896), 10, 40
 "World Movement, The" (1910), 41
Rough Riders, 10, 42
Rowlandson, Mary, 22
Royle, Edwin Milton, 3, 5, 16, 17, 78, 140, 141–156, 166, 167, 169, 179, 180, 198–199, 201, 203–204, 244 (n 9), 245 (n 11), 246 (n 19), 247 (n 37)
 Silent Call, The (novel, 1910, and play), 244–245 (n 9), 247 (n 37)

Squaw Man, The (1905), 3, 16, 17, 78, 140, 141–156, 169, 203–204, 245 (nn 10, 11, 12); compared with *The Girl of the Golden West*, 166, 167; with *The Great Divide*, 170, 175, 176, 179, 180, 252 (n 17); with Shaw's plays, 246 (n 13); with *The Three of Us*, 196

Schiller, Friedrich, 56
Scott, Sir Walter, 66
Shaw, George Bernard, 144, 246 (n 13)
Shipman, Louis Evans, 17, 83, 109, 111, 112, 115–124, 148, 201
  John Ermine of the Yellowstone (1903), 17, 73, 83–84, 107, 109, 111–112, 115–124, 142–143, 239 (n 26), 239–240 (n 28), 240 (nn 29 & 40); compared with *The Girl of the Golden West*, 156, 157, 158, 159, 160, 161, 164, 167; with *The Squaw Man*, 144, 146, 148, 149, 153, 154, 155, 156; with *The Three of Us*, 191, 195–196; with *The Virginian* (play), 129, 133, 137, 138–140
Shuberts brothers, 71, 72, 73, 185–186, 230 (n 61), 235 (n 30)
Sierra Club, 27, 38
Slotkin, Richard, 2, 14, 42, 49, 93, 94, 211 (n 27), 218 (n 28), 222 (n 85), 224 (n 103), 243–244 (n 65), 258 (n 5)
Smith, Edgar, 141–142
  Squawman's Girl of the Golden West, The (1906), 3, 141–142
Smith, Henry Nash, 2, 86, 226 (n 19)
Spanish-American War, 10, 42, 84, 100, 105, 205, 235 (n 30), 236 (nn 41 & 47)
Spencer, Herbert, 34, 41, 49

Stone, John Augustus, 5, 23, 59, 210 (n 18)
  Metamora, or The Last of the Wampanoags (1829), 5, 23, 59, 83, 210 (n 18)

"ten-twenty-thirty" melodramas, 74, 75, 78, 231 (n 74)
"theatrical formations" (McConachie), 15, 55, 64, 225 (n 4)
Theatrical Syndicate, 71–73, 111, 185–186, 197, 230 (n 61), 235 (n 30), 255 (n 36)
  Erlanger, Abraham, 71
  Frohman, Charles, 71, 111, 185, 238 (n 12)
  Hayman, Al, 71
  Klaw, Marc, 71
  Nixon, S.F., 71
  Zimmerman, J.F. 71
Thomas, Augustus, 3, 5, 11, 16, 17, 74, 78, 83–84, 95–107, 108, 111, 115, 139, 148, 199, 201, 235 (nn 30 & 34), 235–236 (n 39), 236 (n 41)
  Alabama (1898), 96
  Arizona (1899), 3, 16, 17, 78, 84, 95–107, **105**, 108, 111, 139, 199, 235 (n 30), 236 (n 45); compared with *The Girl of the Golden West*, 250 (n 59); with *John Ermine of the Yellowstone* (novel), 115, 239 (n 25); with *John Ermine of the Yellowstone* (play), 117, 121; with *The Squaw Man*, 148
  Capitol, The (1895), 96
  Colorado (1901), 235 (n 34)
  In Mizzoura (1893), 96, 235 (n 34)
  New Blood (1894), 96
  Print of My Remembrance, The (1922), 96, 98–99, 104
Thoreau, Henry David, 25, 38
ticket prices (theater), 74

Times Square, 74, 84
Tompkins, Jane, 2, 45, 139, 244 (n 70)
tourism, 26–28, 41, 147, 150, 177
Tribe of Woodcraft Indians, 27
Tully, Richard Walton, 156, 169
Turner, Frederick Jackson, 3, 9–10, 11, 22, 30–38, 40, 41, 42, 43–44, 49–52, 54, 57, 68, 83, 220 (n 47), 221 (n 72), 254–255 (n 3)
   "Problem of the West, The" (1896), 35
   "Significance of the Frontier in American History, The" (1893), 3, 9–10, 22, 30–33, 36–37, 48, 133, 201
   "West and American Ideals, The" (1914), 254–255 (n 33)
Turner Frontier Thesis, 3, 9–10, 30–33, 36, 37–38, 201, 205, 212 (n 34), 213 (n 44), 219 (n 38), 252 (n 15)
   in *Arizona*, 101–102, 106, 202
   in *The Cowboy and the Lady*, 95, 202
   in *The Girl of the Golden West*, 142, 158–164, 165, 167–168, 202
   in *The Great Divide, The*, 170, 172–181, 182, 183–184, 187, 201, 202, 205–206, 252 (n 17)
   in *John Ermine of the Yellowstone* (play), 123, 139, 140, 202
   in *The Squaw Man*, 142, 146–148, 151, 154, 155, 168, 202, 252 (n 17)
   in *The Three of Us*, 170, 190, 193–194, 196–197, 201, 202, 205–206
   in *The Virginian* (play), 128, 129, 133–136, 139, 140, 168, 202
TV westerns, 1
   Bonanza (1959–1973), 256 (n 51)
   Deadwood (2004–2006), 1

Union Square Theatre, 73, 230 (n 63)

vigilante justice, 67
   in *Arizona*, 103, 139, 250 (n 39)
   in *The Cowboy and the Lady*, 89, 90, 91, 93–94, 139, 243 (n 64), 250 (n 59)
   in *The Girl of the Golden West*, 164, 250 (n 59)
   in *My Partner*, 68
   in *The Virginian* (play) 132, 134–135, 139, 240–241 (n 44), 241–242 (n 47), 243 (n 64)

Walker, Charlotte, 122, 240 (n 41)
Wallack's Theatre, 69, 78, 139, 156
Wheeler, Edward J., 222–223 (n 92)
   Deadwood Dick, The Prince of the Road (1877), 222–223 (n 92)
White, Baco, 149
White, Richard, 2, 51, 207
"wilderness cult," 25–26, 27, 29, 38, 49, 120, 123, 127, 131, 154, 243 (n 56)
Wild West Shows, 2, 10, 22, 46–48, 106, 237 (n 49)
Winter, William, 131, 240 (n 28, 29, 41), 241 (n 45), 248 (n 42)
Wister, Owen, 3, 5, 10–11, 16, 17, 45–46, 48, 74, 78, 83–84, 95, 96, 98, 107, 109–112, 123–140, 142, 144, 146, 147, 148, 151, 155, 157, 158, 159, 160, 163, 167, 191, 198–199, 201, 206, 238 (n 12), 240–241 (n 44), 242 (n 55), 243 (nn 57 & 64), 243–244 (n 65), 244 (n 70)
   "Concerning 'Bad Men'" (1901), 127
   "Evolution of the Cow-Puncher, The" (1895), 11, 127, 136
   Lin McLean (1897), 109, 110
   "Open-Air Education, The" (1902), 127
   Red Men and White (1895), 11, 110, 136

"Theodore Roosevelt: The Sportsman and the Man" (1901), 243 (n 57)
Virginian, The (novel, 1902), 45–46, 74, 109–111, 124–129, 132–142, 158, 163, 243 (n 56)
Virginian, The (play with Kirke La Shelle, 1904), 3, 11, 16, 17, 74, 78, 79, 83–84, 107, 109, 111–112, 124–140, **130**, 142, 238 (n 12), 241 (n 45), 241–242 (n 47), 242 (n 54), 243 (n 44); compared with *The Girl of the Golden West*, 56, 57, 58, 59, 60, 61, 63, 64, 67–68; with *The Squaw Man*, 144, 146, 147, 148, 151, 153, 154, 155, 256; with *The Three of Us*, 191, 196
working class culture, 25, 46, 57, 74–75, 77, 216–217 (n 10), 222–223 (n 92)
Worster, Donald, 207

Yellow Bird (John Rollin Ridge), 162

Zola, Emile, 257–258 (n 61)

GPSR Compliance

The European Union's (EU) General Product Safety Regulation (GPSR) is a set of rules that requires consumer products to be safe and our obligations to ensure this.

If you have any concerns about our products, you can contact us on

ProductSafety@springernature.com

In case Publisher is established outside the EU, the EU authorized representative is:

Springer Nature Customer Service Center GmbH
Europaplatz 3
69115 Heidelberg, Germany

www.ingramcontent.com/pod-product-compliance
Lightning Source LLC
LaVergne TN
LVHW051914060526
838200LV00004B/137